2014–2015
BANKRUPTCY CODE
AND RELATED SOURCE MATERIALS

Selected and Annotated by

DAVID G. EPSTEIN

George E. Allen Chair in Law
Richmond University

STEVE H. NICKLES

C.C. Hope Chair in Law and Management
Wake Forest University

**WEST
ACADEMIC
PUBLISHING**

Mat #41483147

© West, a Thomson business, 2007, 2008, 2009 Thomson Reuters
© 2010, 2011, 2012 Thomson Reuters
© 2014 LEG, Inc. d/b/a West Academic

    444 Cedar Street, Suite 700
    St. Paul, MN 55101
    1-877-888-1330

Printed in the United States of America

ISBN: 978-0-314-28888-2

TABLE OF CONTENTS

2014–2015

BANKRUPTCY CODE

AND RELATED SOURCE MATERIALS

PART 1

BANKRUPTCY CODE (TITLE 11 OF THE UNITED STATES CODE)

FIRST COMMENT TO STUDENTS

Richard Dooling's WHITE MAN'S GRAVE is the best[1] novel in which the protagonist is a bankruptcy lawyer. The first page of the novel describes Randall Killigan as the "best bankruptcy lawyer in Indianapolis." The second page explains why he is the best bankruptcy lawyer:

> Randall lived and breathed the Bankruptcy Code and intimidated anybody who crossed him by quoting it chapter, section and verse. * * * When Randall Killigan slept, he dreamed sections of the U.S. Bankruptcy Code, and woke up to discover money—lots of it—eagerly paid by clients who had insatiable appetites for his special insights into the Code.

The Bankruptcy Code is not only important to lawyers in novels but also to lawyers in the real world. And to law students in class and on exams.

Unless your bankruptcy prof is really twisted, she is not going to expect you to dream sections of the Bankruptcy Code. She will, however, expect you to read and understand sections of the Bankruptcy Code.

The Bankruptcy Code is title 11 of the United States Code. It was written in the 1970's by people who were experts in bankruptcy law for people who are experts in bankruptcy law. It was not "user friendly" when it was enacted in 1978. And, amendments through the years—especially the 2005 amendments[2]—have made the various sections of the Bankruptcy Code even more difficult for law students to read and understand.

This book emphasizes those sections of the Bankruptcy Code that your professor emphasizes. And, we make those sections more accessible (law prof talk for "easier") by deleting stuff that is not important, providing a context, and, from time to time, providing hints.

---

[1] You are right. "best" does not mean much here. Not a lot of competition, not a lot of novels featuring bankruptcy lawyers.

[2] The 2005 amendments are (mis)named Bankruptcy Abuse Prevention Consumer Protection Act and commonly referred to as BAPCPA (or worse).

TITLE 11
BANKRUPTCY

CHAPTER 1—GENERAL PROVISIONS

CHAPTER 3—CASE ADMINISTRATION

SUBCHAPTER I—COMMENCEMENT OF A CASE

SUBCHAPTER II—OFFICERS

---

[1]   Sections that are in bold are the sections that are most important in most law school bankruptcy courses. Most of these sections have been annotated or edited or both.

Sections that are in italics have been omitted. These sections are largely ignored in law school bankruptcy classes and completely ignored on law school bankruptcy exams.

CHAPTER 1—GENERAL PROVISIONS

§ 101. Definitions

In this title the following definitions shall apply:

* * *

(2) The term "affiliate" means—

(A) entity that directly or indirectly owns, controls, or holds with power to vote, 20 percent or more of the outstanding voting securities of the debtor, other than an entity that holds such securities—

(i) in a fiduciary or agency capacity without sole discretionary power to vote such securities; or

(ii) solely to secure a debt, if such entity has not in fact exercised such power to vote;

(B) corporation 20 percent or more of whose outstanding voting securities are directly or indirectly owned, controlled, or held with power to vote, by the debtor, or by an entity that directly or indirectly owns, controls, or holds with power to vote, 20 percent or more of the outstanding voting securities of the debtor, other than an entity that holds such securities—

(i) in a fiduciary or agency capacity without sole discretionary power to vote such securities; or

(ii) solely to secure a debt, if such entity has not in fact exercised such power to vote;

(C) person whose business is operated under a lease or operating agreement by a debtor, or person substantially all of whose property is operated under an operating agreement with the debtor; or

(D) entity that operates the business or substantially all of the property of the debtor under a lease or operating agreement.

(3) The term "assisted person" means any person whose debts consist primarily of consumer debts and the value of whose nonexempt property is less than $164,250.

(4) The term "attorney" means attorney, professional law association, corporation, or partnership, authorized under applicable law to practice law.

(4A) The term "bankruptcy assistance" means any goods or services sold or otherwise provided to an assisted person with the express or implied purpose of providing information, advice, counsel, document preparation, or filing, or attendance at a creditors' meeting or appearing in a case or proceeding on behalf of another or providing legal representation with respect to a case or proceeding under this title.

(5) The term "claim" means—

(A) right to payment, whether or not such right is reduced to judgment, liquidated, unliquidated, fixed, contingent, matured, unmatured, disputed, undisputed, legal, equitable, secured, or unsecured; or

(B) right to an equitable remedy for breach of performance if such breach gives rise to a right to payment, whether or not such right to an equitable remedy is reduced to judgment, fixed, contingent, matured, unmatured, disputed, undisputed, secured, or unsecured.

* * *

(7) The term "community claim" means claim that arose before the commencement of the case concerning the debtor for which property of the kind specified in *section 541(a)(2)* of this title is liable, whether or not there is any such property at the time of the commencement of the case.

(8) The term "consumer debt" means debt incurred by an individual primarily for a personal, family, or household purpose.

* * *

(10) The term "creditor" means—

　(A) entity that has a claim against the debtor that arose at the time of or before the order for relief concerning the debtor;

　(B) entity that has a claim against the estate of a kind specified in section 348(d), 502(f), 502(g), 502(h) or 502(i) of this title; or

　(C) entity that has a community claim.

(10A) The term "current monthly income"—

　(A) means the average monthly income from all sources that the debtor receives (or in a joint case the debtor and the debtor's spouse receive) without regard to whether such income is taxable income, derived during the 6-month period ending on—

　　(i) the last day of the calendar month immediately preceding the date of the commencement of the case if the debtor files the schedule of current income required by section 521(a)(1)(B)(ii); or

　　(ii) the date on which current income is determined by the court for purposes of this title if the debtor does not file the schedule of current income required by section 521(a)(1)(B)(ii); and

　(B) includes any amount paid by any entity other than the debtor (or in a joint case the debtor and the debtor's spouse), on a regular basis for the household expenses of the debtor or the debtor's dependents (and in a joint case the debtor's spouse if not otherwise a dependent), but excludes benefits received under the Social Security Act, * * *

(11) The term "custodian" means—

　(A) receiver or trustee of any of the property of the debtor, appointed in a case or proceeding not under this title;

　(B) assignee under a general assignment for the benefit of the debtor's creditors; or

　(C) trustee, receiver, or agent under applicable law, or under a contract, that is appointed or authorized to take charge of property of the debtor for the purpose of enforcing a lien against such property, or for the purpose of general administration of such property for the benefit of the debtor's creditors.

(12) The term "debt" means liability on a claim.

(12A) The term "debt relief agency" means any person who provides any bankruptcy assistance to an assisted person in return for the payment of money or other valuable consideration, or who is a bankruptcy petition preparer under section 110, but does not include— *lawyers are debt relief agency*

12

(A) any person who is an officer, director, employee, or agent of a person who provides such assistance or of the bankruptcy petition preparer;

* * *

(13) The term "debtor" means person or municipality concerning which a case under this title has been commenced.

(13A) The term "debtor's principal residence"—

(A) means a residential structure, if used as the principal residence of the debtor including incidental property, without regard to whether that structure is attached to real property; and

(B) includes an individual condominium or cooperative unit, a mobile or manufactured home, or trailer if used as the principal residence of the debt.

(14) The term "disinterested person" means a person that—

(A) is not a creditor, an equity security holder, or an insider;

(B) is not and was not, within 2 years before the date of the filing of the petition, a director, officer, or employee of the debtor; and

(C) does not have an interest materially adverse to the interest of the estate or of any class of creditors or equity security holders, by reason of any direct or indirect relationship to, connection with, or interest in, the debtor, or for any other reason.

(14A) The term "domestic support obligation" means a debt that accrues before, on, or after the date of the order for relief in a case under this title, including interest that accrues on that debt as provided under applicable nonbankruptcy law notwithstanding any other provision of this title, that is—

(A) owed to or recoverable by—

(i) a spouse, former spouse, or child of the debtor or such child's parent, legal guardian, or responsible relative; or

(ii) a governmental unit;

(B) in the nature of alimony, maintenance, or support (including assistance provided by a governmental unit) of such spouse, former spouse, or child of the debtor or such child's parent, without regard to whether such debt is expressly so designated;

(C) established or subject to establishment before, on, or after the date of the order for relief in a case under this title, by reason of applicable provisions of—

(i) a separation agreement, divorce decree, or property settlement agreement;

(ii) an order of a court of record; or

(iii) a determination made in accordance with applicable nonbankruptcy law by a governmental unit; and

(D) not assigned to a nongovernmental entity, unless that obligation is assigned voluntarily by the spouse, former spouse, child of the debtor, or such child's parent, legal guardian, or responsible relative for the purpose of collecting the debt.

(15) The term "entity" includes person, estate, trust, governmental unit, and United States trustee.

(16) The term "equity security" means—

(A) share in a corporation, whether or not transferable or denominated "stock", or similar security;

(B) interest of a limited partner in a limited partnership; or

(C) warrant or right, other than a right to convert, to purchase, sell, or subscribe to a share, security, or interest of a kind specified in subparagraph (A) or (B) of this paragraph.

(17) The term "equity security holder" means holder of an equity security of the debtor.

(18) The term "family farmer" means—

(A) individual or individual and spouse engaged in a farming operation whose aggregate debts do not exceed $3,792,650+ and not less than 50 percent of whose aggregate noncontingent, liquidated debts (excluding a debt for the principal residence of such individual or such individual and spouse unless such debt arises out of a farming operation), on the date the case is filed, arise out of a farming operation owned or operated by such individual or such individual and spouse, and such individual or such individual and spouse receive from such farming operation more than 50 percent of such individual's or such individual and spouse's gross income for—

(i) the taxable year preceding; or

(ii) each of the 2d and 3d taxable years preceding;

the taxable year in which the case concerning such individual or such individual and spouse was filed; or

(B) corporation or partnership in which more than 50 percent of the outstanding stock or equity is held by one family, or by one family and the relatives of the members of such family, and such family or such relatives conduct the farming operation, and

(i) more than 80 percent of the value of its assets consists of assets related to the farming operation;

(ii) its aggregate debts do not exceed $3,544,525 and not less than 50 percent of its aggregate noncontingent, liquidated debts (excluding a debt for one dwelling which is owned by such corporation or partnership and which a shareholder or partner maintains as a principal residence, unless such debt arises out of a farming operation), on the date the case is filed, arise out of the farming operation owned or operated by such corporation or such partnership; and

(iii) if such corporation issues stock, such stock is not publicly traded.

(19) The term "family farmer with regular annual income" means family farmer whose annual income is sufficiently stable and regular to enable such family farmer to make payments under a plan under chapter 12 of this title.

* * *

(20) The term "farmer" means (except when such term appears in the term "family farmer") person that received more than 80 percent of such person's gross income during the taxable year of such person immediately preceding the taxable year of such person during which the case under this title concerning such person was commenced from a farming operation owned or operated by such person.

(21) The term "farming operation" includes farming, tillage of the soil, dairy farming, ranching, production or raising of crops, poultry, or livestock, and production of poultry or livestock products in an unmanufactured state.

* * *

(23) The term "foreign proceeding" means a collective judicial or administrative proceeding in a foreign country, including an interim proceeding, under a law relating to insolvency or adjustment of debt in which proceeding the assets and affairs of the debtor are subject to control or supervision by a foreign court, for the purpose of reorganization or liquidation.

(24) The term "foreign representative" means a person or body, including a person or body appointed on an interim basis, authorized in a foreign proceeding to administer the reorganization or the liquidation of the debtor's assets or affairs or to act as a representative of such foreign proceeding.

* * *

(27) The term "governmental unit" means United States; State; Commonwealth; District; Territory; municipality; foreign state; department, agency, or instrumentality of the United States (but not a United States trustee while serving as a trustee in a case under this title), a State, a Commonwealth, a District, a Territory, a municipality, or a foreign state; or other foreign or domestic government.

(27B) The term "incidental property" means, with respect to a debtor's principal residence—

    (A) property commonly conveyed with a principal residence in the area where the real property is located;

    (B) all easements, rights, appurtenances, fixtures, rents, royalties, mineral rights, oil or gas rights or profits, water rights, escrow funds, or insurance proceeds; and

    (C) all replacements or additions.

(28) The term "indenture" means mortgage, deed of trust, or indenture, under which there is outstanding a security, other than a voting-trust certificate, constituting a claim against the debtor, a claim secured by a lien on any of the debtor's property, or an equity security of the debtor.

(29) The term "indenture trustee" means trustee under an indenture.

(30) The term "individual with regular income" means individual whose income is sufficiently stable and regular to enable such individual to make payments under a plan under chapter 13 of this title, other than a stockbroker or a commodity broker.

(31) The term "insider" includes—

(A) if the debtor is an individual—

    (i) relative of the debtor or of a general partner of the debtor;

    (ii) partnership in which the debtor is a general partner;

    (iii) general partner of the debtor; or

    (iv) corporation of which the debtor is a director, officer, or person in control;

(B) if the debtor is a corporation—

    (i) director of the debtor;

    (ii) officer of the debtor;

    (iii) person in control of the debtor;

    (iv) partnership in which the debtor is a general partner;

    (v) general partner of the debtor; or

    (vi) relative of a general partner, director, officer, or person in control of the debtor;

(C) if the debtor is a partnership—

    (i) general partner in the debtor;

    (ii) relative of a general partner in, general partner of, or person in control of the debtor;

    (iii) partnership in which the debtor is a general partner;

    (iv) general partner of the debtor; or

    (v) person in control of the debtor;

(D) if the debtor is a municipality, elected official of the debtor or relative of an elected official of the debtor;

(E) affiliate, or insider of an affiliate as if such affiliate were the debtor; and

(F) managing agent of the debtor.

(32) The term "insolvent" means—

(A) with reference to an entity other than a partnership and a municipality, financial condition such that the sum of such entity's debts is greater than all of such entity's property, at a fair valuation, exclusive of—

    (i) property transferred, concealed, or removed with intent to hinder, delay, or defraud such entity's creditors; and

    (ii) property that may be exempted from property of the estate under section 522 of this title; * * *

(35A) The term "intellectual property" means—

(A) trade secret;

(B) invention, process, design, or plant protected under title 35;

(C) patent application;

(D) plant variety;

(E) work of authorship protected under title 17; or

(F) mask work protected under chapter 9 of title 17;

to the extent protected by applicable nonbankruptcy law.

(36) The term "judicial lien" means lien obtained by judgment, levy, sequestration, or other legal or equitable process or proceeding.

(37) The term "lien" means charge against or interest in property to secure payment of a debt or performance of an obligation.

* * *

(39A) The term "median family income" means for any year—

(A) the median family income both calculated and reported by the Bureau of the Census in the then most recent year; and

(B) if not so calculated and reported in the then current year, adjusted annually after such most recent year until the next year in which median family income is both calculated and reported by the Bureau of the Census, to reflect the percentage change in the Consumer Price Index for All Urban Consumers during the period of years occurring after such most recent year and before such current year.

* * *

(40) The term "municipality" means political subdivision or public agency or instrumentality of a State.

(41) The term "person" includes individual, partnership, and corporation, but does not include governmental unit, except * * *

* * *

(42) The term "petition" means petition filed under section 301, 302, 303, or 1504 of this title, as the case may be, commencing a case under this title.

* * *

(43) The term "purchaser" means transferee of a voluntary transfer, and includes immediate or mediate transferee of such a transferee.

* * *

(45) The term "relative" means individual related by affinity or consanguinity within the third degree as determined by the common law, or individual in a step or adoptive relationship within such third degree.

* * *

(49) The term "security"—

(A) includes—

(i) note;

(ii) stock;

(iii) treasury stock;

(iv) bond;

(v) debenture;

(vi) collateral trust certificate;

(vii) pre-organization certificate or subscription;

(viii) transferable share;

(ix) voting-trust certificate;

(x) certificate of deposit;

(xi) certificate of deposit for security;

(xii) investment contract or certificate of interest or participation in a profit-sharing agreement or in an oil, gas, or mineral royalty or lease, if such contract or interest is required to be the subject of a registration statement filed with the Securities and Exchange Commission under the provisions of the Securities Act of 1933, or is exempt under section 3(b) of such Act from the requirement to file such a statement;

(xiii) interest of a limited partner in a limited partnership;

(xiv) other claim or interest commonly known as "security"; and

(xv) certificate of interest or participation in, temporary or interim certificate for, receipt for, or warrant or right to subscribe to or purchase or sell, a security; but

(B) does not include—

(i) currency, check, draft, bill of exchange, or bank letter of credit;

(ii) leverage transaction, as defined in section 761 of this title;

(iii) commodity futures contract or forward contract;

(iv) option, warrant, or right to subscribe to or purchase or sell a commodity futures contract;

(v) option to purchase or sell a commodity;

(vi) contract or certificate of a kind specified in subparagraph (A)(xii) of this paragraph that is not required to be the subject of a registration statement filed with the Securities and Exchange Commission and is not exempt under section 3(b) of the Securities Act of 1933 from the requirement to file such a statement; or

(vii) debt or evidence of indebtedness for goods sold and delivered or services rendered.

(50) The term "security agreement" means agreement that creates or provides for a security interest.

(51) The term "security interest" means lien created by an agreement.

* * *

(51B) The term "single asset real estate" means real property constituting a single property or project, other than residential real property with fewer than 4 residential units, which generates substantially all of the gross income of a debtor who is not a family farmer and on which no substantial business is being conducted by a debtor other than the business of operating the real property and activities incidental thereto.

(51C) The term "small business case" means a case filed under chapter 11 of this title in which the debtor is a small business debtor.

(51D) The term "small business debtor"—

    (A) subject to subparagraph **(B)**, means a person engaged in commercial or business activities (including any affiliate of such person that is also a debtor under this title and excluding a person whose primary activity is the business of owning or operating real property or activities incidental thereto) that has aggregate noncontingent liquidated secured and unsecured debts as of the date of the filing of the petition or the date of the order for relief in an amount not more than $2,490,925 (excluding debts owed to 1 or more affiliates or insiders) for a case in which the United States trustee has not appointed under section 1102(a)(1) a committee of unsecured creditors or where the court has determined that the committee of unsecured creditors is not sufficiently active and representative to provide effective oversight of the debtor; and

    (B) does not include any member of a group of affiliated debtors that has aggregate noncontingent liquidated secured and unsecured debts in an amount greater than $2,490,925 (excluding debt owed to 1 or more affiliates or insiders).

* * *

(53) The term "statutory lien" means lien arising solely by force of a statute on specified circumstances or conditions, or lien of distress for rent, whether or not statutory, but does not include security interest or judicial lien, whether or not such interest or lien is provided by or is dependent on a statute and whether or not such interest or lien is made fully effective by statute.

* * *

(54) The term "transfer" means—

    (A) the creation of a lien;

    (B) the retention of title as a security interest;

    (C) the foreclosure of a debtor's equity of redemption; or

    (D) each mode, direct or indirect, absolute or conditional, voluntary or involuntary, of disposing of or parting with—

        (i) property; or

        (ii) an interest in property.

UNOFFICIAL COMMENTS

Looking for statutory definitions is essential to success in working with the Bankruptcy Code, to succeed in a law school bankruptcy course. Section 101 is the first place to look.

The most important section 101 definitions are

— claim

— debtor

— insolvent

— transfer

Notice how broad the definitions of "claim" and "transfer" are. And, notice the important limitations in the definitions of "debtor" and "insolvent." Not everyone who is in debt is a "debtor." Not everyone who is not able to pay her bills is "insolvent."

While section 101 is the first place to look for definitions of terms used in the Bankruptcy Code, it is not the only place. Definitions are scattered through the Code. For example, the important term "secured claim" is defined in section 506(a), and the terms "commencement of a case" and "order for relief" are explained in section 301(b) and section 303(a) and (h).

§ 102. Rules of construction

In this title—

(1) "after notice and a hearing", or a similar phrase—

(A) means after such notice as is appropriate in the particular circumstances, and such opportunity for a hearing as is appropriate in the particular circumstances; but

(B) authorizes an act without an actual hearing if such notice is given properly and if—

(i) such a hearing is not requested timely by a party in interest; or

(ii) there is insufficient time for a hearing to be commenced before such act must be done, and the court authorizes such act;

(2) "claim against the debtor" includes claim against property of the debtor;

(3) "includes" and "including" are not limiting;

(4) "may not" is prohibitive, and not permissive;

(5) "or" is not exclusive;

* * *

§ 103. Applicability of chapters

(a) * * * chapters 1, 3, and 5 of this title apply in a case under chapter 7, 11, 12, or 13 of this title, and this chapter, sections 307, 362(*o*), 555 through 557, and 559 through 562 apply in a case under chapter 15.

(b) Subchapters I and II of chapter 7 of this title apply only in a case under such chapter.

(c) Subchapter III of chapter 7 of this title applies only in a case under such chapter concerning a stockbroker.

(d) Subchapter IV of chapter 7 of this title applies only in a case under such chapter concerning a commodity broker.

* * *

(g) * * * subchapters I, II, and III of chapter 11 of this title apply only in a case under such chapter.

(h) Subchapter IV of chapter 11 of this title applies only in a case under such chapter concerning a railroad.

(i) Chapter 13 of this title applies only in a case under such chapter.

(j) Chapter 12 of this title applies only in a case under such chapter.

(k) Chapter 15 applies only in a case under such chapter, except that—

> **(1)** sections 1505, 1513, and 1514 apply in all cases under this title; and

> **(2)** section 1509 applies whether or not a case under this title is pending.

§ 104. Adjustment of dollar amounts

* * *

(b)(1) On April 1, 1998, and at each 3-year interval ending on April 1 thereafter, each dollar amount in effect under sections 101(3), 101(18), 101(19A), 101(51D), 109(e), 303(b), 507(a), 522(d), 522(f)(3) and 522(f)(4), 522(n), 522(p), 522(q), 523(a)(2)(C), 541(b), 547(c)(9), 707(b), 1322(d), 1325(b), and 1326(b)(3) of this title and section 1409(b) of title 28 immediately before such April 1 shall be adjusted—

> **(A)** to reflect the change in the Consumer Price Index for All Urban Consumers, published by the Department of Labor, for the most recent 3-year period ending immediately before January 1 preceding such April 1, and

> **(B)** to round to the nearest $25 the dollar amount that represents such change.

* * *

§ 105. Power of court

(a) The court may issue any order, process, or judgment that is necessary or appropriate to carry out the provisions of this title. No provision of this title providing for the raising of an issue by a party in interest shall be construed to preclude the court from, sua sponte, taking any action or making any determination necessary or appropriate to enforce or implement court orders or rules, or to prevent an abuse of process.

* * *

UNOFFICIAL COMMENTS

When lawyers cannot find any specific statutory basis for an action that they are urging a bankruptcy judge to take, they rely on section 105—more specifically the phrase "necessary or appropriate" in section 105. For example, "Judge, use your 105 power to enjoin creditors of the corporate debtor from suing the CEO of the corporate debtor for breach of her corporate duty. It is 'necessary and appropriate' so that she can devote all of her time and energy to saving the corporate debtor."

Lawyers opposing such action tend to focus on the phrase "provisions of this title." For example, "Judge, 105 does not authorize you to protect non-debtors. The relevant 'provisions of this title'—section 362—is limited to protecting the debtor in the bankruptcy case."

OTHER SECTIONS

As the above paragraphs indicate, section 105 is often read together with section 362. Section 105 protection, unlike section 362 protection, is not "automatic"; section 105 protection, unlike section 362 protection, is not limited to the debtor in the bankruptcy case and his property and property of the estate.

And, the use of section 105 is not limited to protecting persons, who, unlike the debtor, are not protected by the automatic stay. If your class covers exceptions to discharge, you will talk about section 105 in connection with "partial discharge.". And, if your class covers business reorganizations under chapter 11, you will talk about section 105 in connection with "substantive consolidation."

Litigation over section 105(a) protection is an adversary proceeding under Rule 7001(7), infra at page 231.

§ 106. Waiver of sovereign immunity

(a) Notwithstanding an assertion of sovereign immunity, sovereign immunity is abrogated as to a governmental unit to the extent set forth in this section with respect to the following:

> **(1)** Sections 105, 106, 107, 108, 303, 346, 362, 363, 364, 365, 366, 502, 503, 505, 506, 510, 522, 523, 524, 525, 542, 543, 544, 545, 546, 547, 548, 549, 550, 551, 552, 553, 722, 724, 726, 744, 749, 764, 901, 922, 926, 928, 929, 944, 1107, 1141, 1142, 1143, 1146, 1201, 1203, 1205, 1206, 1227, 1231, 1301, 1303, 1305, and 1327 of this title.

> **(2)** The court may hear and determine any issue arising with respect to the application of such sections to governmental units.

> **(3)** The court may issue against a governmental unit an order, process, or judgment under such sections or the Federal Rules of Bankruptcy Procedure, including an order or judgment awarding a money recovery, but not including an award of punitive damages. Such order or judgment for costs or fees under this title or the Federal Rules of Bankruptcy Procedure against any governmental unit shall be consistent with the provisions and limitations of section 2412(d)(2)(A) of title 28.

> **(4)** The enforcement of any such order, process, or judgment against any governmental unit shall be consistent with appropriate nonbankruptcy law applicable to such governmental unit and, in the case of a money judgment against the United States, shall be paid as if it is a judgment rendered by a district court of the United States.

> **(5)** Nothing in this section shall create any substantive claim for relief or cause of action not otherwise existing under this title, the Federal Rules of Bankruptcy Procedure, or nonbankruptcy law.

(b) A governmental unit that has filed a proof of claim in the case is deemed to have waived sovereign immunity with respect to a claim against such governmental unit that is property of the estate and that arose out of the same transaction or occurrence out of which the claim of such governmental unit arose.

(c) Notwithstanding any assertion of sovereign immunity by a governmental unit, there shall be offset against a claim or interest of a governmental unit any claim against such governmental unit that is property of the estate.

* * *

§ 109. Who may be a debtor *eligibility to be a debtor*

(a) Notwithstanding any other provision of this section, only a person that resides or has a domicile, a place of business, or property in the United States, or a municipality, may be a debtor under this title.

(b) A person may be a debtor under chapter 7 of this title only if such person is not—

(1) a railroad;

(2) a domestic insurance company, bank, savings bank, cooperative bank, savings and loan association * * *

(c) An entity may be a debtor under chapter 9 of this title if and only if such entity—

(1) is a municipality:

(2) is specifically authorized, in its capacity as a municipality or by name, to be a debtor under such chapter by State law, or by a governmental officer or organization empowered by State law to authorize such entity to be a debtor under such chapter;

(3) is insolvent;

(4) desires to effect a plan to adjust such debts; and

(5) (A) has obtained the agreement of creditors holding at least a majority in amount of the claims of each class that such entity intends to impair under a plan in a case under such chapter;

(B) has negotiated in good faith with creditors and has failed to obtain the agreement of creditors holding at least a majority in amount of the claims of each class that such entity intends to impair under a plan in a case under such chapter;

(C) is unable to negotiate with creditors because such negotiation is impracticable; or

(D) reasonably believes that a creditor may attempt to obtain a transfer that is avoidable under section 547 of this title

(d) Only a railroad, a person that may be a debtor under chapter 7 of this title (except a stockbroker or a commodity broker), and an uninsured State member bank, or a corporation organized under section 25A of the Federal Reserve Act, which operates, or operates as, a multilateral clearing organization pursuant to section 409 of the Federal Deposit Insurance Corporation Improvement Act of 1991 may be a debtor under chapter 11 of this title.

(e) Only an individual with regular income that owes, on the date of the filing of the petition, noncontingent, liquidated, unsecured debts of less than $383,175 and noncontingent, liquidated, secured debts of less than $1,149,525, or an individual with regular income and such individual's spouse, except a stockbroker or a commodity broker, that owe, on the date of the filing of the petition, noncontingent, liquidated, unsecured debts that aggregate less than $383,175 and noncontingent, liquidated, secured debts of less than $1,149,525 may be a debtor under chapter 13 of this title.

(f) Only a family farmer or family fisherman with regular annual income may be a debtor under chapter 12 of this title.

(g) Notwithstanding any other provision of this section, no individual or family farmer may be a debtor under this title who has been a debtor in a case pending under this title at any time in the preceding 180 days if—

(1) the case was dismissed by the court for willful failure of the debtor to abide by orders of the court, or to appear before the court in proper prosecution of the case; or

(2) the debtor requested and obtained the voluntary dismissal of the case following the filing of a request for relief from the automatic stay provided by section 362 of this title.

(h)(1) Subject to paragraphs (2) and (3), and notwithstanding any other provision of this section, an individual may not be a debtor under this title unless such individual has, during the 180-day period preceding the date of filing of the petition by such individual, received from an approved nonprofit budget and credit counseling agency described in section 111(a) an individual or group briefing (including a briefing conducted by telephone or on the Internet) that outlined the opportunities for available credit counseling and assisted such individual in performing a related budget analysis.

* * *

(3)(A) * * * The requirements of paragraph (1) shall not apply with respect to a debtor who submits to the court a certification that—

(i) describes exigent circumstances that merit a waiver of the requirements of paragraph (1);

(ii) states that the debtor requested credit counseling services from an approved nonprofit budget and credit counseling agency, but was unable to obtain the services referred to in paragraph (1) during the 5-day period beginning on the date on which the debtor made that request; and

(iii) is satisfactory to the court.

(B) With respect to a debtor, an exemption under subparagraph (A) shall cease to apply to that debtor on the date on which the debtor meets the requirements of paragraph (1), but in no case may the exemption apply to that debtor after the date that is 30 days after the debtor files a petition, except that the court, for cause, may order an additional 15 days.

* * *

OTHER SECTIONS

It is always important to look to section 101 definitions: debtor, entity, individual with regular income, insolvent, person, transfer.

Read section 109 with sections 301, 302, and 303 on commencement of voluntary, joint, and involuntary cases. The phrase "commencement of the case" is explained in sections 301(b) and 303(a). The phrase "order for relief" is explained in sections 301(b) and 303(h).

Also, read section 109(b) together with section 707 which governs dismissal of chapter 7 cases.

* * *

CHAPTER 3—CASE ADMINISTRATION

SUBCHAPTER I—COMMENCEMENT OF A CASE

SUBCHAPTER I—COMMENCEMENT OF A CASE

§ 301. Voluntary cases

(a) A voluntary case under a chapter of this title is commenced by the filing with the bankruptcy court of a petition under such chapter by an entity that may be a debtor under such chapter.

(b) The commencement of a voluntary case under a chapter of this title constitutes an order for relief under such chapter.

UNOFFICIAL COMMENTS

Notice that this section uses both the phrase "commencement of a * * * case" and the phrase "order for relief." Other Code provisions use one but not both phrases. For voluntary, i.e., debtor-filed, cases, the two phrases have the same meaning. You will see in section 303 (if you look carefully) that the two phrases do not have the same meaning in involuntary, i.e., creditor-filed, cases.

OTHER SECTIONS

The term "entity" is defined in section 101. That definition makes sense only if you also look at the section 101 definition of "person."

You need to read section 301 together with section 109 which explains the section 301(a) phrase "entity that may be a debtor under such chapter."

And, compare sections 301 and 303.

Section 342 requires notice of the order for relief. Looking at Official Form 9 on pages 274–275 infra might help your understanding of the notice requirement.

Section 301 requires that a "petition" be filed. And, looking at Official Form 1, the section 301 "petition", on page 234 infra, might be helpful in understanding section 301.

§ 302. Joint cases

(a) A joint case under a chapter of this title is commenced by the filing with the bankruptcy court of a single petition under such chapter by an individual that may be a debtor under such chapter and such individual's spouse. The commencement of a joint case under a chapter of this title constitutes an order for relief under such chapter.

(b) After the commencement of a joint case, the court shall determine the extent, if any, to which the debtors' estates shall be consolidated.

UNOFFICIAL COMMENTS

You need to see the difference between joint administration under section 302(a) and Rule 1015 on page 223 infra and substantive consolidation under section 302(b) [and section 105.] As the terms suggest, joint administration is merely administrative while substantive consolidation affects substantive rights. In essence, in section 302(b) substantive consolidation, the court is baking one large mixed fruit pie to be eaten by the husband's creditors and the wife's creditors. In joint administration, there is a peach pie for the wife's creditors and a banana pie for the husband's creditors being baked by the court in the same oven at the same time.

OTHER SECTIONS

Spouses' decision to file a joint petition under section 302 affects their choices as to what law determines what property will be exempt under section 522(b) but not how much property will be exempt under that law, section 522(m).

§ 303. Involuntary cases

(a) An involuntary case may be commenced only under chapter 7 or 11 of this title, and only against a person, except a farmer, family farmer, or a corporation that is not a moneyed, business, or commercial corporation, that may be a debtor under the chapter under which such case is commenced.

(b) An involuntary case against a person is commenced by the filing with the bankruptcy court of a petition under chapter 7 or 11 of this title—

    (1) by three or more entities, each of which is either a holder of a claim against such person that is not contingent as to liability or the subject of a bona fide dispute as to liability or amount, or an indenture trustee representing such a holder, if such noncontingent, undisputed claims aggregate at least $15,325 more than the value of any lien on property of the debtor securing such claims held by the holders of such claims;

(2) if there are fewer than 12 such holders, excluding any employee or insider of such person and any transferee of a transfer that is voidable under section 544, 545, 547, 548, 549, or 724(a) of this title, by one or more of such holders that hold in the aggregate at least $15,325 of such claims;

(3) if such person is a partnership—

(A) by fewer than all of the general partners in such partnership; or

(B) if relief has been ordered under this title with respect to all of the general partners in such partnership, by a general partner in such partnership, the trustee of such a general partner, or a holder of a claim against such partnership; or

(4) by a foreign representative of the estate in a foreign proceeding concerning such person.

(c) After the filing of a petition under this section but before the case is dismissed or relief is ordered, a creditor holding an unsecured claim that is not contingent, other than a creditor filing under subsection (b) of this section, may join in the petition with the same effect as if such joining creditor were a petitioning creditor under subsection (b) of this section.

(d) The debtor, or a general partner in a partnership debtor that did not join in the petition, may file an answer to a petition under this section.

(e) After notice and a hearing, and for cause, the court may require the petitioners under this section to file a bond to indemnify the debtor for such amounts as the court may later allow under subsection (i) of this section.

(f) Notwithstanding section 363 of this title, except to the extent that the court orders otherwise, and until an order for relief in the case, any business of the debtor may continue to operate, and the debtor may continue to use, acquire, or dispose of property as if an involuntary case concerning the debtor had not been commenced.

(g) At any time after the commencement of an involuntary case under chapter 7 of this title but before an order for relief in the case, the court, on request of a party in interest, after notice to the debtor and a hearing, and if necessary to preserve the property of the estate or to prevent loss to the estate, may order the United States trustee to appoint an interim trustee under section 701 of this title to take possession of the property of the estate and to operate any business of the debtor. Before an order for relief, the debtor may regain possession of property in the possession of a trustee ordered appointed under this subsection if the debtor files such bond as the court requires, conditioned on the debtor's accounting for and delivering to the trustee, if there is an order for relief in the case, such property, or the value, as of the date the debtor regains possession, of such property.

(h) If the petition is not timely controverted, the court shall order relief against the debtor in an involuntary case under the chapter under which the petition was filed. Otherwise, after trial, the court shall order relief against the debtor in an involuntary case under the chapter under which the petition was filed, only if—

(1) the debtor is generally not paying such debtor's debts as such debts become due unless such debts are the subject of a bona fide dispute as to liability or amount; or

(2) within 120 days before the date of the filing of the petition, a custodian, other than a trustee, receiver, or agent appointed or authorized to take charge of less than substantially all of the property of the debtor for the purpose of enforcing a lien against such property, was appointed or took possession.

(i) If the court dismisses a petition under this section other than on consent of all petitioners and the debtor, and if the debtor does not waive the right to judgment under this subsection, the court may grant judgment—

    (1) against the petitioners and in favor of the debtor for—

        (A) costs; or

        (B) a reasonable attorney's fee; or

    (2) against any petitioner that filed the petition in bad faith, for—

        (A) any damages proximately caused by such filing; or

        (B) punitive damages.

(j) Only after notice to all creditors and a hearing may the court dismiss a petition filed under this section—

    (1) on the motion of a petitioner;

    (2) on consent of all petitioners and the debtor; or

    (3) for want of prosecution.

UNOFFICIAL COMMENTS

Don't use the word "insolvent" in discussing section 303(h)(1), to describe failure to pay debts. That is not how the Bankruptcy Code uses the word "insolvent" in section 101.

Note that the date of the commencement of the case and the date of the order for relief are not the same in involuntary cases. There is a gap period in involuntary cases between commencement and order for relief. Remember that other Code provisions use one but not both terms.

OTHER SECTIONS

Again, look to section 101 for definitions: debtor, entity, person.

Because of section 104, the dollar amounts in section 303 change every three years to reflect changes in the Consumer Price Index.

Section 502(f) deals with claims that arise during the gap period between commencement of an involuntary cases and the order for relief.

Section 549(b) governs transfers of property of the estate that occur during that gap period.

* * *

§ 305. Abstention

(a) The court, after notice and a hearing, may dismiss a case under this title, or may suspend all proceedings in a case under this title, at any time if—

    (1) the interests of creditors and the debtor would be better served by such dismissal or suspension; or

    (2)(A) a petition under section 1515 for recognition of a foreign proceeding has been granted; and

(B) the purposes of chapter 15 of this title would be best served by such dismissal or suspension.

(b) A foreign representative may seek dismissal or suspension under subsection (a)(2) of this section.

(c) An order under subsection (a) of this section dismissing a case or suspending all proceedings in a case, or a decision not so to dismiss or suspend, is not reviewable by appeal or otherwise by the court of appeals under section 158(d), 1291, or 1292 of title 28 or by the Supreme Court of the United States under section 1254 of title 28.

UNOFFICIAL COMMENTS

Even though the section title is "Abstention" the operative verb is "dismiss". Not used much. Note the conjunction "and" in section 305(a)(1). Hard to envision a situation in which the court would find that dismissal of a voluntary petition, i.e., a petition filed by the debtor, was in the "interests" of that filing debtor.

OTHER SECTIONS

In chapter 7 cases, most dismissal issues arise under 707; in chapter 11, it is 1112; in chapter 13, it is 1307.

* * *

§ 307.   United States trustee

The United States trustee may raise and may appear and be heard on any issue in any case or proceeding under this title but may not file a plan pursuant to section 1121(c) of this title.

§ 308.   Debtor reporting requirements

(a) For purposes of this section, the term "profitability" means, with respect to a debtor, the amount of money that the debtor has earned or lost during current and recent fiscal periods.

(b) A debtor in a small business case shall file periodic financial and other reports containing information including—

    (1) the debtor's profitability;

    (2) reasonable approximations of the debtor's projected cash receipts and cash disbursements over a reasonable period;

    (3) comparisons of actual cash receipts and disbursements with projections in prior reports;

    (4) whether the debtor is—

        (A) in compliance in all material respects with postpetition requirements imposed by this title and the Federal Rules of Bankruptcy Procedure; and

        (B) timely filing tax returns and other required government filings and paying taxes and other administrative expenses when due;

    (5) if the debtor is not in compliance with the requirements referred to in paragraph (A) or filing tax returns and other required government filings and making the payments referred to in paragraph (B), what the failures are and how, at what cost, and when the debtor intends to remedy such failures; and

(6) such other matters as are in the best interests of the debtor and creditors, and in the public interest in fair and efficient procedures under chapter 11 of this title.

UNOFFICIAL COMMENTS

The title for this section is at best incomplete. This section only applies to a small business debtor. And, probably, will only be applied in a small business debtor chapter 11 case even though the section is in chapter 3.

* * *

SUBCHAPTER II—OFFICERS

§ 321. Eligibility to serve as trustee

(a) A person may serve as trustee in a case under this title only if such person is—

(1) an individual that is competent to perform the duties of trustee and, in a case under chapter 7, 12, or 13 of this title, resides or has an office in the judicial district within which the case is pending, or in any judicial district adjacent to such district; or

(2) a corporation authorized by such corporation's charter or bylaws to act as trustee, and, in a case under chapter 7, 12, or 13 of this title, having an office in at least one of such districts.

(b) A person that has served as an examiner in the case may not serve as trustee in the case.

(c) The United States trustee for the judicial district in which the case is pending is eligible to serve as trustee in the case if necessary.

* * *

§ 323. Role and capacity of trustee

(a) The trustee in a case under this title is the representative of the estate.

(b) The trustee in a case under this title has capacity to sue and be sued.

* * *

§ 326. Limitation on compensation of trustee

(a) In a case under chapter 7 or 11, the court may allow reasonable compensation under section 330 of this title of the trustee for the trustee's services, payable after the trustee renders such services, not to exceed 25 percent on the first $5,000 or less, 10 percent on any amount in excess of $5,000 but not in excess of $50,000, 5 percent on any amount in excess of $50,000 but not in excess of $1,000,000, and reasonable compensation not to exceed 3 percent of such moneys in excess of $1,000,000, upon all moneys disbursed or turned over in the case by the trustee to parties in interest, excluding the debtor, but including holders of secured claims.

(b) In a case under chapter 12 or 13 of this title, the court may not allow compensation for services or reimbursement of expenses of the United States trustee or of a standing trustee appointed under section 586(b) of title 28, but may allow reasonable compensation under section 330 of this title of a trustee appointed under section 1202(a) or 1302(a) of this title for the trustee's services, payable after the trustee renders such services, not to exceed five percent upon all payments under the plan.

* * *

§ 327. Employment of professional persons

(a) Except as otherwise provided in this section, the trustee, with the court's approval, may employ one or more attorneys, accountants, appraisers, auctioneers, or other professional persons, that do not hold or represent an interest adverse to the estate, and that are disinterested persons, to represent or assist the trustee in carrying out the trustee's duties under this title.

(b) If the trustee is authorized to operate the business of the debtor under section 721, 1202, or 1108 of this title, and if the debtor has regularly employed attorneys, accountants, or other professional persons on salary, the trustee may retain or replace such professional persons if necessary in the operation of such business.

(c) In a case under chapter 7, 12, or 11 of this title, a person is not disqualified for employment under this section solely because of such person's employment by or representation of a creditor, unless there is objection by another creditor or the United States trustee, in which case the court shall disapprove such employment if there is an actual conflict of interest.

(d) The court may authorize the trustee to act as attorney or accountant for the estate if such authorization is in the best interest of the estate.

(e) The trustee, with the court's approval, may employ, for a specified special purpose, other than to represent the trustee in conducting the case, an attorney that has represented the debtor, if in the best interest of the estate, and if such attorney does not represent or hold any interest adverse to the debtor or to the estate with respect to the matter on which such attorney is to be employed.

(f) The trustee may not employ a person that has served as an examiner in the case.

§ 328. Limitation on compensation of professional persons

(a) The trustee, or a committee appointed under section 1102 of this title, with the court's approval, may employ or authorize the employment of a professional person under section 327 or 1103 of this title, as the case may be, on any reasonable terms and conditions of employment, including on a retainer, on an hourly basis, on a fixed or percentage fee basis, or on a contingent fee basis. Notwithstanding such terms and conditions, the court may allow compensation different from the compensation provided under such terms and conditions after the conclusion of such employment, if such terms and conditions prove to have been improvident in light of developments not capable of being anticipated at the time of the fixing of such terms and conditions.

(b) If the court has authorized a trustee to serve as an attorney or accountant for the estate under section 327(d) of this title, the court may allow compensation for the trustee's services as such attorney or accountant only to the extent that the trustee performed services as attorney or accountant for the estate and not for performance of any of the trustee's duties that are generally performed by a trustee without the assistance of an attorney or accountant for the estate.

(c) Except as provided in section 327(c), 327(e), or 1107(b) of this title, the court may deny allowance of compensation for services and reimbursement of expenses of a professional person employed under section 327 or 1103 of this title if, at any time during such professional person's employment under section 327 or 1103 of this title, such professional person is not a disinterested person, or represents or holds an interest adverse to the interest of the estate with respect to the matter on which such professional person is employed.

§ 329. Debtor's transactions with attorneys

(a) Any attorney representing a debtor in a case under this title, or in connection with such a case, whether or not such attorney applies for compensation under this title, shall file with the court a statement of the compensation paid or agreed to be paid, if such payment or agreement was made after one year before the date of the filing of the petition, for services rendered or to be rendered in contemplation of or in connection with the case by such attorney, and the source of such compensation.

(b) If such compensation exceeds the reasonable value of any such services, the court may cancel any such agreement, or order the return of any such payment, to the extent excessive, to—

    (1) the estate, if the property transferred—

        (A) would have been property of the estate; or

        (B) was to be paid by or on behalf of the debtor under a plan under chapter 11, 12, or 13 of this title; or

    (2) the entity that made such payment.

§ 330. Compensation of officers

(a)(1) After notice to the parties in interest and the United States Trustee and a hearing, and subject to sections 326, 328, and 329, the court may award to a trustee, a consumer privacy ombudsman appointed under section 332, an examiner, an ombudsman appointed under section 333, or a professional person employed under section 327 or 1103—

        (A) reasonable compensation for actual, necessary services rendered by the trustee, examiner, ombudsman, professional person, or attorney and by any paraprofessional person employed by any such person; and

        (B) reimbursement for actual, necessary expenses.

    (2) The court may, on its own motion or on the motion of the United States Trustee, the United States Trustee for the District or Region, the trustee for the estate, or any other party in interest, award compensation that is less than the amount of compensation that is requested.

    (3) In determining the amount of reasonable compensation to be awarded to an examiner, trustee under chapter 11, or professional person, the court shall consider the nature, the extent, and the value of such services, taking into account all relevant factors, including—

        (A) the time spent on such services;

        (B) the rates charged for such services;

(C) whether the services were necessary to the administration of, or beneficial at the time at which the service was rendered toward the completion of, a case under this title;

(D) whether the services were performed within a reasonable amount of time commensurate with the complexity, importance, and nature of the problem, issue, or task addressed;

(E) with respect to a professional person, whether the person is board certified or otherwise has demonstrated skill and experience in the bankruptcy field; and

(F) whether the compensation is reasonable based on the customary compensation charged by comparably skilled practitioners in cases other than cases under this title.

(4)(A) Except as provided in subparagraph (B), the court shall not allow compensation for—

(i) unnecessary duplication of services; or

(ii) services that were not—

(I) reasonably likely to benefit the debtor's estate; or

(II) necessary to the administration of the case.

(B) In a chapter 12 or chapter 13 case in which the debtor is an individual, the court may allow reasonable compensation to the debtor's attorney for representing the interests of the debtor in connection with the bankruptcy case based on a consideration of the benefit and necessity of such services to the debtor and the other factors set forth in this section.

(5) The court shall reduce the amount of compensation awarded under this section by the amount of any interim compensation awarded under section 331, and, if the amount of such interim compensation exceeds the amount of compensation awarded under this section, may order the return of the excess to the estate.

(6) Any compensation awarded for the preparation of a fee application shall be based on the level and skill reasonably required to prepare the application.

(7) In determining the amount of reasonable compensation to be awarded to a trustee, the court shall treat such compensation as a commission, based on section 326.

(b)(1) There shall be paid from the filing fee in a case under chapter 7 of this title $45 to the trustee serving in such case, after such trustee's services are rendered.

(2) The Judicial Conference of the United States—

(A) shall prescribe additional fees of the same kind as prescribed under section 1914(b) of title 28; and

(B) may prescribe notice of appearance fees and fees charged against distributions in cases under this title;

to pay $15 to trustees serving in cases after such trustees' services are rendered. Beginning 1 year after the date of the enactment of the Bankruptcy Reform Act of 1994, such $15 shall be paid in addition to the amount paid under paragraph (1).

* * *

UNOFFICIAL COMMENT

In reading a statute, it is sometimes important to notice what is missing. If your prof covers Lamie v. U.S. Trustee, 540 U.S. 526 (2004), the Court emphasized that a reference to "Chapter 7" was missing from section 330(b)(4).

§ 333. Appointment of patient care ombudsman

(a)(1) If the debtor in a case under chapter 7, 9, or 11 is a health care business, the court shall order, not later than 30 days after the commencement of the case, the appointment of an ombudsman to monitor the quality of patient care and to represent the interests of the patients of the health care business unless the court finds that the appointment of such ombudsman is not necessary for the protection of patients under the specific facts of the case.

(2)(A) If the court orders the appointment of an ombudsman under paragraph (1), the United States trustee shall appoint 1 disinterested person (other than the United States trustee) to serve as such ombudsman. * * *

(b) An ombudsman appointed under subsection (a) shall—

(1) monitor the quality of patient care provided to patients of the debtor, to the extent necessary under the circumstances, including interviewing patients and physicians;

(2) not later than 60 days after the date of appointment, and not less frequently than at 60-day intervals thereafter, report to the court after notice to the parties in interest, at a hearing or in writing, regarding the quality of patient care provided to patients of the debtor; and

(3) if such ombudsman determines that the quality of patient care provided to patients of the debtor is declining significantly or is otherwise being materially compromised, file with the court a motion or a written report, with notice to the parties in interest immediately upon making such determination.

* * *

SUBCHAPTER III—ADMINISTRATION

§ 341. Meetings of creditors and equity security holders

(a) Within a reasonable time after the order for relief in a case under this title, the United States trustee shall convene and preside at a meeting of creditors.

(b) The United States trustee may convene a meeting of any equity security holders.

(c) The court may not preside at, and may not attend, any meeting under this section including any final meeting of creditors. Notwithstanding any local court rule, provision of a State constitution, any otherwise applicable nonbankruptcy law, or any other requirement that representation at the meeting of creditors under subsection (a) be by an attorney, a creditor holding a consumer debt or any representative of the creditor (which may include an entity or an employee of an entity and may be a representative for more than 1 creditor) shall be permitted to appear at and participate in the meeting of creditors in a case under chapter 7 or 13, either alone or in conjunction with an attorney for the creditor. Nothing in this subsection shall be construed to require any creditor to be represented by an attorney at any meeting of creditors.

(d) Prior to the conclusion of the meeting of creditors or equity security holders, the trustee shall orally examine the debtor to ensure that the debtor in a case under chapter 7 of this title is aware of—

(1) the potential consequences of seeking a discharge in bankruptcy, including the effects on credit history;

(2) the debtor's ability to file a petition under a different chapter of this title;

(3) the effect of receiving a discharge of debts under this title; and

(4) the effect of reaffirming a debt, including the debtor's knowledge of the provisions of section 524(d) of this title.

(e) Notwithstanding subsections (a) and (b), the court, on the request of a party in interest and after notice and a hearing, for cause may order that the United States trustee not convene a meeting of creditors or equity security holders if the debtor has filed a plan as to which the debtor solicited acceptances prior to the commencement of the case.

UNOFFICIAL COMMENTS

The meeting required by section 341, generally (and, cleverly) referred to as the "341 meeting", provides an opportunity for creditors to question the debtor under oath. For example, creditors can ask the debtor to explain what happened to all of the assets listed on the financial statements that the debtor gave them when applying for credit that are not listed on the schedules that the debtor filed with the bankruptcy court clerk's office when she filed her bankruptcy petition. Note that the US Trustee presides at the 341 meeting. Judges do not attend.

Other Statutes and . . .

Section 343 should be a part of section 341. It explains what happens at the 341 meeting (albeit not as clearly as I just have).

Section 521(a)(4) requires the debtor to provide books and records to the trustee. Section 521(e)(2) requires that the debtor provide tax returns at least 7 days before the 341 meeting.

It might be helpful to look at Rule 2004 on page 225 infra and the United States Bankruptcy Court Central District of California General Order, 93-01, In re Automatic Dismissal of Cases for Failure of Debtor(s) to Appear at Scheduled Section 341(a) Meetings of Creditors, on page 338.

§ 342. Notice

(a) There shall be given such notice as is appropriate, * * * of an order for relief in a case under this title.

(b) Before the commencement of a case under this title by an individual whose debts are primarily consumer debts, the clerk shall give to such individual written notice containing—

(1) a brief description of—

(A) chapters 7, 11, 12, and 13 and the general purpose, benefits, and costs of proceeding under each of those chapters; and

(B) the types of services available from credit counseling agencies; and

(2) statements specifying that—

(A) a person who knowingly and fraudulently conceals assets or makes a false oath or statement under penalty of perjury in connection with a case under this title shall be subject to fine, imprisonment, or both; and

(B) all information supplied by a debtor in connection with a case under this title is subject to examination by the Attorney General.

* * *

(d) In a case under chapter 7 of this title in which the debtor is an individual and in which the presumption of abuse arises under section 707(b), the clerk shall give written notice to all creditors not later than 10 days after the date of the filing of the petition that the presumption of abuse has arisen.

UNOFFICIAL COMMENTS

Notice to creditors under section 342(a) only makes sense if you know that (1) a bankruptcy petition is accompanied by various forms, including a Form 6, Schedule D, Schedule E and Schedule F listing creditors and (2) creditors can participate in a bankruptcy case in various meaningful ways.

Official Form 9, infra at page 274, is the form of notice.

§ 343. Examination of the debtor

The debtor shall appear and submit to examination under oath at the meeting of creditors under section 341(a) of this title. Creditors, any indenture trustee, any trustee or examiner in the case, or the United States trustee may examine the debtor. The United States trustee may administer the oath required under this section.

OTHER SECTIONS

Under section 344, a debtor may (not must) be given immunity from prosecution.

Section 521(a)(4) requires the debtor to provide books and records to the trustee. Section 521(e)(2) requires that the debtor provide tax returns at least 7 days before the 341 meeting.

A debtor's failure to appear at the section 341 meeting for questioning may be cause for dismissal of the case under sections 707(a), 1112(b), and 1307(c).

A Rule 2004 examination is similar in scope to a section 343 examination. The differences are that a Rule 2004 examination may be held at any time during the pendency of the case; may be conducted upon any entity connected with the bankruptcy, not just the debtor; contemplates an order by the court upon motion of the requesting party; and is presided over by the requesting party without the presence of the U.S. Trustee.

§ 344. Self-incrimination; immunity

Immunity for persons required to submit to examination, to testify, or to provide information in a case under this title may be granted under part V of title 18.

* * *

§ 348. Effect of conversion

(a) Conversion of a case from a case under one chapter of this title to a case under another chapter of this title constitutes an order for relief under the chapter to which the case is converted, but, except as provided in subsections (b) and (c) of this section, does not effect a change in the date of the filing of the petition, the commencement of the case, or the order for relief.

(b) Unless the court for cause orders otherwise, in sections 701(a), 727(a)(10), 727(b), 1102(a), 1110(a)(1), 1121(b), 1121(c), 1141(d)(4), 1201(a), 1221, 1228(a), 1301(a), and 1305(a) of this title, "the order for relief under this chapter" in a chapter to which a case has been converted under section 706, 1112, 1208, or 1307 of this title means the conversion of such case to such chapter.

(c) Sections 342 and 365(d) of this title apply in a case that has been converted under section 706, 1112, 1208, or 1307 of this title, as if the conversion order were the order for relief.

(d) A claim against the estate or the debtor that arises after the order for relief but before conversion in a case that is converted under section 1112, 1208, or 1307 of this title, other than a claim specified in section 503(b) of this title, shall be treated for all purposes as if such claim had arisen immediately before the date of the filing of the petition.

(e) Conversion of a case under section 706, 1112, 1208, or 1307 of this title terminates the service of any trustee or examiner that is serving in the case before such conversion.

(f)(1) Except as provided in paragraph (2), when a case under chapter 13 of this title is converted to a case under another chapter under this title—

    (A) property of the estate in the converted case shall consist of property of the estate, as of the date of filing of the petition, that remains in the possession of or is under the control of the debtor on the date of conversion;

    (B) valuations of property and of allowed secured claims in the chapter 13 case shall apply only in a case converted to a case under chapter 11 or 12, but not in a case converted to a case under chapter 7, with allowed secured claims in cases under chapters 11 and 12 reduced to the extent that they have been paid in accordance with the chapter 13 plan; and

    (C) with respect to cases converted from chapter 13—

        (i) the claim of any creditor holding security as of the date of filing of the petition shall continue to be secured by that security unless the full amount of such claim determined under applicable nonbankruptcy law has been paid in full as of the date of conversion, notwithstanding any valuation or determination of the amount of an allowed secured claim made for the purposes of the case under chapter 13; and

        (ii) unless a prebankruptcy default has been fully cured under the plan at the time of conversion, in any proceeding under this title or otherwise, the default shall have the effect given under applicable nonbankruptcy law.

(2) If the debtor converts a case under chapter 13 of this title to a case under another chapter under this title in bad faith, the property of the estate in the converted case shall consist of the property of the estate as of the date of conversion.

UNOFFICIAL COMMENT

The section title is descriptive. The section becomes applicable only after the court has ordered conversion of a bankruptcy case from one chapter to another and deals only with questions as to the effect of such conversion. The question of whether a court should order conversion is answered in sections 706, 1112, and 1307.

§ 349. Effect of dismissal

(a) Unless the court, for cause, orders otherwise, the dismissal of a case under this title does not bar the discharge, in a later case under this title, of debts that were dischargeable in the case dismissed; nor does the dismissal of a case under this title prejudice the debtor with regard to the filing of a subsequent petition under this title, except as provided in section 109(g) of this title.

(b) Unless the court, for cause, orders otherwise, a dismissal of a case other than under section 742 of this title—

(1) reinstates—

(A) any proceeding or custodianship superseded under section 543 of this title;

(B) any transfer avoided under section 522, 544, 545, 547, 548, 549, or 724(a) of this title, or preserved under section 510(c)(2), 522(i)(2), or 551 of this title; and

(C) any lien voided under section 506(d) of this title;

(2) vacates any order, judgment, or transfer ordered, under section 522(i)(1), 542, 550, or 553 of this title; and

(3) revests the property of the estate in the entity in which such property was vested immediately before the commencement of the case under this title.

UNOFFICIAL COMMENTS

Again, the section title is descriptive. The section becomes applicable only after the court has ordered dismissal of a bankruptcy case and deals only with questions as to the effect of such dismissal. The question of whether a court should order dismissal is answered in sections 706, 1112, and 1307.

* * *

SUBCHAPTER IV—ADMINISTRATIVE POWERS

§ 361. Adequate protection

When adequate protection is required under section 362, 363, or 364 of this title of an interest of an entity in property, such adequate protection may be provided by—

(1) requiring the trustee to make a cash payment or periodic cash payments to such entity, to the extent that the stay under section 362 of this title, use, sale, or lease under section 363 of this title, or any grant of a lien under section 364 of this title results in a decrease in the value of such entity's interest in such property;

(2) providing to such entity an additional or replacement lien to the extent that such stay, use, sale, lease, or grant results in a decrease in the value of such entity's interest in such property; or

(3) granting such other relief, other than entitling such entity to compensation allowable under section 503(b)(1) of this title as an administrative expense, as will result in the realization by such entity of the indubitable equivalent of such entity's interest in such property.

UNOFFICIAL COMMENTS

When you think "adequate protection", think about secured creditors and their rights in their collateral. "Adequate protection" is about recognition and preservation of a creditor's collateral value. That is what the oblique references to "interest of an entity in property" mean.

Section 361 gives three examples of what "may be" "adequate protection" of such rights in collateral. The third such example, "indubitable equivalent", is obviously the most comprehensive (and the most likely to be involved in a law school exam question).

OTHER SECTIONS

The introduction to section 361 indicates the connection between section 361 and section 362 and section 363 and section 364. You also need to read section 361 together with section 507(b) which explains what happens when the protection that the bankruptcy court thought would be adequate turns out to be inadequate.

The 2005 amendments added "adequate protection" provisions to sections 521(a)(6), 1325(a)(5) and section 1326(a).

Sections 365 and 366 use the phrase "adequate assurance" which is different from "adequate protection."

You will see the phrase "indubitable equivalent" again in your studying cram down of secured claims in section 1129.

§ 362.   Automatic stay

(a) Except as provided in subsection (b) of this section, a petition filed under section 301, 302, or 303 of this title, or ＊ ＊ ＊ operates as a stay, applicable to all entities of—

    (1) the commencement or continuation, including the issuance or employment of process, of a judicial, administrative, or other action or proceeding against the debtor that was or could have been commenced before the commencement of the case under this title, or to recover a claim against the debtor that arose before the commencement of the case under this title;

    (2) the enforcement, against the debtor or against property of the estate, of a judgment obtained before the commencement of the case under this title; *garnishment*

    (3) *blc wages made earned before filing petition* any act to obtain possession of property of the estate or of property from the estate or to exercise control over property of the estate; *(eviction)*

    (4) any act to create, perfect, or enforce any lien against property of the estate;

    (5) any act to create, perfect, or enforce against property of the debtor any lien to the extent that such lien secures a claim that arose before the commencement of the case under this title;

    (6) any act to collect, assess, or recover a claim against the debtor that arose before the commencement of the case under this title;

    (7) the setoff of any debt owing to the debtor that arose before the commencement of the case under this title against any claim against the debtor; and

    (8) the commencement or continuation of a proceeding before the United States Tax Court concerning tax liability of a debtor that is a corporation for a taxable period the bankruptcy court may determine or concerning the tax liability of a debtor who is an individual for a taxable period ending before the date of the order for relief under this title.

Exceptions **(b)** The filing of a petition under section 301, 302, or 303 of this title, * * * does not operate as a stay—

(1) under subsection (a) of this section, of the commencement or continuation of a criminal action or proceeding against the debtor;

(2) under subsection (a)—

(A) of the commencement or continuation of a civil action or proceeding—

(i) for the establishment of paternity;

(ii) for the establishment or modification of an order for domestic support obligations;

(iii) concerning child custody or visitation;

(iv) for the dissolution of a marriage, except to the extent that such proceeding seeks to determine the division of property that is property of the estate; or

(v) regarding domestic violence;

(B) of the collection of a domestic support obligation from property that is not property of the estate;

(C) with respect to the withholding of income that is property of the estate or property of the debtor for payment of a domestic support obligation under a judicial or administrative order or a statute; *garnishment w/ child domestic support*

(D) of the withholding, suspension, or restriction of a driver's license, a professional or occupational license, or a recreational license, under State law, as specified in section 466(a)(16) of the Social Security Act; * * *

(3) under subsection (a) of this section, of any act to perfect, or to maintain or continue the perfection of, an interest in property to the extent that the trustee's rights and powers are subject to such perfection under section 546(b) of this title or to the extent that such act is accomplished within the period provided under section 547(e)(2)(A) of this title;

(4) under paragraph (1), (2), (3), or (6) of subsection (a) of this section, of the commencement or continuation of an action or proceeding by a governmental unit or any organization exercising authority under the Convention on the Prohibition of the Development, Production, Stockpiling and Use of Chemical Weapons and on Their Destruction, opened for signature on January 13, 1993, to enforce such governmental unit's or organization's police and regulatory power, including the enforcement of a judgment other than a money judgment, obtained in an action or proceeding by the governmental unit to enforce such governmental unit's or organization's police or regulatory power;

* * *

(10) under subsection (a) of this section, of any act by a lessor to the debtor under a lease of nonresidential real property that has terminated by the expiration of the stated term of the lease before the commencement of or during a case under this title to obtain possession of such property;

(11) under subsection (a) of this section, of the presentment of a negotiable instrument and the giving of notice of and protesting dishonor of such an instrument;

Take steps against debtor to show steps are futile just so creditor can go after guaranter

* * *

(20) under subsection (a), of any act to enforce any lien against or security interest in real property following entry of the order under subsection (d)(4) as to such real property in any prior case under this title, for a period of 2 years after the date of the entry of such an order, except that the debtor, in a subsequent case under this title, may move for relief from such order based upon changed circumstances or for other good cause shown, after notice and a hearing;

(21) under subsection (a), of any act to enforce any lien against or security interest in real property—

   (A) if the debtor is ineligible under section 109(g) to be a debtor in a case under this title; or

   (B) if the case under this title was filed in violation of a bankruptcy court order in a prior case under this title prohibiting the debtor from being a debtor in another case under this title;

(22) subject to subsection (*l*), under subsection (a)(3), of the continuation of any eviction, unlawful detainer action, or similar proceeding by a lessor against a debtor involving residential property in which the debtor resides as a tenant under a lease or rental agreement and with respect to which the lessor has obtained before the date of the filing of the bankruptcy petition, a judgment for possession of such property against the debtor;

If landlord got judgment of eviction, cant file bankruptcy case to stop the eviction. unless threat to the building

(24) under subsection (a), any transfer that is not avoidable under section 544 and that is not avoidable under section 549;

* * *

(c) Except as provided in subsections (d), (e), (f), and (h) of this section—

(1) the stay of an act against property of the estate under subsection (a) of this section continues until such property is no longer property of the estate;

(2) the stay of any other act under subsection (a) of this section continues until the earliest of—

   (A) the time the case is closed;

   (B) the time the case is dismissed; or

   (C) if the case is a case under chapter 7 of this title concerning an individual or a case under chapter 9, 11, 12, or 13 of this title, the time a discharge is granted or denied;

(3) if a single or joint case is filed by or against a debtor who is an individual in a case under chapter 7, 11, or 13, and if a single or joint case of the debtor was pending within the preceding 1-year period but was dismissed, other than a case refiled under a chapter other than chapter 7 after dismissal under section 707(b)—

   (A) the stay under subsection (a) with respect to any action taken with respect to a debt or property securing such debt or with respect to any lease shall terminate with respect to the debtor on the 30th day after the filing of the later case;

(B) on the motion of a party in interest for continuation of the automatic stay and upon notice and a hearing, the court may extend the stay in particular cases as to any or all creditors (subject to such conditions or limitations as the court may then impose) after notice and a hearing completed before the expiration of the 30-day period only if the party in interest demonstrates that the filing of the later case is in good faith as to the creditors to be stayed; and

(C) for purposes of subparagraph (B), a case is presumptively filed not in good faith (but such presumption may be rebutted by clear and convincing evidence to the contrary)—

(i) as to all creditors, if—

(I) more than 1 previous case under any of chapters 7, 11, and 13 in which the individual was a debtor was pending within the preceding 1-year period;

(II) a previous case under any of chapters 7, 11, and 13 in which the individual was a debtor was dismissed within such 1-year period, after the debtor failed to—

(aa) file or amend the petition or other documents as required by this title or the court without substantial excuse (but mere inadvertence or negligence shall not be a substantial excuse unless the dismissal was caused by the negligence of the debtor's attorney);

(bb) provide adequate protection as ordered by the court; or

(cc) perform the terms of a plan confirmed by the court; or

(III) there has not been a substantial change in the financial or personal affairs of the debtor since the dismissal of the next most previous case under chapter 7, 11, or 13 or any other reason to conclude that the later case will be concluded—

(aa) if a case under chapter 7, with a discharge; or

(bb) if a case under chapter 11 or 13, with a confirmed plan that will be fully performed; and

(ii) as to any creditor that commenced an action under subsection (d) in a previous case in which the individual was a debtor if, as of the date of dismissal of such case, that action was still pending or had been resolved by terminating, conditioning, or limiting the stay as to actions of such creditor; and

(4)(A)(i) if a single or joint case is filed by or against a debtor who is an individual under this title, and if 2 or more single or joint cases of the debtor were pending within the previous year but were dismissed, other than a case refiled under a chapter other than chapter 7 after dismissal under section 707(b), the stay under subsection (a) shall not go into effect upon the filing of the later case; and

(ii) on request of a party in interest, the court shall promptly enter an order confirming that no stay is in effect;

(B) if, within 30 days after the filing of the later case, a party in interest requests the court may order the stay to take effect in the case as to any or all creditors (subject to such conditions or limitations as the court may impose), after notice and a hearing, only if the party in interest demonstrates that the filing of the later case is in good faith as to the creditors to be stayed;

(C) a stay imposed under subparagraph (B) shall be effective on the date of the entry of the order allowing the stay to go into effect; and

(D) for purposes of subparagraph (B), a case is presumptively filed not in good faith (but such presumption may be rebutted by clear and convincing evidence to the contrary)—

    (i) as to all creditors if—

        (I) 2 or more previous cases under this title in which the individual was a debtor were pending within the 1-year period;

        (II) a previous case under this title in which the individual was a debtor was dismissed within the time period stated in this paragraph after the debtor failed to file or amend the petition or other documents as required by this title or the court without substantial excuse (but mere inadvertence or negligence shall not be substantial excuse unless the dismissal was caused by the negligence of the debtor's attorney), failed to provide adequate protection as ordered by the court, or failed to perform the terms of a plan confirmed by the court; or

        (III) there has not been a substantial change in the financial or personal affairs of the debtor since the dismissal of the next most previous case under this title, or any other reason to conclude that the later case will not be concluded, if a case under chapter 7, with a discharge, and if a case under chapter 11 or 13, with a confirmed plan that will be fully performed; or

    (ii) as to any creditor that commenced an action under subsection (d) in a previous case in which the individual was a debtor if, as of the date of dismissal of such case, such action was still pending or had been resolved by terminating, conditioning, or limiting the stay as to such action of such creditor.

(d) On request of a party in interest and after notice and a hearing, the court shall grant relief from the stay provided under subsection (a) of this section, such as by terminating, annulling, modifying, or conditioning such stay—

    (1) for cause, including the lack of adequate protection of an interest in property of such party in interest; *when collateral more than has equity it's adequate protected*

    (2) with respect to a stay of an act against property under subsection (a) of this section, if—

        (A) the debtor does not have an equity in such property; and   *In Re Radden*

        (B) such property is not necessary to an effective reorganization; *Ct only needs to find that property is necessary for effective reorganization*

    (3) with respect to a stay of an act against single asset real estate under subsection (a), by a creditor whose claim is secured by an interest in such real estate, unless, not later than the date that is 90 days after the entry of the order for relief (or such later date as the court may determine for cause by order entered within that 90-day period) or 30 days after the court determines that the debtor is subject to this paragraph, whichever is later—

    (A) the debtor has filed a plan of reorganization that has a reasonable possibility of being confirmed within a reasonable time; or

    (B) the debtor has commenced monthly payments that—

        (i) may, in the debtor's sole discretion, notwithstanding section 363(c)(2), be made from rents or other income generated before, on, or after the date of the commencement of the case by or from the property to each creditor whose claim is secured by such real estate (other than a claim secured by a judgment lien or by an unmatured statutory lien); and

        (ii) are in an amount equal to interest at the then applicable nondefault contract rate of interest on the value of the creditor's interest in the real estate; or

  (4) with respect to a stay of an act against real property under subsection (a), by a creditor whose claim is secured by an interest in such real property, if the court finds that the filing of the petition was part of a scheme to delay, hinder, or defraud creditors that involved either—

    (A) transfer of all or part ownership of, or other interest in, such real property without the consent of the secured creditor or court approval; or

    (B) multiple bankruptcy filings affecting such real property. If recorded in compliance with applicable State laws governing notices of interests or liens in real property, an order entered under paragraph (4) shall be binding in any other case under this title purporting to affect such real property filed not later than 2 years after the date of the entry of such order by the court, except that a debtor in a subsequent case under this title may move for relief from such order based upon changed circumstances or for good cause shown, after notice and a hearing. Any Federal, State, or local governmental unit that accepts notices of interests or liens in real property shall accept any certified copy of an order described in this subsection for indexing and recording.

  (e)(1) Thirty days after a request under subsection (d) of this section for relief from the stay of any act against property of the estate under subsection (a) of this section, such stay is terminated with respect to the party in interest making such request, unless the court, after notice and a hearing, orders such stay continued in effect pending the conclusion of, or as a result of, a final hearing and determination under subsection (d) of this section. A hearing under this subsection may be a preliminary hearing, or may be consolidated with the final hearing under subsection (d) of this section. The court shall order such stay continued in effect pending the conclusion of the final hearing under subsection (d) of this section if there is a reasonable likelihood that the party opposing relief from such stay will prevail at the conclusion of such final hearing. If the hearing under this subsection is a preliminary hearing, then such final hearing shall be concluded not later than thirty days after the conclusion of such preliminary hearing, unless the 30-day period is extended with the consent of the parties in interest or for a specific time which the court finds is required by compelling circumstances.

    (2) Notwithstanding paragraph (1), in a case under chapter 7, 11, or 13 in which the debtor is an individual, the stay under subsection (a) shall terminate on the date that is 60 days after a request is made by a party in interest under subsection (d), unless—

    (A) a final decision is rendered by the court during the 60-day period beginning on the date of the request; or

    (B) such 60-day period is extended—

        (i) by agreement of all parties in interest; or

        (ii) by the court for such specific period of time as the court finds is required for good cause, as described in findings made by the court.

* * *

    (g) In any hearing under subsection (d) or (e) of this section concerning relief from the stay of any act under subsection (a) of this section—

    (1) the party requesting such relief has the burden of proof on the issue of the debtor's equity in property; and

    (2) the party opposing such relief has the burden of proof on all other issues.

    (h)(1) In a case in which the debtor is an individual, the stay provided by subsection (a) is terminated with respect to personal property of the estate or of the debtor securing in whole or in part a claim, or subject to an unexpired lease, and such personal property shall no longer be property of the estate if the debtor fails within the applicable time set by section 521(a)(2)—

    (A) to file timely any statement of intention required under section 521(a)(2) with respect to such personal property or to indicate in such statement that the debtor will either surrender such personal property or retain it and, if retaining such personal property, either redeem such personal property pursuant to section 722, enter into an agreement of the kind specified in section 524(c) applicable to the debt secured by such personal property, or assume such unexpired lease pursuant to section 365(p) if the trustee does not do so, as applicable; and

    (B) to take timely the action specified in such statement, as it may be amended before expiration of the period for taking action, unless such statement specifies the debtor's intention to reaffirm such debt on the original contract terms and the creditor refuses to agree to the reaffirmation on such terms.

    (2) Paragraph (1) does not apply if the court determines, on the motion of the trustee filed before the expiration of the applicable time set by section 521(a)(2), after notice and a hearing, that such personal property is of consequential value or benefit to the estate, and orders appropriate adequate protection of the creditor's interest, and orders the debtor to deliver any collateral in the debtor's possession to the trustee. If the court does not so determine, the stay provided by subsection (a) shall terminate upon the conclusion of the hearing on the motion.

* * *

    (k)(1) Except as provided in paragraph (2), an individual injured by any willful violation of a stay provided by this section shall recover actual damages, including costs and attorneys' fees, and, in appropriate circumstances, may recover punitive damages.

    (2) If such violation is based on an action taken by an entity in the good faith belief that subsection (h) applies to the debtor, the recovery under paragraph (1) of this subsection against such entity shall be limited to actual damages.

UNOFFICIAL COMMENTS

Subsection (a) answers the questions (1) when does the automatic stay become effective and (2) what is covered by the automatic stay. The best short answer I have heard to the second question was the statement by a creditor client: "What you are telling me is that anything that might be helpful in collecting from the debtor is covered by that stay."

Subsection (b) answers the related question: what is not covered by the automatic stay. There is nothing in the parts of subsection (b) that might be covered in a basic bankruptcy course that helps a creditor of a business debtor. The most meaningful limitations on the scope of the automatic stay are not in subsection (b) but in subsection (a). For example, note the limiting phrase "before the commencement of the case" in section 362(a)(1), (2), (3), (5), (6), and (7).

Subsection (c) answers the question of when does the automatic stay end. In a business chapter 11 case, it may be years before any of the section 362(c) events that end the automatic stay occurs. Accordingly, it can be important (especially in such chapter 11 cases) to answer the question of what a creditor can do to obtain relief from the stay.

And subsection (d) answers that important question of what a creditor can do to obtain relief from the automatic stay. And, in using section 362(d) to answer questions (especially exam questions) it is important that you understand that

— the word "request" in the Code is a motion under the Bankruptcy Rules (see Rule 4001 on page 226 infra and Rule 9014 on page 232 infra);

— section 362(g) fixes the burden of proof in section 362(d) litigation;

— "cause" in section 362(d)(1) encompasses more than simply a lack of adequate protection of an interest in property and that "cause" is the only statutory basis for a holder of an unsecured claim to seek relief from the stay;

— relief from stay is often different from termination of the automatic stay.

OTHER SECTIONS

Section 1301 expands the scope of the automatic stay for a chapter 13 debtor.

Some courts use section 105 to provide similar, albeit not automatic, protection to third parties.

Understanding abandonment under section 554 is necessary to understanding 362(c)(1).

"Adequate protection of an interest in property" in section 362(d)(1) is explained in section 361.

Section 363 explains what the debtor can do with its property, including property in which a creditor has an interest, while the automatic stay is in effect.

Again, stay litigation is governed by Rule 4001, infra at page 226 and Rule 9014 on page 232.

The form of order used by the Central District of California to deny a motion for relief from stay is on page 340.

§ 363. Use, sale, or lease of property

(a) In this section, "cash collateral" means cash, negotiable instruments, documents of title, securities, deposit accounts, or other cash equivalents whenever acquired in which the estate and an entity other than the estate have an interest and includes the proceeds, products, offspring, rents, or profits of property and the fees, charges, accounts or other payments for the use or occupancy of rooms and other public facilities in hotels, motels, or other lodging properties subject to a security interest as provided in section 552(b) of this title, whether existing before or after the commencement of a case under this title.

(b)(1) The trustee, after notice and a hearing, may use, sell, or lease, other than in the ordinary course of business, property of the estate, * * *

(c)(1) If the business of the debtor is authorized to be operated under section 721, 1108, 1203, 1204, or 1304 of this title and unless the court orders otherwise, the trustee may enter into transactions, including the sale or lease of property of the estate, in the ordinary course of business, without notice or a hearing, and may use property of the estate in the ordinary course of business without notice or a hearing.

(2) The trustee may not use, sell, or lease cash collateral under paragraph (1) of this subsection unless—

(A) each entity that has an interest in such cash collateral consents; or

(B) the court, after notice and a hearing, authorizes such use, sale, or lease in accordance with the provisions of this section. * * *

(4) Except as provided in paragraph (2) of this subsection, the trustee shall segregate and account for any cash collateral in the trustee's possession, custody, or control.

(d) The trustee may use, sell, or lease property under subsection (b) or (c) of this section—

(1) in the case of a debtor that is a corporation or trust that is not a moneyed business, commercial corporation, or trust, only in accordance with nonbankruptcy law applicable to the transfer of property by a debtor that is such a corporation or trust; and

(2) to the extent not inconsistent with any relief granted under subsection (c), (d), (e), or (f) of section 362.

(e) Notwithstanding any other provision of this section, at any time, on request of an entity that has an interest in property used, sold, or leased, or proposed to be used, sold, or leased, by the trustee, the court, with or without a hearing, shall prohibit or condition such use, sale, or lease as is necessary to provide adequate protection of such interest. This subsection also applies to property that is subject to any unexpired lease of personal property (to the exclusion of such property being subject to an order to grant relief from the stay under section 362).

(f) The trustee may sell property under subsection (b) or (c) of this section free and clear of any interest in such property of an entity other than the estate, only if—

(1) applicable nonbankruptcy law permits sale of such property free and clear of such interest;

(2) such entity consents;

(3) such interest is a lien and the price at which such property is to be sold is greater than the aggregate value of all liens on such property;

(4) such interest is in bona fide dispute; or

(5) such entity could be compelled, in a legal or equitable proceeding, to accept a money satisfaction of such interest.

(g) Notwithstanding subsection (f) of this section, the trustee may sell property under subsection (b) or (c) of this section free and clear of any vested or contingent right in the nature of dower or curtesy.

(h) Notwithstanding subsection (f) of this section, the trustee may sell both the estate's interest, under subsection (b) or (c) of this section, and the interest of any co-owner in property in which the debtor had, at the time of the commencement of the case, an undivided interest as a tenant in common, joint tenant, or tenant by the entirety, only if—

(1) partition in kind of such property among the estate and such co-owners is impracticable;

(2) sale of the estate's undivided interest in such property would realize significantly less for the estate than sale of such property free of the interests of such co-owners;

(3) the benefit to the estate of a sale of such property free of the interests of co-owners outweighs the detriment, if any, to such co-owners; and

(4) such property is not used in the production, transmission, or distribution, for sale, of electric energy or of natural or synthetic gas for heat, light, or power.

(i) Before the consummation of a sale of property to which subsection (g) or (h) of this section applies, or of property of the estate that was community property of the debtor and the debtor's spouse immediately before the commencement of the case, the debtor's spouse, or a co-owner of such property, as the case may be, may purchase such property at the price at which such sale is to be consummated.

(j) After a sale of property to which subsection (g) or (h) of this section applies, the trustee shall distribute to the debtor's spouse or the co-owners of such property, as the case may be, and to the estate, the proceeds of such sale, less the costs and expenses, not including any compensation of the trustee, of such sale, according to the interests of such spouse or co-owners, and of the estate.

(k) At a sale under subsection (b) of this section of property that is subject to a lien that secures an allowed claim, unless the court for cause orders otherwise the holder of such claim may bid at such sale, and, if the holder of such claim purchases such property, such holder may offset such claim against the purchase price of such property.

(l) Subject to the provisions of section 365, the trustee may use, sell, or lease property under subsection (b) or (c) of this section, or a plan under chapter 11, 12, or 13 of this title may provide for the use, sale, or lease of property, notwithstanding any provision in a contract, a lease, or applicable law that is conditioned on the insolvency or financial condition of the debtor, on the commencement of a case under this title concerning the debtor, or on the appointment of or the taking possession by a trustee in a case under this title or a custodian, and that effects, or gives an option to effect, a forfeiture, modification, or termination of the debtor's interest in such property.

(m) The reversal or modification on appeal of an authorization under subsection (b) or (c) of this section of a sale or lease of property does not affect the validity of a sale or lease under such authorization to an entity that purchased or leased such property in good faith, whether or not such entity knew of the pendency of the appeal, unless such authorization and such sale or lease were stayed pending appeal.

(n) The trustee may avoid a sale under this section if the sale price was controlled by an agreement among potential bidders at such sale, or may recover from a party to such agreement any amount by which the value of the property sold exceeds the price at which such sale was consummated, and may recover any costs, attorneys' fees, or expenses incurred in avoiding such sale or recovering such amount. In addition to any recovery under the preceding sentence, the court may grant judgment for punitive damages in favor of the estate and against any such party that entered into such an agreement in willful disregard of this subsection.

(*o*) Notwithstanding subsection (f), if a person purchases any interest in a consumer credit transaction that is subject to the Truth in Lending Act or any interest in a consumer credit contract (as defined in section 433.1 of title 16 of the Code of Federal Regulations (January 1, 2004), as amended from time to time), and if such interest is purchased through a sale under this section, then such person shall remain subject to all claims and defenses that are related to such consumer credit transaction or such consumer credit contract, to the same extent as such person would be subject to such claims and defenses of the consumer had such interest been purchased at a sale not under this section.

(p) In any hearing under this section—

(1) the trustee has the burden of proof on the issue of adequate protection; and

(2) the entity asserting an interest in property has the burden of proof on the issue of the validity, priority, or extent of such interest.

UNOFFICIAL COMMENTS

Everywhere the word "trustee" appears in section 363 think "debtor in possession" because (1) almost all 363 questions arise in chapter 11 cases, and (2) almost all chapter 11 cases have a debtor in possession—not a trustee, and (3) almost all statutory powers of trustees are also statutory powers of chapter 11 debtors in possession under section 1107(a).

Subsections (b) and (c) distinguish between doing stuff that is in the "ordinary course of business" and doing stuff that is not, without defining "ordinary course." Under subsection (b) "other than in the ordinary course" requires a "hearing" but does not indicate what the court wants to hear about at that hearing.

Subsection (c) further distinguishes between property that is cash collateral and property that is not. Section 363(c)(2)(B) requires a "hearing" but does not indicate what the court wants to hear about at that hearing.

Generally, what the court wants to hear about at a hearing involving section 363 use of cash collateral (or other collateral) is whether the property interests of the creditor whose collateral is being used, is adequately protected. Re-read section 363(e). Also re-read section 363(p) on allocation of burdens of proof at such a hearing.

[And if that creditor has an Article 9 security interest and your teacher has covered floating liens, you will also need to read section 552 to understand cash collateral use and adequate protection. Section 552(a) limits the effectiveness in bankruptcy of an after-acquired property clause in a pre-petition credit agreement. This has the effect of enabling the debtor in possession to use assets acquired postpetition as adequate protection for using cash collateral.]

Assets can be sold either under section 363 or as a part of a chapter 11 plan. See Section 1123 (b)(4).

In doing section 363(k), lawyers generally use the phrase "credit bidding" (although only creditors with liens can do section 363(k)).

OTHER SECTIONS

Section 361 is necessary to an understanding of "adequate protection of an interest in property." And, section 503(b)(7) is necessary to understanding what happens when what a court thought would be "adequate protection" turns out to be inadequate.

Delaware Local Rule 6004–1, page 342, is helpful, if not necessary, to understanding how a 363 sale of assets happens. A debtor's sale of its property can also be accomplished in a chapter 11 plan, section 1123(b)(4). The chapter 11 plan approach is much more time-consuming and expensive.

Section 9–204 of the Uniform Commercial Code on page 324 infra authorizes a "floating lien", i.e., a security interest that reaches property that the debtor acquires after the agreement. Again, if your teacher has covered UCC floating liens, then understanding section 552 is necessary to understanding section 363 and use of cash collateral.

If your professor has spent time talking about cash collateral use, then you should spend time looking at the Delaware local rule 4001–2 on page 350.

§ 364. Obtaining credit

(a) If the trustee is authorized to operate the business of the debtor under section 721, 1108, 1203, 1204, or 1304 of this title, unless the court orders otherwise, the trustee may obtain unsecured credit and incur unsecured debt in the ordinary course of business allowable under section 503(b)(1) of this title as an administrative expense.

(b) The court, after notice and a hearing, may authorize the trustee to obtain unsecured credit or to incur unsecured debt other than under subsection (a) of this section, allowable under section 503(b)(1) of this title as an administrative expense.

(c) If the trustee is unable to obtain unsecured credit allowable under section 503(b)(1) of this title as an administrative expense, the court, after notice and a hearing, may authorize the obtaining of credit or the incurring of debt—

    (1) with priority over any or all administrative expenses of the kind specified in section 503(b) or 507(b) of this title;

    (2) secured by a lien on property of the estate that is not otherwise subject to a lien; or

    (3) secured by a junior lien on property of the estate that is subject to a lien.

(d)(1) The court, after notice and a hearing, may authorize the obtaining of credit or the incurring of debt secured by a senior or equal lien on property of the estate that is subject to a lien only if—

    (A) the trustee is unable to obtain such credit otherwise; and

    (B) there is adequate protection of the interest of the holder of the lien on the property of the estate on which such senior or equal lien is proposed to be granted.

    (2) In any hearing under this subsection, the trustee has the burden of proof on the issue of adequate protection.

(e) The reversal or modification on appeal of an authorization under this section to obtain credit or incur debt, or of a grant under this section of a priority or a lien, does not affect the validity of any debt so incurred, or any priority or lien so granted, to an entity that extended such credit in good faith, whether or not such entity knew of the pendency of the appeal, unless such authorization and the incurring of such debt, or the granting of such priority or lien, were stayed pending appeal.

(f) Except with respect to an entity that is an underwriter as defined in section 1145(b) of this title, section 5 of the Securities Act of 1933, the Trust Indenture Act of 1939, and any State or local law requiring registration for offer or sale of a security or registration or licensing of an issuer of, underwriter of, or broker or dealer in, a security does not apply to the offer or sale under this section of a security that is not an equity security.

UNOFFICIAL COMMENTS

Everywhere the word "trustee" appears in section 364 think "debtor in possession" because (1) almost all 364 questions arise in chapter 11 cases and (2) almost all chapter 11 cases have a debtor in possession and not a trustee and (3) almost all statutory powers of trustees are also statutory powers of chapter 11 debtors in possession under section 1107(a).

Even though you see section 364 in Chapter 3, you will see section 364 used only in chapter 11 cases. Accordingly, to understand the significance of the "administrative expense" priority provided by section 364. It is necessary to understand that (1) full payment of all administrative expense priority claims is a confirmation requirement, section 1129(a)(9)(A) and (2) most chapter 11 cases end without a confirmed plan.

OTHER SECTIONS

Section 361 is necessary to an understanding of "adequate protection of an interest in property." And, section 503(b)(7) is necessary to understanding what happens when what a court thought would be "adequate protection" turns out to be inadequate.

Section 9–204 of the Uniform Commercial Code on page 324 infra authorizes a "floating lien", i.e., a security interest that reaches property that the debtor acquires after the agreement. If your teacher has covered UCC floating liens, then understanding section 552 is necessary to understanding section 364. Section 552(a) limits the effectiveness in bankruptcy of after-acquired property clauses in pre-petition credit agreements which enables the debtor in possession to use assets acquired postpetition as collateral for section 364(c) postpetition loans.

§ 365. Executory contracts and unexpired leases

(a) Except as provided in * * * subsections (b), (c), and (d) of this section, the trustee, subject to the court's approval, may assume or reject any executory contract or unexpired lease of the debtor.

(b)(1) If there has been a default in an executory contract or unexpired lease of the debtor, the trustee may not assume such contract or lease unless, at the time of assumption of such contract or lease, the trustee—

    (A) cures, or provides adequate assurance that the trustee will promptly cure, such default other than a default that is a breach of a provision relating to the satisfaction of any provision (other than a penalty rate or penalty provision) relating to a default arising from any failure to perform nonmonetary obligations under an unexpired lease of real property, if it is impossible for the trustee to cure such default by performing nonmonetary acts at and after the time of assumption, except that if such default arises from a failure to operate in accordance with a nonresidential real property lease, then such default shall be cured by performance at and after the time of assumption in accordance with such lease, and pecuniary losses resulting from such default shall be compensated in accordance with the provisions of this paragraph;

    (B) compensates, or provides adequate assurance that the trustee will promptly compensate, a party other than the debtor to such contract or lease, for any actual pecuniary loss to such party resulting from such default; and

    (C) provides adequate assurance of future performance under such contract or lease.

(2) Paragraph (1) of this subsection does not apply to a default that is a breach of a provision relating to—

    (A) the insolvency or financial condition of the debtor at any time before the closing of the case;

    (B) the commencement of a case under this title;

(C) the appointment of or taking possession by a trustee in a case under this title or a custodian before such commencement; or

(D) the satisfaction of any penalty rate or penalty provision relating to a default arising from any failure by the debtor to perform nonmonetary obligations under the executory contract or unexpired lease.

(3) For the purposes of paragraph (1) of this subsection and paragraph (2)(B) of subsection (f), adequate assurance of future performance of a lease of real property in a shopping center includes adequate assurance—

(A) of the source of rent and other consideration due under such lease, and in the case of an assignment, that the financial condition and operating performance of the proposed assignee and its guarantors, if any, shall be similar to the financial condition and operating performance of the debtor and its guarantors, if any, as of the time the debtor became the lessee under the lease;

(B) that any percentage rent due under such lease will not decline substantially;

(C) that assumption or assignment of such lease is subject to all the provisions thereof, including (but not limited to) provisions such as a radius, location, use, or exclusivity provision, and will not breach any such provision contained in any other lease, financing agreement, or master agreement relating to such shopping center; and

(D) that assumption or assignment of such lease will not disrupt any tenant mix or balance in such shopping center.

(4) Notwithstanding any other provision of this section, if there has been a default in an unexpired lease of the debtor, other than a default of a kind specified in paragraph (2) of this subsection, the trustee may not require a lessor to provide services or supplies incidental to such lease before assumption of such lease unless the lessor is compensated under the terms of such lease for any services and supplies provided under such lease before assumption of such lease.

(c) The trustee may not assume or assign any executory contract or unexpired lease of the debtor, whether or not such contract or lease prohibits or restricts assignment of rights or delegation of duties, if—

(1)(A) applicable law excuses a party, other than the debtor, to such contract or lease from accepting performance from or rendering performance to an entity other than the debtor or the debtor in possession, whether or not such contract or lease prohibits or restricts assignment of rights or delegation of duties; and

(B) such party does not consent to such assumption or assignment; or

(2) such contract is a contract to make a loan, or extend other debt financing or financial accommodations, to or for the benefit of the debtor, or to issue a security of the debtor; or

(3) such lease is of nonresidential real property and has been terminated under applicable nonbankruptcy law prior to the order for relief.

(d)(1) In a case under chapter 7 of this title, if the trustee does not assume or reject an executory contract or unexpired lease of residential real property or of personal property of the debtor within 60 days after the order for relief, or within such additional time as the court, for cause, within such 60-day period, fixes, then such contract or lease is deemed rejected.

(2) In a case under chapter 9, 11, 12, or 13 of this title, the trustee may assume or reject an executory contract or unexpired lease of residential real property or of personal property of the debtor at any time before the confirmation of a plan but the court, on the request of any party to such contract or lease, may order the trustee to determine within a specified period of time whether to assume or reject such contract or lease.

(3) The trustee shall timely perform all the obligations of the debtor, except those specified in section 365(b)(2), arising from and after the order for relief under any unexpired lease of nonresidential real property, until such lease is assumed or rejected, notwithstanding section 503(b)(1) of this title. The court may extend, for cause, the time for performance of any such obligation that arises within 60 days after the date of the order for relief, but the time for performance shall not be extended beyond such 60-day period. This subsection shall not be deemed to affect the trustee's obligations under the provisions of subsection (b) or (f) of this section. Acceptance of any such performance does not constitute waiver or relinquishment of the lessor's rights under such lease or under this title.

(4)(A) Subject to subparagraph (B), an unexpired lease of nonresidential real property under which the debtor is the lessee shall be deemed rejected, and the trustee shall immediately surrender that nonresidential real property to the lessor, if the trustee does not assume or reject the unexpired lease by the earlier of—

(i) the date that is 120 days after the date of the order for relief; or

(ii) the date of the entry of an order confirming a plan.

(B)(i) The court may extend the period determined under subparagraph (A), prior to the expiration of the 120-day period, for 90 days on the motion of the trustee or lessor for cause.

(ii) If the court grants an extension under clause (i), the court may grant a subsequent extension only upon prior written consent of the lessor in each instance.

(5) The trustee shall timely perform all of the obligations of the debtor, except those specified in section 365(b)(2), first arising from or after 60 days after the order for relief in a case under chapter 11 of this title under an unexpired lease of personal property (other than personal property leased to an individual primarily for personal, family, or household purposes), until such lease is assumed or rejected notwithstanding section 503(b)(1) of this title, unless the court, after notice and a hearing and based on the equities of the case, orders otherwise with respect to the obligations or timely performance thereof. This subsection shall not be deemed to affect the trustee's obligations under the provisions of subsection (b) or (f). Acceptance of any such performance does not constitute waiver or relinquishment of the lessor's rights under such lease or under this title.

(e)(1) Notwithstanding a provision in an executory contract or unexpired lease, or in applicable law, an executory contract or unexpired lease of the debtor may not be terminated or modified, and any right or obligation under such contract or lease may not be terminated or modified, at any time after the commencement of the case solely because of a provision in such contract or lease that is conditioned on—

bankruptcy termination unenforceable

(A) the insolvency or financial condition of the debtor at any time before the closing of the case;

(B) the commencement of a case under this title; or

(C) the appointment of or taking possession by a trustee in a case under this title or a custodian before such commencement.

(2) Paragraph (1) of this subsection does not apply to an executory contract or unexpired lease of the debtor, whether or not such contract or lease prohibits or restricts assignment of rights or delegation of duties, if—

(A)(i) applicable law excuses a party, other than the debtor, to such contract or lease from accepting performance from or rendering performance to the trustee or to an assignee of such contract or lease, whether or not such contract or lease prohibits or restricts assignment of rights or delegation of duties; and

(ii) such party does not consent to such assumption or assignment; or

(B) such contract is a contract to make a loan, or extend other debt financing or financial accommodations, to or for the benefit of the debtor, or to issue a security of the debtor.

(f)(1) Except as provided in subsections (b) and (c) of this section, notwithstanding a provision in an executory contract or unexpired lease of the debtor, or in applicable law, that prohibits, restricts, or conditions the assignment of such contract or lease, the trustee may assign such contract or lease under paragraph (2) of this subsection.

(2) The trustee may assign an executory contract or unexpired lease of the debtor only if—

(A) the trustee assumes such contract or lease in accordance with the provisions of this section; and

(B) adequate assurance of future performance by the assignee of such contract or lease is provided, whether or not there has been a default in such contract or lease.

(3) Notwithstanding a provision in an executory contract or unexpired lease of the debtor, or in applicable law that terminates or modifies, or permits a party other than the debtor to terminate or modify, such contract or lease or a right or obligation under such contract or lease on account of an assignment of such contract or lease, such contract, lease, right, or obligation may not be terminated or modified under such provision because of the assumption or assignment of such contract or lease by the trustee.

(g) Except as provided in subsections (h)(2) and (i)(2) of this section, the rejection of an executory contract or unexpired lease of the debtor constitutes a breach of such contract or lease—

(1) if such contract or lease has not been assumed under this section or under a plan confirmed under chapter 9, 11, 12, or 13 of this title, immediately before the date of the filing of the petition; or

(2) if such contract or lease has been assumed under this section or under a plan confirmed under chapter 9, 11, 12, or 13 of this title—

(A) if before such rejection the case has not been converted under section 1112, 1208, or 1307 of this title, at the time of such rejection; or

(B) if before such rejection the case has been converted under section 1112, 1208, or 1307 of this title—

(i) immediately before the date of such conversion, if such contract or lease was assumed before such conversion; or

(ii) at the time of such rejection, if such contract or lease was assumed after such conversion.

(h)(1)(A) If the trustee rejects an unexpired lease of real property under which the debtor is the lessor and—

(i) if the rejection by the trustee amounts to such a breach as would entitle the lessee to treat such lease as terminated by virtue of its terms, applicable nonbankruptcy law, or any agreement made by the lessee, then the lessee under such lease may treat such lease as terminated by the rejection; or

(ii) if the term of such lease has commenced, the lessee may retain its rights under such lease (including rights such as those relating to the amount and timing of payment of rent and other amounts payable by the lessee and any right of use, possession, quiet enjoyment, subletting, assignment, or hypothecation) that are in or appurtenant to the real property for the balance of the term of such lease and for any renewal or extension of such rights to the extent that such rights are enforceable under applicable nonbankruptcy law.

(B) If the lessee retains its rights under subparagraph (A)(ii), the lessee may offset against the rent reserved under such lease for the balance of the term after the date of the rejection of such lease and for the term of any renewal or extension of such lease, the value of any damage caused by the nonperformance after the date of such rejection, of any obligation of the debtor under such lease, but the lessee shall not have any other right against the estate or the debtor on account of any damage occurring after such date caused by such nonperformance. *Cant get more than what you pay*

(C) The rejection of a lease of real property in a shopping center with respect to which the lessee elects to retain its rights under subparagraph (A)(ii) does not affect the enforceability under applicable nonbankruptcy law of any provision in the lease pertaining to radius, location, use, exclusivity, or tenant mix or balance.

(D) In this paragraph, "lessee" includes any successor, assign, or mortgagee permitted under the terms of such lease.

(2)(A) If the trustee rejects a timeshare interest under a timeshare plan under which the debtor is the timeshare interest seller and—

(i) if the rejection amounts to such a breach as would entitle the timeshare interest purchaser to treat the timeshare plan as terminated under its terms, applicable nonbankruptcy law, or any agreement made by timeshare interest purchaser, the timeshare interest purchaser under the timeshare plan may treat the timeshare plan as terminated by such rejection; or

(ii) if the term of such timeshare interest has commenced, then the timeshare interest purchaser may retain its rights in such timeshare interest for the balance of such term and for any term of renewal or extension of such timeshare interest to the extent that such rights are enforceable under applicable nonbankruptcy law.

(B) If the timeshare interest purchaser retains its rights under subparagraph (A), such timeshare interest purchaser may offset against the moneys due for such timeshare interest for the balance of the term after the date of the rejection of such timeshare interest, and the term of any renewal or extension of such timeshare interest, the value of any damage caused by the nonperformance after the date of such rejection, of any obligation of the debtor under such timeshare plan, but the timeshare interest purchaser shall not have any right against the estate or the debtor on account of any damage occurring after such date caused by such nonperformance.

(i)(1) If the trustee rejects an executory contract of the debtor for the sale of real property or for the sale of a timeshare interest under a timeshare plan, under which the purchaser is in possession, such purchaser may treat such contract as terminated, or, in the alternative, may remain in possession of such real property or timeshare interest.

(2) If such purchaser remains in possession—

(A) such purchaser shall continue to make all payments due under such contract, but may, offset against such payments any damages occurring after the date of the rejection of such contract caused by the nonperformance of any obligation of the debtor after such date, but such purchaser does not have any rights against the estate on account of any damages arising after such date from such rejection, other than such offset; and

(B) the trustee shall deliver title to such purchaser in accordance with the provisions of such contract, but is relieved of all other obligations to perform under such contract.

(j) A purchaser that treats an executory contract as terminated under subsection (i) of this section, or a party whose executory contract to purchase real property from the debtor is rejected and under which such party is not in possession, has a lien on the interest of the debtor in such property for the recovery of any portion of the purchase price that such purchaser or party has paid.

(k) Assignment by the trustee to an entity of a contract or lease assumed under this section relieves the trustee and the estate from any liability for any breach of such contract or lease occurring after such assignment.

(*l*) If an unexpired lease under which the debtor is the lessee is assigned pursuant to this section, the lessor of the property may require a deposit or other security for the performance of the debtor's obligations under the lease substantially the same as would have been required by the landlord upon the initial leasing to a similar tenant.

* * *

(n)(1) If the trustee rejects an executory contract under which the debtor is a licensor of a right to intellectual property, the licensee under such contract may elect—

    (A) to treat such contract as terminated by such rejection if such rejection by the trustee amounts to such a breach as would entitle the licensee to treat such contract as terminated by virtue of its own terms, applicable nonbankruptcy law, or an agreement made by the licensee with another entity; or

    (B) to retain its rights (including a right to enforce any exclusivity provision of such contract, but excluding any other right under applicable nonbankruptcy law to specific performance of such contract) under such contract and under any agreement supplementary to such contract, to such intellectual property (including any embodiment of such intellectual property to the extent protected by applicable nonbankruptcy law), as such rights existed immediately before the case commenced, for—

        (i) the duration of such contract; and

        (ii) any period for which such contract may be extended by the licensee as of right under applicable nonbankruptcy law.

(2) If the licensee elects to retain its rights, as described in paragraph (1)(B) of this subsection, under such contract—

    (A) the trustee shall allow the licensee to exercise such rights;

    (B) the licensee shall make all royalty payments due under such contract for the duration of such contract and for any period described in paragraph (1)(B) of this subsection for which the licensee extends such contract; and

    (C) the licensee shall be deemed to waive—

        (i) any right of setoff it may have with respect to such contract under this title or applicable nonbankruptcy law; and

        (ii) any claim allowable under section 503(b) of this title arising from the performance of such contract.

(3) If the licensee elects to retain its rights, as described in paragraph (1)(B) of this subsection, then on the written request of the licensee the trustee shall—

    (A) to the extent provided in such contract, or any agreement supplementary to such contract, provide to the licensee any intellectual property (including such embodiment) held by the trustee; and

    (B) not interfere with the rights of the licensee as provided in such contract, or any agreement supplementary to such contract, to such intellectual property (including such embodiment) including any right to obtain such intellectual property (or such embodiment) from another entity.

(4) Unless and until the trustee rejects such contract, on the written request of the licensee the trustee shall—

    (A) to the extent provided in such contract or any agreement supplementary to such contract—

        (i) perform such contract; or

        (ii) provide to the licensee such intellectual property (including any embodiment of such intellectual property to the extent protected by applicable nonbankruptcy law) held by the trustee; and

(B) not interfere with the rights of the licensee as provided in such contract, or any agreement supplementary to such contract, to such intellectual property (including such embodiment), including any right to obtain such intellectual property (or such embodiment) from another entity.

* * *

(p)(1) If a lease of personal property is rejected or not timely assumed by the trustee under subsection (d), the leased property is no longer property of the estate and the stay under section 362(a) is automatically terminated.

(2)(A) If the debtor in a case under chapter 7 is an individual, the debtor may notify the creditor in writing that the debtor desires to assume the lease. Upon being so notified, the creditor may, at its option, notify the debtor that it is willing to have the lease assumed by the debtor and may condition such assumption on cure of any outstanding default on terms set by the contract.

(B) If, not later than 30 days after notice is provided under subparagraph (A), the debtor notifies the lessor in writing that the lease is assumed, the liability under the lease will be assumed by the debtor and not by the estate.

(C) The stay under section 362 and the injunction under section 524(a)(2) shall not be violated by notification of the debtor and negotiation of cure under this subsection.

(3) In a case under chapter 11 in which the debtor is an individual and in a case under chapter 13, if the debtor is the lessee with respect to personal property and the lease is not assumed in the plan confirmed by the court, the lease is deemed rejected as of the conclusion of the hearing on confirmation. If the lease is rejected, the stay under section 362 and any stay under section 1301 is automatically terminated with respect to the property subject to the lease.

UNOFFICIAL COMMENTS

Everywhere the word "trustee" appears in section 365 think "debtor in possession" because (1) almost all 365 questions arise in chapter 11 cases and (2) almost all chapter 11 cases have a debtor in possession and not a trustee and (3) almost all statutory powers of trustees are also statutory powers of chapter 11 debtors in possession under section 1107(a).

Section 365 is important—almost certain to be on your exam. Section 365 is poorly organized. You need to understand that the section deals with two different transactions—(1) unexpired leases and (2) executory contracts—and generally provides that one of three things can happen to a debtor's unexpired leases and executory contracts—trustee or chapter 11 debtor in possession can either (1) keep without change, i.e., "assume" or (2) sell, i.e., "assign" or (3) breach, i.e., "reject."

You will need to look to section 365(d) to see how soon a decision must be made as among the three and what happens during the "gap period" before such a decision is made. Section 365(a) deals with the role of the bankruptcy judge in that decision.

You will look to subsections (c), (e) and (f) when the question is whether there is some limitation on assuming or assigning. And you will be looking to subsection (b) when the question is what is required in order to assume or assign.

Using section 365 is further complicated by special rules for special types of leases and contracts. For example, lessors of commercial real estate have greater section 365 rights than lessors of residential real estate; and, lessors of shopping centers have greater section 365 rights than lessors of other commercial real estate.

OTHER SECTIONS

Definitions in section 101 are always important. "Intellectual property", an important term in section 365(n), is defined in section 101. Note that the section 101 definition of "intellectual property" does not include trademarks.

And, notice that section 101 does not define "executory contract" or "nonmonetary obligation" or "adequate protection." The last phrase also appears in UCC section 2–609.

Section 503 is important to section 365. Assumption of a lease or executory contract creates a section 503(b)(1) administrative expense (although neither section 365 nor section 503 say that. Cf. section 503(b)(7)).

Under section 502(g), a rejection (breach) of a lease or executory contract which occurs post-petition is treated as creating a pre-petition claim. And, section 502(b)(6) caps the amount of an allowable claim for postpetition rent when a lease of real property is rejected by the debtor/tenant.

Less important in law school is the section 502(b)(7) cap on the amount of an allowable claim when an executory employment contract is rejected by the debtor/employer.

Sections 1123(b)(2) and 1322(b)(7) deal with how a chapter 11 or chapter 13 plan can deal with leases and executory contracts. These sections are somewhat misleading. They state that a chapter 11 plan or a chapter 13 plan can provide for the rejection, assumption, or assignment of leases and executory contracts, without expressly reminding you about the section 365(d)(4) time limit for nonresidential real property leases. Consider yourself reminded.

While a collective bargaining agreement is an executory contract, rejection of collective bargaining agreements in a chapter 11 case is governed by section 1113, not section 365. Similarly, sections 555–562, 744–784, 1114, and 1168–1169 provide for special treatment for certain types of executory contracts and leases.

§ 366. Utility service

(a) Except as provided in subsections (b) and (c) of this section, a utility may not alter, refuse, or discontinue service to, or discriminate against, the trustee or the debtor solely on the basis of the commencement of a case under this title or that a debt owed by the debtor to such utility for service rendered before the order for relief was not paid when due.

(b) Such utility may alter, refuse, or discontinue service if neither the trustee nor the debtor, within 20 days after the date of the order for relief, furnishes adequate assurance of payment, in the form of a deposit or other security, for service after such date. On request of a party in interest and after notice and a hearing, the court may order reasonable modification of the amount of the deposit or other security necessary to provide adequate assurance of payment.

(c)(1)(A) For purposes of this subsection, the term "assurance of payment" means—

   (i) a cash deposit;

   (ii) a letter of credit;

   (iii) a certificate of deposit;

   (iv) a surety bond;

   (v) a prepayment of utility consumption; or

   (vi) another form of security that is mutually agreed on between the utility and the debtor or the trustee.

(B) For purposes of this subsection an administrative expense priority shall not constitute an assurance of payment.

(2) Subject to paragraphs (3) and (4), with respect to a case filed under chapter 11, a utility referred to in subsection (a) may alter, refuse, or discontinue utility service, if during the 30-day period beginning on the date of the filing of the petition, the utility does not receive from the debtor or the trustee adequate assurance of payment for utility service that is satisfactory to the utility.

(3)(A) On request of a party in interest and after notice and a hearing, the court may order modification of the amount of an assurance of payment under paragraph (2).

(B) In making a determination under this paragraph whether an assurance of payment is adequate, the court may not consider—

(i) the absence of security before the date of the filing of the petition;

(ii) the payment by the debtor of charges for utility service in a timely manner before the date of the filing of the petition; or

(iii) the availability of an administrative expense priority.

(4) Notwithstanding any other provision of law, with respect to a case subject to this subsection, a utility may recover or set off against a security deposit provided to the utility by the debtor before the date of the filing of the petition without notice or order of the court.

CHAPTER 5—CREDITORS, THE DEBTOR, AND THE ESTATE

SUBCHAPTER I—CREDITORS AND CLAIMS

SUBCHAPTER II—DEBTOR'S DUTIES AND BENEFITS

SUBCHAPTER III—THE ESTATE

SUBCHAPTER I—CREDITORS AND CLAIMS

§ 501. Filing of proofs of claims or interests

(a) A creditor or an indenture trustee may file a proof of claim. An equity security holder may file a proof of interest.

(b) If a creditor does not timely file a proof of such creditor's claim, an entity that is liable to such creditor with the debtor, or that has secured such creditor, may file a proof of such claim.

(c) If a creditor does not timely file a proof of such creditor's claim, the debtor or the trustee may file a proof of such claim.

* * *

UNOFFICIAL COMMENTS

Whether a proof of claim is filed can affect whether a creditor shares in any bankruptcy distribution. Whether a proof of claim is filed generally has no effect on whether the claim is covered by a bankruptcy discharge.

OTHER SECTIONS

Always look for definitions in section 101. Here, it is especially important that you see the definition of "claim" and the definition of "creditor."

Understanding section 501 requires understanding later Bankruptcy Code sections and Bankruptcy Rules. Section 521 requires the debtor to file a list of creditors, and the Rules require that the creditors receive notice about filing proofs of claim. Filing a proof of claim under section 501 is important to allowance of claims under section 502. And, section 1111 provides for deeming (i.e., pretending) that a proof of claim has been filed in chapter 11 cases.

Less important for a basic bankruptcy course, section 106(b) provides that a governmental unit's filing a proof of claim waives sovereign immunity with respect to that claim.

Official Form 10, infra at page 276 is the proof of claim form and is to be accompanied by documents supporting the claim. In chapter 7 and 13 cases, the deadline for filing a proof of claim is governed by Rule 3002(c), and is generally "not later than 90 days after the first date set for the meeting of creditors called under section 341(a)" In chapter 11 cases, the deadline for filing a proof of claim is governed by Rule 3003(c)(3) and is to be fixed by the court.

§ 502. Allowance of claims or interests

(a) A claim or interest, proof of which is filed under section 501 of this title, is deemed allowed, unless a party in interest, including a creditor of a general partner in a partnership that is a debtor in a case under chapter 7 of this title, objects. Debtor in Possession to or trustee

(b) Except as provided in subsections (e)(2), (f), (g), (h) and (i) of this section, if such objection to a claim is made, the court, after notice and a hearing, shall determine the amount of such claim in lawful currency of the United States as of the date of the filing of the petition, and shall allow such claim in such amount, except to the extent that—

(1) such claim is unenforceable against the debtor and property of the debtor, under any agreement or applicable law for a reason other than because such claim is contingent or unmatured;

(2) such claim is for unmatured interest; Interest accrued after filing bankrupty

(3) if such claim is for a tax assessed against property of the estate, such claim exceeds the value of the interest of the estate in such property;

(4) if such claim is for services of an insider or attorney of the debtor, such claim exceeds the reasonable value of such services;

(5) such claim is for a debt that is unmatured on the date of the filing of the petition and that is excepted from discharge under section 523(a)(5) of this title;

(6) if such claim is the claim of a lessor for damages resulting from the termination of a lease of real property, such claim exceeds—

(A) the rent reserved by such lease, without acceleration, for the greater of one year, or 15 percent, not to exceed three years, of the remaining term of such lease, following the earlier of—

(i) the date of the filing of the petition; and

(ii) the date on which such lessor repossessed, or the lessee surrendered, the leased property; plus

(B) any unpaid rent due under such lease, without acceleration, on the earlier of such dates;

(7) if such claim is the claim of an employee for damages resulting from the termination of an employment contract, such claim exceeds—

(A) the compensation provided by such contract, without acceleration, for one year following the earlier of—

(i) the date of the filing of the petition; or

(ii) the date on which the employer directed the employee to terminate, or such employee terminated, performance under such contract; plus

(B) any unpaid compensation due under such contract, without acceleration, on the earlier of such dates;

(8) such claim results from a reduction, due to late payment, in the amount of an otherwise applicable credit available to the debtor in connection with an employment tax on wages, salaries, or commissions earned from the debtor; or

(9) proof of such claim is not timely filed, except to the extent tardily filed as permitted under paragraph (1), (2), or (3) of section 726(a) of this title or under the Federal Rules of Bankruptcy Procedure, except that a claim of a governmental unit shall be timely filed if it is filed before 180 days after the date of the order for relief or such later time as the Federal Rules of Bankruptcy Procedure may provide, and except that in a case under chapter 13, a claim of a governmental unit for a tax with respect to a return filed under section 1308 shall be timely if the claim is filed on or before the date that is 60 days after the date on which such return was filed as required.

(c) There shall be estimated for purpose of allowance under this section—

(1) any contingent or unliquidated claim, the fixing or liquidation of which, as the case may be, would unduly delay the administration of the case; or

(2) any right to payment arising from a right to an equitable remedy for breach of performance.

(d) Notwithstanding subsections (a) and (b) of this section, the court shall disallow any claim of any entity from which property is recoverable under section 542, 543, 550, or 553 of this title or that is a transferee of a transfer avoidable under section 522(f), 522(h), 544, 545, 547, 548, 549, or 724(a) of this title, unless such entity or transferee has paid the amount, or turned over any such property, for which such entity or transferee is liable under section 522(i), 542, 543, 550, or 553 of this title.

(e)(1) Notwithstanding subsections (a), (b), and (c) of this section and paragraph (2) of this subsection, the court shall disallow any claim for reimbursement or contribution of an entity that is liable with the debtor on or has secured the claim of a creditor, to the extent that—

(A) such creditor's claim against the estate is disallowed;

(B) such claim for reimbursement or contribution is contingent as of the time of allowance or disallowance of such claim for reimbursement or contribution; or

(C) such entity asserts a right of subrogation to the rights of such creditor under section 509 of this title.

(2) A claim for reimbursement or contribution of such an entity that becomes fixed after the commencement of the case shall be determined, and shall be allowed under subsection (a), (b), or (c) of this section, or disallowed under subsection (d) of this section, the same as if such claim had become fixed before the date of the filing of the petition.

(f) In an involuntary case, a claim arising in the ordinary course of the debtor's business or financial affairs after the commencement of the case but before the earlier of the appointment of a trustee and the order for relief shall be determined as of the date such claim arises, and shall be allowed under subsection (a), (b), or (c) of this section or disallowed under subsection (d) or (e) of this section, the same as if such claim had arisen before the date of the filing of the petition.

(g)(1) A claim arising from the rejection, under section 365 of this title or under a plan under chapter 9, 11, 12, or 13 of this title, of an executory contract or unexpired lease of the debtor that has not been assumed shall be determined, and shall be allowed under subsection (a), (b), or (c) of this section or disallowed under subsection (d) or (e) of this section, the same as if such claim had arisen before the date of the filing of the petition.

* * *

(h) A claim arising from the recovery of property under section 522, 550, or 553 of this title shall be determined, and shall be allowed under subsection (a), (b), or (c) of this section, or disallowed under subsection (d) or (e) of this section, the same as if such claim had arisen before the date of the filing of the petition.

(i) A claim that does not arise until after the commencement of the case for a tax entitled to priority under section 507(a)(8) of this title shall be determined, and shall be allowed under subsection (a), (b), or (c) of this section, or disallowed under subsection (d) or (e) of this section, the same as if such claim had arisen before the date of the filing of the petition.

(j) A claim that has been allowed or disallowed may be reconsidered for cause. A reconsidered claim may be allowed or disallowed according to the equities of the case. Reconsideration of a claim under this subsection does not affect the validity of any payment or transfer from the estate made to a holder of an allowed claim on account of such allowed claim that is not reconsidered, but if a reconsidered claim is allowed and is of the same class as such holder's claim, such holder may not receive any additional payment or transfer from the estate on account of such holder's allowed claim until the holder of such reconsidered and allowed claim receives payment on account of such claim proportionate in value to that already received by such other holder. This subsection does not alter or modify the trustee's right to recover from a creditor any excess payment or transfer made to such creditor.

(k)(1) The court, on the motion of the debtor and after a hearing, may reduce a claim filed under this section based in whole on an unsecured consumer debt by not more than 20 percent of the claim, if—

    (A) the claim was filed by a creditor who unreasonably refused to negotiate a reasonable alternative repayment schedule proposed on behalf of the debtor by an approved nonprofit budget and credit counseling agency described in section 111;

    (B) the offer of the debtor under subparagraph (A)—

        (i) was made at least 60 days before the date of the filing of the petition; and

        (ii) provided for payment of at least 60 percent of the amount of the debt over a period not to exceed the repayment period of the loan, or a reasonable extension thereof; and

    (C) no part of the debt under the alternative repayment schedule is nondischargeable.

(2) The debtor shall have the burden of proving, by clear and convincing evidence, that—

   (A) the creditor unreasonably refused to consider the debtor's proposal; and

   (B) the proposed alternative repayment schedule was made prior to expiration of the 60-day period specified in paragraph (1)(B)(i).

UNOFFICIAL COMMENTS

Whether a claim is allowed affects whether a creditor shares in any bankruptcy distribution. Whether a claim is allowed does not generally affect whether the claim is covered by a bankruptcy discharge.

The date of the filing of the petition is an important date for purposes of section 502. With limited exceptions, allowable claims are limited to obligations to pay that existed at the "date of the filing of the petition" and limited to the amount owed at that date.

The phrase "applicable law" in section 502(b)(1) means non-bankruptcy law. For example, if debtor D were sued by creditor C outside of bankruptcy and C would not be able to recover because of D's statute of limitations defense, then C does not have allowable claim in D's bankruptcy.

Read section 502(b)(6) as a "cap" or "ceiling" on the amount of a lessor's claim for future rent. Generally, the landlord is able to re-let the premises and its actual allowable claim is significantly less than the 502(b)(6) cap. In essence, what you have to do is read 502(b)(1) before you read 502(b)(6). If, under state law, the landlord's claim for future rent would be limited to the difference between D's rental rate and the new tenant's rental rate, the allowable claim will be similarly limited.

OTHER SECTIONS

Always look for definitions in section 101. Here, it is especially important that you see the definition of "claim."

Section 501 governs the filing of a proof of claim.

Section 502(b)(3) needs to be read together with section 506(b) and section 726(a)(5). Section 502(b)(3) in essence establishes the general rule that, after a bankruptcy petition has been filed, interest stops accruing on pre-bankruptcy obligations. Section 506(b) and section 726(a)(5) are the exceptions to the rule.

Section 502(d) and section 550(h) need to be read together with the avoiding power provisions, including sections 544, 547, and 548. The former disallows claims of those from whom property is recoverable; the latter recognizes claims of those from whom property has been recovered.

Similarly, section 502(g)(1) needs to be read together with section 365.

Section 704(a)(5) requires chapter 7 trustees to object to the allowance of "improper" claims.

§ 503. Allowance of administrative expenses

(a) An entity may timely file a request for payment of an administrative expense, or may tardily file such request if permitted by the court for cause.

(b) After notice and a hearing, there shall be allowed administrative expenses, other than claims allowed under section 502(f) of this title, including—

   (1)(A) the actual, necessary costs and expenses of preserving the estate including—

      (i) wages, salaries, and commissions for services rendered after the commencement of the case; and * * *

   (B) any tax—

(i) incurred by the estate, whether secured or unsecured, including property taxes for which liability is in rem, in personam, or both, except a tax of a kind specified in section 507(a)(8) of this title; or

(ii) attributable to an excessive allowance of a tentative carryback adjustment that the estate received, whether the taxable year to which such adjustment relates ended before or after the commencement of the case;

* * *

(2) compensation and reimbursement awarded under section 330(a) of this title;

(3) the actual, necessary expenses, other than compensation and reimbursement specified in paragraph (4) of this subsection, incurred by—

(A) a creditor that files a petition under section 303 of this title;

(B) a creditor that recovers, after the court's approval, for the benefit of the estate any property transferred or concealed by the debtor;

(C) a creditor in connection with the prosecution of a criminal offense relating to the case or to the business or property of the debtor;

(D) a creditor, an indenture trustee, an equity security holder, or a committee representing creditors or equity security holders other than a committee appointed under section 1102 of this title, in making a substantial contribution in a case under chapter 9 or 11 of this title; * * *

(F) a member of a committee appointed under section 1102 of this title, if such expenses are incurred in the performance of the duties of such committee;

(4) reasonable compensation for professional services rendered by an attorney or an accountant of an entity whose expense is allowable under subparagraph (A), (B), (C), (D), or (E) of paragraph (3) of this subsection, based on the time, the nature, the extent, and the value of such services, and the cost of comparable services other than in a case under this title, and reimbursement for actual, necessary expenses incurred by such attorney or accountant;

(5) reasonable compensation for services rendered by an indenture trustee in making a substantial contribution in a case under chapter 9 or 11 of this title, based on the time, the nature, the extent, and the value of such services, and the cost of comparable services other than in a case under this title;

* * *

(7) with respect to a nonresidential real property lease previously assumed under section 365, and subsequently rejected, a sum equal to all monetary obligations due, excluding those arising from or relating to a failure to operate or a penalty provision, for the period of 2 years following the later of the rejection date or the date of actual turnover of the premises, without reduction or setoff for any reason whatsoever except for sums actually received or to be received from an entity other than the debtor, and the claim for remaining sums due for the balance of the term of the lease shall be a claim under section 502(b)(6);

* * *

(9) the value of any goods received by the debtor within 20 days before the date of commencement of a case under this title in which the goods have been sold to the debtor in the ordinary course of such debtor's business.

(c) Notwithstanding subsection (b), there shall neither be allowed, nor paid—

(1) a transfer made to, or an obligation incurred for the benefit of, an insider of the debtor for the purpose of inducing such person to remain with the debtor's business, absent a finding by the court based on evidence in the record that—

(A) the transfer or obligation is essential to retention of the person because the individual has a bona fide job offer from another business at the same or greater rate of compensation;

(B) the services provided by the person are essential to the survival of the business; and

(C) either—

(i) the amount of the transfer made to, or obligation incurred for the benefit of, the person is not greater than an amount equal to 10 times the amount of the mean transfer or obligation of a similar kind given to nonmanagement employees for any purpose during the calendar year in which the transfer is made or the obligation is incurred; or

(ii) if no such similar transfers were made to, or obligations were incurred for the benefit of, such nonmanagement employees during such calendar year, the amount of the transfer or obligation is not greater than an amount equal to 25 percent of the amount of any similar transfer or obligation made to or incurred for the benefit of such insider for any purpose during the calendar year before the year in which such transfer is made or obligation is incurred;

(2) a severance payment to an insider of the debtor, unless—

(A) the payment is part of a program that is generally applicable to all full-time employees; and

(B) the amount of the payment is not greater than 10 times the amount of the mean severance pay given to nonmanagement employees during the calendar year in which the payment is made; or

(3) other transfers or obligations that are outside the ordinary course of business and not justified by the facts and circumstances of the case, including transfers made to, or obligations incurred for the benefit of, officers, managers, or consultants hired after the date of the filing of the petition.

UNOFFICIAL COMMENTS

Section 503 tells you what is an administrative expense. Other sections set out below tell you why is it important to be an administrative expense.

The primary litigable (i.e., exam) issue raised by the language of section 503 is what the section 503(b)(1) phrase "necessary" costs and expenses of "preserving the estate" covers. There is also a possible exam issue in section 503(b)(9) of how "value" is to be determined.

Notice section 503(a)(7). You need to understand that assumption of an executory contract or lease gives rise to an administrative expense although neither section 365 nor section 507 directly so state.

OTHER SECTIONS

It is important to determine what is an administrative expense because section 507(a)(2) gives a "second priority" to administrative expenses. Section 726(a) then explains the importance of section 507 priority in a Chapter 7 case. Sections 1123(a)(1) and 1129(a)(9) explain the importance of section 507 priority in a chapter 11 case. And, section 1322(a)(2) plays a similar role in chapter 13 cases.

To understand the importance of the administrative expense priority now afforded to unpaid sellers by section 503(b)(9), it is helpful to read about unpaid sellers' right of reclamation under section 546 and whatever case or commentary your prof provided relating to payment of "critical vendors."

You might find it helpful to read section 503(c) together with section 548(a)(1)(B)(ii)(IV). Both were added in 2005 to address a concern about excessive compensation to management of a financially troubled business.

§ 504. Sharing of compensation

(a) Except as provided in subsection (b) of this section, a person receiving compensation or reimbursement under *section 503(b)(2)* or *503(b)(4)* of this title may not share or agree to share—

> **(1)** any such compensation or reimbursement with another person; or

> **(2)** any compensation or reimbursement received by another person under such sections.

(b)(1) A member, partner, or regular associate in a professional association, corporation, or partnership may share compensation or reimbursement received under *section 503(b)(2)* or *503(b)(4)* of this title with another member, partner, or regular associate in such association, corporation, or partnership, and may share in any compensation or reimbursement received under such sections by another member, partner, or regular associate in such association, corporation, or partnership.

> **(2)** An attorney for a creditor that files a petition under *section 303* of this title may share compensation and reimbursement received under *section 503(b)(4)* of this title with any other attorney contributing to the services rendered or expenses incurred by such creditor's attorney.

(c) This section shall not apply with respect to sharing, or agreeing to share, compensation with a bona fide public service attorney referral program that operates in accordance with non-Federal law regulating attorney referral services and with rules of professional responsibility applicable to attorney acceptance of referrals.

§ 505. Determination of tax liability

(a)(1) Except as provided in paragraph (2) of this subsection, the court may determine the amount or legality of any tax, any fine or penalty relating to a tax, or any addition to tax, whether or not previously assessed, whether or not paid, and whether or not contested before and adjudicated by a judicial or administrative tribunal of competent jurisdiction.

> **(2)** The court may not so determine—

>> **(A)** the amount or legality of a tax, fine, penalty, or addition to tax if such amount or legality was contested before and adjudicated by a judicial or administrative tribunal of competent jurisdiction before the commencement of the case under this title;

>> **(B)** any right of the estate to a tax refund, before the earlier of—

(i) 120 days after the trustee properly requests such refund from the governmental unit from which such refund is claimed; or

(ii) a determination by such governmental unit of such request; or

(C) the amount or legality of any amount arising in connection with an ad valorem tax on real or personal property of the estate, if the applicable period for contesting or redetermining that amount under applicable nonbankruptcy law has expired.

(b)(1)(A) The clerk shall maintain a list under which a Federal, State, or local governmental unit responsible for the collection of taxes within the district may—

(i) designate an address for service of requests under this subsection; and

(ii) describe where further information concerning additional requirements for filing such requests may be found.

(B) If such governmental unit does not designate an address and provide such address to the clerk under subparagraph (A), any request made under this subsection may be served at the address for the filing of a tax return or protest with the appropriate taxing authority of such governmental unit.

(2) A trustee may request a determination of any unpaid liability of the estate for any tax incurred during the administration of the case by submitting a tax return for such tax and a request for such a determination to the governmental unit charged with responsibility for collection or determination of such tax at the address and in the manner designated in paragraph (1). Unless such return is fraudulent, or contains a material misrepresentation, the estate, the trustee, the debtor, and any successor to the debtor are discharged from any liability for such tax—

(A) upon payment of the tax shown on such return, if—

(i) such governmental unit does not notify the trustee, within 60 days after such request, that such return has been selected for examination; or

(ii) such governmental unit does not complete such an examination and notify the trustee of any tax due, within 180 days after such request or within such additional time as the court, for cause, permits;

(B) upon payment of the tax determined by the court, after notice and a hearing, after completion by such governmental unit of such examination; or

(C) upon payment of the tax determined by such governmental unit to be due.

(c) Notwithstanding *section 362* of this title, after determination by the court of a tax under this section, the governmental unit charged with responsibility for collection of such tax may assess such tax against the estate, the debtor, or a successor to the debtor, as the case may be, subject to any otherwise applicable law.

§ 506. Determination of secured status

(a)(1) An allowed claim of a creditor secured by a lien on property in which the estate has an interest, or that is subject to setoff under section 553 of this title, is a secured claim to the extent of the value of such creditor's interest in the estate's interest in such property, or to the extent of the amount subject to setoff, as the case may be, and is an

Secured creditor granted a secured claim up to the value of collateral. If claim is greater than value of collateral, the remaining portion of the initial claim continues as unsecured claim against estate.

unsecured claim to the extent that the value of such creditor's interest or the amount so subject to setoff is less than the amount of such allowed claim. Such value shall be determined in light of the purpose of the valuation and of the proposed disposition or use of such property, and in conjunction with any hearing on such disposition or use or on a plan affecting such creditor's interest.

  (2) If the debtor is an individual in a case under chapter 7 or 13, such value with respect to personal property securing an allowed claim shall be determined based on the replacement value of such property as of the date of the filing of the petition without deduction for costs of sale or marketing. With respect to property acquired for personal, family, or household purposes, replacement value shall mean the price a retail merchant would charge for property of that kind considering the age and condition of the property at the time value is determined.

 (b) To the extent that an allowed secured claim is secured by property the value of which, after any recovery under subsection (c) of this section, is greater than the amount of such claim, there shall be allowed to the holder of such claim, interest on such claim, and any reasonable fees, costs, or charges provided for under the agreement or State statute under which such claim arose. *If oversecured the secured creditor can receive post bankruptcy interest, generally at it's contract rate, until value of collateral is exhausted*

 (c) The trustee may recover from property securing an allowed secured claim the reasonable, necessary costs and expenses of preserving, or disposing of, such property to the extent of any benefit to the holder of such claim, including the payment of all ad valorem property taxes with respect to the property.

 (d) To the extent that a lien secures a claim against the debtor that is not an allowed secured claim, such lien is void, unless—

  (1) such claim was disallowed only under section 502(b)(5) or 502(e) of this title; or

  (2) such claim is not an allowed secured claim due only to the failure of any entity to file a proof of such claim under section 501 of this title.

UNOFFICIAL COMMENTS

 You can't understand bankruptcy if you don't understand section 506. If you understand section 506, you will understand that a single transaction evidenced by a single set of documents can result in two separate claims. Assume, for example, that S loans D 1000 and obtains a first mortgage on Blackacre. One deal, one note, one mortgage. Nonetheless, if Blackacre is valued at 700, then S has a 700 secured claim and a 300 unsecured claim.

 Look at the first sentence of section 506(a)(1) to learn that the amount of the secured claim depends not solely on the amount that is owed but also on the "value" of the collateral.

 Look to the second sentence of section 506(a)(1) [and in some instances to section 506(a)(2)] to determine how to determine the value of the collateral.

 You will rarely need to look to section 506(b). It is used more often in law school than in the "real world." It applies only in the "unreal" situation in which the value of a creditor's collateral is greater than the amount of the creditor's claim, i.e., where the creditor is over-secured.

OTHER SECTIONS

 If the basis for the secured claim is a "lien", read section 506 together with section 541. Under section 541, property of the estate is limited to "interests of the debtor in property." A lien is a property interest. Accordingly, if bankruptcy debtor D owns Blackacre and is indebted to S who has a mortgage on Blackacre, then property of the estate does not include all of Blackacre. Rather, property of the estate is limited to D's interest in Blackacre, i.e., is limited by S's lien interest.

If the basis for the secured claim is a right of "setoff," then read section 506 together with section 553.

Section 506(b) is an exception to section 502(b)(2).

See the similarity between the language of section 506(c) and section 503(b)(1). In essence section 506(c) identifies the administrative expenses that a secured creditor must pay.

Rule 3012, infra at page 225, provides for the determination of the amount of the secured claim by valuing the collateral.

Section 1325(a)(5) governs the treatment of secured claims in chapter 13 plans. In chapter 13 cases, you need to read section 506 together with both section 1325(a)(5) and also section 1325(a) "hanging paragraph". BAPCPA added an unnumbered paragraph after section 1329(a)(9) [generally referred to as the "hanging paragraph", or worse] which affects the applicability of section 506 to most car loans. Unlimited case law but limited clarity on the applicability and effect of the hanging paragraph.

In chapter 11 cases, section 1123(b)(5) governs the treatment of secured claims. Section 1123(b)(5) and section 506(a) need to be read together with section 1111(b). If applicable, section 1111(b) permits a creditor with a 1000 claim secured by Redacre which has a value of 700 to elect to have a 1000 secured claim for certain purposes.

§ 507. Priorities

(a) The following expenses and claims have priority in the following order:

(1) First:

(A) Allowed unsecured claims for domestic support obligations that, as of the date of the filing of the petition in a case under this title, are owed to or recoverable by a spouse, former spouse, or child of the debtor, or such child's parent, legal guardian, or responsible relative, without regard to whether the claim is filed by such person or is filed by a governmental unit on behalf of such person, on the condition that funds received under this paragraph by a governmental unit under this title after the date of the filing of the petition shall be applied and distributed in accordance with applicable nonbankruptcy law.

(B) Subject to claims under subparagraph (A), allowed unsecured claims for domestic support obligations that, as of the date of the filing of the petition, are assigned by a spouse, former spouse, child of the debtor, or such child's parent, legal guardian, or responsible relative to a governmental unit. * * *

(C) If a trustee is appointed or elected under section 701, 702, 703, 1104, 1202, or 1302, the administrative expenses of the trustee allowed under paragraphs (1)(A), (2), and (6) of section 503(b) shall be paid before payment of claims under subparagraphs (A) and (B), to the extent that the trustee administers assets that are otherwise available for the payment of such claims.

(2) Second, administrative expenses allowed under section 503(b) of this title, and any fees and charges assessed against the estate under chapter 123 of title 28. * * *

(4) Fourth, allowed unsecured claims, but only to the extent of $12,475 for each individual or corporation, as the case may be, earned within 180 days before the date of the filing of the petition or the date of the cessation of the debtor's business, whichever occurs first, for—

(A) wages, salaries, or commissions, including vacation, severance, and sick leave pay earned by an individual; or

(B) sales commissions * * *

(5) Fifth, allowed unsecured claims for contributions to an employee benefit plan—

(A) arising from services rendered within 180 days before the date of the filing of the petition or the date of the cessation of the debtor's business, whichever occurs first; but only

(B) for each such plan, to the extent of—

(i) the number of employees covered by each such plan multiplied by $12,475; less

(ii) the aggregate amount paid to such employees under paragraph (4) of this subsection, plus the aggregate amount paid by the estate on behalf of such employees to any other employee benefit plan. * * *

(8) Eighth, allowed unsecured claims of governmental units, only to the extent that such claims are for—

(A) a tax on or measured by income or gross receipts for a taxable year ending on or before the date of the filing of the petition—

(i) for which a return, if required, is last due, including extensions, after three years before the date of the filing of the petition;

(ii) assessed within 240 days before the date of the filing of the petition, exclusive of—

(I) any time during which an offer in compromise with respect to that tax was pending or in effect during that 240-day period, plus 30 days; and

(II) any time during which a stay of proceedings against collections was in effect in a prior case under this title during that 240-day period, plus 90 days or

(iii) other than a tax of a kind specified in section 523(a)(1)(B) or 523(a)(1)(C) of this title, not assessed before, but assessable, under applicable law or by agreement, after, the commencement of the case;

(B) a property tax incurred before the commencement of the case and last payable without penalty after one year before the date of the filing of the petition;

(C) a tax required to be collected or withheld and for which the debtor is liable in whatever capacity;

(D) an employment tax on a wage, salary, or commission of a kind specified in paragraph (4) of this subsection earned from the debtor before the date of the filing of the petition, whether or not actually paid before such date, for which a return is last due, under applicable law or under any extension, after three years before the date of the filing of the petition; * * *

An otherwise applicable time period specified in this paragraph shall be suspended for any period during which a governmental unit is prohibited under applicable nonbankruptcy law from collecting a tax as a result of a request by the debtor for a hearing and an appeal of any collection action taken or proposed against the debtor, plus 90 days; plus any time during which the stay of proceedings was in effect in a prior case under this title or during which collection was precluded by the existence of 1 or more confirmed plans under this title, plus 90 days.

* * *

(b) If the trustee, under section 362, 363, or 364 of this title, provides adequate protection of the interest of a holder of a claim secured by a lien on property of the debtor and if, notwithstanding such protection, such creditor has a claim allowable under subsection (a)(2) of this section arising from the stay of action against such property under section 362 of this title, from the use, sale, or lease of such property under section 363 of this title, or from the granting of a lien under section 364(d) of this title, then such creditor's claim under such subsection shall have priority over every other claim allowable under such subsection.

* * *

UNOFFICIAL COMMENTS

Don't be in such a hurry to get to the numbered provisions that you miss the phrase "in the following order." In other words, the first priority must be paid in full before the second priority gets anything.

And, don't miss the recurring phrase "allowed unsecured claims." Priority under section 507 is limited to certain unsecured claims. No section 507 priority for a secured claim.

Assume, for example, that under non-bankruptcy law, F's first mortgage has "priority" over S's second mortgage. Neither F's secured claim nor S's secured claim, has a "section 507" priority. In the main, section 507 determines which unsecured claims get paid from the debtor's property not encumbered by mortgages or other liens.

If you understand the prior paragraph, then you will understand (at least in part) why federal tax claims only have an 8th priority. As a result of the federal tax lien provisions in the Internal Revenue Code, most federal tax claims are secured claims. Relevant provisions of the Federal Tax Lien Law are set out on page 329 et seq.

OTHER SECTIONS

Section 726(a) explains the importance of section 507 priority in a chapter 7 case. Sections 1123(a)(1) and 1129(a)(9) explain the importance of section 507 priority in a chapter 11 case. And, section 1322(a)(2) plays a similar role in chapter 13 cases.

* * *

§ 509. Claims of codebtors

(a) Except as provided in subsection (b) or (c) of this section, an entity that is liable with the debtor on, or that has secured, a claim of a creditor against the debtor, and that pays such claim, is subrogated to the rights of such creditor to the extent of such payment.

(b) Such entity is not subrogated to the rights of such creditor to the extent that—

(1) a claim of such entity for reimbursement or contribution on account of such payment of such creditor's claim is—

(A) allowed under section 502 of this title;

(B) disallowed other than under section 502(e) of this title; or

(C) subordinated under section 510 of this title; or

73

(2) as between the debtor and such entity, such entity received the consideration for the claim held by such creditor.

(c) The court shall subordinate to the claim of a creditor and for the benefit of such creditor an allowed claim, by way of subrogation under this section, or for reimbursement or contribution, of an entity that is liable with the debtor on, or that has secured, such creditor's claim, until such creditor's claim is paid in full, either through payments under this title or otherwise.

§ 510. Subordination

(a) A subordination agreement is enforceable in a case under this title to the same extent that such agreement is enforceable under applicable nonbankruptcy law.

(b) For the purpose of distribution under this title, a claim arising from rescission of a purchase or sale of a security of the debtor or of an affiliate of the debtor, for damages arising from the purchase or sale of such a security, or for reimbursement or contribution allowed under section 502 on account of such a claim, shall be subordinated to all claims or interests that are senior to or equal the claim or interest represented by such security, except that if such security is common stock, such claim has the same priority as common stock.

(c) Notwithstanding subsections (a) and (b) of this section, after notice and a hearing, the court may—

    (1) under principles of equitable subordination, subordinate for purposes of distribution all or part of an allowed claim to all or part of another allowed claim or all or part of an allowed interest to all or part of another allowed interest; or

    (2) order that any lien securing such a subordinated claim be transferred to the estate.

UNOFFICIAL COMMENTS

In a sense, section 510, which provides bases for moving claims to the "end of the line," is the exact opposite of section 507, which provides bases for moving claims to the "front of the line."

And, in a sense, section 510 subordination generally has the same practical effect as section 502 disallowance. A disallowed claim gets nothing from the bankruptcy distribution, and a subordinated claim generally gets nothing from the bankruptcy distribution.

* * *

SUBCHAPTER II—DEBTOR'S DUTIES AND BENEFITS

§ 521. Debtor's duties

(a) The debtor shall—

    (1) file—

        (A) a list of creditors; and

        (B) unless the court orders otherwise—

            (i) a schedule of assets and liabilities;

            (ii) a schedule of current income and current expenditures;

(iii) a statement of the debtor's financial affairs and, if section 342(b) applies, a certificate—

(I) of an attorney whose name is indicated on the petition as the attorney for the debtor, or a bankruptcy petition preparer signing the petition under section 110(b)(1), indicating that such attorney or the bankruptcy petition preparer delivered to the debtor the notice required by section 342(b); or

(II) if no attorney is so indicated, and no bankruptcy petition preparer signed the petition, of the debtor that such notice was received and read by the debtor;

(iv) copies of all payment advices or other evidence of payment received within 60 days before the date of the filing of the petition, by the debtor from any employer of the debtor; *Pay stubs*

(v) a statement of the amount of monthly net income, itemized to show how the amount is calculated; and

(vi) a statement disclosing any reasonably anticipated increase in income or expenditures over the 12-month period following the date of the filing of the petition;

(2) if an individual debtor's schedule of assets and liabilities includes debts which are secured by property of the estate—

(A) within thirty days after the date of the filing of a petition under chapter 7 of this title or on or before the date of the meeting of creditors, whichever is earlier, or within such additional time as the court, for cause, within such period fixes, file with the clerk a statement of his intention with respect to the retention or surrender of such property and, if applicable, specifying that such property is claimed as exempt, that the debtor intends to redeem such property, or that the debtor intends to reaffirm debts secured by such property and

(B) within 30 days after the first date set for the meeting of creditors under section 341(a), or within such additional time as the court, for cause, within such 30-day period fixes, perform his intention with respect to such property, as specified by subparagraph (A) of this paragraph;

except that nothing in subparagraphs (A) and (B) of this paragraph shall alter the debtor's or the trustee's rights with regard to such property under this title, except as provided in section 362(h);

(3) if a trustee is serving in the case * * * cooperate with the trustee as necessary to enable the trustee to perform the trustee's duties under this title;

(4) if a trustee is serving in the case * * * surrender to the trustee all property of the estate and any recorded information, including books, documents, records, and papers, relating to property of the estate, whether or not immunity is granted under section 344 of this title;

(5) appear at the hearing required under section 524(d) of this title;

(6) in a case under chapter 7 of this title in which the debtor is an individual, not retain possession of personal property as to which a creditor has an allowed claim for the purchase price secured in whole or in part by an interest in such personal property unless the debtor, not later than 45 days after the first meeting of creditors under section 341(a), either—

>   **(A)** enters into an agreement with the creditor pursuant to section 524(c) with respect to the claim secured by such property; or

>   **(B)** redeems such property from the security interest pursuant to section 722.

If the debtor fails to so act within the 45-day period referred to in paragraph (6), the stay under section 362(a) is terminated with respect to the personal property of the estate or of the debtor which is affected, such property shall no longer be property of the estate, and the creditor may take whatever action as to such property as is permitted by applicable nonbankruptcy law, unless the court determines on the motion of the trustee filed before the expiration of such 45-day period, and after notice and a hearing, that such property is of consequential value or benefit to the estate, orders appropriate adequate protection of the creditor's interest, and orders the debtor to deliver any collateral in the debtor's possession to the trustee; and

Filing for bankruptcy is an event of default (nonbankruptcy law)

Eliminates ride through w/ respect to personal property, but not real property

(b) In addition to the requirements under subsection (a), a debtor who is an individual shall file with the court—

>   **(1)** a certificate from the approved nonprofit budget and credit counseling agency that provided the debtor services under section 109(h) describing the services provided to the debtor; and

>   **(2)** a copy of the debt repayment plan, if any, developed under section 109(h) through the approved nonprofit budget and credit counseling agency referred to in paragraph (1).

* * *

(d) If the debtor fails timely to take the action specified in subsection (a)(6) of this section, or in paragraphs (1) and (2) of section 362(h), with respect to property which a lessor or bailor owns and has leased, rented, or bailed to the debtor or as to which a creditor holds a security interest not otherwise voidable under section 522(f), 544, 545, 547, 548, or 549, nothing in this title shall prevent or limit the operation of a provision in the underlying lease or agreement that has the effect of placing the debtor in default under such lease or agreement by reason of the occurrence, pendency, or existence of a proceeding under this title or the insolvency of the debtor. Nothing in this subsection shall be deemed to justify limiting such a provision in any other circumstance.

(e) * * *

>   **(2)(A)** The debtor shall provide—

>>   **(i)** not later than 7 days before the date first set for the first meeting of creditors, to the trustee a copy of the Federal income tax return required under applicable law (or at the election of the debtor, a transcript of such return) for the most recent tax year ending immediately before the commencement of the case and for which a Federal income tax return was filed; and

(ii) at the same time the debtor complies with clause (i), a copy of such return (or if elected under clause (i), such transcript) to any creditor that timely requests such copy.

(B) If the debtor fails to comply with clause (i) or (ii) of subparagraph (A), the court shall dismiss the case unless the debtor demonstrates that the failure to so comply is due to circumstances beyond the control of the debtor. * * *

(h) If requested by the United States trustee or by the trustee, the debtor shall provide—

(1) a document that establishes the identity of the debtor, including a driver's license, passport, or other document that contains a photograph of the debtor; or

(2) such other personal identifying information relating to the debtor that establishes the identity of the debtor.

(i)(1) Subject to paragraphs (2) and (4) and notwithstanding section 707(a), if an individual debtor in a voluntary case under chapter 7 or 13 fails to file all of the information required under subsection (a)(1) within 45 days after the date of the filing of the petition, the case shall be automatically dismissed effective on the 46th day after the date of the filing of the petition.

(2) Subject to paragraph (4) and with respect to a case described in paragraph (1), any party in interest may request the court to enter an order dismissing the case. If requested, the court shall enter an order of dismissal not later than 5 days after such request.

(3) Subject to paragraph (4) and upon request of the debtor made within 45 days after the date of the filing of the petition described in paragraph (1), the court may allow the debtor an additional period of not to exceed 45 days to file the information required under subsection (a)(1) if the court finds justification for extending the period for the filing.

(4) Notwithstanding any other provision of this subsection, on the motion of the trustee filed before the expiration of the applicable period of time specified in paragraph (1), (2), or (3), and after notice and a hearing, the court may decline to dismiss the case if the court finds that the debtor attempted in good faith to file all the information required by subsection (a)(1)(B)(iv) and that the best interests of creditors would be served by administration of the case.

(j)(1) Notwithstanding any other provision of this title, if the debtor fails to file a tax return that becomes due after the commencement of the case or to properly obtain an extension of the due date for filing such return, the taxing authority may request that the court enter an order converting or dismissing the case.

(2) If the debtor does not file the required return or obtain the extension referred to in paragraph (1) within 90 days after a request is filed by the taxing authority under that paragraph, the court shall convert or dismiss the case, whichever is in the best interests of creditors and the estate.

UNOFFICIAL COMMENTS

Be sure you understand section 521(a)(2) and (6). That is what you are most likely to see on your exam.

OTHER SECTIONS

Understanding section 521(a)(2) and (6) requires an understanding of section 524(c) and (d), section 722, and section 524(a). A discharge does not affect the rights of lien creditors to enforce their liens by foreclosing on their collateral. Accordingly, a chapter 7 debtor who wants to keep her encumbered personal property must now either elect under section 521 to reaffirm or redeem.

And, under section 362(h)(1), a debtor who wants to keep the automatic stay intact must make a section 521(a)(2)(A) election.

You might find it helpful to look at Rule 4002, infra at page 228.

§ 522. Exemptions

(a) In this section—

    (1) "dependent" includes spouse, whether or not actually dependent; and

    (2) "value" means fair market value as of the date of the filing of the petition or, with respect to property that becomes property of the estate after such date, as of the date such property becomes property of the estate.

[handwritten margin note: equivalent to liquidation value (Wb/sh)]

(b)(1) Notwithstanding section 541 of this title, an individual debtor may exempt from property of the estate the property listed in either paragraph (2) or, in the alternative, paragraph (3) of this subsection. In joint cases filed under section 302 of this title and individual cases filed under section 301 or 303 of this title by or against debtors who are husband and wife, and whose estates are ordered to be jointly administered under Rule 1015(b) of the Federal Rules of Bankruptcy Procedure, one debtor may not elect to exempt property listed in paragraph (2) and the other debtor elect to exempt property listed in paragraph (3) of this subsection. If the parties cannot agree on the alternative to be elected, they shall be deemed to elect paragraph (2), where such election is permitted under the law of the jurisdiction where the case is filed.

    (2) Property listed in this paragraph is property that is specified under subsection (d), unless the State law that is applicable to the debtor under paragraph (3)(A) specifically does not so authorize. *[handwritten: Can't use para. 2 if state law prohibits federal exemptions.]*

    (3) Property listed in this paragraph is—

        (A) subject to subsections (*o*) and (p), any property that is exempt under Federal law, other than subsection (d) of this section, or State or local law that is applicable on the date of the filing of the petition at the place in which the debtor's domicile has been located for the 730 days immediately preceding the date of the filing of the petition or if the debtor's domicile has not been located at a single State for such 730-day period, the place in which the debtor's domicile was located for 180 days immediately preceding the 730-day period or for a longer portion of such 180-day period than in any other place; *[handwritten: look to (o)]*

[handwritten margin note: Anything exempt under non bankruptcy law. Federal law other than subsection D]

        (B) any interest in property in which the debtor had, immediately before the commencement of the case, an interest as a tenant by the entirety or joint tenant to the extent that such interest as a tenant by the entirety or joint tenant is exempt from process under applicable nonbankruptcy law; and

        (C) retirement funds to the extent that those funds are in a fund or account that is exempt from taxation under section 401, 403, 408, 408A, 414, 457, or 501(a) of the Internal Revenue Code of 1986.

[handwritten: IRA, 401K 403B]

If the effect of the domiciliary requirement under subparagraph (A) is to render the debtor ineligible for any exemption, the debtor may elect to exempt property that is specified under subsection (d).

(4) For purposes of paragraph (3)(C) and subsection (d)(12), the following shall apply:

(A) If the retirement funds are in a retirement fund that has received a favorable determination under section 7805 of the Internal Revenue Code of 1986, and that determination is in effect as of the date of the filing of the petition in a case under this title, those funds shall be presumed to be exempt from the estate.

(B) If the retirement funds are in a retirement fund that has not received a favorable determination under such section 7805, those funds are exempt from the estate if the debtor demonstrates that—

(i) no prior determination to the contrary has been made by a court or the Internal Revenue Service; and

(ii)(I) the retirement fund is in substantial compliance with the applicable requirements of the Internal Revenue Code of 1986; or

(II) the retirement fund fails to be in substantial compliance with the applicable requirements of the Internal Revenue Code of 1986 and the debtor is not materially responsible for that failure.

(C) A direct transfer of retirement funds from 1 fund or account that is exempt from taxation under section 401, 403, 408, 408A, 414, 457, or 501(a) of the Internal Revenue Code of 1986, under section 401(a)(31) of the Internal Revenue Code of 1986, or otherwise, shall not cease to qualify for exemption under paragraph (3)(C) or subsection (d)(12) by reason of such direct transfer.

(D)(i) Any distribution that qualifies as an eligible rollover distribution within the meaning of section 402(c) of the Internal Revenue Code of 1986 or that is described in clause (ii) shall not cease to qualify for exemption under paragraph (3)(C) or subsection (d)(12) by reason of such distribution.

(ii) A distribution described in this clause is an amount that—

(I) has been distributed from a fund or account that is exempt from taxation under section 401, 403, 408, 408A, 414, 457, or 501(a) of the Internal Revenue Code of 1986; and

(II) to the extent allowed by law, is deposited in such a fund or account not later than 60 days after the distribution of such amount.

(c) Unless the case is dismissed, property exempted under this section is not liable during or after the case for any debt of the debtor that arose, or that is determined under section 502 of this title as if such debt had arisen, before the commencement of the case, except—

(1) a debt of a kind specified in paragraph (1) or (5) of section 523(a) (in which case, notwithstanding any provision of applicable nonbankruptcy law to the contrary, such property shall be liable for a debt of a kind specified in such paragraph;

(2) a debt secured by a lien that is— lien ahead of exemption rights.

(A)(i) not avoided under subsection (f) or (g) of this section or under section 544, 545, 547, 548, 549, or 724(a) of this title; and

(ii) not void under section 506(d) of this title; or

(B) a tax lien, notice of which is properly filed; * * *

Federal Exemptions

Double for Couples

(d) The following property may be exempted under subsection (b)(2) of this section:

(1) The debtor's aggregate interest, not to exceed $22,975 in value, in real property or personal property that the debtor or a dependent of the debtor uses as a residence, in a cooperative that owns property that the debtor or a dependent of the debtor uses as a residence, or in a burial plot for the debtor or a dependent of the debtor.

(2) The debtor's interest, not to exceed $3,675 in value, in one motor vehicle.

(3) The debtor's interest, not to exceed $575 in value in any particular item or $12,250 in aggregate value, in household furnishings, household goods, wearing apparel, appliances, books, animals, crops, or musical instruments, that are held primarily for the personal, family, or household use of the debtor or a dependent of the debtor.

(4) The debtor's aggregate interest, not to exceed $1,550 in value, in jewelry held primarily for the personal, family, or household use of the debtor or a dependent of the debtor.

Wildcard

(5) The debtor's aggregate interest in any property, not to exceed in value $1,225 plus up to $11,500 of any unused amount of the exemption provided under paragraph (1) of this subsection.

(6) The debtor's aggregate interest, not to exceed $2,300 in value, in any implements, professional books, or tools, of the trade of the debtor or the trade of a dependent of the debtor.

(7) Any unmatured life insurance contract owned by the debtor, other than a credit life insurance contract.

(8) The debtor's aggregate interest, not to exceed in value $12,250 less any amount of property of the estate transferred in the manner specified in section 542(d) of this title, in any accrued dividend or interest under, or loan value of, any unmatured life insurance contract owned by the debtor under which the insured is the debtor or an individual of whom the debtor is a dependent.

(9) Professionally prescribed health aids for the debtor or a dependent of the debtor.

(10) The debtor's right to receive—

(A) a social security benefit, unemployment compensation, or a local public assistance benefit;

(B) a veterans' benefit;

(C) a disability, illness, or unemployment benefit;

(D) alimony, support, or separate maintenance, to the extent reasonably necessary for the support of the debtor and any dependent of the debtor;

(E) a payment under a stock bonus, pension, profitsharing, annuity, or similar plan or contract on account of illness, disability, death, age, or length of service, to the extent reasonably necessary for the support of the debtor and any dependent of the debtor, unless—

(i) such plan or contract was established by or under the auspices of an insider that employed the debtor at the time the debtor's rights under such plan or contract arose;

(ii) such payment is on account of age or length of service; and

(iii) such plan or contract does not qualify under section 401(a), 403(a), 403(b), or 408 of the Internal Revenue Code of 1986.

(11) The debtor's right to receive, or property that is traceable to—

(A) an award under a crime victim's reparation law [restitution]

(B) a payment on account of the wrongful death of an individual of whom the debtor was a dependent, to the extent reasonably necessary for the support of the debtor and any dependent of the debtor;

(C) a payment under a life insurance contract that insured the life of an individual of whom the debtor was a dependent on the date of such individual's death, to the extent reasonably necessary for the support of the debtor and any dependent of the debtor;

(D) a payment, not to exceed $22,975 on account of personal bodily injury, not including pain and suffering or compensation for actual pecuniary loss, of the debtor or an individual of whom the debtor is a dependent; or

(E) a payment in compensation of loss of future earnings of the debtor or an individual of whom the debtor is or was a dependent, to the extent reasonably necessary for the support of the debtor and any dependent of the debtor.

[handwritten margin note: Structured settlement makes to be or to be a difference]

(12) Retirement funds to the extent that those funds are in a fund or account that is exempt from taxation under section 401, 403, 408, 408A, 414, 457, or 501(a) of the Internal Revenue Code of 1986.

(e) A waiver of an exemption executed in favor of a creditor that holds an unsecured claim against the debtor is unenforceable in a case under this title with respect to such claim against property that the debtor may exempt under subsection (b) of this section. A waiver by the debtor of a power under subsection (f) or (h) of this section to avoid a transfer, under subsection (g) or (i) of this section to exempt property, or under subsection (i) of this section to recover property or to preserve a transfer, is unenforceable in a case under this title.

[handwritten margin note: Exemption cant be waived only way is to give creditor scanty lien.]

(f)(1) Notwithstanding any waiver of exemptions but subject to paragraph (3), the debtor may avoid the fixing of a lien on an interest of the debtor in property to the extent that such lien impairs an exemption to which the debtor would have been entitled under subsection (b) of this section, if such lien is—

(A) a judicial lien, other than a judicial lien that secures a debt of a kind that is specified in section 523(a)(5); or *[handwritten: B/c state law would exempt under a judgment lien.]*

(B) a nonpossessory, nonpurchase-money security interest in any— *[handwritten: Domestic support]*

(i) household furnishings, household goods, wearing apparel, appliances, books, animals, crops, musical instruments, or jewelry that are

[handwritten at bottom: Certain liens can be avoided 81 if impair your exemption Collateral is a hostage they can kill if you don't pay the ransom Avoid that type of leverage on debtors]

held primarily for the personal, family, or household use of the debtor or a dependent of the debtor;

       (ii) implements, professional books, or tools, of the trade of the debtor or the trade of a dependent of the debtor; or

       (iii) professionally prescribed health aids for the debtor or a dependent of the debtor.

    (2)(A) For the purposes of this subsection, a lien shall be considered to impair an exemption to the extent that the sum of—

       (i) the lien;

       (ii) all other liens on the property; and

       (iii) the amount of the exemption that the debtor could claim if there were no liens on the property;

exceeds the value that the debtor's interest in the property would have in the absence of any liens.

       (B) In the case of a property subject to more than 1 lien, a lien that has been avoided shall not be considered in making the calculation under subparagraph (A) with respect to other liens.

       (C) This paragraph shall not apply with respect to a judgment arising out of a mortgage foreclosure.

    (3) In a case in which State law that is applicable to the debtor—

       (A) permits a person to voluntarily waive a right to claim exemptions under subsection (d) or prohibits a debtor from claiming exemptions under subsection (d); and

       (B) either permits the debtor to claim exemptions under State law without limitation in amount, except to the extent that the debtor has permitted the fixing of a consensual lien on any property or prohibits avoidance of a consensual lien on property otherwise eligible to be claimed as exempt property;

the debtor may not avoid the fixing of a lien on an interest of the debtor or a dependent of the debtor in property if the lien is a nonpossessory, nonpurchase-money security interest in implements, professional books, or tools of the trade of the debtor or a dependent of the debtor or farm animals or crops of the debtor or a dependent of the debtor to the extent the value of such implements, professional books, tools of the trade, animals, and crops exceeds $6,225.

    (4)(A) Subject to subparagraph (B), for purposes of paragraph (1)(B), the term "household goods" means—

       (i) clothing;

       (ii) furniture;

       (iii) appliances;

       (iv) 1 radio;

       (v) 1 television;

(vi) 1 VCR;

(vii) linens;

(viii) china;

(ix) crockery;

(x) kitchenware;

(xi) educational materials and educational equipment primarily for the use of minor dependent children of the debtor;

(xii) medical equipment and supplies;

(xiii) furniture exclusively for the use of minor children, or elderly or disabled dependents of the debtor;

(xiv) personal effects (including the toys and hobby equipment of minor dependent children and wedding rings) of the debtor and the dependents of the debtor; and

(xv) 1 personal computer and related equipment.

(B) The term "household goods" does not include—

(i) works of art (unless by or of the debtor, or any relative of the debtor);

(ii) electronic entertainment equipment with a fair market value of more than $650 in the aggregate (except 1 television, 1 radio, and 1 VCR);

(iii) items acquired as antiques with a fair market value of more than $650 in the aggregate;

(iv) jewelry with a fair market value of more than $650 in the aggregate (except wedding rings); and

(v) a computer (except as otherwise provided for in this section), motor vehicle (including a tractor or lawn tractor), boat, or a motorized recreational device, conveyance, vehicle, watercraft, or aircraft.

(g) Notwithstanding sections 550 and 551 of this title, the debtor may exempt under subsection (b) of this section property that the trustee recovers under section 510(c)(2), 542, 543, 550, 551, or 553 of this title, to the extent that the debtor could have exempted such property under subsection (b) of this section if such property had not been transferred, if—

(1)(A) such transfer was not a voluntary transfer of such property by the debtor; and

(B) the debtor did not conceal such property; or

(2) the debtor could have avoided such transfer under subsection (f)(1)(B) of this section.

(h) The debtor may avoid a transfer of property of the debtor or recover a setoff to the extent that the debtor could have exempted such property under subsection (g)(1) of this section if the trustee had avoided such transfer, if—

(1) such transfer is avoidable by the trustee under section 544, 545, 547, 548, 549, or 724(a) of this title or recoverable by the trustee under section 553 of this title; and

(2) the trustee does not attempt to avoid such transfer.

(i)(1) If the debtor avoids a transfer or recovers a setoff under subsection (f) or (h) of this section, the debtor may recover in the manner prescribed by, and subject to the limitations of, section 550 of this title, the same as if the trustee had avoided such transfer, and may exempt any property so recovered under subsection (b) of this section.

(2) Notwithstanding section 551 of this title, a transfer avoided under section 544, 545, 547, 548, 549, or 724(a) of this title, under subsection (f) or (h) of this section, or property recovered under section 553 of this title, may be preserved for the benefit of the debtor to the extent that the debtor may exempt such property under subsection (g) of this section or paragraph (1) of this subsection.

(j) Notwithstanding subsections (g) and (i) of this section, the debtor may exempt a particular kind of property under subsections (g) and (i) of this section only to the extent that the debtor has exempted less property in value of such kind than that to which the debtor is entitled under subsection (b) of this section.

(k) Property that the debtor exempts under this section is not liable for payment of any administrative expense except—

(1) the aliquot share of the costs and expenses of avoiding a transfer of property that the debtor exempts under subsection (g) of this section, or of recovery of such property, that is attributable to the value of the portion of such property exempted in relation to the value of the property recovered; and

(2) any costs and expenses of avoiding a transfer under subsection (f) or (h) of this section, or of recovery of property under subsection (i)(1) of this section, that the debtor has not paid.

(*l*) The debtor shall file a list of property that the debtor claims as exempt under subsection (b) of this section. If the debtor does not file such a list, a dependent of the debtor may file such a list, or may claim property as exempt from property of the estate on behalf of the debtor. Unless a party in interest objects, the property claimed as exempt on such list is exempt.

(m) Subject to the limitation in subsection (b), this section shall apply separately with respect to each debtor in a joint case. *Each use the exemption. Double exemptions*

(n) For assets in individual retirement accounts described in section 408 or 408A of the Internal Revenue Code of 1986, other than a simplified employee pension under section 408(k) of such Code or a simple retirement account under section 408(p) of such Code, the aggregate value of such assets exempted under this section, without regard to amounts attributable to rollover contributions under section 402(c), 402(e)(6), 403(a)(4), 403(a) (5), and 403(b)(8) of the Internal Revenue Code of 1986, and earnings thereon, shall not exceed $1,245,475 in a case filed by a debtor who is an individual, except that such amount may be increased if the interests of justice so require.

(o) For purposes of subsection (b)(3)(A), and notwithstanding subsection (a), the value of an interest in—

(1) real or personal property that the debtor or a dependent of the debtor uses as a residence;

(2) a cooperative that owns property that the debtor or a dependent of the debtor uses as a residence;

(3) a burial plot for the debtor or a dependent of the debtor; or

(4) real or personal property that the debtor or a dependent of the debtor claims as a homestead;

shall be reduced to the extent that such value is attributable to any portion of any property that the debtor disposed of in the 10-year period ending on the date of the filing of the petition with the intent to hinder, delay, or defraud a creditor and that the debtor could not exempt, or that portion that the debtor could not exempt, under subsection (b), if on such date the debtor had held the property so disposed of.

(p)(1) Except as provided in paragraph (2) of this subsection and sections 544 and 548, as a result of electing under subsection (b)(3)(A) to exempt property under State or local law, a debtor may not exempt any amount of interest that was acquired by the debtor during the 1215-day period preceding the date of the filing of the petition that exceeds in the aggregate $155,675 in value in—

(A) real or personal property that the debtor or a dependent of the debtor uses as a residence;

(B) a cooperative that owns property that the debtor or a dependent of the debtor uses as a residence;

(C) a burial plot for the debtor or a dependent of the debtor; or

(D) real or personal property that the debtor or dependent of the debtor claims as a homestead.

(2)(A) The limitation under paragraph (1) shall not apply to an exemption claimed under subsection (b)(3)(A) by a family farmer for the principal residence of such farmer.

(B) For purposes of paragraph (1), any amount of such interest does not include any interest transferred from a debtor's previous principal residence (which was acquired prior to the beginning of such 1215-day period) into the debtor's current principal residence, if the debtor's previous and current residences are located in the same State.

* * *

UNOFFICIAL COMMENTS

The hard law school question on exemption law is determining what law determines what property is exempt in bankruptcy. Section 522(b)(1) indicates that the individual can choose the law from section 522(b)(2) "or in the alternative" the law from section 522(b)(3).

The section 522(b)(2) alternative is to choose the exemptions established by the Bankruptcy Code—by section 522(d). That alternative, however, is not available to most debtors because most states have enacted a law "that specifically does not so authorize." Such laws are generally referred to as "opt-out" laws. Accordingly, the most important aspect of section 522(b)(2) and 522(d) is how unimportant each is.

Section 522(b)(3) then determines what property is exempt in bankruptcy by determining what property would be exempt outside of bankruptcy, i.e., property that would be exempt under federal laws other than the Bankruptcy Code, and, more important, under relevant state law. And, section 523(b)(3) determines which state's law is relevant, based on the "debtor's domicile." Neither section

522 nor any other provision of title II speaks to what constitutes a "debtor's domicile" for purposes of title II.

OTHER SECTIONS

Because of the definition of "insolvent" in section 101, determination of what property is exempt under section 522 can affect whether a debtor is "insolvent" as that term is used in the Bankruptcy Code.

Schedule 6c on page 245 infra is what a debtor prepares in order to claim property as exempt property. Rule 4003(b) on page 229 infra governs objections to such a claim of exemptions. Read Rule 4003(b) together with 522(*l*). More specifically, read the 30 day deadline in Rule 4003(b) together with the last sentence of section 522(*l*).

Section 522 also needs to be read together with section 541 which describes "property of the estate." Think about the relationship between the two provisions. Some property of the estate is exempt property; in essence, section 522 determines what property of the estate is exempted from creditors, i.e., what property the debtor gets to keep. Pay particular attention to section 541(b)—especially 541(b)(5)–(8). It identifies interests in property that the debtor gets to keep because it is not even "property of the estate." While the practical effect of section 541(b) is to identify property that the debtor gets to keep, section 541(b) property is not exempt property.

Section 522 often needs to be read together with section 548. An individual debtor's acquiring more exempt property on the eve of bankruptcy (sometimes referred to as "insolvency planning") is often challenged as a fraudulent conveyance under section 548.

Section 522 also often needs to be read together with section 722. Redemption under section 722 is limited to property that is exempt under section 522 or abandoned under section 554.

§ 523. Exceptions to discharge

(a) A discharge under section 727, 1141, 1228(a), 1228(b), or 1328(b) of this title does not discharge an individual debtor from any debt—

    (1) for a tax or a customs duty—

        (A) of the kind and for the periods specified in section 507(a)(3) or 507(a)(8) of this title, whether or not a claim for such tax was filed or allowed;

        (B) with respect to which a return, or equivalent report or notice, if required—

            (i) was not filed or given; or

            (ii) was filed or given after the date on which such return, report, or notice was last due, under applicable law or under any extension, and after two years before the date of the filing of the petition; or

        (C) with respect to which the debtor made a fraudulent return or willfully attempted in any manner to evade or defeat such tax;

    (2) for money, property, services, or an extension, renewal, or refinancing of credit, to the extent obtained by—

        (A) false pretenses, a false representation, or actual fraud, other than a statement respecting the debtor's or an insider's financial condition;

        (B) use of a statement in writing—

            (i) that is materially false;

            (ii) respecting the debtor's or an insider's financial condition;

(iii) on which the creditor to whom the debtor is liable for such money, property, services, or credit reasonably relied; and

(iv) that the debtor caused to be made or published with intent to deceive; or

(C)(i) for purposes of subparagraph (A)—

(I) consumer debts owed to a single creditor and aggregating more than $650 for luxury goods or services incurred by an individual debtor on or within 90 days before the order for relief under this title are presumed to be nondischargeable; and

(II) cash advances aggregating more than $925 that are extensions of consumer credit under an open end credit plan obtained by an individual debtor on or within 70 days before the order for relief under this title, are presumed to be nondischargeable; and

(ii) for purposes of this subparagraph—

* * *

(II) the term "luxury goods or services" does not include goods or services reasonably necessary for the support or maintenance of the debtor or a dependent of the debtor;

(3) neither listed nor scheduled under section 521(a)(1) of this title, with the name, if known to the debtor, of the creditor to whom such debt is owed, in time to permit— *Claims not listed by the debtor*

(A) if such debt is not of a kind specified in paragraph (2), (4), or (6) of this subsection, timely filing of a proof of claim, unless such creditor had notice or actual knowledge of the case in time for such timely filing; or

(B) if such debt is of a kind specified in paragraph (2), (4), or (6) of this subsection, timely filing of a proof of claim and timely request for a determination of dischargeability of such debt under one of such paragraphs, unless such creditor had notice or actual knowledge of the case in time for such timely filing and request;

(4) for fraud or defalcation while acting in a fiduciary capacity, embezzlement, or larceny; *or fraud*

(5) for a domestic support obligation;

(6) for willful and malicious injury by the debtor to another entity or to the property of another entity;

(7) to the extent such debt is for a fine, penalty, or forfeiture payable to and for the benefit of a governmental unit, and is not compensation for actual pecuniary loss, other than a tax penalty—

(A) relating to a tax of a kind not specified in paragraph (1) of this subsection; or

(B) imposed with respect to a transaction or event that occurred before three years before the date of the filing of the petition;

(8) unless excepting such debt from discharge under this paragraph would impose an undue hardship on the debtor and the debtor's dependents, for—

(A)(i) an educational benefit overpayment or loan made, insured, or guaranteed by a governmental unit, or made under any program funded in whole or in part by a governmental unit or nonprofit institution; or

(ii) an obligation to repay funds received as an educational benefit, scholarship, or stipend; or

(B) any other educational loan that is a qualified education loan, as defined in section 221(d)(1) of the Internal Revenue Code of 1986, incurred by a debtor who is an individual;

(9) for death or personal injury caused by the debtor's operation of a motor vehicle, vessel, or aircraft if such operation was unlawful because the debtor was intoxicated from using alcohol, a drug, or another substance;

(10) that was or could have been listed or scheduled by the debtor in a prior case concerning the debtor under this title * * * in which the debtor waived discharge, or was denied a discharge under section 727(a)(2), (3), (4), (5), (6), or (7) of this title * * *

* * *

(14) incurred to pay a tax to the United States that would be nondischargeable pursuant to paragraph (1);

(15) to a spouse, former spouse, or child of the debtor and not of the kind described in paragraph (5) that is incurred by the debtor in the course of a divorce or separation or in connection with a separation agreement, divorce decree or other order of a court of record, or a determination made in accordance with State or territorial law by a governmental unit;

* * *

(c)(1) Except as provided in subsection (a)(3)(B) of this section, the debtor shall be discharged from a debt of a kind specified in paragraph (2), (4), or (6) of subsection (a) of this section, unless, on request of the creditor to whom such debt is owed, and after notice and a hearing, the court determines such debt to be excepted from discharge under paragraph (2), (4), or (6), as the case may be, of subsection (a) of this section.

* * *

(d) If a creditor requests a determination of dischargeability of a consumer debt under subsection (a)(2) of this section, and such debt is discharged, the court shall grant judgment in favor of the debtor for the costs of, and a reasonable attorney's fee for, the proceeding if the court finds that the position of the creditor was not substantially justified, except that the court shall not award such costs and fees if special circumstances would make the award unjust.

* * *

UNOFFICIAL COMMENTS

Notice that the words "credit card" nowhere appear in section 523 (or anywhere else in the Bankruptcy Code). Most dischargeability litigation *(that is what litigation under section 523 is generally called) involving credit cards involves section 523(a)(2) and so do most law school exam questions on dischargeability.

Section 523(a)(2) is a mess. For starters, (a)(2)(C) should be a part of (a)(2)(B) and you should add the conjunction "or" to connect (a)(2)(A) with (a)(2)(B).

Most cases and most law school exam questions involve (a)(2)(A) rather than (a)(2)(B) since (a)(2)(B) applies only where the debtor used a written statement. Most courts, however, look to the numbered requirements of (a)(2)(B) in litigation involving (a)(2)(A).

OTHER SECTIONS

All of section 523(a) applies in chapter 7 cases, individual debtor chapter 11 cases, and chapter 13 cases in which there is a section 1328(b) hardship discharge. Most of section 523(a) applies in chapter 13 cases in which there is a section 1328(a) discharge. Section 523(a) does not apply to business entity debtors in chapter 11 cases.

Litigation over whether a particular debt is excepted from discharge by section 523 can and does occur in state court. The Congressional grant of jurisdiction over bankruptcy related litigation in 28 USC 1334(b) is "original but not exclusive jurisdiction of all civil proceedings arising under title 11 * * * Accordingly, except for dischargeability litigation based on one of the subsections enumerated in section 523(c), dischargeability litigation can occur either in bankruptcy court during the bankruptcy case or state court."

Rule 7001 on page 231 infra provides that section 523 litigation is an adversary proceeding. Rule 4007 on page 230 infra provides further guidance about dischargeability litigation.

§ 524. Effect of discharge

(a) A discharge in a case under this title—

(1) voids any judgment at any time obtained, to the extent that such judgment is a determination of the personal liability of the debtor with respect to any debt discharged under section 727, 944, 1141, 1228, or 1328 of this title, whether or not discharge of such debt is waived; *σ*

(2) operates as an injunction against the commencement or continuation of an action, the employment of process, or an act, to collect, recover or offset any such debt as a personal liability of the debtor, whether or not discharge of such debt is waived; and

(3) operates as an injunction against the commencement or continuation of an action, the employment of process, or an act, to collect or recover from, or offset against, property of the debtor of the kind specified in section 541(a)(2) of this title that is acquired after the commencement of the case, on account of any allowable community claim, except a community claim that is excepted from discharge under section 523, 1228(a)(1), or 1328(a)(1), or that would be so excepted, determined in accordance with the provisions of sections 523(c) and 523(d) of this title, in a case concerning the debtor's spouse commenced on the date of the filing of the petition in the case concerning the debtor, whether or not discharge of the debt based on such community claim is waived.

(b) Subsection (a)(3) of this section does not apply if—

(1)(A) the debtor's spouse is a debtor in a case under this title, or a bankrupt or a debtor in a case under the Bankruptcy Act, commenced within six years of the date of the filing of the petition in the case concerning the debtor; and

(B) the court does not grant the debtor's spouse a discharge in such case concerning the debtor's spouse; or

(2)(A) the court would not grant the debtor's spouse a discharge in a case under chapter 7 of this title concerning such spouse commenced on the date of the filing of the petition in the case concerning the debtor; and

(B) a determination that the court would not so grant such discharge is made by the bankruptcy court within the time and in the manner provided for a determination under section 727 of this title of whether a debtor is granted a discharge.

(c) An agreement between a holder of a claim and the debtor, the consideration for which, in whole or in part, is based on a debt that is dischargeable in a case under this title is enforceable only to any extent enforceable under applicable nonbankruptcy law, whether or not discharge of such debt is waived, only if—

(1) such agreement was made before the granting of the discharge under section 727, 1141, 1228, or 1328 of this title;

(2) the debtor received the disclosures described in subsection (k) at or before the time at which the debtor signed the agreement;

(3) such agreement has been filed with the court and, if applicable, accompanied by a declaration or an affidavit of the attorney that represented the debtor during the course of negotiating an agreement under this subsection, which states that—

(A) such agreement represents a fully informed and voluntary agreement by the debtor;

(B) such agreement does not impose an undue hardship on the debtor or a dependent of the debtor; and

(C) the attorney fully advised the debtor of the legal effect and consequences of—

(i) an agreement of the kind specified in this subsection; and

(ii) any default under such an agreement;

(4) the debtor has not rescinded such agreement at any time prior to discharge or within sixty days after such agreement is filed with the court, whichever occurs later, by giving notice of rescission to the holder of such claim;

(5) the provisions of subsection (d) of this section have been complied with; and

(6)(A) in a case concerning an individual who was not represented by an attorney during the course of negotiating an agreement under this subsection, the court approves such agreement as—

(i) not imposing an undue hardship on the debtor or a dependent of the debtor; and

(ii) in the best interest of the debtor.

(B) Subparagraph (A) shall not apply to the extent that such debt is a consumer debt secured by real property.

(d) In a case concerning an individual, when the court has determined whether to grant or not to grant a discharge under section 727, 1141, 1228, or 1328 of this title, the court may hold a hearing at which the debtor shall appear in person. At any such hearing, the court shall inform the debtor that a discharge has been granted or the reason why a discharge has not been granted. If a discharge has been granted and if the debtor desires to make an agreement of the kind specified in subsection (c) of this section and was not represented by an attorney during the course of negotiating such agreement, then the court shall hold a hearing at which the debtor shall appear in person and at such hearing the court shall—

(1) inform the debtor—

(A) that such an agreement is not required under this title, under nonbankruptcy law, or under any agreement not made in accordance with the provisions of subsection (c) of this section; and

(B) of the legal effect and consequences of—

(i) an agreement of the kind specified in subsection (c) of this section; and

(ii) a default under such an agreement; and

(2) determine whether the agreement that the debtor desires to make complies with the requirements of subsection (c)(6) of this section, if the consideration for such agreement is based in whole or in part on a consumer debt that is not secured by real property of the debtor.

(e) Except as provided in subsection (a)(3) of this section, discharge of a debt of the debtor does not affect the liability of any other entity on, or the property of any other entity for, such debt.

(f) Nothing contained in subsection (c) or (d) of this section prevents a debtor from voluntarily repaying any debt.

* * *

(j) Subsection (a)(2) does not operate as an injunction against an act by a creditor that is the holder of a secured claim, if—

(1) such creditor retains a security interest in real property that is the principal residence of the debtor;

(2) such act is in the ordinary course of business between the creditor and the debtor; and

(3) such act is limited to seeking or obtaining periodic payments associated with a valid security interest in lieu of pursuit of in rem relief to enforce the lien.

(k)(1) The disclosures required under subsection (c)(2) shall consist of the disclosure statement described in paragraph (3), completed as required in that paragraph, together with the agreement specified in subsection (c), statement, declaration, motion and order described, respectively, in paragraphs (4) through (8), and shall be the only disclosures required in connection with entering into such agreement.

(2) Disclosures made under paragraph (1) shall be made clearly and conspicuously and in writing. The terms "Amount Reaffirmed" and "Annual Percentage Rate" shall be disclosed more conspicuously than other terms, data or information provided in connection with this disclosure, except that the phrases "Before agreeing to reaffirm a debt, review these important disclosures" and "Summary of Reaffirmation Agreement" may be equally conspicuous. Disclosures may be made in a different order and may use terminology different from that set forth in paragraphs (2) through (8), except that the terms "Amount Reaffirmed" and "Annual Percentage Rate" must be used where indicated.

(3) The disclosure statement required under this paragraph shall consist of the following:

(A) The statement: "Part A: Before agreeing to reaffirm a debt, review these important disclosures:";

(B) Under the heading "Summary of Reaffirmation Agreement", the statement: "This Summary is made pursuant to the requirements of the Bankruptcy Code";

(C) The "Amount Reaffirmed", using that term, which shall be—

(i) the total amount of debt that the debtor agrees to reaffirm by entering into an agreement of the kind specified in subsection (c), and

(ii) the total of any fees and costs accrued as of the date of the disclosure statement, related to such total amount.

(D) In conjunction with the disclosure of the "Amount Reaffirmed", the statements—

(i) "The amount of debt you have agreed to reaffirm"; and

(ii) "Your credit agreement may obligate you to pay additional amounts which may come due after the date of this disclosure. Consult your credit agreement."

(E) The "Annual Percentage Rate", using that term, which shall be disclosed as—

(i) if, at the time the petition is filed, the debt is an extension of credit under an open end credit plan, as the terms "credit" and "open end credit plan" are defined in section 103 of the Truth in Lending Act, then—

(I) the annual percentage rate determined under paragraphs (5) and (6) of section 127(b) of the Truth in Lending Act, as applicable, as disclosed to the debtor in the most recent periodic statement prior to entering into an agreement of the kind specified in subsection (c) or, if no such periodic statement has been given to the debtor during the prior 6 months, the annual percentage rate as it would have been so disclosed at the time the disclosure statement is given to the debtor, or to the extent this annual percentage rate is not readily available or not applicable, then

(II) the simple interest rate applicable to the amount reaffirmed as of the date the disclosure statement is given to the debtor, or if different simple interest rates apply to different balances, the simple interest rate applicable to each such balance, identifying the amount of each such balance included in the amount reaffirmed, or

(III) if the entity making the disclosure elects, to disclose the annual percentage rate under subclause (I) and the simple interest rate under subclause (II); or

(ii) if, at the time the petition is filed, the debt is an extension of credit other than under an open end credit plan, as the terms "credit" and "open end credit plan" are defined in section 103 of the Truth in Lending Act, then—

(I) the annual percentage rate under section 128(a)(4) of the Truth in Lending Act, as disclosed to the debtor in the most recent disclosure statement given to the debtor prior to the entering into an agreement of the kind specified in subsection (c) with respect to the debt, or, if no such disclosure statement was given to the debtor, the annual percentage rate as it would have been so disclosed at the time the disclosure statement is given to the debtor, or to the extent this annual percentage rate is not readily available or not applicable, then

(II) the simple interest rate applicable to the amount reaffirmed as of the date the disclosure statement is given to the debtor, or if different simple interest rates apply to different balances, the simple interest rate applicable to each such balance, identifying the amount of such balance included in the amount reaffirmed, or

(III) if the entity making the disclosure elects, to disclose the annual percentage rate under (I) and the simple interest rate under (II).

(F) If the underlying debt transaction was disclosed as a variable rate transaction on the most recent disclosure given under the Truth in Lending Act, by stating "The interest rate on your loan may be a variable interest rate which changes from time to time, so that the annual percentage rate disclosed here may be higher or lower."

(G) If the debt is secured by a security interest which has not been waived in whole or in part or determined to be void by a final order of the court at the time of the disclosure, by disclosing that a security interest or lien in goods or property is asserted over some or all of the debts the debtor is reaffirming and listing the items and their original purchase price that are subject to the asserted security interest, or if not a purchase-money security interest then listing by items or types and the original amount of the loan.

(H) At the election of the creditor, a statement of the repayment schedule using 1 or a combination of the following—

(i) by making the statement: "Your first payment in the amount of $____ is due on ____ but the future payment amount may be different. Consult your reaffirmation agreement or credit agreement, as applicable.", and stating the amount of the first payment and the due date of that payment in the places provided;

(ii) by making the statement: "Your payment schedule will be:", and describing the repayment schedule with the number, amount, and due dates or period of payments scheduled to repay the debts reaffirmed to the extent then known by the disclosing party; or

(iii) by describing the debtor's repayment obligations with reasonable specificity to the extent then known by the disclosing party.

(I) The following statement: "Note: When this disclosure refers to what a creditor 'may' do, it does not use the word 'may' to give the creditor specific permission. The word 'may' is used to tell you what might occur if the law permits the creditor to take the action. If you have questions about your reaffirming a debt or what the law requires, consult with the attorney who helped you negotiate this agreement reaffirming a debt. If you don't have an attorney helping you, the judge will explain the effect of your reaffirming a debt when the hearing on the reaffirmation agreement is held."

(J)(i) The following additional statements:

"Reaffirming a debt is a serious financial decision. The law requires you to take certain steps to make sure the decision is in your best interest. If these steps are not completed, the reaffirmation agreement is not effective, even though you have signed it.

"1. Read the disclosures in this Part A carefully. Consider the decision to reaffirm carefully. Then, if you want to reaffirm, sign the reaffirmation agreement in Part B (or you may use a separate agreement you and your creditor agree on).

"2. Complete and sign Part D and be sure you can afford to make the payments you are agreeing to make and have received a copy of the disclosure statement and a completed and signed reaffirmation agreement.

"3. If you were represented by an attorney during the negotiation of your reaffirmation agreement, the attorney must have signed the certification in Part C.

"4. If you were not represented by an attorney during the negotiation of your reaffirmation agreement, you must have completed and signed Part E.

"5. The original of this disclosure must be filed with the court by you or your creditor. If a separate reaffirmation agreement (other than the one in Part B) has been signed, it must be attached.

"6. If you were represented by an attorney during the negotiation of your reaffirmation agreement, your reaffirmation agreement becomes effective upon filing with the court unless the reaffirmation is presumed to be an undue hardship as explained in Part D.

"7. If you were not represented by an attorney during the negotiation of your reaffirmation agreement, it will not be effective unless the court approves it. The court will notify you of the hearing on your reaffirmation agreement. You must attend this hearing in bankruptcy court where the judge will review your reaffirmation agreement. The bankruptcy court must approve your reaffirmation agreement as consistent with your best interests, except that no court approval is required if your reaffirmation agreement is for a consumer debt secured by a mortgage, deed of trust, security deed, or other lien on your real property, like your home.

"Your right to rescind (cancel) your reaffirmation agreement. You may rescind (cancel) your reaffirmation agreement at any time before the bankruptcy court enters a discharge order, or before the expiration of the 60-day period that begins on the date your reaffirmation agreement is filed with the court, whichever occurs later. To rescind (cancel) your reaffirmation agreement, you must notify the creditor that your reaffirmation agreement is rescinded (or canceled).

"What are your obligations if you reaffirm the debt? A reaffirmed debt remains your personal legal obligation. It is not discharged in your bankruptcy case. That means that if you default on your reaffirmed debt after your bankruptcy case is over, your creditor may be able to take your property or your wages. Otherwise, your obligations will be determined by the reaffirmation agreement which may have changed the terms of the original agreement. For example, if you are reaffirming an open end credit agreement, the creditor may be permitted by that agreement or applicable law to change the terms of that agreement in the future under certain conditions.

"Are you required to enter into a reaffirmation agreement by any law? No, you are not required to reaffirm a debt by any law. Only agree to reaffirm a debt if it is in your best interest. Be sure you can afford the payments you agree to make.

"What if your creditor has a security interest or lien? Your bankruptcy discharge does not eliminate any lien on your property. A 'lien' is often referred to as a security interest, deed of trust, mortgage or security deed. Even if you do not reaffirm and your personal liability on the debt is discharged, because of the lien your creditor may still have the right to take the security property if you do not pay the debt or default on it. If the lien is on an item of personal property that is exempt under your State's law or that the trustee has abandoned, you may be able to redeem the item rather than reaffirm the debt. To redeem, you must make a single payment to the creditor equal to the amount of the allowed secured claim, as agreed by the parties or determined by the court."

(ii) In the case of a reaffirmation under subsection (m)(2), numbered paragraph 6 in the disclosures required by clause (i) of this subparagraph shall read as follows:

"6. If you were represented by an attorney during the negotiation of your reaffirmation agreement, your reaffirmation agreement becomes effective upon filing with the court."

(4) The form of such agreement required under this paragraph shall consist of the following:

"Part B: Reaffirmation Agreement. I (we) agree to reaffirm the debts arising under the credit agreement described below.

"Brief description of credit agreement:

"Description of any changes to the credit agreement made as part of this reaffirmation agreement:

"Signature: Date:

"Borrower:

"Co-borrower, if also reaffirming these debts:

"Accepted by creditor:

"Date of creditor acceptance:".

(5) The declaration shall consist of the following:

(A) The following certification:

"Part C: Certification by Debtor's Attorney (If Any).

"I hereby certify that (1) this agreement represents a fully informed and voluntary agreement by the debtor; (2) this agreement does not impose an undue hardship on the debtor or any dependent of the debtor; and (3) I have fully advised the debtor of the legal effect and consequences of this agreement and any default under this agreement.

"Signature of Debtor's Attorney: Date:".

(B) If a presumption of undue hardship has been established with respect to such agreement, such certification shall state that in the opinion of the attorney, the debtor is able to make the payment.

(C) In the case of a reaffirmation agreement under subsection (m)(2), subparagraph (B) is not applicable.

(6)(A) The statement in support of such agreement, which the debtor shall sign and date prior to filing with the court, shall consist of the following:

"Part D: Debtor's Statement in Support of Reaffirmation Agreement.

"1. I believe this reaffirmation agreement will not impose an undue hardship on my dependents or me. I can afford to make the payments on the reaffirmed debt because my monthly income (take home pay plus any other income received) is $___, and my actual current monthly expenses including monthly payments on post-bankruptcy debt and other reaffirmation agreements total $___, leaving $___ to make the required payments on this reaffirmed debt. I understand that if my income less my monthly expenses does not leave enough to make the payments, this reaffirmation agreement is presumed to be an undue hardship on me and must be reviewed by the court. However, this presumption may be overcome if I explain to the satisfaction of the court how I can afford to make the payments here: ___.

"2. I received a copy of the Reaffirmation Disclosure Statement in Part A and a completed and signed reaffirmation agreement."

(B) Where the debtor is represented by an attorney and is reaffirming a debt owed to a creditor defined in section 19(b)(1)(A)(iv) of the Federal Reserve Act, the statement of support of the reaffirmation agreement, which the debtor shall sign and date prior to filing with the court, shall consist of the following:

"I believe this reaffirmation agreement is in my financial interest. I can afford to make the payments on the reaffirmed debt. I received a copy of the Reaffirmation Disclosure Statement in Part A and a completed and signed reaffirmation agreement."

(7) The motion that may be used if approval of such agreement by the court is required in order for it to be effective, shall be signed and dated by the movant and shall consist of the following:

"Part E: Motion for Court Approval (To be completed only if the debtor is not represented by an attorney.). I (we), the debtor(s), affirm the following to be true and correct:

"I am not represented by an attorney in connection with this reaffirmation agreement.

"I believe this reaffirmation agreement is in my best interest based on the income and expenses I have disclosed in my Statement in Support of this reaffirmation agreement, and because (provide any additional relevant reasons the court should consider):

"Therefore, I ask the court for an order approving this reaffirmation agreement."

(8) The court order, which may be used to approve such agreement, shall consist of the following:

"Court Order: The court grants the debtor's motion and approves the reaffirmation agreement described above."

(l) Notwithstanding any other provision of this title the following shall apply:

(1) A creditor may accept payments from a debtor before and after the filing of an agreement of the kind specified in subsection (c) with the court.

(2) A creditor may accept payments from a debtor under such agreement that the creditor believes in good faith to be effective.

(3) The requirements of subsections (c)(2) and (k) shall be satisfied if disclosures required under those subsections are given in good faith.

(m)(1) Until 60 days after an agreement of the kind specified in subsection (c) is filed with the court (or such additional period as the court, after notice and a hearing and for cause, orders before the expiration of such period), it shall be presumed that such agreement is an undue hardship on the debtor if the debtor's monthly income less the debtor's monthly expenses as shown on the debtor's completed and signed statement in support of such agreement required under subsection (k)(6)(A) is less than the scheduled payments on the reaffirmed debt. This presumption shall be reviewed by the court. The presumption may be rebutted in writing by the debtor if the statement includes an explanation that identifies additional sources of funds to make the payments as agreed upon under the terms of such agreement. If the presumption is not rebutted to the satisfaction of the court, the court may disapprove such agreement. No agreement shall be disapproved without notice and a hearing to the debtor and creditor, and such hearing shall be concluded before the entry of the debtor's discharge.

(2) This subsection does not apply to reaffirmation agreements where the creditor is a credit union, as defined in section 19(b)(1)(A)(iv) of the Federal Reserve Act.

UNOFFICIAL COMMENTS

Think of section 524 as three separate provisions.

First, section 524(a) deals with the effect of a discharge generally. Notice the use of the phrase "as a personal liability" in section 524(a)(1).

Second, section 524(c) and (d) [and (l) and (m)] deal very specifically with post-bankruptcy agreements to pay debts that would otherwise be affected by a discharge.

The post-bankruptcy agreements to pay governed by section 524(c) and (d) are generally referred to as "reaffirmation agreements." The important word is "agreement." Section 524(c) and (d) only apply if the "debtor" and creditor both have agreed.

And notice the word "debtor." Remember that term is defined in section 101. No one is a "debtor" for purposes of the Bankruptcy Code until there has been a bankruptcy filing. Accordingly by using the word "debtor", section 524(c) and (d) limit its scope to agreements entered into after a bankruptcy filing.

Third, omitted section 524(g) and (h) detail a procedure for dealing with asbestos claims in chapter 11 cases.

OTHER SECTIONS

Generally, post-bankruptcy efforts by creditors to collect are barred by the section 362 automatic stay until discharge, and then section 524 after the discharge. Section 362(c) contains some exceptions to the automatic stay but there is no section 362(c) exception for reaffirmation efforts. The question of the relationship between sections 362 and 524 is addressed by courts (and perhaps your professor) but not the Bankruptcy Code.

Rule 4008 on page 231 will help you understand the bankruptcy court's role in the reaffirmation agreement process.

Compare reaffirmation under section 524 with redemption under section 712.

§ 525. Protection against discriminatory treatment

(a) * * *[A] governmental unit may not deny, revoke, suspend, or refuse to renew a license, permit, charter, franchise, or other similar grant to, condition such a grant to, discriminate with respect to such a grant against, deny employment to, terminate the employment of, or discriminate with respect to employment against, a person that is * * * or has been a debtor under this title * * * or another person with whom such debtor has been associated, solely because such * * * debtor is or has been a debtor under this title * * *, has been insolvent before the commencement of the case under this title, or during the case but before the debtor is granted or denied a discharge, or has not paid a debt that is dischargeable in the case under this title. * * *

(b) No private employer may terminate the employment of, or discriminate with respect to employment against, an individual who is or has been a debtor under this title, * * * a debtor or an individual associated with such debtor * * * solely because such debtor * * *

    (1) is or has been a debtor under this title * * *.

    (2) has been insolvent before the commencement of a case under this title or during the case but before the grant or denial of a discharge; or

    (3) has not paid a debt that is dischargeable in a case under this title. * * *

(c)(1) A governmental unit that operates a student grant or loan program and a person engaged in a business that includes the making of loans guaranteed or insured under a student loan program may not deny a student grant, loan, loan guarantee, or loan insurance to a person that is or has been a debtor under this title * * * or another person with whom the debtor * * * has been associated, because the debtor * * * has been a debtor under this title * * * has been insolvent before the commencement of a case under this title or during the pendency of the case but before the debtor is granted or denied a discharge, or has not paid a debt that is dischargeable in the case under this title * * *.

    (2) In this section, "student loan program" means any program operated under title IV of the Higher Education Act of 1965 or a similar program operated under State or local law.

UNOFFICIAL COMMENTS

The title to this section is incomplete, if not misleading. "Discriminatory treatment" by whom? Part (a) is limited to "a governmental unit". Part (b) is limited to "private employers." And, Part (c) is limited to student loan program operators.

§ 526. Restrictions on debt relief agencies

(a) A debt relief agency shall not—

(1) fail to perform any service that such agency informed an assisted person or prospective assisted person it would provide in connection with a case or proceeding under this title;

(2) make any statement, or counsel or advise any assisted person or prospective assisted person to make a statement in a document filed in a case or proceeding under this title, that is untrue and misleading, or that upon the exercise of reasonable care, should have been known by such agency to be untrue or misleading;

(3) misrepresent to any assisted person or prospective assisted person, directly or indirectly, affirmatively or by material omission, with respect to—

    (A) the services that such agency will provide to such person; or

    (B) the benefits and risks that may result if such person becomes a debtor in a case under this title; or

(4) advise an assisted person or prospective assisted person to incur more debt in contemplation of such person filing a case under this title or to pay an attorney or bankruptcy petition preparer a fee or charge for services performed as part of preparing for or representing a debtor in a case under this title. *Don't tell him to buy new car*

(b) Any waiver by any assisted person of any protection or right provided under this section shall not be enforceable against the debtor by any Federal or State court or any other person, but may be enforced against a debt relief agency.

(c)(1) Any contract for bankruptcy assistance between a debt relief agency and an assisted person that does not comply with the material requirements of this section, section 527, or section 528 shall be void and may not be enforced by any Federal or State court or by any other person, other than such assisted person.

(2) Any debt relief agency shall be liable to an assisted person in the amount of any fees or charges in connection with providing bankruptcy assistance to such person that such debt relief agency has received, for actual damages, and for reasonable attorneys' fees and costs if such agency is found, after notice and a hearing, to have—

    (A) intentionally or negligently failed to comply with any provision of this section, section 527, or section 528 with respect to a case or proceeding under this title for such assisted person;

    (B) provided bankruptcy assistance to an assisted person in a case or proceeding under this title that is dismissed or converted to a case under another chapter of this title because of such agency's intentional or negligent failure to file any required document including those specified in section 521; or

    (C) intentionally or negligently disregarded the material requirements of this title or the Federal Rules of Bankruptcy Procedure applicable to such agency.

(3) In addition to such other remedies as are provided under State law, whenever the chief law enforcement officer of a State, or an official or agency designated by a State, has reason to believe that any person has violated or is violating this section, the State—

    (A) may bring an action to enjoin such violation;

(B) may bring an action on behalf of its residents to recover the actual damages of assisted persons arising from such violation, including any liability under paragraph (2); and

(C) in the case of any successful action under subparagraph (A) or (B), shall be awarded the costs of the action and reasonable attorneys' fees as determined by the court.

(4) The district courts of the United States for districts located in the State shall have concurrent jurisdiction of any action under subparagraph (A) or (B) of paragraph (3).

(5) Notwithstanding any other provision of Federal law and in addition to any other remedy provided under Federal or State law, if the court, on its own motion or on the motion of the United States trustee or the debtor, finds that a person intentionally violated this section, or engaged in a clear and consistent pattern or practice of violating this section, the court may—

(A) enjoin the violation of such section; or

(B) impose an appropriate civil penalty against such person.

(d) No provision of this section, section 527, or section 528 shall—

(1) annul, alter, affect, or exempt any person subject to such sections from complying with any law of any State except to the extent that such law is inconsistent with those sections, and then only to the extent of the inconsistency; or

(2) be deemed to limit or curtail the authority or ability—

(A) of a State or subdivision or instrumentality thereof, to determine and enforce qualifications for the practice of law under the laws of that State; or

(B) of a Federal court to determine and enforce the qualifications for the practice of law before that court.

§ 527. Disclosures

(a) A debt relief agency providing bankruptcy assistance to an assisted person shall provide—

(1) the written notice required under section 342(b)(1); and

(2) to the extent not covered in the written notice described in paragraph (1), and not later than 3 business days after the first date on which a debt relief agency first offers to provide any bankruptcy assistance services to an assisted person, a clear and conspicuous written notice advising assisted persons that—

(A) all information that the assisted person is required to provide with a petition and thereafter during a case under this title is required to be complete, accurate, and truthful;

(B) all assets and all liabilities are required to be completely and accurately disclosed in the documents filed to commence the case, and the replacement value of each asset as defined in section 506 must be stated in those documents where requested after reasonable inquiry to establish such value;

(C) current monthly income, the amounts specified in section 707(b)(2), and, in a case under chapter 13 of this title, disposable income (determined in accordance with section 707(b)(2)), are required to be stated after reasonable inquiry; and

    (D) information that an assisted person provides during their case may be audited pursuant to this title, and that failure to provide such information may result in dismissal of the case under this title or other sanction, including a criminal sanction.

(b) A debt relief agency providing bankruptcy assistance to an assisted person shall provide each assisted person at the same time as the notices required under subsection (a)(1) the following statement, to the extent applicable, or one substantially similar. The statement shall be clear and conspicuous and shall be in a single document separate from other documents or notices provided to the assisted person:

"IMPORTANT INFORMATION ABOUT BANKRUPTCY ASSISTANCE SERVICES FROM AN ATTORNEY OR BANKRUPTCY PETITION PREPARER.

"If you decide to seek bankruptcy relief, you can represent yourself, you can hire an attorney to represent you, or you can get help in some localities from a bankruptcy petition preparer who is not an attorney. THE LAW REQUIRES AN ATTORNEY OR BANKRUPTCY PETITION PREPARER TO GIVE YOU A WRITTEN CONTRACT SPECIFYING WHAT THE ATTORNEY OR BANKRUPTCY PETITION PREPARER WILL DO FOR YOU AND HOW MUCH IT WILL COST. Ask to see the contract before you hire anyone.

"The following information helps you understand what must be done in a routine bankruptcy case to help you evaluate how much service you need. Although bankruptcy can be complex, many cases are routine.

"Before filing a bankruptcy case, either you or your attorney should analyze your eligibility for different forms of debt relief available under the Bankruptcy Code and which form of relief is most likely to be beneficial for you. Be sure you understand the relief you can obtain and its limitations. To file a bankruptcy case, documents called a Petition, Schedules and Statement of Financial Affairs, and in some cases a Statement of Intention need to be prepared correctly and filed with the bankruptcy court. You will have to pay a filing fee to the bankruptcy court. Once your case starts, you will have to attend the required first meeting of creditors where you may be questioned by a court official called a 'trustee' and by creditors.

"If you choose to file a chapter 7 case, you may be asked by a creditor to reaffirm a debt. You may want help deciding whether to do so. A creditor is not permitted to coerce you into reaffirming your debts.

"If you choose to file a chapter 13 case in which you repay your creditors what you can afford over 3 to 5 years, you may also want help with preparing your chapter 13 plan and with the confirmation hearing on your plan which will be before a bankruptcy judge.

"If you select another type of relief under the Bankruptcy Code other than chapter 7 or chapter 13, you will want to find out what should be done from someone familiar with that type of relief.

"Your bankruptcy case may also involve litigation. You are generally permitted to represent yourself in litigation in bankruptcy court, but only attorneys, not bankruptcy petition preparers, can give you legal advice.".

* * *

§ 528. Requirements for debt relief agencies

(a) A debt relief agency shall—

(1) not later than 5 business days after the first date on which such agency provides any bankruptcy assistance services to an assisted person, but prior to such assisted person's petition under this title being filed, execute a written contract with such assisted person that explains clearly and conspicuously—

(A) the services such agency will provide to such assisted person; and

(B) the fees or charges for such services, and the terms of payment;

* * *

SUBCHAPTER III—THE ESTATE

§ 541. Property of the estate

(a) The commencement of a case under section 301, 302, or 303 of this title creates an estate. Such estate is comprised of all the following property, wherever located and by whomever held:

(1) Except as provided in subsections (b) and (c)(2) of this section, all legal or equitable interests of the debtor in property as of the commencement of the case.

Only legal or equitable included

(2) All interests of the debtor and the debtor's spouse in community property as of the commencement of the case that is—

(A) under the sole, equal, or joint management and control of the debtor; or

(B) liable for an allowable claim against the debtor, or for both an allowable claim against the debtor and an allowable claim against the debtor's spouse, to the extent that such interest is so liable.

(3) Any interest in property that the trustee recovers under section 329(b), 363(n), 543, 550, 553, or 723 of this title.

(4) Any interest in property preserved for the benefit of or ordered transferred to the estate under section 510(c) or 551 of this title.

(5) Any interest in property that would have been property of the estate if such interest had been an interest of the debtor on the date of the filing of the petition, and that the debtor acquires or becomes entitled to acquire within 180 days after such date—

(A) by bequest, devise, or inheritance;

(B) as a result of a property settlement agreement with the debtor's spouse, or of an interlocutory or final divorce decree; or

(C) as a beneficiary of a life insurance policy or of a death benefit plan.

(6) Proceeds, product, offspring, rents, or profits of or from property of the estate, except such as are earnings from services performed by an individual debtor after the commencement of the case.

Wages, commissions earned after the petition is filed will not become property of the estate.

102

(7) Any interest in property that the estate acquires after the commencement of the case.

(b) Property of the estate does not include—

(1) any power that the debtor may exercise solely for the benefit of an entity other than the debtor;

(2) any interest of the debtor as a lessee under a lease of nonresidential real property that has terminated at the expiration of the stated term of such lease before the commencement of the case under this title, and ceases to include any interest of the debtor as a lessee under a lease of nonresidential real property that has terminated at the expiration of the stated term of such lease during the case;

(3) any eligibility of the debtor to participate in programs authorized under the Higher Education Act of 1965 (20 U.S.C. 1001 et seq.; 42 U.S.C. 2751 et seq.), or any accreditation status or State licensure of the debtor as an educational institution;

* * *

(5) funds placed in an education individual retirement account (as defined in section 530(b)(1) of the Internal Revenue Code of 1986) not later than 365 days before the date of the filing of the petition in a case under this title, but—

(A) only if the designated beneficiary of such account was a child, stepchild, grandchild, or stepgrandchild of the debtor for the taxable year for which funds were placed in such account;

* * *

(7) any amount—

(A) withheld by an employer from the wages of employees for payment as contributions— *companies bankruptcy estate will not include this money*

(i) to—

(I) an employee benefit plan that is subject to title I of the Employee Retirement Income Security Act of 1974 or under an employee benefit plan which is a governmental plan under section 414(d) of the Internal Revenue Code of 1986;

(II) a deferred compensation plan under section 457 of the Internal Revenue Code of 1986; or

(III) a tax-deferred annuity under section 403(b) of the Internal Revenue Code of 1986; except that such amount under this subparagraph shall not constitute disposable income as defined in section 1325(b)(2); or

(ii) to a health insurance plan regulated by State law whether or not subject to such title; or

Exceptions excluded from the estate.

(B) received by an employer from employees for payment as contributions—

(i) to—

(I) an employee benefit plan that is subject to title I of the Employee Retirement Income Security Act of 1974 or under an employee benefit plan which is a governmental plan under section 414(d) of the Internal Revenue Code of 1986;

    (II) a deferred compensation plan under section 457 of the Internal Revenue Code of 1986; or

    (III) a tax-deferred annuity under section 403(b) of the Internal Revenue Code of 1986; except that such amount under this subparagraph shall not constitute disposable income, as defined in section 1325(b)(2); or

    (ii) to a health insurance plan regulated by State law whether or not subject to such title;

* * *

(c)(1) Except as provided in paragraph (2) of this subsection, an interest of the debtor in property becomes property of the estate under subsection (a)(1), (a)(2), or (a)(5) of this section notwithstanding any provision in an agreement, transfer instrument, or applicable nonbankruptcy law—

    (A) that restricts or conditions transfer of such interest by the debtor; or

    (B) that is conditioned on the insolvency or financial condition of the debtor, on the commencement of a case under this title, or on the appointment of or taking possession by a trustee in a case under this title or a custodian before such commencement, and that effects or gives an option to effect a forfeiture, modification, or termination of the debtor's interest in property.

    (2) A restriction on the transfer of a beneficial interest of the debtor in a trust that is enforceable under applicable nonbankruptcy law is enforceable in a case under this title.

[handwritten margin note: Spendthrift Trust]

(d) Property in which the debtor holds, as of the commencement of the case, only legal title and not an equitable interest, such as a mortgage secured by real property, or an interest in such a mortgage, sold by the debtor but as to which the debtor retains legal title to service or supervise the servicing of such mortgage or interest, becomes property of the estate under subsection (a)(1) or (2) of this section only to the extent of the debtor's legal title to such property, but not to the extent of any equitable interest in such property that the debtor does not hold.

[handwritten margin note: Wouldn't limit if it was a universal rule]

UNOFFICIAL COMMENTS

Bankruptcy automatically and immediately creates a new entity—an "estate." Most "property of the estate" is property of the estate because of section 541(a)(1) or section 541(a)(6).

Note the two limiting phrases in section 541(a)(1): (i) "interests of the debtor in" and (ii) "as of the commencement of the case."

Because of the phrase "interest of the debtor in," Blackacre is not property of the estate; only the debtor's interest in Blackacre is property of the estate. And, the debtor's interest in Blackacre might be limited by a co-owner or a mortgage holder or. . . .

The impact of the second limitation—"as of the commencement of the case"—is limited by the term "proceeds" in section 541(a)(6). If the debtor finds a lottery ticket the day after she files for bankruptcy and that lottery ticket is the winner in that week's lottery drawing, the lottery money is not property of the estate. On the other hand, if the debtor has a lottery ticket when she files for bankruptcy, and that ticket is the winner in that week's lottery drawing, the lottery money is property of the estate.

OTHER SECTIONS

"Commencement of the case" turns on sections 301, 302, and 303.

The last part of section 541(a)(6)—"except such as are earnings from services performed by an individual debtor after commencement of the case"—needs to be read together with section 1115 for individuals in chapter 11 and with section 1306 for chapter 13 debtors.

During bankruptcy, section 362 limits creditor recourse to property of the estate. Section 363 addresses questions relating to the debtor's use and sale of property of the estate.

Section 522 tells you what property of the estate will be treated as exempt property. Think about the relationship between the two provisions. Some property of the estate is exempt property; in essence, section 522 determines what property of the estate is exempted from creditors, i.e., what property of the estate the debtor gets to keep.

Pay particular attention to section 541(b)—especially section 541(b)(5)–(8). It identifies interests in property that the debtor gets to keep because it is not even "property of the estate." While the practical effect of section 541(b) is to identify property that the debtor gets to keep, section 541(b) property is not exempt property.

Section 521 and Rule 1007 require a debtor to file schedules. The Official Form 6 Schedule A, Real Property, Schedule B, Personal Property and Schedule C, Property Claimed As Exempt are set out on page 237 et seq.

Sections 1129(a)(7) and 1325(a)(4) look to property of the estate to determine the minimum possible plan distribution to unsecured creditors.

§ 542. Turnover of property to the estate

(a) Except as provided in subsection (c) or (d) of this section, an entity, other than a custodian, in possession, custody, or control, during the case, of property that the trustee may use, sell, or lease under section 363 of this title, or that the debtor may exempt under section 522 of this title, shall deliver to the trustee, and account for, such property or the value of such property, unless such property is of inconsequential value or benefit to the estate.

(b) Except as provided in subsection (c) or (d) of this section, an entity that owes a debt that is property of the estate and that is matured, payable on demand, or payable on order, shall pay such debt to, or on the order of, the trustee, except to the extent that such debt may be offset under section 553 of this title against a claim against the debtor.

(c) Except as provided in section 362(a)(7) of this title, an entity that has neither actual notice nor actual knowledge of the commencement of the case concerning the debtor may transfer property of the estate, or pay a debt owing to the debtor, in good faith and other than in the manner specified in subsection (d) of this section, to an entity other than the trustee, with the same effect as to the entity making such transfer or payment as if the case under this title concerning the debtor had not been commenced.

(d) A life insurance company may transfer property of the estate or property of the debtor to such company in good faith, with the same effect with respect to such company as if the case under this title concerning the debtor had not been commenced, if such transfer is to pay a premium or to carry out a nonforfeiture insurance option, and is required to be made automatically, under a life insurance contract with such company that was entered into before the date of the filing of the petition and that is property of the estate.

(e) Subject to any applicable privilege, after notice and a hearing, the court may order an attorney, accountant, or other person that holds recorded information, including books, documents, records, and papers, relating to the debtor's property or financial affairs, to turn over or disclose such recorded information to the trustee.

UNOFFICIAL COMMENTS

The most common application of section 542 is to a real property mortgagee or Article 9 secured party who repossessed but did not re-sell its collateral before the debtor filed for bankruptcy.

OTHER SECTIONS

Property of the estate is established by section 541.

When you see the word "trustee", you need to think trustee or debtor in possession. Under section 1107, a debtor in possession has the same powers as a trustee. And, in most chapter 11 cases, there is a debtor in possession and not a trustee.

Section 362(a)(4) stays a creditor who repossessed but did not re-sell pre-petition from selling post-petition. Such a post-petition sale would be covered by the phrase "enforce the lien."

§ 543. Turnover of property by a custodian

(a) A custodian with knowledge of the commencement of a case under this title concerning the debtor may not make any disbursement from, or take any action in the administration of, property of the debtor, proceeds, product, offspring, rents, or profits of such property, or property of the estate, in the possession, custody, or control of such custodian, except such action as is necessary to preserve such property.

(b) A custodian shall—

(1) deliver to the trustee any property of the debtor held by or transferred to such custodian, or proceeds, product, offspring, rents, or profits of such property, that is in such custodian's possession, custody, or control on the date that such custodian acquires knowledge of the commencement of the case; and

(2) file an accounting of any property of the debtor, or proceeds, product, offspring, rents, or profits of such property, that, at any time, came into the possession, custody, or control of such custodian.

* * *

§ 544. Trustee as lien creditor and as successor to certain creditors and purchasers

(a) The trustee shall have, as of the commencement of the case, and without regard to any knowledge of the trustee or of any creditor, the rights and powers of, or may avoid any transfer of property of the debtor or any obligation incurred by the debtor that is voidable by—

(1) a creditor that extends credit to the debtor at the time of the commencement of the case, and that obtains, at such time and with respect to such credit, a judicial lien on all property on which a creditor on a simple contract could have obtained such a judicial lien, whether or not such a creditor exists;

(2) a creditor that extends credit to the debtor at the time of the commencement of the case, and obtains, at such time and with respect to such credit, an execution against the debtor that is returned unsatisfied at such time, whether or not such a creditor exists; or

106

(3) a bona fide purchaser of real property, other than fixtures, from the debtor, against whom applicable law permits such transfer to be perfected, that obtains the status of a bona fide purchaser and has perfected such transfer at the time of the commencement of the case, whether or not such a purchaser exists.

(b)(1) Except as provided in paragraph (2), the trustee may avoid any transfer of an interest of the debtor in property or any obligation incurred by the debtor that is voidable under applicable law by a creditor holding an unsecured claim that is allowable under section 502 of this title or that is not allowable only under section 502(e) of this title.

[handwritten: Trustee can bring claim under the UFTA.]

[handwritten margin note: Transfers recorded before bankrupcy]

(2) Paragraph (1) shall not apply to a transfer of a charitable contribution (as that term is defined in section 548(d)(3)) that is not covered under section 548(a)(1)(B), by reason of section 548(a)(2). Any claim by any person to recover a transferred contribution described in the preceding sentence under Federal or State law in a Federal or State court shall be preempted by the commencement of the case.

UNOFFICIAL COMMENTS

The words "avoidance action" are commonly used to refer to section 544 (and section 545, 547–49, and 553) although those words do not appear in the Bankruptcy Code.

Section 544 is in many ways two very different statutes. Subsection (a) is used to deal with unrecorded transfers. Subsection (b) is used to (i) deal with transfers that are recorded before bankruptcy that are not timely recorded and (ii) to deal with fraudulent transfers.

What both subsection (a) and subsection (b) have in common is that each gives the bankruptcy trustee rights and powers that a private creditor would have under nonbankruptcy law. In using section 544(a), you will most often also be using section 9–317 of the Uniform Commercial Code, infra at page 325. In using section 544(b), you will most often be using a state fraudulent conveyance law based on the Uniform Fraudulent Transfer Act, set out infra at page 307 et seq.

Subsection (a) is commonly referred to as the "strong arm clause," although those words do not appear in the Bankruptcy Code. The most common section 544(a) exam fact pattern is one in which (i) the debtor transfers real property or mortgages real property or grants a security interest in personal property and (ii) there is no recordation or perfection (even though there is no mention of recordation or perfection in section 544(a)).

And subsection (b) is commonly used in connection with state fraudulent conveyance law (even though the words "fraudulent conveyance" do not appear in subsection (b)). The most common section 544(b) exam fact pattern is one in which (i) more than two years before the bankruptcy filing (ii) there was a transfer of the debtor's property that was a fraudulent conveyance under state law and (iii) at least one of the creditors with an allowable claim is a creditor protected by that state fraudulent conveyance law. While there is no mention of fraudulent conveyances in section 544(b), "applicable law" means law other than the Bankruptcy Code and so includes state fraudulent conveyance law.

OTHER SECTIONS

Always look to section 101 for definitions. Here it is important that you see the definition of "transfer."

When you see the word "trustee" in section 544 and other sections in chapter 3 and chapter 5, think "debtor in possession", think section 1107(a) for chapter 11 cases.

Section 544 needs to be read together with section 546(a) and section 550 to see how soon after bankruptcy an action must be brought to avoid a transfer under section 544, and how soon an action must be brought to recover and what can be recovered from whom.

Section 502(d) disallows claims of creditors from whom transfers are avoidable under section 544. Section 502(h) recognizes claims of those as to whom transfers have been avoided.

544(a) also needs to be read together with section 545(2) which applies to unfiled statutory liens such as federal tax liens. And with section 547(e) and section 548(d)(1) which deal with fact patterns in which (i) the debtor transfers real property or mortgages real property or grants a security interest in personal property and (ii) there is recordation or perfection before the bankruptcy filing but (iii) the recordation or perfection is not timely.

§ 545. Statutory liens

The trustee may avoid the fixing of a statutory lien on property of the debtor to the extent that such lien—

(1) first becomes effective against the debtor—

(A) when a case under this title concerning the debtor is commenced;

(B) when an insolvency proceeding other than under this title concerning the debtor is commenced;

(C) when a custodian is appointed or authorized to take or takes possession;

(D) when the debtor becomes insolvent;

(E) when the debtor's financial condition fails to meet a specified standard; or

(F) at the time of an execution against property of the debtor levied at the instance of an entity other than the holder of such statutory lien;

(2) is not perfected or enforceable at the time of the commencement of the case against a bona fide purchaser that purchases such property at the time of the commencement of the case, whether or not such a purchaser exists, except in any case in which a purchaser is a purchaser described in section 6323 of the Internal Revenue Code of 1986, or in any other similar provision of State or local law;

(3) is for rent; or

(4) is a lien of distress for rent.

UNOFFICIAL COMMENTS

In a sense, section 545 is three separate sections.

Section 545(1) is designed to avoid state-created bankruptcy priorities. A "lien" that doesn't become effective until bankruptcy or insolvency is more like a "priority" than like a lien and section 507 sets out which unsecured claims have priority in bankruptcy.

Section 545(2) has a different purpose. It, like section 544, reaches liens that are not recorded or otherwise perfected.

Section 545(3) and (4) have a third purpose—avoiding statutory liens for rent. Note that these provisions do not affect security deposits or other contractual landlord's liens—only statutory landlord's liens for rent.

OTHER SECTIONS

Here it is important that you see the definitions of "statutory lien" and "transfer."

When you see the word "trustee" in section 545 and other sections in chapter 3 and chapter 5, think "debtor in possession," think section 1107(a).

And section 545 needs to be read together with section 546(a) and section 550 to see how soon after bankruptcy an action must be brought to avoid a transfer under section 545 and how soon an action must be brought to recover and what can be recovered from whom.

Section 502(d) disallows claims of creditors from whom transfers are avoidable under section 545. Section 502(h) recognizes claims of those as to whom transfers have been avoided.

As indicated above, read section 545(1) together with section 507 and read section 545(2) together with section 544(a) and read section 545(3) and (4) together with section 365.

Statutory liens cannot be avoided as a preference, section 547(c)(6).

The most important statutory lien is the federal tax lien. The most important sections of the Federal Tax Lien Act are set out infra at page 329–336.

§ 546. Limitations on avoiding powers

(a) An action or proceeding under section 544, 545, 547, 548, or 553 of this title may not be commenced after the earlier of—

    (1) the later of—

        (A) 2 years after the entry of the order for relief; or

        (B) 1 year after the appointment or election of the first trustee under section 702, 1104, 1163, 1202, or 1302 of this title if such appointment or such election occurs before the expiration of the period specified in subparagraph (A); or

    (2) the time the case is closed or dismissed.

(b)(1) The rights and powers of a trustee under sections 544, 545, and 549 of this title are subject to any generally applicable law that—

    (A) permits perfection of an interest in property to be effective against an entity that acquires rights in such property before the date of perfection; or

    (B) provides for the maintenance or continuation of perfection of an interest in property to be effective against an entity that acquires rights in such property before the date on which action is taken to effect such maintenance or continuation.

    (2) If—

    (A) a law described in paragraph (1) requires seizure of such property or commencement of an action to accomplish such perfection, or maintenance or continuation of perfection of an interest in property; and

    (B) such property has not been seized or such an action has not been commenced before the date of the filing of the petition;

such interest in such property shall be perfected, or perfection of such interest shall be maintained or continued, by giving notice within the time fixed by such law for such seizure or such commencement.

(c)(1) Except as provided in subsection (d) of this section and in section 507(c), and subject to the prior rights of a holder of a security interest in such goods or the proceeds thereof, the rights and powers of the trustee under sections 544(a), 545, 547, and 549 are subject to the right of a seller of goods that has sold goods to the debtor, in the ordinary course of such seller's business, to reclaim such goods if the debtor has received such goods while insolvent, within 45 days before the date of the commencement of a case under this title, but such seller may not reclaim such goods unless such seller demands in writing reclamation of such goods—

    (A) not later than 45 days after the date of receipt of such goods by the debtor; or

(B) not later than 20 days after the date of commencement of the case, if the 45-day period expires after the commencement of the case.

(2) If a seller of goods fails to provide notice in the manner described in paragraph (1), the seller still may assert the rights contained in section 503(b)(9).

* * *

(h) Notwithstanding the rights and powers of a trustee under sections 544(a), 545, 547, 549, and 553, if the court determines on a motion by the trustee made not later than 120 days after the date of the order for relief in a case under chapter 11 of this title and after notice and a hearing, that a return is in the best interests of the estate, the debtor, with the consent of a creditor and subject to the prior rights of holders of security interests in such goods or the proceeds of such goods, may return goods shipped to the debtor by the creditor before the commencement of the case, and the creditor may offset the purchase price of such goods against any claim of the creditor against the debtor that arose before the commencement of the case.

* * *

UNOFFICIAL COMMENTS

As the title suggests, section 546 limits the trustee's avoiding powers. The two most important such limits to a law student are (1) the time limits in section 546(a) and (2) the limits on avoidance of a right of reclamation in section 546(c).

The structure of section 546(c) is somewhat unusual. Instead of stating when a right of reclamation is valid, section 546(c) states when a right of reclamation cannot be avoided.

OTHER SECTIONS

You need to understand the relationship between the two year time period of section 546(a) and the one year period of section 550(f). The former tells you how soon the action to avoid the transfer must be brought; the latter tells you how soon the action to recover for an avoided transfer must be brought.

And you need to see the relationship (and, in places, the seeming lack of a relationship) between (i) section 546(c) and Uniform Commercial Code section 2–702, set out on page 320 infra and (ii) section 546(c) and section 503(b)(9).

§ 547. Preferences

(a) In this section—

(1) "inventory" means personal property leased or furnished, held for sale or lease, or to be furnished under a contract for service, raw materials, work in process, or materials used or consumed in a business, including farm products such as crops or livestock, held for sale or lease;

(2) "new value" means money or money's worth in goods, services, or new credit, or release by a transferee of property previously transferred to such transferee in a transaction that is neither void nor voidable by the debtor or the trustee under any applicable law, including proceeds of such property, but does not include an obligation substituted for an existing obligation;

* * *

(b) Except as provided in subsections (c) and (i) of this section, the trustee may avoid any transfer of an interest of the debtor in property—

(1) to or for the benefit of a creditor;

(2) for or on account of an antecedent debt owed by the debtor before such transfer was made; *[prior]*

[See 547(f) as well.]
[Need all 5]

(3) made while the debtor was insolvent;

(4) made—

    (A) on or within 90 days before the date of the filing of the petition; or

    (B) between ninety days and one year before the date of the filing of the petition, if such creditor at the time of such transfer was an insider; and

(5) that enables such creditor to receive more than such creditor would receive

[If unsecured creditor obtains judicial lien he has received a preference]

    (A) the case were a case under chapter 7 of this title; *[— Did you get more if this was a 7 liquidation]*

    (B) the transfer had not been made; and

    (C) such creditor received payment of such debt to the extent provided by the provisions of this title.

(c) The trustee may not avoid under this section a transfer— *[Creditor affirmative defenses]*

    (1) to the extent that such transfer was—

        (A) intended by the debtor and the creditor to or for whose benefit such transfer was made to be a contemporaneous exchange for new value given to the debtor; and

        (B) in fact a substantially contemporaneous exchange;

    (2) to the extent that such transfer was in payment of a debt incurred by the debtor in the ordinary course of business or financial affairs of the debtor and the transferee, and such transfer was—

        (A) made in the ordinary course of business or financial affairs of the debtor and the transferee; or *[Is the way debtor/creditor did business]* *[as long as not last minute change]*

        (B) made according to ordinary business terms; *[Consistent w/ payments made]* *[ordinary to terms of industry]*

[Not for long term lenders]

    (3) that creates a security interest in property acquired by the debtor— *[only by the creditor prior yr]*

        (A) to the extent such security interest secures new value that was—

            (i) given at or after the signing of a security agreement that contains a description of such property as collateral;

            (ii) given by or on behalf of the secured party under such agreement;

            (iii) given to enable the debtor to acquire such property; and

            (iv) in fact used by the debtor to acquire such property; and

        (B) that is perfected on or before 30 days after the debtor receives possession of such property;

    (4) to or for the benefit of a creditor, to the extent that, after such transfer, such creditor gave new value to or for the benefit of the debtor—

        (A) not secured by an otherwise unavoidable security interest; and

[Look at first payment then credit (new value) as defense. Creditor must sue if they give no more new value from last payment]

(B) on account of which new value the debtor did not make an otherwise unavoidable transfer to or for the benefit of such creditor;

(5) that creates a perfected security interest in inventory or a receivable or the proceeds of either, except to the extent that the aggregate of all such transfers to the transferee caused a reduction, as of the date of the filing of the petition and to the prejudice of other creditors holding unsecured claims, of any amount by which the debt secured by such security interest exceeded the value of all security interests for such debt on the later of—

    (A)(i) with respect to a transfer to which subsection (b)(4)(A) of this section applies, 90 days before the date of the filing of the petition; or

        (ii) with respect to a transfer to which subsection (b)(4)(B) of this section applies, one year before the date of the filing of the petition; or

    (B) the date on which new value was first given under the security agreement creating such security interest;

(6) that is the fixing of a statutory lien that is not avoidable under section 545 of this title;

(7) to the extent such transfer was a bona fide payment of a debt for a domestic support obligation;

(8) if, in a case filed by an individual debtor whose debts are primarily consumer debts, the aggregate value of all property that constitutes or is affected by such transfer is less than $600; or

(9) if, in a case filed by a debtor whose debts are not primarily consumer debts, the aggregate value of all property that constitutes or is affected by such transfer is less than $6,225.

(d) The trustee may avoid a transfer of an interest in property of the debtor transferred to or for the benefit of a surety to secure reimbursement of such a surety that furnished a bond or other obligation to dissolve a judicial lien that would have been avoidable by the trustee under subsection (b) of this section. The liability of such surety under such bond or obligation shall be discharged to the extent of the value of such property recovered by the trustee or the amount paid to the trustee.

(e)(1) For the purposes of this section—

    (A) a transfer of real property other than fixtures, but including the interest of a seller or purchaser under a contract for the sale of real property, is perfected when a bona fide purchaser of such property from the debtor against whom applicable law permits such transfer to be perfected cannot acquire an interest that is superior to the interest of the transferee; and

    (B) a transfer of a fixture or property other than real property is perfected when a creditor on a simple contract cannot acquire a judicial lien that is superior to the interest of the transferee.

(2) For the purposes of this section, except as provided in paragraph (3) of this subsection, a transfer is made—

    (A) at the time such transfer takes effect between the transferor and the transferee, if such transfer is perfected at, or within 30 days after, such time, except as provided in subsection (c)(3)(B);

(B) at the time such transfer is perfected, if such transfer is perfected after such 30 days; or

(C) immediately before the date of the filing of the petition, if such transfer is not perfected at the later of—

(i) the commencement of the case; or

(ii) 30 days after such transfer takes effect between the transferor and the transferee.

(3) For the purposes of this section, a transfer is not made until the debtor has acquired rights in the property transferred.

(f) For the purposes of this section, the debtor is presumed to have been insolvent on and during the 90 days immediately preceding the date of the filing of the petition.

(g) For the purposes of this section, the trustee has the burden of proving the avoidability of a transfer under subsection (b) of this section, and the creditor or party in interest against whom recovery or avoidance is sought has the burden of proving the nonavoidability of a transfer under subsection (c) of this section.

(h) The trustee may not avoid a transfer if such transfer was made as a part of an alternative repayment schedule between the debtor and any creditor of the debtor created by an approved nonprofit budget and credit counseling agency.

(i) If the trustee avoids under subsection (b) a transfer made between 90 days and 1 year before the date of the filing of the petition, by the debtor to an entity that is not an insider for the benefit of a creditor that is an insider, such transfer shall be considered to be avoided under this section only with respect to the creditor that is an insider.

UNOFFICIAL COMMENTS

This is one of the most important provisions of the Bankruptcy Code. Especially for law students. Almost certain to be covered by your exam.

The keys to understanding section 547 are (i) understanding the relationship among the various subsections and paragraphs of section 547 and (ii) understanding the purposes of the section.

Subsection (a) is definitional. Subsection (b) sets out the elements of (your teacher might say "requirements for") a preference. Five numbered elements. Notice that the conjunction in section 547(b) is "and". Need to have all five numbered elements.

Even more important, notice that there are two other requirements in section 547(b) before you even get to the numbered elements. Two other requirements in the phrase "transfer of an interest of the debtor in property." First, there must be a "transfer", as that term is defined in section 101. Second, what is being transferred to the creditor must be the debtor's stuff. If D owes C 1,000, and M., D's momma, pays C, and then 89 days later D files for bankruptcy, that payment by M of M's money to C is not a preference in D's bankruptcy case.

In doing section 547(b)(3), be sure and do section 547(f). And law professors love to ask questions that test your understanding of the relationship of 547(b)(3), 547(f) and 547(b)(4). Warning: only do section 547(f)—only assume insolvency—when you are doing section 547. Note the prefatory language in section 547(f): "For purposes of this section." See also 553(c).

In the main, section 547(b) is about a creditor's doing better than other creditors with similar legal status as a result of a transfer before bankruptcy. In essence, the primary purpose of section 547(b) is a retroactive application of the bankruptcy policy of equality of distribution.

Because of section 547(e), section 547 serves a second purpose. It provides a basis for avoiding a transfer that (i) must be recorded or otherwise perfected under state law, (ii) was recorded or otherwise perfected before a bankruptcy filing but (iii) was not timely recorded or perfected.

If, for example, on January 15, D borrows 1000 from C and at the time of the loan D grants C a mortgage, no basis for a preference attack—no "antecedent debt" as required by section 547(b)(2). If you have the additional facts that C did not record the January 15 mortgage until December 7 and bankruptcy was filed on December 12, then there would be a section 547(b) preference. Because of section 547(e), the mortgage which was actually transferred to C on January 15 would be treated as a December 7th transfer for purposes of applying the various requirements of section 547(b).

Always do section 547(b) before you do (c). Only if you have a preference under (b), do you look for an exception under (c).

The parts of (c) that you will most often look at are section 547(c)(2) and section 547(c)(4).

In looking at (c)(2), pay special attention to the word "or" connecting 547(c)(2)(A) with (B). In looking at (c)(4), focus on the word "after."

OTHER SECTIONS

Definitions in section 101 are always important: "consumer debt," "insolvent," and, especially, "transfer."

When you see the word "trustee" in section 547 and other sections in chapter 3 and chapter 5, think "debtor in possession," think section 1107(a).

And section 547 needs to be read together with section 546(a) and section 550 to see how soon after bankruptcy an action must be brought to avoid a transfer under section 547 and how soon an action must be brought to recover and what can be recovered from whom.

Section 502(d) disallows claims of creditors from whom transfers are avoidable under section 547. Section 502(h) recognizes claims of creditors as to whom transfers have been avoided.

Under section 547(c)(6), section 547 does not apply to the creation of statutory liens. Under the introductory language of section 553, section 547 does not apply to the exercise of a right of setoff.

§ 548. Fraudulent transfers and obligations

(a)(1) The trustee may avoid any transfer (including any transfer to or for the benefit of an insider under an employment contract) of an interest of the debtor in property, or any obligation (including any obligation to or for the benefit of an insider under an employment contract) incurred by the debtor, that was made or incurred on or within 2 years before the date of the filing of the petition, if the debtor voluntarily or involuntarily—

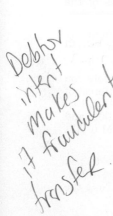

> **(A)** made such transfer or incurred such obligation with actual intent to hinder, delay, or defraud any entity to which the debtor was or became, on or after the date that such transfer was made or such obligation was incurred, indebted; or

> **(B)(i)** received less than a reasonably equivalent value in exchange for such transfer or obligation; and

>> **(ii)(I)** was insolvent on the date that such transfer was made or such obligation was incurred, or became insolvent as a result of such transfer or obligation;

>> **(II)** was engaged in business or a transaction, or was about to engage in business or a transaction, for which any property remaining with the debtor was an unreasonably small capital;

>> **(III)** intended to incur, or believed that the debtor would incur, debts that would be beyond the debtor's ability to pay as such debts matured; or

(IV) made such transfer to or for the benefit of an insider, or incurred such obligation to or for the benefit of an insider, under an employment contract and not in the ordinary course of business. *[handwritten: golden parachute]*

[handwritten: Could be challenged as fraudulent transfers.]

(2) A transfer of a charitable contribution to a qualified religious or charitable entity or organization shall not be considered to be a transfer covered under paragraph (1)(B) in any case in which—

> **(A)** the amount of that contribution does not exceed 15 percent of the gross annual income of the debtor for the year in which the transfer of the contribution is made; or

> **(B)** the contribution made by a debtor exceeded the percentage amount of gross annual income specified in subparagraph (A), if the transfer was consistent with the practices of the debtor in making charitable contributions.

(b) The trustee of a partnership debtor may avoid any transfer of an interest of the debtor in property, or any obligation incurred by the debtor, that was made or incurred on or within 2 years before the date of the filing of the petition, to a general partner in the debtor, if the debtor was insolvent on the date such transfer was made or such obligation was incurred, or became insolvent as a result of such transfer or obligation.

(c) Except to the extent that a transfer or obligation voidable under this section is voidable under section 544, 545, or 547 of this title, a transferee or obligee of such a transfer or obligation that takes for value and in good faith has a lien on or may retain any interest transferred or may enforce any obligation incurred, as the case may be, to the extent that such transferee or obligee gave value to the debtor in exchange for such transfer or obligation. *[handwritten: lien on what you paid for transfer]*

(d)(1) For the purposes of this section, a transfer is made when such transfer is so perfected that a bona fide purchaser from the debtor against whom applicable law permits such transfer to be perfected cannot acquire an interest in the property transferred that is superior to the interest in such property of the transferee, but if such transfer is not so perfected before the commencement of the case, such transfer is made immediately before the date of the filing of the petition.

(2) In this section—

> **(A)** "value" means property, or satisfaction or securing of a present or antecedent debt of the debtor, but does not include an unperformed promise to furnish support to the debtor or to a relative of the debtor;

* * *

(4) In this section, the term "qualified religious or charitable entity or organization" means—

> **(A)** an entity described in section 170(c)(1) of the Internal Revenue Code of 1986; or

> **(B)** an entity or organization described in section 170(c)(2) of the Internal Revenue Code of 1986.

(e)(1) In addition to any transfer that the trustee may otherwise avoid, the trustee may avoid any transfer of an interest of the debtor in property that was made on or within 10 years before the date of the filing of the petition, if—

> **(A)** such transfer was made to a self-settled trust or similar device;

(B) such transfer was by the debtor;

(C) the debtor is a beneficiary of such trust or similar device; and

(D) the debtor made such transfer with actual intent to hinder, delay, or defraud any entity to which the debtor was or became, on or after the date that such transfer was made, indebted.

* * *

UNOFFICIAL COMMENTS

Note from the title and text that section 548 applies to both transfers and obligations.

Pay special attention to the conjunctions in section 548(a)(1). "Or" connects 548(a)(1)(A) with (B). Trustee can win by either proving the requirement of (A) or the requirements of (B). (A) requires proof of "**actual** [emphasis added] intent to hinder, delay or defraud." (B) does not. Instead, (B) requires proof of two things: (i) the debtor received less than reasonably equivalent value as value is defined in section 548(d)(2)(A) and (ii) the debtor's financial condition comes within one of the four situations listed under (ii).

Because of section 548(d), section 548, like section 547, provides a basis for avoiding a transfer that (i) must be recorded or otherwise perfected under state law, (ii) was recorded or otherwise perfected before a bankruptcy filing but (iii) was not timely recorded or perfected.

OTHER SECTIONS

Definitions in section 101 are always important: "insolvent" and, especially, "transfer."

When you see the word "trustee" in section 548 and other sections in chapter 3 and chapter 5, think "debtor in possession," think section 1107(a). And section 548 needs to be read together with section 546(a) and section 550 to see how soon after bankruptcy an action must be brought to avoid a transfer under section 548 and how soon an action must be brought to recover and what can be recovered from whom.

Section 502(d) disallows claims of creditors from whom transfers are avoidable under section 548 Section 502(h) recognizes claims of those as to whom transfers have been avoided.

When you see the words "two years" in section 548 and see that your facts occurred more than two years before the bankruptcy filing, look to section 544(b). Even where your facts occurred within two years of bankruptcy, looking to section 544(b) and state law can be important when the definitions or requirements of state law differ from section 548.

Certain section 548 transfers may be a basis for withholding a discharge under section 727(a)(2). For example, when you see an individual debtor transferring property so as to maximize the amount of property that she can claim as exempt, then you need to look also at section 522 and section 727(a)(2).

§ 549. Postpetition transactions

(a) Except as provided in subsection (b) or (c) of this section, the trustee may avoid a transfer of property of the estate—

(1) that occurs after the commencement of the case; and

(2)(A) that is authorized only under section 303(f) or 542(c) of this title; or

(B) that is not authorized under this title or by the court.

(b) In an involuntary case, the trustee may not avoid under subsection (a) of this section a transfer made after the commencement of such case but before the order for relief to the extent any value, including services, but not including satisfaction or securing of a debt that arose before the commencement of the case, is given after the commencement of the case in exchange for such transfer, notwithstanding any notice or knowledge of the case that the transferee has.

(c) The trustee may not avoid under subsection (a) of this section a transfer of an interest in real property to a good faith purchaser without knowledge of the commencement of the case and for present fair equivalent value unless a copy or notice of the petition was filed, where a transfer of an interest in such real property may be recorded to perfect such transfer, before such transfer is so perfected that a bona fide purchaser of such real property, against whom applicable law permits such transfer to be perfected, could not acquire an interest that is superior to such interest of such good faith purchaser. A good faith purchaser without knowledge of the commencement of the case and for less than present fair equivalent value has a lien on the property transferred to the extent of any present value given, unless a copy or notice of the petition was so filed before such transfer was so perfected.

(d) An action or proceeding under this section may not be commenced after the earlier of—

    (1) two years after the date of the transfer sought to be avoided; or

    (2) the time the case is closed or dismissed.

UNOFFICIAL COMMENTS

Section 549 only applies to transfers that happen after bankruptcy happened—postpetition. Subsection (b) is further limited to transfers that happened after the filing of an involuntary bankruptcy (which almost never happens). And, subsection (a) is limited by the "not authorized by this title" requirement of section 549(a)(2)(B). Most postpetition transfers in chapter 11 business cases are authorized under section 363(b) or (c).

Section 549(c) further limits the use of section 549(a) only to avoid a transfer of real estate.

The most significant limitation of section 549 is more subtle. Use section 549 when (1) there has been a postpetition transfer and (2) the question is whether the trustee has any legal rights against the transferee. Do not use section 549 when (1) there has been a postpetition transfer and (2) the question is whether the trustee has any legal rights against the debtor/transferor. No section 549 question—indeed no question—as to whether the trustee has legal rights against the debtor/transferor. Unless the postpetition transfer was authorized, such a transfer was a conversion by the debtor of section 541 property of the estate.

OTHER SECTIONS

Definitions in section 101 are always important. Here the section 101 definition of "transfer" can be important.

When you see the word "trustee" in section 549 and other sections in chapter 3 and chapter 5, think "debtor in possession", think section 1107(a).

Section 550 determines how the trustee or debtor in possession can recover and from whom. More specifically, section 549(d) must be read together with section 550(f).

Section 502(d) disallows claims of creditors from whom transfers are avoidable under section 549. Section 502(h) recognizes claims of those as to whom transfers have been avoided.

Section 549 also needs to be read together with section 362. Some section 549 transfers are also violations of the automatic stay.

If a third party transfers property of the estate post-bankruptcy, look to section 542(c). A common example of a post-bankruptcy transfer of property of the estate by a third party is the bank where the debtor has her checking account paying funds from the account to a payee on a debtor's check post-bankruptcy.

Again, section 363 is the most important other section to read in connection with section 549—especially in cases involving businesses operating in chapter 11. Most post-bankruptcy transfers will be authorized by section 363, and so not avoidable by section 549.

§ 550. Liability of transferee of avoided transfer

(a) Except as otherwise provided in this section, to the extent that a transfer is avoided under section 544, 545, 547, 548, 549, 553(b), or 724(a) of this title, the trustee may recover, for the benefit of the estate, the property transferred, or, if the court so orders, the value of such property, from—

    (1) the initial transferee of such transfer or the entity for whose benefit such transfer was made; or

    (2) any immediate or mediate transferee of such initial transferee.

(b) The trustee may not recover under section[1] (a)(2) of this section from—

    (1) a transferee that takes for value, including satisfaction or securing of a present or antecedent debt, in good faith, and without knowledge of the voidability of the transfer avoided; or

    (2) any immediate or mediate good faith transferee of such transferee.

(c) If a transfer made between 90 days and one year before the filing of the petition—

    (1) is avoided under section 547(b) of this title; and

    (2) was made for the benefit of a creditor that at the time of such transfer was an insider;

the trustee may not recover under subsection (a) from a transferee that is not an insider.

(d) The trustee is entitled to only a single satisfaction under subsection (a) of this section.

(e)(1) A good faith transferee from whom the trustee may recover under subsection (a) of this section has a lien on the property recovered to secure the lesser of—

    (A) the cost, to such transferee, of any improvement made after the transfer, less the amount of any profit realized by or accruing to such transferee from such property; and

    (B) any increase in the value of such property as a result of such improvement, of the property transferred.

    (2) In this subsection, "improvement" includes—

        (A) physical additions or changes to the property transferred;

        (B) repairs to such property;

        (C) payment of any tax on such property;

        (D) payment of any debt secured by a lien on such property that is superior or equal to the rights of the trustee; and

        (E) preservation of such property.

---

[1]   So in original. Probably should be "subsection".

(f) An action or proceeding under this section may not be commenced after the earlier of—

    (1) one year after the avoidance of the transfer on account of which recovery under this section is sought; or

    (2) the time the case is closed or dismissed.

UNOFFICIAL COMMENTS

Section 550 applies only after you have applied either section 544 or section 547 or section 548 or section 549 or section 553 to avoid a transfer. And, it has to be applied within one year thereafter.

OTHER SECTIONS

Definitions in section 101 are always important, especially "transfer."

When you see the word "trustee" in section 549 and other sections in chapter 3 and chapter 5, think "debtor in possession," think section 1107(a).

Whatever is recovered under section 550 is property of the estate under section 541 and may be exempt under section 522. And, such recovery can result in an allowable prepetition claim under section 502(h).

An action under section 550 is an adversary proceeding under Rule 7001 set out infra at 231.

§ 551. Automatic preservation of avoided transfer

Any transfer avoided under section 522, 544, 545, 547, 548, 549, or 724(a) of this title, or any lien void under section 506(d) of this title, is preserved for the benefit of the estate but only with respect to property of the estate. *If estate can avoid lien, the lien continues to exist but is now within the estate*

§ 552. Postpetition effect of security interest

(a) Except as provided in subsection (b) of this section, property acquired by the estate or by the debtor after the commencement of the case is not subject to any lien resulting from any security agreement entered into by the debtor before the commencement of the case.

(b)(1) Except as provided in sections 363, 506(c), 522, 544, 545, 547, and 548 of this title, if the debtor and an entity entered into a security agreement before the commencement of the case and if the security interest created by such security agreement extends to property of the debtor acquired before the commencement of the case and to proceeds, products, offspring, or profits of such property, then such security interest extends to such proceeds, products, offspring, or profits acquired by the estate after the commencement of the case to the extent provided by such security agreement and by applicable nonbankruptcy law, except to any extent that the court, after notice and a hearing and based on the equities of the case, orders otherwise.

    (2) Except as provided in sections 363, 506(c), 522, 544, 545, 547, and 548 of this title, and notwithstanding section 546(b) of this title, if the debtor and an entity entered into a security agreement before the commencement of the case and if the security interest created by such security agreement extends to property of the debtor acquired before the commencement of the case and to amounts paid as rents of such property or the fees, charges, accounts, or other payments for the use or occupancy of rooms and other public facilities in hotels, motels, or other lodging properties, then such security interest extends to such rents and such fees, charges, accounts, or other payments acquired by the estate after the commencement of the case to the extent provided in such security agreement, except to any extent that the court, after notice and a hearing and based on the equities of the case, orders otherwise.

UNOFFICIAL COMMENTS

This section makes sense only if you understand the basics of Article 9 of the Uniform Commercial Code. UCC section 9–204, infra at page 324, permits a creditor to obtain a lien that "floats"—that encumbers not only stuff that the debtor now has but also stuff that the debtor might later acquire.

Section 552 limits the effect of such a floating lien in bankruptcy. Subsection (a) establishes the general rule that a security interest obtained before bankruptcy only encumbers stuff that the debtor has rights in before it filed for bankruptcy. Subsection (b) creates an exception for proceeds and the like.

To illustrate, on January 2, D obtains financing from S and grants S a security interest in its present and future inventory. D files for bankruptcy on January 15. Under section 552(a), S's lien would not reach inventory that D acquired after January 15th. Under section 552(b), S's lien would reach the cash and accounts receivable that result from post-January 15th sales of pre-January 15th inventory.

OTHER SECTIONS

Section 552 is generally applied together with sections 361 and 363 or 364. In the above example, D could offer S a security interest in the inventory that it acquires postpetition as adequate protection for D's section 363 sale of prepetition collateral and D's use of cash collateral resulting therefrom.

Read section 552(b) together with section 541(a)(6): both cover proceeds. Similarly, read section 552(b) together with section 363(a); some section 552(b) proceeds are also section 363(a) "cash collateral."

Again, it might be helpful to look at section 9–204, infra at page 324.

§ 553. Setoff

(a) Except as otherwise provided in this section and in sections 362 and 363 of this title, this title does not affect any right of a creditor to offset a mutual debt owing by such creditor to the debtor that arose before the commencement of the case under this title against a claim of such creditor against the debtor that arose before the commencement of the case, except to the extent that—

    (1) the claim of such creditor against the debtor is disallowed;

    (2) such claim was transferred, by an entity other than the debtor, to such creditor—

        (A) after the commencement of the case; or

        (B)(i) after 90 days before the date of the filing of the petition; and

            (ii) while the debtor was insolvent * * *

    (3) the debt owed to the debtor by such creditor was incurred by such creditor—

        (A) after 90 days before the date of the filing of the petition;

        (B) while the debtor was insolvent; and

        (C) for the purpose of obtaining a right of setoff against the debtor * * *

(b)(1) If a creditor offsets a mutual debt owing to the debtor against a claim against the debtor on or within 90 days before the date of the filing of the petition, then the trustee may recover from such creditor the amount so offset to the extent that any insufficiency on the date of such setoff is less than the insufficiency on the later of—

    (A) 90 days before the date of the filing of the petition; and

    (B) the first date during the 90 days immediately preceding the date of the filing of the petition on which there is an insufficiency.

    (2) In this subsection, "insufficiency" means amount, if any, by which a claim against the debtor exceeds a mutual debt owing to the debtor by the holder of such claim.

    (c) For the purposes of this section, the debtor is presumed to have been insolvent on and during the 90 days immediately preceding the date of the filing of the petition.

UNOFFICIAL COMMENTS

Section 553 does not create a right of setoff. Rather, it recognizes a right of setoff established by nonbankruptcy law and establishes limits on the exercise of that right before bankruptcy or during bankruptcy.

Note that the limits in section 553(b) look very much like section 547(c)(5). And, note that the limits in section 553(b), unlike the limits in section 553(a), only apply to a pre-petition setoff.

OTHER SECTIONS

A postpetition setoff is stayed by section 362(a)(7).

Under the definition of "secured claim" in section 506, a creditor with a right of setoff has a secured claim to the extent of its right of setoff.

Because of the introductory phrase in section 553(a)—"Except . . . this title does not apply," section 547 does not apply to the right of setoff.

§ 554. Abandonment of property of the estate

    (a) After notice and a hearing, the trustee may abandon any property of the estate that is burdensome to the estate or that is of inconsequential value and benefit to the estate.

    (b) On request of a party in interest and after notice and a hearing, the court may order the trustee to abandon any property of the estate that is burdensome to the estate or that is of inconsequential value and benefit to the estate.

    (c) Unless the court orders otherwise, any property scheduled under section 521(a)(1) of this title not otherwise administered at the time of the closing of a case is abandoned to the debtor and administered for purposes of section 350 of this title.

    (d) Unless the court orders otherwise, property of the estate that is not abandoned under this section and that is not administered in the case remains property of the estate.

UNOFFICIAL COMMENT

Section 554 sort of answers the question, when can property be abandoned. The language of section 554 is of less help (no help?) in answering the question, to whom is property abandoned. Cases' and commentators' answer to that question is that property is abandoned to the debtor.

OTHER SECTIONS

As abandoned property becomes property of the debtor, it continues to be protected by the automatic stay by reason of section 362(a)(5).

Abandoned property can be redeemed under section 722.

28 USC section 959(b) requires a trustee to follow state law requirements in his actions as trustee. State environmental law can affect whether and how property of the estate with environmental problems can be abandoned. Title 11

CHAPTER 7—LIQUIDATION

SUBCHAPTER I—OFFICERS AND ADMINISTRATION

* * *

SUBCHAPTER I—OFFICERS AND ADMINISTRATION

§ 701. Interim trustee

(a)(1) Promptly after the order for relief under this chapter, the United States trustee shall appoint one disinterested person that is a member of the panel of private trustees established under section 586(a)(1) of title 28 or that is serving as trustee in the case immediately before the order for relief under this chapter to serve as interim trustee in the case.

(2) If none of the members of such panel is willing to serve as interim trustee in the case, then the United States trustee may serve as interim trustee in the case.

(b) The service of an interim trustee under this section terminates when a trustee elected or designated under section 702 of this title to serve as trustee in the case qualifies under section 322 of this title.

(c) An interim trustee serving under this section is a trustee in a case under this title.

§ 702. Election of trustee

(a) A creditor may vote for a candidate for trustee only if such creditor—

(1) holds an allowable, undisputed, fixed, liquidated, unsecured claim of a kind entitled to distribution under section 726(a)(2), 726(a)(3), 726(a)(4), 752(a), 766(h), or 766(i) of this title;

(2) does not have an interest materially adverse, other than an equity interest that is not substantial in relation to such creditor's interest as a creditor, to the interest of creditors entitled to such distribution; and

(3) is not an insider.

(b) At the meeting of creditors held under section 341 of this title, creditors may elect one person to serve as trustee in the case if election of a trustee is requested by creditors that may vote under subsection (a) of this section, and that hold at least 20 percent in amount of the claims specified in subsection (a)(1) of this section that are held by creditors that may vote under subsection (a) of this section.

(c) A candidate for trustee is elected trustee if—

(1) creditors holding at least 20 percent in amount of the claims of a kind specified in subsection (a)(1) of this section that are held by creditors that may vote under subsection (a) of this section vote; and

(2) such candidate receives the votes of creditors holding a majority in amount of claims specified in subsection (a)(1) of this section that are held by creditors that vote for a trustee.

(d) If a trustee is not elected under this section, then the interim trustee shall serve as trustee in the case.

§ 704. Duties of trustee

(a) The trustee shall—

(1) collect and reduce to money the property of the estate for which such trustee serves, and close such estate as expeditiously as is compatible with the best interests of parties in interest;

(2) be accountable for all property received;

(3) ensure that the debtor shall perform his intention as specified in section 521(a)(2)(B) of this title;

(4) investigate the financial affairs of the debtor;

(5) if a purpose would be served, examine proofs of claims and object to the allowance of any claim that is improper;

(6) if advisable, oppose the discharge of the debtor;

(7) unless the court orders otherwise, furnish such information concerning the estate and the estate's administration as is requested by a party in interest;

(8) if the business of the debtor is authorized to be operated, file with the court, with the United States trustee, and with any governmental unit charged with responsibility for collection or determination of any tax arising out of such operation, periodic reports and summaries of the operation of such business, including a statement of receipts and disbursements, and such other information as the United States trustee or the court requires;

(9) make a final report and file a final account of the administration of the estate with the court and with the United States trustee;

* * *

(b)(1) With respect to a debtor who is an individual in a case under this chapter—

    (A) the United States trustee (or the bankruptcy administrator, if any) shall review all materials filed by the debtor and, not later than 10 days after the date of the first meeting of creditors, file with the court a statement as to whether the debtor's case would be presumed to be an abuse under section 707(b); and

    (B) not later than 5 days after receiving a statement under subparagraph (A), the court shall provide a copy of the statement to all creditors.

    (2) The United States trustee (or bankruptcy administrator, if any) shall, not later than 30 days after the date of filing a statement under paragraph (1), either file a motion to dismiss or convert under section 707(b) or file a statement setting forth the reasons the United States trustee (or the bankruptcy administrator, if any) does not consider such a motion to be appropriate, if the United States trustee (or the bankruptcy administrator, if any) determines that the debtor's case should be presumed to be an abuse under section 707(b) and the product of the debtor's current monthly income, multiplied by 12 is not less than—

    (A) in the case of a debtor in a household of 1 person, the median family income of the applicable State for 1 earner; or

    (B) in the case of a debtor in a household of 2 or more individuals, the highest median family income of the applicable State for a family of the same number or fewer individuals.

* * *

Unofficial Comment

It should be obvious from section 704(a) that the trustee is the most important professional in most chapter 7 cases. She collects and sells property of the estate.

Other Sections

Section 704 should be read together with section 726. The former provides for the trustee's sale of property of the estate; the latter provides for the distribution of the sale proceeds.

§ 706. Conversion

(a) The debtor may convert a case under this chapter to a case under chapter 11, 12, or 13 of this title at any time, if the case has not been converted under section 1112, 1208, or 1307 of this title. Any waiver of the right to convert a case under this subsection is unenforceable.

(b) On request of a party in interest and after notice and a hearing, the court may convert a case under this chapter to a case under chapter 11 of this title at any time.

(c) The court may not convert a case under this chapter to a case under chapter 12 or 13 of this title unless the debtor requests or consents to such conversion.

(d) Notwithstanding any other provision of this section, a case may not be converted to a case under another chapter of this title unless the debtor may be a debtor under such chapter.

§ 707. Dismissal of a case or conversion to a case under chapter 11 or 13

(a) The court may dismiss a case under this chapter only after notice and a hearing and only for cause, including—

(1) unreasonable delay by the debtor that is prejudicial to creditors; [handwritten: Don't want debtor declaring bankruptcy just to avoid creditors]

(2) nonpayment of any fees or charges required under chapter 123 of title 28; and [handwritten: Don't pay ct fees trustee fees]

(3) failure of the debtor in a voluntary case to file, within fifteen days or such additional time as the court may allow after the filing of the petition commencing such case, the information required by paragraph (1) of section 521(a), but only on a motion by the United States trustee. [handwritten: Don't necessarily get 45 days if trustee files a motion]

(b)(1) After notice and a hearing, the court, on its own motion or on a motion by the United States trustee, trustee (or bankruptcy administrator, if any), or any party in interest, may dismiss a case filed by an individual debtor under this chapter whose debts are primarily consumer debts, or, with the debtor's consent, convert such a case to a case under chapter 11 or 13 of this title, if it finds that the granting of relief would be an abuse of the provisions of this chapter. In making a determination whether to dismiss a case under this section, the court may not take into consideration whether a debtor has made, or continues to make, charitable contributions (that meet the definition of "charitable contribution" under section 548(d)(3)) to any qualified religious or charitable entity or organization (as that term is defined in section 548(d)(4)). [handwritten: Either Dismiss or convert to ch 13]

(2)(A)(i) In considering under paragraph (1) whether the granting of relief would be an abuse of the provisions of this chapter, the court shall presume abuse exists if the debtor's current monthly income reduced by the amounts determined under clauses (ii), (iii), and (iv), and multiplied by 60 is not less than the lesser of—

(I) 25 percent of the debtor's nonpriority unsecured claims in the case, or $7,475, whichever is greater; or

(II) $12,475. [handwritten: # adjusted for inflation]

(ii)(I) The debtor's monthly expenses shall be the debtor's applicable monthly expense amounts specified under the National Standards and Local Standards, and the debtor's actual monthly expenses for the categories specified as Other Necessary Expenses issued by the Internal Revenue Service for the area in which the debtor resides, as in effect on the date of the order for relief, for the debtor, the dependents of the debtor, and the spouse of the debtor in a joint case, if the spouse is not otherwise a dependent. Such expenses shall include reasonably necessary health insurance, disability insurance, and health savings account expenses for the debtor, the spouse of the debtor, or the dependents of the debtor. Notwithstanding any other provision of this clause, the monthly expenses of the debtor shall not include any payments for debts. In addition, the debtor's monthly expenses shall include the debtor's reasonably necessary expenses incurred to maintain the safety of the debtor and the family of the debtor from family violence as identified under section 309 of the Family Violence Prevention and Services Act, or other applicable Federal law. The expenses included in the debtor's monthly expenses described in the preceding sentence shall be kept confidential by the court. In addition, if it is

[handwritten: Monthly income − II, III, IV × 60]

demonstrated that it is reasonable and necessary, the debtor's monthly expenses may also include an additional allowance for food and clothing of up to 5 percent of the food and clothing categories as specified by the National Standards issued by the Internal Revenue Service.

(II) In addition, the debtor's monthly expenses may include, if applicable, the continuation of actual expenses paid by the debtor that are reasonable and necessary for care and support of an elderly, chronically ill, or disabled household member or member of the debtor's immediate family (including parents, grandparents, siblings, children, and grandchildren of the debtor, the dependents of the debtor, and the spouse of the debtor in a joint case who is not a dependent) and who is unable to pay for such reasonable and necessary expenses.

(III) In addition, for a debtor eligible for chapter 13, the debtor's monthly expenses may include the actual administrative expenses of administering a chapter 13 plan for the district in which the debtor resides, up to an amount of 10 percent of the projected plan payments, as determined under schedules issued by the Executive Office for United States Trustees.

(IV) In addition, the debtor's monthly expenses may include the actual expenses for each dependent child less than 18 years of age, not to exceed $1,875 per year per child, to attend a private or public elementary or secondary school if the debtor provides documentation of such expenses and a detailed explanation of why such expenses are reasonable and necessary, and why such expenses are not already accounted for in the National Standards, Local Standards, or Other Necessary Expenses referred to in subclause (I).

(V) In addition, the debtor's monthly expenses may include an allowance for housing and utilities, in excess of the allowance specified by the Local Standards for housing and utilities issued by the Internal Revenue Service, based on the actual expenses for home energy costs if the debtor provides documentation of such actual expenses and demonstrates that such actual expenses are reasonable and necessary.

(iii) The debtor's average monthly payments on account of secured debts shall be calculated as the sum of—

(I) the total of all amounts scheduled as contractually due to secured creditors in each month of the 60 months following the date of the filing of the petition; and

(II) any additional payments to secured creditors necessary for the debtor, in filing a plan under chapter 13 of this title, to maintain possession of the debtor's primary residence, motor vehicle, or other property necessary for the support of the debtor and the debtor's dependents, that serves as collateral for secured debts; divided by 60.

(iv) The debtor's expenses for payment of all priority claims (including priority child support and alimony claims) shall be calculated as the total amount of debts entitled to priority, divided by 60.

126

[handwritten: presumption can be rebutted]

(B)(i) In any proceeding brought under this subsection, the presumption of abuse may only be rebutted by demonstrating special circumstances, such as a serious medical condition or a call or order to active duty in the Armed Forces, to the extent such special circumstances that justify additional expenses or adjustments of current monthly income for which there is no reasonable alternative.

(ii) In order to establish special circumstances, the debtor shall be required to itemize each additional expense or adjustment of income and to provide—

(I) documentation for such expense or adjustment to income; and

(II) a detailed explanation of the special circumstances that make such expenses or adjustment to income necessary and reasonable.

(iii) The debtor shall attest under oath to the accuracy of any information provided to demonstrate that additional expenses or adjustments to income are required.

(iv) The presumption of abuse may only be rebutted if the additional expenses or adjustments to income referred to in clause (i) cause the product of the debtor's current monthly income reduced by the amounts determined under clauses (ii), (iii), and (iv) of subparagraph (A) when multiplied by 60 to be less than the lesser of—

(I) 25 percent of the debtor's nonpriority unsecured claims, or $7,475, whichever is greater; or

(II) $12,475.   *[handwritten: #adjusted for inflation]*

(C) As part of the schedule of current income and expenditures required under section 521, the debtor shall include a statement of the debtor's current monthly income, and the calculations that determine whether a presumption arises under subparagraph (A)(i), that show how each such amount is calculated.

(D) Subparagraphs (A) through (C) shall not apply, and the court may not dismiss or convert a case based on any form of means testing, if the debtor is a disabled veteran (as defined in section 3741(1) of title 38), and the indebtedness occurred primarily during a period during which he or she was—

(i) on active duty (as defined in section 101(d)(1) of title 10); or

(ii) performing a homeland defense activity (as defined in section 901(1) of title 32).

(3) In considering under paragraph (1) whether the granting of relief would be an abuse of the provisions of this chapter in a case in which the presumption in paragraph (2)(A)(i) of such paragraph does not arise or is rebutted, the court shall consider—

(A) whether the debtor filed the petition in bad faith; or

(B) the totality of the circumstances (including whether the debtor seeks to reject a personal services contract and the financial need for such rejection as sought by the debtor) of the debtor's financial situation demonstrates abuse.

[handwritten left margin: Must have an effect that can be quantified and extensively documented]

[handwritten right margin: not matter for judicial discretion will soon create a medical test]

[handwritten bottom: Catch all categories w/ no clear guidelines]

(4)(A) The court, on its own initiative or on the motion of a party in interest, in accordance with the procedures described in rule 9011 of the Federal Rules of Bankruptcy Procedure, may order the attorney for the debtor to reimburse the trustee for all reasonable costs in prosecuting a motion filed under section 707(b), including reasonable attorneys' fees, if—

     (i) a trustee files a motion for dismissal or conversion under this subsection; and

     (ii) the court—

         (I) grants such motion; and

         (II) finds that the action of the attorney for the debtor in filing a case under this chapter violated rule 9011 of the Federal Rules of Bankruptcy Procedure.

(B) If the court finds that the attorney for the debtor violated rule 9011 of the Federal Rules of Bankruptcy Procedure, the court, on its own initiative or on the motion of a party in interest, in accordance with such procedures, may order—

     (i) the assessment of an appropriate civil penalty against the attorney for the debtor; and

     (ii) the payment of such civil penalty to the trustee, the United States trustee (or the bankruptcy administrator, if any).

(C) The signature of an attorney on a petition, pleading, or written motion shall constitute a certification that the attorney has—

     (i) performed a reasonable investigation into the circumstances that gave rise to the petition, pleading, or written motion; and

     (ii) determined that the petition, pleading, or written motion—

         (I) is well grounded in fact; and

         (II) is warranted by existing law or a good faith argument for the extension, modification, or reversal of existing law and does not constitute an abuse under paragraph (1).

(D) The signature of an attorney on the petition shall constitute a certification that the attorney has no knowledge after an inquiry that the information in the schedules filed with such petition is incorrect.

(5)(A) Except as provided in subparagraph (B) and subject to paragraph (6), the court, on its own initiative or on the motion of a party in interest, in accordance with the procedures described in rule 9011 of the Federal Rules of Bankruptcy Procedure, may award a debtor all reasonable costs (including reasonable attorneys' fees) in contesting a motion filed by a party in interest (other than a trustee or United States trustee (or bankruptcy administrator, if any)) under this subsection if—

     (i) the court does not grant the motion; and

     (ii) the court finds that—

         (I) the position of the party that filed the motion violated rule 9011 of the Federal Rules of Bankruptcy Procedure; or

(II) the attorney (if any) who filed the motion did not comply with the requirements of clauses (i) and (ii) of paragraph (4)(C), and the motion was made solely for the purpose of coercing a debtor into waiving a right guaranteed to the debtor under this title.

(B) A small business that has a claim of an aggregate amount less than $1,250 shall not be subject to subparagraph (A)(ii)(I).

(C) For purposes of this paragraph—

(i) the term "small business" means an unincorporated business, partnership, corporation, association, or organization that—

(I) has fewer than 25 full-time employees as determined on the date on which the motion is filed; and

(II) is engaged in commercial or business activity; and

(ii) the number of employees of a wholly owned subsidiary of a corporation includes the employees of—

(I) a parent corporation; and

(II) any other subsidiary corporation of the parent corporation.

(6) Only the judge or United States trustee (or bankruptcy administrator, if any) may file a motion under section 707(b), if the current monthly income of the debtor, or in a joint case, the debtor and the debtor's spouse, as of the date of the order for relief, when multiplied by 12, is equal to or less than— *below the median*

Can't file motion Abuse

(A) in the case of a debtor in a household of 1 person, the median family income of the applicable State for 1 earner; *median income household w/ 1 earner*

(B) in the case of a debtor in a household of 2, 3, or 4 individuals, the highest median family income of the applicable State for a family of the same number or fewer individuals; or *This is family size*

(C) in the case of a debtor in a household exceeding 4 individuals, the highest median family income of the applicable State for a family of 4 or fewer individuals, plus $675 per month for each individual in excess of 4.

(7)(A) No judge, United States trustee (or bankruptcy administrator, if any), trustee, or other party in interest may file a motion under paragraph (2) if the current monthly income of the debtor, including a veteran (as that term is defined in section 101 of title 38), and the debtor's spouse combined, as of the date of the order for relief when multiplied by 12, is equal to or less than— *below the median*

Can't file motion presumption of Abuse (Means Test)

(i) in the case of a debtor in a household of 1 person, the median family income of the applicable State for 1 earner;

(ii) in the case of a debtor in a household of 2, 3, or 4 individuals, the highest median family income of the applicable State for a family of the same number or fewer individuals; or

(iii) in the case of a debtor in a household exceeding 4 individuals, the highest median family income of the applicable State for a family of 4 or fewer individuals, plus $625 per month for each individual in excess of 4.

(B) In a case that is not a joint case, current monthly income of the debtor's spouse shall not be considered for purposes of subparagraph (A) if—

(i)(I) the debtor and the debtor's spouse are separated under applicable nonbankruptcy law; or

(II) the debtor and the debtor's spouse are living separate and apart, other than for the purpose of evading subparagraph (A); and

(ii) the debtor files a statement under penalty of perjury—

(I) specifying that the debtor meets the requirement of subclause (I) or (II) of clause (i); and

(II) disclosing the aggregate, or best estimate of the aggregate, amount of any cash or money payments received from the debtor's spouse attributed to the debtor's current monthly income.

(c)(1) In this subsection—

(A) the term "crime of violence" has the meaning given such term in section 16 of title 18; and

(B) the term "drug trafficking crime" has the meaning given such term in section 924(c)(2) of title 18.

(2) Except as provided in paragraph (3), after notice and a hearing, the court, on a motion by the victim of a crime of violence or a drug trafficking crime, may when it is in the best interest of the victim dismiss a voluntary case filed under this chapter by a debtor who is an individual if such individual was convicted of such crime.

(3) The court may not dismiss a case under paragraph (2) if the debtor establishes by a preponderance of the evidence that the filing of a case under this chapter is necessary to satisfy a claim for a domestic support obligation.

UNOFFICIAL COMMENTS

Under section 707(a), the general standard for dismissal is "cause", more specifically "only for cause." Accordingly, if a debtor files a chapter 7 petition and then he changes his mind, he must prove "cause" in order to dismiss.

Subsection (b) only applies if the debtor is (1) an individual and (2) his debts are "primarily consumer debts." Under section 707(b), the standard is "abuse of the provisions of this chapter."

Section 707(b)(2) provides a complex "means test" to establish whether there is a presumption of abuse. Happily most debtors do not have to "take" this "means test" (and hopefully, the means test will not be on your test) because of the comparison of their current monthly income with the average monthly income under section 707(b)(7).

OTHER SECTIONS

Section 101 defines "consumer debt," "current monthly income," "median family income."

Look to section 349 for the effect of dismissal. And to section 362(c)(3) and (4) for the effect of dismissal on the automatic stay in later bankruptcy cases.

You can get a better sense of what "means testing" means by looking at Official Form 22A. Individual debtors filing for chapter 7 relief will complete this form for "means testing" purposes.

Some of the information needed to complete this form, such as the debtor's current monthly income, will come from the debtor's own personal records. Other information comes from Census Bureau and Internal Revenue Service data. The U.S. Trustee website, www.usdoj.gov/ust/eo/bapcpa/meanstesting.htm reproduces this data, such as Census Bureau Median Family Income By Family Size.

SUBCHAPTER II—COLLECTION, LIQUIDATION, AND DISTRIBUTION OF THE ESTATE

§ 721. Authorization to operate business

The court may authorize the trustee to operate the business of the debtor for a limited period, if such operation is in the best interest of the estate and consistent with the orderly liquidation of the estate.

§ 722. Redemption

An individual debtor may, whether or not the debtor has waived the right to redeem under this section, redeem tangible personal property intended primarily for personal, family, or household use, from a lien securing a dischargeable consumer debt, if such property is exempted under section 522 of this title or has been abandoned under section 554 of this title, by paying the holder of such lien the amount of the allowed secured claim of such holder that is secured by such lien in full at the time of redemption.

UNOFFICIAL COMMENTS

Understanding section 722 requires an understanding of the limited effect of discharge. Discharge only affects the debtor's payment obligations, only protects a debtor from being compelled to pay discharged debts. Discharge does not protect a debtor from losing property encumbered by liens.

Section 722 permits certain debtors to keep encumbered property. There are basically two different section 722 questions: (1) when does it apply? (2) what does it require?

First, section 722 only applies if

— the debtor is "an individual debtor," and

— the encumbered property is "tangible personal property," not real property such as a house, and

— the encumbered property is "intended primarily for personal, family or household use," and

— the encumbered property is "exempted under section 522" or "abandoned under section 544," and

— the secured debt is "a dischargeable consumer debt."

Second, section 722 requires a payment

— the amount of which depends not on the amount that is owed but the by the amount of the allowed secured claim, an amount determined by section 506, and

— that must be made "in full at the time of redemption."

OTHER SECTIONS

Section 722 redemption must be compared with section 524 reaffirmation. Reaffirmation but not redemption requires (1) an agreement between the debtor and the affected creditor and (2) court approval.

Section 722 should also be read together with

— section 101 which defines important terms such as "consumer debt," and

— section 506(a)(2) which tells you how to determine the amount of the secured claim which is the amount that must be paid under section 722,

(Notice the relationship between the second sentence of section 506(a)(2) which uses the phrase "property ACQUIRED for personal, family or household purposes" and section 722 which uses the similar but not identical language "INTENDED PRIMARILY for personal, family or household purposes").

— section 521 which requires the debtor to state whether she intends to redeem.

You might find it helpful to look at Rule 4002, infra at page 228.

Section 9–623 of the Uniform Commercial Code, infra at page 327 provides a right of redemption that is similar to section 722 in concept but different in terms of when it applies and what amount it requires be paid.

* * *

§ 724. Treatment of certain liens

(a) The trustee may avoid a lien that secures a claim of a kind specified in section 726(a)(4) of this title.

(b) Property in which the estate has an interest and that is subject to a lien that is not avoidable under this title (other than to the extent that there is a properly perfected unavoidable tax lien arising in connection with an ad valorem tax on real or personal property of the estate) and that secures an allowed claim for a tax, or proceeds of such property, shall be distributed—

(1) first, to any holder of an allowed claim secured by a lien on such property that is not avoidable under this title and that is senior to such tax lien;

(2) second, to any holder of a claim of a kind specified in section 507(a)(1)(C) or 507(a)(2) (except that such expenses, other than claims for wages, salaries, or commissions that arise after the date of the filing of the petition, shall be limited to expenses incurred under this chapter and shall not include expenses incurred under chapter 11 of this title), 507(a)(1)(A), 507(a)(1)(B), 507(a)(3), 507(a)(4), 507(a)(5), 507(a)(6), or 507(a)(7) of this title, to the extent of the amount of such allowed tax claim that is secured by such tax lien;

(3) third, to the holder of such tax lien, to any extent that such holder's allowed tax claim that is secured by such tax lien exceeds any amount distributed under paragraph (2) of this subsection;

(4) fourth, to any holder of an allowed claim secured by a lien on such property that is not avoidable under this title and that is junior to such tax lien;

(5) fifth, to the holder of such tax lien, to the extent that such holder's allowed claim secured by such tax lien is not paid under paragraph (3) of this subsection; and

(6) sixth, to the estate.

(c) If more than one holder of a claim is entitled to distribution under a particular paragraph of subsection (b) of this section, distribution to such holders under such paragraph shall be in the same order as distribution to such holders would have been other than under this section.

(d) A statutory lien the priority of which is determined in the same manner as the priority of a tax lien under section 6323 of the Internal Revenue Code of 1986 shall be treated under subsection (b) of this section the same as if such lien were a tax lien.

(e) Before subordinating a tax lien on real or personal property of the estate, the trustee shall—

(1) exhaust the unencumbered assets of the estate; and

(2) in a manner consistent with section 506(c), recover from property securing an allowed secured claim the reasonable, necessary costs and expenses of preserving or disposing of such property.

(f) Notwithstanding the exclusion of ad valorem tax liens under this section and subject to the requirements of subsection (e), the following may be paid from property of the estate which secures a tax lien, or the proceeds of such property:

(1) Claims for wages, salaries, and commissions that are entitled to priority under section 507(a)(4).

(2) Claims for contributions to an employee benefit plan entitled to priority under section 507(a)(5).

§ 725. Disposition of certain property

After the commencement of a case under this chapter, but before final distribution of property of the estate under section 726 of this title, the trustee, after notice and a hearing, shall dispose of any property in which an entity other than the estate has an interest, such as a lien, and that has not been disposed of under another section of this title.

OTHER SECTIONS

The section 725 phrase "disposed of under another section of this title" refers to (1) foreclosure after relief from stay under section 362(d) and (2) sale under section 363 and (3) exemption under section 522 and (4) abandonment under section 554.

§ 726. Distribution of property of the estate

(a) Except as provided in section 510 of this title, property of the estate shall be distributed—

(1) first, in payment of claims of the kind specified in, and in the order specified in, section 507 of this title, proof of which is timely filed under section 501 of this title or tardily filed on or before the earlier of—

(A) the date that is 10 days after the mailing to creditors of the summary of the trustee's final report; or

(B) the date on which the trustee commences final distribution under this section;

(2) second, in payment of any allowed unsecured claim, other than a claim of a kind specified in paragraph (1), (3), or (4) of this subsection, proof of which is—

(A) timely filed under section 501(a) of this title;

(B) timely filed under section 501(b) or 501(c) of this title; or

(C) tardily filed under section 501(a) of this title, if—

(i) the creditor that holds such claim did not have notice or actual knowledge of the case in time for timely filing of a proof of such claim under section 501(a) of this title; and

(ii) proof of such claim is filed in time to permit payment of such claim;

(3) third, in payment of any allowed unsecured claim proof of which is tardily filed under section 501(a) of this title, other than a claim of the kind specified in paragraph (2)(C) of this subsection;

(4) fourth, in payment of any allowed claim, whether secured or unsecured, for any fine, penalty, or forfeiture, or for multiple, exemplary, or punitive damages, arising before the earlier of the order for relief or the appointment of a trustee, to the extent that such fine, penalty, forfeiture, or damages are not compensation for actual pecuniary loss suffered by the holder of such claim;

(5) fifth, in payment of interest at the legal rate from the date of the filing of the petition, on any claim paid under paragraph (1), (2), (3), or (4) of this subsection; and

(6) sixth, to the debtor.

(b) Payment on claims of a kind specified in paragraph (1), (2), (3), (4), (5), (6), (7), (8), (9), or (10) of section 507(a) of this title, or in paragraph (2), (3), (4), or (5) of subsection (a) of this section, shall be made pro rata among claims of the kind specified in each such particular paragraph, except that in a case that has been converted to this chapter under section 1112, 1208, or 1307 of this title, a claim allowed under section 503(b) of this title incurred under this chapter after such conversion has priority over a claim allowed under section 503(b) of this title incurred under any other chapter of this title or under this chapter before such conversion and over any expenses of a custodian superseded under section 543 of this title.

(c) Notwithstanding subsections (a) and (b) of this section, if there is property of the kind specified in section 541(a)(2) of this title, or proceeds of such property, in the estate, such property or proceeds shall be segregated from other property of the estate, and such property or proceeds and other property of the estate shall be distributed as follows:

(1) Claims allowed under section 503 of this title shall be paid either from property of the kind specified in section 541(a)(2) of this title, or from other property of the estate, as the interest of justice requires.

(2) Allowed claims, other than claims allowed under section 503 of this title, shall be paid in the order specified in subsection (a) of this section, and, with respect to claims of a kind specified in a particular paragraph of section 507 of this title or subsection (a) of this section, in the following order and manner:

(A) First, community claims against the debtor or the debtor's spouse shall be paid from property of the kind specified in section 541(a)(2) of this title, except to the extent that such property is solely liable for debts of the debtor.

(B) Second, to the extent that community claims against the debtor are not paid under subparagraph (A) of this paragraph, such community claims shall be paid from property of the kind specified in section 541(a)(2) of this title that is solely liable for debts of the debtor.

(C) Third, to the extent that all claims against the debtor including community claims against the debtor are not paid under subparagraph (A) or (B) of this paragraph such claims shall be paid from property of the estate other than property of the kind specified in section 541(a)(2) of this title.

(D) Fourth, to the extent that community claims against the debtor or the debtor's spouse are not paid under subparagraph (A), (B), or (C) of this paragraph, such claims shall be paid from all remaining property of the estate.

UNOFFICIAL COMMENTS

In chapter 7 cases, unsecured creditors get paid from property of the estate (more accurately, from the proceeds resulting from the chapter 7 trustee's liquidation (i.e. sale) of property of the estate). Section 726 sets out how this money is to be distributed.

Pay special attention to section 726(b)(2). If a case starts out as a chapter 11 or 13 case and is then converted to chapter 7, the chapter 7 administrative expenses are paid first.

OTHER SECTIONS

Section 541 determines what is property of the estate—the debtor's interest in property. A creditor who has a lien also has an interest in property. Look to section 725 to see what happens to the property encumbered by a lien.

And look to section 502 for allowable claims, section 503 for administrative claims, section 507 for other priority claims, and section 510 for subordinated claims.

You might also be looking back to section 726 when you are doing the "best interests of creditors" test in section 1129(a)(7) or section 1325(a)(4).

§ 727. Discharge

(a) The court shall grant the debtor a discharge, unless—

(1) the debtor is not an individual;

(2) the debtor, with intent to hinder, delay, or defraud a creditor or an officer of the estate charged with custody of property under this title, has transferred, removed, destroyed, mutilated, or concealed, or has permitted to be transferred, removed, destroyed, mutilated, or concealed—

(A) property of the debtor, within one year before the date of the filing of the petition; or

(B) property of the estate, after the date of the filing of the petition;

(3) the debtor has concealed, destroyed, mutilated, falsified, or failed to keep or preserve any recorded information, including books, documents, records, and papers, from which the debtor's financial condition or business transactions might be ascertained, unless such act or failure to act was justified under all of the circumstances of the case;

(4) the debtor knowingly and fraudulently, in or in connection with the case—

(A) made a false oath or account;

(B) presented or used a false claim;

(C) gave, offered, received, or attempted to obtain money, property, or advantage, or a promise of money, property, or advantage, for acting or forbearing to act; or

(D) withheld from an officer of the estate entitled to possession under this title, any recorded information, including books, documents, records, and papers, relating to the debtor's property or financial affairs;

135

(5) the debtor has failed to explain satisfactorily, before determination of denial of discharge under this paragraph, any loss of assets or deficiency of assets to meet the debtor's liabilities;

(6) the debtor has refused, in the case—

    (A) to obey any lawful order of the court, other than an order to respond to a material question or to testify;

    (B) on the ground of privilege against self-incrimination, to respond to a material question approved by the court or to testify, after the debtor has been granted immunity with respect to the matter concerning which such privilege was invoked; or

    (C) on a ground other than the properly invoked privilege against self-incrimination, to respond to a material question approved by the court or to testify;

(7) the debtor has committed any act specified in paragraph (2), (3), (4), (5), or (6) of this subsection, on or within one year before the date of the filing of the petition, or during the case, in connection with another case, under this title or under the Bankruptcy Act, concerning an insider;

(8) the debtor has been granted a discharge under this section [or] under section 1141 of this title, * * *in a case commenced within 8 years before the date of the filing of the petition;

(9) the debtor has been granted a discharge under section 1228 or 1328 of this title, * * * in a case commenced within six years before the date of the filing of the petition, unless payments under the plan in such case totaled at least—

    (A) 100 percent of the allowed unsecured claims in such case; or

    (B)(i) 70 percent of such claims; and

        (ii) the plan was proposed by the debtor in good faith, and was the debtor's best effort;

(10) the court approves a written waiver of discharge executed by the debtor after the order for relief under this chapter;

(11) after filing the petition, the debtor failed to complete an instructional course concerning personal financial management described in section 111, except that this paragraph shall not apply with respect to a debtor who is a person described in section 109(h)(4) or who resides in a district for which the United States trustee (or the bankruptcy administrator, if any) determines that the approved instructional courses are not adequate to service the additional individuals who would otherwise be required to complete such instructional courses under this section (The United States trustee (or the bankruptcy administrator, if any) who makes a determination described in this paragraph shall review such determination not later than 1 year after the date of such determination, and not less frequently than annually thereafter.); or

(12) the court after notice and a hearing held not more than 10 days before the date of the entry of the order granting the discharge finds that there is reasonable cause to believe that—

    (A) section 522(q)(1) may be applicable to the debtor; and

(B) there is pending any proceeding in which the debtor may be found guilty of a felony of the kind described in section 522(q)(1)(A) or liable for a debt of the kind described in section 522(q)(1)(B).

(b) Except as provided in section 523 of this title, a discharge under subsection (a) of this section discharges the debtor from all debts that arose before the date of the order for relief under this chapter, and any liability on a claim that is determined under section 502 of this title as if such claim had arisen before the commencement of the case, whether or not a proof of claim based on any such debt or liability is filed under section 501 of this title, and whether or not a claim based on any such debt or liability is allowed under section 502 of this title.

(c)(1) The trustee, a creditor, or the United States trustee may object to the granting of a discharge under subsection (a) of this section.

(2) On request of a party in interest, the court may order the trustee to examine the acts and conduct of the debtor to determine whether a ground exists for denial of discharge.

(d) On request of the trustee, a creditor, or the United States trustee, and after notice and a hearing, the court shall revoke a discharge granted under subsection (a) of this section if—

(1) such discharge was obtained through the fraud of the debtor, and the requesting party did not know of such fraud until after the granting of such discharge;

(2) the debtor acquired property that is property of the estate, or became entitled to acquire property that would be property of the estate, and knowingly and fraudulently failed to report the acquisition of or entitlement to such property, or to deliver or surrender such property to the trustee;

(3) the debtor committed an act specified in subsection (a)(6) of this section; or

(4) the debtor has failed to explain satisfactorily—

(A) a material misstatement in an audit referred to in section 586(f) of title 28; or

(B) a failure to make available for inspection all necessary accounts, papers, documents, financial records, files, and all other papers, things, or property belonging to the debtor that are requested for an audit referred to in section 586(f) of title 28.

(e) The trustee, a creditor, or the United States trustee may request a revocation of a discharge—

(1) under subsection (d)(1) of this section within one year after such discharge is granted; or

(2) under subsection (d)(2) or (d)(3) of this section before the later of—

(A) one year after the granting of such discharge; and

(B) the date the case is closed.

UNOFFICIAL COMMENT

Subsection (a) is the most important part of section 727. It lists the grounds for withholding a discharge from a chapter 7 debtor; these numbered grounds are generally referred to as objections to discharge.

Subsection (c) then tells you who can file a complaint pursuant to Rule 7001 objecting to discharge.

And, subsection (b) tells you which debts are covered by the discharge. Note the limiting phrase in section 727(b): "that arose before the date of the order for relief."

Subsections (d) and (e) deal with the different question of when a discharge should be revoked. Most law school courses do not deal with revocation of a chapter 7 discharge. Most bankruptcy practitioners never deal with revocation of a chapter 7 discharge.

OTHER SECTIONS

Definitions in section 101 are always important, especially "claim" and "debt." Sections 301 and 303 explain the phrase "order for relief."

The term "discharge" is not defined. Section 524 describes the effect of discharge.

Be sure you see the relationship between the section 362 automatic stay which protects any debtor during the bankruptcy case and the section 727 discharge which protects a chapter 7 debtor after the bankruptcy case. And the relationship between section 523 exceptions which affect a particular debt and section 727 objections which affect all debts.

And, if you are working with section 727(a)(2), see how it is both similar to and different from section 548. A common section 727(a)(2) fact pattern involves an individual making transfers on the eve of bankruptcy to maximize her exempt property. Such a fact pattern implicates sections 727(a)(2), 548 and 522.

And, if you are working with section 727(a)(5), see why you don't have to see section 344.

And, if you are working with section 727(d), think about how a waiver of discharge differs from a section 524(b) reaffirmation agreement.

Because of language in section 1141(d)(3)(c), section 727 applies in some chapter 11 cases.

You might find it helpful to find Form 18, on page 285 infra. especially the explanation of discharge that is a part of that form.

* * *

CHAPTER 11—REORGANIZATION

SUBCHAPTER I—OFFICERS AND ADMINISTRATION

SUBCHAPTER I—OFFICERS AND ADMINISTRATION

§ 1101. Definitions for this chapter

In this chapter—

(1) "debtor in possession" means debtor except when a person that has qualified under section 322 of this title is serving as trustee in the case;

(2) "substantial consummation" means—

　(A) transfer of all or substantially all of the property proposed by the plan to be transferred;

　(B) assumption by the debtor or by the successor to the debtor under the plan of the business or of the management of all or substantially all of the property dealt with by the plan; and

　(C) commencement of distribution under the plan.

UNOFFICIAL COMMENTS

A "debtor in possession" is the same as "debtor-in-possession", the same as the "dip" or "DIP." A "debtor in possession" is generally viewed as different from the pre-bankruptcy "debtor." There is some confusion in the case law about differences between the "debtor in possession" and chapter 11 "debtor."

OTHER SECTIONS

When you think about a debtor in possession, you need to think about section 1107 which gives the debtor in possession the rights and powers and duties of a trustee and section 1108 which provides for authority for a trustee (and so a debtor in possession) to operate the chapter 11 debtor's business as a matter of course without court authority.

§ 1102. Creditors' and equity security holders' committees

(a)(1) Except as provided in paragraph (3), as soon as practicable after the order for relief under chapter 11 of this title, the United States trustee shall appoint a committee of creditors holding unsecured claims and may appoint additional committees of creditors or of equity security holders as the United States trustee deems appropriate.

(2) On request of a party in interest, the court may order the appointment of additional committees of creditors or of equity security holders if necessary to assure adequate representation of creditors or of equity security holders. The United States trustee shall appoint any such committee.

(3) On request of a party in interest in a case in which the debtor is a small business debtor and for cause, the court may order that a committee of creditors not be appointed.

(4) On request of a party in interest and after notice and a hearing, the court may order the United States trustee to change the membership of a committee appointed under this subsection, if the court determines that the change is necessary to ensure adequate representation of creditors or equity security holders. The court may order the United States trustee to increase the number of members of a committee to include a creditor that is a small business concern (as described in section 3(a)(1) of the Small Business Act), if the court determines that the creditor holds claims (of the kind represented by the committee) the aggregate amount of which, in comparison to the annual gross revenue of that creditor, is disproportionately large.

(b)(1) A committee of creditors appointed under subsection (a) of this section shall ordinarily consist of the persons, willing to serve, that hold the seven largest claims against the debtor of the kinds represented on such committee, or of the members of a committee organized by creditors before the commencement of the case under this chapter, if such committee was fairly chosen and is representative of the different kinds of claims to be represented.

(2) A committee of equity security holders appointed under subsection (a)(2) of this section shall ordinarily consist of the persons, willing to serve, that hold the seven largest amounts of equity securities of the debtor of the kinds represented on such committee.

(3) A committee appointed under subsection (a) shall—

(A) provide access to information for creditors who—

(i) hold claims of the kind represented by that committee; and

(ii) are not appointed to the committee;

(B) solicit and receive comments from the creditors described in subparagraph (A); and

(C) be subject to a court order that compels any additional report or disclosure to be made to the creditors described in subparagraph (A).

UNOFFICIAL COMMENT

Be sure that you understand the roles of (i) statutory language and (ii) the United States Trustee and (iii) the bankruptcy judge in answering questions about who serves on the committee.

§ 1103. Powers and duties of committees

(a) At a scheduled meeting of a committee appointed under section 1102 of this title, at which a majority of the members of such committee are present, and with the court's approval, such committee may select and authorize the employment by such committee of one or more attorneys, accountants, or other agents, to represent or perform services for such committee.

(b) An attorney or accountant employed to represent a committee appointed under section 1102 of this title may not, while employed by such committee, represent any other entity having an adverse interest in connection with the case. Representation of one or more creditors of the same class as represented by the committee shall not per se constitute the representation of an adverse interest.

(c) A committee appointed under section 1102 of this title may—

(1) consult with the trustee or debtor in possession concerning the administration of the case;

(2) investigate the acts, conduct, assets, liabilities, and financial condition of the debtor, the operation of the debtor's business and the desirability of the continuance of such business, and any other matter relevant to the case or to the formulation of a plan;

(3) participate in the formulation of a plan, advise those represented by such committee of such committee's determinations as to any plan formulated, and collect and file with the court acceptances or rejections of a plan;

(4) request the appointment of a trustee or examiner under section 1104 of this title; and

(5) perform such other services as are in the interest of those represented.

(d) As soon as practicable after the appointment of a committee under section 1102 of this title, the trustee shall meet with such committee to transact such business as may be necessary and proper.

§ 1104. Appointment of trustee or examiner

(a) At any time after the commencement of the case but before confirmation of a plan, on request of a party in interest or the United States trustee, and after notice and a hearing, the court shall order the appointment of a trustee—

(1) for cause, including fraud, dishonesty, incompetence, or gross mismanagement of the affairs of the debtor by current management, either before or after the commencement of the case, or similar cause, but not including the number of holders of securities of the debtor or the amount of assets or liabilities of the debtor; or

(2) if such appointment is in the interests of creditors, any equity security holders, and other interests of the estate, without regard to the number of holders of securities of the debtor or the amount of assets or liabilities of the debtor.

(b)(1) Except as provided in section 1163 of this title, on the request of a party in interest made not later than 30 days after the court orders the appointment of a trustee under subsection (a), the United States trustee shall convene a meeting of creditors for the purpose of electing one disinterested person to serve as trustee in the case. The election of a trustee shall be conducted in the manner provided in subsections (a), (b), and (c) of section 702 of this title.

(2)(A) If an eligible, disinterested trustee is elected at a meeting of creditors under paragraph (1), the United States trustee shall file a report certifying that election.

(B) Upon the filing of a report under subparagraph (A)—

(i) the trustee elected under paragraph (1) shall be considered to have been selected and appointed for purposes of this section; and

(ii) the service of any trustee appointed under subsection (a) shall terminate.

(C) The court shall resolve any dispute arising out of an election described in subparagraph (A).

(c) If the court does not order the appointment of a trustee under this section, then at any time before the confirmation of a plan, on request of a party in interest or the United States trustee, and after notice and a hearing, the court shall order the appointment of an examiner to conduct such an investigation of the debtor as is appropriate, including an investigation of any allegations of fraud, dishonesty, incompetence, misconduct, mismanagement, or irregularity in the management of the affairs of the debtor of or by current or former management of the debtor, if—

(1) such appointment is in the interests of creditors, any equity security holders, and other interests of the estate; or

(2) the debtor's fixed, liquidated, unsecured debts, other than debts for goods, services, or taxes, or owing to an insider, exceed $5,000,000.

(d) If the court orders the appointment of a trustee or an examiner, if a trustee or an examiner dies or resigns during the case or is removed under section 324 of this title, or if a trustee fails to qualify under section 322 of this title, then the United States trustee, after consultation with parties in interest, shall appoint, subject to the court's approval, one disinterested person other than the United States trustee to serve as trustee or examiner, as the case may be, in the case.

(e) The United States trustee shall move for the appointment of a trustee under subsection (a) if there are reasonable grounds to suspect that current members of the governing body of the debtor, the debtor's chief executive or chief financial officer, or members of the governing body who selected the debtor's chief executive or chief financial officer, participated in actual fraud, dishonesty, or criminal conduct in the management of the debtor or the debtor's public financial reporting.

UNOFFICIAL COMMENTS

Section 1104 governs the appointment of a trustee or an examiner in chapter 11 cases. A trustee replaces the debtor in possession; there cannot be both a trustee and a debtor in possession in a chapter 11 case. An examiner does not replace the debtor. A trustee or examiner must be a "disinterested person."

OTHER SECTIONS

Definitions in section 101 are always important: "disinterested person."

Under section 1121, the appointment or election of a trustee terminates the debtor's exclusive period for filing a plan.

§ 1105. Termination of trustee's appointment

At any time before confirmation of a plan, on request of a party in interest or the United States trustee, and after notice and a hearing, the court may terminate the trustee's appointment and restore the debtor to possession and management of the property of the estate and of the operation of the debtor's business.

§ 1106. Duties of trustee and examiner

(a) A trustee shall—

(1) perform the duties of the trustee, as specified in paragraphs (2), (5), (7), (8), (9), (10), (11), and (12) of section 704(a);

(2) if the debtor has not done so, file the list, schedule, and statement required under section 521(a)(1) of this title;

(3) except to the extent that the court orders otherwise, investigate the acts, conduct, assets, liabilities, and financial condition of the debtor, the operation of the debtor's business and the desirability of the continuance of such business, and any other matter relevant to the case or to the formulation of a plan;

(4) as soon as practicable—

(A) file a statement of any investigation conducted under paragraph (3) of this subsection, including any fact ascertained pertaining to fraud, dishonesty, incompetence, misconduct, mismanagement, or irregularity in the management of the affairs of the debtor, or to a cause of action available to the estate; and

(B) transmit a copy or a summary of any such statement to any creditors' committee or equity security holders' committee, to any indenture trustee, and to such other entity as the court designates;

(5) as soon as practicable, file a plan under section 1121 of this title, file a report of why the trustee will not file a plan, or recommend conversion of the case to a case under chapter 7, 12, or 13 of this title or dismissal of the case;

(6) for any year for which the debtor has not filed a tax return required by law, furnish, without personal liability, such information as may be required by the governmental unit with which such tax return was to be filed, in light of the condition of the debtor's books and records and the availability of such information;

(7) after confirmation of a plan, file such reports as are necessary or as the court orders; and

(8) if with respect to the debtor there is a claim for a domestic support obligation, provide the applicable notice specified in subsection (c).

(b) An examiner appointed under section 1104(d) of this title shall perform the duties specified in paragraphs (3) and (4) of subsection (a) of this section, and, except to the extent that the court orders otherwise, any other duties of the trustee that the court orders the debtor in possession not to perform.

* * *

OTHER SECTIONS

Look also to section 1116 if there is a trustee in a "small business" case.

§ 1107. Rights, powers, and duties of debtor in possession

(a) Subject to any limitations on a trustee serving in a case under this chapter, and to such limitations or conditions as the court prescribes, a debtor in possession shall have all the rights, other than the right to compensation under section 330 of this title, and powers, and shall perform all the functions and duties, except the duties specified in sections 1106(a)(2), (3), and (4) of this title, of a trustee serving in a case under this chapter.

* * *

§ 1108. Authorization to operate business

Unless the court, on request of a party in interest and after notice and a hearing, orders otherwise, the trustee may operate the debtor's business.

§ 1109. Right to be heard

(a) The Securities and Exchange Commission may raise and may appear and be heard on any issue in a case under this chapter, but the Securities and Exchange Commission may not appeal from any judgment, order, or decree entered in the case.

(b) A party in interest, including the debtor, the trustee, a creditors' committee, an equity security holders' committee, a creditor, an equity security holder, or any indenture trustee, may raise and may appear and be heard on any issue in a case under this chapter.

* * *

§ 1111. Claims and interests

(a) A proof of claim or interest is deemed filed under section 501 of this title for any claim or interest that appears in the schedules filed under section 521(a)(1) or 1106(a)(2) of this title, except a claim or interest that is scheduled as disputed, contingent, or unliquidated.

(b)(1)(A) A claim secured by a lien on property of the estate shall be allowed or disallowed under section 502 of this title the same as if the holder of such claim had recourse against the debtor on account of such claim, whether or not such holder has such recourse, unless—

> **(i)** the class of which such claim is a part elects, by at least two-thirds in amount and more than half in number of allowed claims of such class, application of paragraph (2) of this subsection; or

> **(ii)** such holder does not have such recourse and such property is sold under section 363 of this title or is to be sold under the plan.

(B) A class of claims may not elect application of paragraph (2) of this subsection if—

> **(i)** the interest on account of such claims of the holders of such claims in such property is of inconsequential value; or

> **(ii)** the holder of a claim of such class has recourse against the debtor on account of such claim and such property is sold under section 363 of this title or is to be sold under the plan.

(2) If such an election is made, then notwithstanding section 506(a) of this title, such claim is a secured claim to the extent that such claim is allowed.

UNOFFICIAL COMMENTS

This section should be at least two different sections. No significant connection between section 1111(a) and section 1111(b).

Section 1111(a) is a part of the claims allowance process. In limited situations, section 1111(a) ignores the section 501 requirement of filing a proof of claim.

Section 1111(b) is a part of the plan confirmation process. In limited situations, section 1111(b) ignores the section 506 definition of secured claim. More specifically, a creditor with a lien can elect to have its entire claim treated as secured, regardless of the value of its collateral. This is cleverly called the "eleven eleven b election."

OTHER SECTIONS

Section 1111(a) should be read together with sections 501 and 502.

It is imperative that section 1111(b) be read together with section 506 and section 1129(b)(2)(A)(i)(II) and that section 1129(b)(2)(A)(i)(II) be read very carefully and thoughtfully. Hard stuff (if you are not using our course materials).

Rule 3014, infra at page 225, sets out the procedure for the section 1111(b) election.

§ 1112. Conversion or dismissal

(a) The debtor may convert a case under this chapter to a case under chapter 7 of this title unless—

(1) the debtor is not a debtor in possession;

(2) the case originally was commenced as an involuntary case under this chapter; or

(3) the case was converted to a case under this chapter other than on the debtor's request.

(b)(1) Except as provided in paragraph (2) and subsection (c), on request of a party in interest, and after notice and a hearing, the court shall convert a case under this chapter to a case under chapter 7 or dismiss a case under this chapter, whichever is in the best interests of creditors and the estate, for cause unless the court determines that the appointment under section 1104(a) of a trustee or an examiner is in the best interests of creditors and the estate.

(2) The court may not convert a case under this chapter to a case under chapter 7 or dismiss a case under this chapter if the court finds and specifically identifies unusual circumstances establishing that converting or dismissing the case is not in the best interests of creditors and the estate, and the debtor or any other party in interest establishes that—

(A) there is a reasonable likelihood that a plan will be confirmed within the timeframes established in sections 1121(e) and 1129(e) of this title, or if such sections do not apply, within a reasonable period of time; and

(B) the grounds for granting such relief include an act or omission of the debtor other than under paragraph (4)(A)—

(i) for which there exists a reasonable justification for the act or omission; and

　　(ii) that will be cured within a reasonable period of time fixed by the court.

(3) The court shall commence the hearing on a motion under this subsection not later than 30 days after filing of the motion, and shall decide the motion not later than 15 days after commencement of such hearing, unless the movant expressly consents to a continuance for a specific period of time or compelling circumstances prevent the court from meeting the time limits established by this paragraph.

(4) For purposes of this subsection, the term "cause" includes—

　　(A) substantial or continuing loss to or diminution of the estate and the absence of a reasonable likelihood of rehabilitation;

　　(B) gross mismanagement of the estate;

　　(C) failure to maintain appropriate insurance that poses a risk to the estate or to the public;

　　(D) unauthorized use of cash collateral substantially harmful to 1 or more creditors;

　　(E) failure to comply with an order of the court;

　　(F) unexcused failure to satisfy timely any filing or reporting requirement established by this title or by any rule applicable to a case under this chapter;

　　(G) failure to attend the meeting of creditors convened under section 341(a) or an examination ordered under rule 2004 of the Federal Rules of Bankruptcy Procedure without good cause shown by the debtor;

　　(H) failure timely to provide information or attend meetings reasonably requested by the United States trustee (or the bankruptcy administrator, if any);

　　(I) failure timely to pay taxes owed after the date of the order for relief or to file tax returns due after the date of the order for relief;

　　(J) failure to file a disclosure statement, or to file or confirm a plan, within the time fixed by this title or by order of the court;

　　(K) failure to pay any fees or charges required under chapter 123 of title 28;

　　(L) revocation of an order of confirmation under section 1144;

　　(M) inability to effectuate substantial consummation of a confirmed plan;

　　(N) material default by the debtor with respect to a confirmed plan;

　　(O) termination of a confirmed plan by reason of the occurrence of a condition specified in the plan; and

　　(P) failure of the debtor to pay any domestic support obligation that first becomes payable after the date of the filing of the petition.

(c) The court may not convert a case under this chapter to a case under chapter 7 of this title if the debtor is a farmer or a corporation that is not a moneyed, business, or commercial corporation, unless the debtor requests such conversion.

(d) The court may convert a case under this chapter to a case under chapter 12 or 13 of this title only if—

　　(1) the debtor requests such conversion;

(2) the debtor has not been discharged under section 1141(d) of this title; and

(3) if the debtor requests conversion to chapter 12 of this title, such conversion is equitable.

(e) Except as provided in subsections (c) and (f), the court, on request of the United States trustee, may convert a case under this chapter to a case under chapter 7 of this title or may dismiss a case under this chapter, whichever is in the best interest of creditors and the estate if the debtor in a voluntary case fails to file, within fifteen days after the filing of the petition commencing such case or such additional time as the court may allow, the information required by paragraph (1) of section 521, including a list containing the names and addresses of the holders of the twenty largest unsecured claims (or of all unsecured claims if there are fewer than twenty unsecured claims), and the approximate dollar amounts of each of such claims.

(f) Notwithstanding any other provision of this section, a case may not be converted to a case under another chapter of this title unless the debtor may be a debtor under such chapter.

OTHER SECTIONS

Section 348 governs the effect of conversion. Section 349 governs the effect of dismissal.

§ 1113. Rejection of collective bargaining agreements

(a) The debtor in possession, or the trustee if one has been appointed under the provisions of this chapter, other than a trustee in a case covered by subchapter IV of this chapter and by title I of the Railway Labor Act, may assume or reject a collective bargaining agreement only in accordance with the provisions of this section.

(b)(1) Subsequent to filing a petition and prior to filing an application seeking rejection of a collective bargaining agreement, the debtor in possession or trustee (hereinafter in this section "trustee" shall include a debtor in possession), shall—

> **(A)** make a proposal to the authorized representative of the employees covered by such agreement, based on the most complete and reliable information available at the time of such proposal, which provides for those necessary modifications in the employees benefits and protections that are necessary to permit the reorganization of the debtor and assures that all creditors, the debtor and all of the affected parties are treated fairly and equitably; and

> **(B)** provide, subject to subsection (d)(3), the representative of the employees with such relevant information as is necessary to evaluate the proposal.

(2) During the period beginning on the date of the making of a proposal provided for in paragraph (1) and ending on the date of the hearing provided for in subsection (d)(1), the trustee shall meet, at reasonable times, with the authorized representative to confer in good faith in attempting to reach mutually satisfactory modifications of such agreement.

(c) The court shall approve an application for rejection of a collective bargaining agreement only if the court finds that—

> **(1)** the trustee has, prior to the hearing, made a proposal that fulfills the requirements of subsection (b)(1);

(2) the authorized representative of the employees has refused to accept such proposal without good cause; and

(3) the balance of the equities clearly favors rejection of such agreement.

(d)(1) Upon the filing of an application for rejection the court shall schedule a hearing to be held not later than fourteen days after the date of the filing of such application. All interested parties may appear and be heard at such hearing. Adequate notice shall be provided to such parties at least ten days before the date of such hearing. The court may extend the time for the commencement of such hearing for a period not exceeding seven days where the circumstances of the case, and the interests of justice require such extension, or for additional periods of time to which the trustee and representative agree.

(2) The court shall rule on such application for rejection within thirty days after the date of the commencement of the hearing. In the interests of justice, the court may extend such time for ruling for such additional period as the trustee and the employees' representative may agree to. If the court does not rule on such application within thirty days after the date of the commencement of the hearing, or within such additional time as the trustee and the employees' representative may agree to, the trustee may terminate or alter any provisions of the collective bargaining agreement pending the ruling of the court on such application.

(3) The court may enter such protective orders, consistent with the need of the authorized representative of the employee to evaluate the trustee's proposal and the application for rejection, as may be necessary to prevent disclosure of information provided to such representative where such disclosure could compromise the position of the debtor with respect to its competitors in the industry in which it is engaged.

(e) If during a period when the collective bargaining agreement continues in effect, and if essential to the continuation of the debtor's business, or in order to avoid irreparable damage to the estate, the court, after notice and a hearing, may authorize the trustee to implement interim changes in the terms, conditions, wages, benefits, or work rules provided by a collective bargaining agreement. Any hearing under this paragraph shall be scheduled in accordance with the needs of the trustee. The implementation of such interim changes shall not render the application for rejection moot.

(f) No provision of this title shall be construed to permit a trustee to unilaterally terminate or alter any provisions of a collective bargaining agreement prior to compliance with the provisions of this section.

§ 1114. Payment of insurance benefits to retired employees

(a) For purposes of this section, the term "retiree benefits" means payments to any entity or person for the purpose of providing or reimbursing payments for retired employees and their spouses and dependents, for medical, surgical, or hospital care benefits, or benefits in the event of sickness, accident, disability, or death under any plan, fund, or program (through the purchase of insurance or otherwise) maintained or established in whole or in part by the debtor prior to filing a petition commencing a case under this title.

(b)(1) For purposes of this section, the term "authorized representative" means the authorized representative designated pursuant to subsection (c) for persons receiving any retiree benefits covered by a collective bargaining agreement or subsection (d) in the case of persons receiving retiree benefits not covered by such an agreement.

(2) Committees of retired employees appointed by the court pursuant to this section shall have the same rights, powers, and duties as committees appointed under sections 1102 and 1103 of this title for the purpose of carrying out the purposes of sections 1114 and 1129(a)(13) and, as permitted by the court, shall have the power to enforce the rights of persons under this title as they relate to retiree benefits.

(c)(1) A labor organization shall be, for purposes of this section, the authorized representative of those persons receiving any retiree benefits covered by any collective bargaining agreement to which that labor organization is signatory, unless (A) such labor organization elects not to serve as the authorized representative of such persons, or (B) the court, upon a motion by any party in interest, after notice and hearing, determines that different representation of such persons is appropriate.

(2) In cases where the labor organization referred to in paragraph (1) elects not to serve as the authorized representative of those persons receiving any retiree benefits covered by any collective bargaining agreement to which that labor organization is signatory, or in cases where the court, pursuant to paragraph (1) finds different representation of such persons appropriate, the court, upon a motion by any party in interest, and after notice and a hearing, shall appoint a committee of retired employees if the debtor seeks to modify or not pay the retiree benefits or if the court otherwise determines that it is appropriate, from among such persons, to serve as the authorized representative of such persons under this section.

(d) The court, upon a motion by any party in interest, and after notice and a hearing, shall order the appointment of a committee of retired employees if the debtor seeks to modify or not pay the retiree benefits or if the court otherwise determines that it is appropriate, to serve as the authorized representative, under this section, of those persons receiving any retiree benefits not covered by a collective bargaining agreement. The United States trustee shall appoint any such committee.

(e)(1) Notwithstanding any other provision of this title, the debtor in possession, or the trustee if one has been appointed under the provisions of this chapter (hereinafter in this section "trustee" shall include a debtor in possession), shall timely pay and shall not modify any retiree benefits, except that—

> **(A)** the court, on motion of the trustee or authorized representative, and after notice and a hearing, may order modification of such payments, pursuant to the provisions of subsections (g) and (h) of this section, or

> **(B)** the trustee and the authorized representative of the recipients of those benefits may agree to modification of such payments,

after which such benefits as modified shall continue to be paid by the trustee.

(2) Any payment for retiree benefits required to be made before a plan confirmed under section 1129 of this title is effective has the status of an allowed administrative expense as provided in section 503 of this title.

(f)(1) Subsequent to filing a petition and prior to filing an application seeking modification of the retiree benefits, the trustee shall—

> **(A)** make a proposal to the authorized representative of the retirees, based on the most complete and reliable information available at the time of such proposal, which provides for those necessary modifications in the retiree benefits that are necessary to permit the reorganization of the debtor and assures that all

creditors, the debtor and all of the affected parties are treated fairly and equitably; and

(B) provide, subject to subsection (k)(3), the representative of the retirees with such relevant information as is necessary to evaluate the proposal.

(2) During the period beginning on the date of the making of a proposal provided for in paragraph (1), and ending on the date of the hearing provided for in subsection (k)(1), the trustee shall meet, at reasonable times, with the authorized representative to confer in good faith in attempting to reach mutually satisfactory modifications of such retiree benefits.

(g) The court shall enter an order providing for modification in the payment of retiree benefits if the court finds that—

(1) the trustee has, prior to the hearing, made a proposal that fulfills the requirements of subsection (f);

(2) the authorized representative of the retirees has refused to accept such proposal without good cause; and

(3) such modification is necessary to permit the reorganization of the debtor and assures that all creditors, the debtor, and all of the affected parties are treated fairly and equitably, and is clearly favored by the balance of the equities;

except that in no case shall the court enter an order providing for such modification which provides for a modification to a level lower than that proposed by the trustee in the proposal found by the court to have complied with the requirements of this subsection and subsection (f): *Provided, however,* That at any time after an order is entered providing for modification in the payment of retiree benefits, or at any time after an agreement modifying such benefits is made between the trustee and the authorized representative of the recipients of such benefits, the authorized representative may apply to the court for an order increasing those benefits which order shall be granted if the increase in retiree benefits sought is consistent with the standard set forth in paragraph (3): *Provided further,* That neither the trustee nor the authorized representative is precluded from making more than one motion for a modification order governed by this subsection.

(h)(1) Prior to a court issuing a final order under subsection (g) of this section, if essential to the continuation of the debtor's business, or in order to avoid irreparable damage to the estate, the court, after notice and a hearing, may authorize the trustee to implement interim modifications in retiree benefits.

(2) Any hearing under this subsection shall be scheduled in accordance with the needs of the trustee.

(3) The implementation of such interim changes does not render the motion for modification moot.

(i) No retiree benefits paid between the filing of the petition and the time a plan confirmed under section 1129 of this title becomes effective shall be deducted or offset from the amounts allowed as claims for any benefits which remain unpaid, or from the amounts to be paid under the plan with respect to such claims for unpaid benefits, whether such claims for unpaid benefits are based upon or arise from a right to future unpaid benefits or from any benefits not paid as a result of modifications allowed pursuant to this section.

(j) No claim for retiree benefits shall be limited by section 502(b)(7) of this title.

(k)(1) Upon the filing of an application for modifying retiree benefits, the court shall schedule a hearing to be held not later than fourteen days after the date of the filing of such application. All interested parties may appear and be heard at such hearing. Adequate notice shall be provided to such parties at least ten days before the date of such hearing. The court may extend the time for the commencement of such hearing for a period not exceeding seven days where the circumstances of the case, and the interests of justice require such extension, or for additional periods of time to which the trustee and the authorized representative agree.

(2) The court shall rule on such application for modification within ninety days after the date of the commencement of the hearing. In the interests of justice, the court may extend such time for ruling for such additional period as the trustee and the authorized representative may agree to. If the court does not rule on such application within ninety days after the date of the commencement of the hearing, or within such additional time as the trustee and the authorized representative may agree to, the trustee may implement the proposed modifications pending the ruling of the court on such application.

(3) The court may enter such protective orders, consistent with the need of the authorized representative of the retirees to evaluate the trustee's proposal and the application for modification, as may be necessary to prevent disclosure of information provided to such representative where such disclosure could compromise the position of the debtor with respect to its competitors in the industry in which it is engaged.

(l) If the debtor, during the 180-day period ending on the date of the filing of the petition—

(1) modified retiree benefits; and

(2) was insolvent on the date such benefits were modified;

the court, on motion of a party in interest, and after notice and a hearing, shall issue an order reinstating as of the date the modification was made, such benefits as in effect immediately before such date unless the court finds that the balance of the equities clearly favors such modification.

(m) This section shall not apply to any retiree, or the spouse or dependents of such retiree, if such retiree's gross income for the twelve months preceding the filing of the bankruptcy petition equals or exceeds $250,000, unless such retiree can demonstrate to the satisfaction of the court that he is unable to obtain health, medical, life, and disability coverage for himself, his spouse, and his dependents who would otherwise be covered by the employer's insurance plan, comparable to the coverage provided by the employer on the day before the filing of a petition under this title.

§ 1115. Property of the estate

(a) In a case in which the debtor is an individual, property of the estate includes, in addition to the property specified in section 541—

(1) all property of the kind specified in section 541 that the debtor acquires after the commencement of the case but before the case is closed, dismissed, or converted to a case under chapter 7, 12, or 13, whichever occurs first; and

(2) earnings from services performed by the debtor after the commencement of the case but before the case is closed, dismissed, or converted to a case under chapter 7, 12, or 13, whichever occurs first.

(b) Except as provided in section 1104 or a confirmed plan or order confirming a plan, the debtor shall remain in possession of all property of the estate.

OTHER SECTIONS

Section 1115 was taken from section 1306.

When you are using section 1115, you also need to use section 541 which governs property of the estate generally and section 522 which provides for the exemption of certain property of the estate.

And, depending on what issues your professor chooses to cover, you may also need to decide whether a chapter 11 debtor's property consists of only section 115 property or both section 541 property and section 1115 in discussing section 1129(b)(2)(B)(ii) and the application of the absolute priority rule to individual chapter 11 debtors.

§ 1116. Duties of trustee or debtor in possession in small business cases

In a small business case, a trustee or the debtor in possession, in addition to the duties provided in this title and as otherwise required by law, shall—

(1) append to the voluntary petition or, in an involuntary case, file not later than 7 days after the date of the order for relief—

(A) its most recent balance sheet, statement of operations, cash-flow statement, and Federal income tax return; or

(B) a statement made under penalty of perjury that no balance sheet, statement of operations, or cash-flow statement has been prepared and no Federal tax return has been filed;

(2) attend, through its senior management personnel and counsel, meetings scheduled by the court or the United States trustee, including initial debtor interviews, scheduling conferences, and meetings of creditors convened under section 341 unless the court, after notice and a hearing, waives that requirement upon a finding of extraordinary and compelling circumstances;

(3) timely file all schedules and statements of financial affairs, unless the court, after notice and a hearing, grants an extension, which shall not extend such time period to a date later than 30 days after the date of the order for relief, absent extraordinary and compelling circumstances;

(4) file all postpetition financial and other reports required by the Federal Rules of Bankruptcy Procedure or by local rule of the district court;

(5) subject to section 363(c)(2), maintain insurance customary and appropriate to the industry;

(6)(A) timely file tax returns and other required government filings; and

(B) subject to section 363(c)(2), timely pay all taxes entitled to administrative expense priority except those being contested by appropriate proceedings being diligently prosecuted; and

(7) allow the United States trustee, or a designated representative of the United States trustee, to inspect the debtor's business premises, books, and records at reasonable times, after reasonable prior written notice, unless notice is waived by the debtor.

SUBCHAPTER II—THE PLAN

§ 1121. Who may file a plan

(a) The debtor may file a plan with a petition commencing a voluntary case, or at any time in a voluntary case or an involuntary case.

(b) Except as otherwise provided in this section, only the debtor may file a plan until after 120 days after the date of the order for relief under this chapter.

(c) Any party in interest, including the debtor, the trustee, a creditors' committee, an equity security holders' committee, a creditor, an equity security holder, or any indenture trustee, may file a plan if and only if—

　(1) a trustee has been appointed under this chapter;

　(2) the debtor has not filed a plan before 120 days after the date of the order for relief under this chapter; or

　(3) the debtor has not filed a plan that has been accepted, before 180 days after the date of the order for relief under this chapter, by each class of claims or interests that is impaired under the plan.

(d)(1) Subject to paragraph (2), on request of a party in interest made within the respective periods specified in subsections (b) and (c) of this section and after notice and a hearing, the court may for cause reduce or increase the 120-day period or the 180-day period referred to in this section.

　(2)(A) The 120-day period specified in paragraph (1) may not be extended beyond a date that is 18 months after the date of the order for relief under this chapter.

　　(B) The 180-day period specified in paragraph (1) may not be extended beyond a date that is 20 months after the date of the order for relief under this chapter.

(e) In a small business case—

　(1) only the debtor may file a plan until after 180 days after the date of the order for relief, unless that period is—

　　(A) extended as provided by this subsection, after notice and a hearing; or

　　(B) the court, for cause, orders otherwise;

　(2) the plan and a disclosure statement (if any) shall be filed not later than 300 days after the date of the order for relief; and

　(3) the time periods specified in paragraphs (1) and (2), and the time fixed in section 1129(e) within which the plan shall be confirmed, may be extended only if—

　　(A) the debtor, after providing notice to parties in interest (including the United States trustee), demonstrates by a preponderance of the evidence that it is more likely than not that the court will confirm a plan within a reasonable period of time;

    (B) a new deadline is imposed at the time the extension is granted; and

    (C) the order extending time is signed before the existing deadline has expired.

UNOFFICIAL COMMENTS

Section 1121 indicates who can file a chapter 11 plan and the time period in which only the debtor in possession can file a plan. That period is commonly referred as to the "exclusivity period."

Note that the 180-day period, like the 120-day period, starts running from the date of the order for relief.

More important, note the words "at any time" in section 1121(a). Expiration of a section 1121 time period only ends the debtor's exclusive right to file a plan, not the debtor's right to file a plan. Increasingly, the important time constraints on filing a petition can be found in the debtors in possession financing agreement, not section 1121.

OTHER SECTIONS

Recall that section 301 and 303 establish the "date of the order for relief."

Section 307 prohibits the U.S. trustee from filing a plan.

Section 1123 governs the content of a plan. Section 1126 and section 1129 govern creditor approval and court approval of plans.

§ 1122. Classification of claims or interests

    (a) Except as provided in subsection (b) of this section, a plan may place a claim or an interest in a particular class only if such claim or interest is substantially similar to the other claims or interests of such class.

    (b) A plan may designate a separate class of claims consisting only of every unsecured claim that is less than or reduced to an amount that the court approves as reasonable and necessary for administrative convenience.

UNOFFICIAL COMMENTS

Read section 1122(a) so carefully that you not only see what section 1122(a) says but also what it does not say. Here is what is not said that is important. First, neither section 1122(a) nor any other Bankruptcy Code provision defines or explains what makes claims "substantially similar." Second, section 1122 (a) does not explain whether all claims that are "substantially similar" must be in the same class.

OTHER SECTIONS

Classification of claims is an important part of the plan process—important in terms of section 1123 "contents of the plan", important in terms of section 1126 "acceptance of the plan," important in terms of section 1129 "confirmation of the plan."

§ 1123. Contents of plan

    (a) Notwithstanding any otherwise applicable nonbankruptcy law, a plan shall—

    (1) designate, subject to section 1122 of this title, classes of claims, other than claims of a kind specified in section 507(a)(2), 507(a)(3), or 507(a)(8) of this title, and classes of interests;

(2) specify any class of claims or interests that is not impaired under the plan;

(3) specify the treatment of any class of claims or interests that is impaired under the plan;

(4) provide the same treatment for each claim or interest of a particular class, unless the holder of a particular claim or interest agrees to a less favorable treatment of such particular claim or interest;

(5) provide adequate means for the plan's implementation, such as—

    (A) retention by the debtor of all or any part of the property of the estate;

    (B) transfer of all or any part of the property of the estate to one or more entities, whether organized before or after the confirmation of such plan;

    (C) merger or consolidation of the debtor with one or more persons;

    (D) sale of all or any part of the property of the estate, either subject to or free of any lien, or the distribution of all or any part of the property of the estate among those having an interest in such property of the estate;

    (E) satisfaction or modification of any lien;

    (F) cancellation or modification of any indenture or similar instrument;

    (G) curing or waiving of any default;

    (H) extension of a maturity date or a change in an interest rate or other term of outstanding securities;

    (I) amendment of the debtor's charter; or

    (J) issuance of securities of the debtor, or of any entity referred to in subparagraph (B) or (C) of this paragraph, for cash, for property, for existing securities, or in exchange for claims or interests, or for any other appropriate purpose;

(6) provide for the inclusion in the charter of the debtor, if the debtor is a corporation, or of any corporation referred to in paragraph (5)(B) or (5)(C) of this subsection, of a provision prohibiting the issuance of nonvoting equity securities, and providing, as to the several classes of securities possessing voting power, an appropriate distribution of such power among such classes, including, in the case of any class of equity securities having a preference over another class of equity securities with respect to dividends, adequate provisions for the election of directors representing such preferred class in the event of default in the payment of such dividends;

(7) contain only provisions that are consistent with the interests of creditors and equity security holders and with public policy with respect to the manner of selection of any officer, director, or trustee under the plan and any successor to such officer, director, or trustee; and

(8) in a case in which the debtor is an individual, provide for the payment to creditors under the plan of all or such portion of earnings from personal services performed by the debtor after the commencement of the case or other future income of the debtor as is necessary for the execution of the plan.

(b) Subject to subsection (a) of this section, a plan may—

(1) impair or leave unimpaired any class of claims, secured or unsecured, or of interests;

(2) subject to section 365 of this title, provide for the assumption, rejection, or assignment of any executory contract or unexpired lease of the debtor not previously rejected under such section;

(3) provide for—

　　(A) the settlement or adjustment of any claim or interest belonging to the debtor or to the estate; or

　　(B) the retention and enforcement by the debtor, by the trustee, or by a representative of the estate appointed for such purpose, of any such claim or interest;

(4) provide for the sale of all or substantially all of the property of the estate, and the distribution of the proceeds of such sale among holders of claims or interests;

(5) modify the rights of holders of secured claims, other than a claim secured only by a security interest in real property that is the debtor's principal residence, or of holders of unsecured claims, or leave unaffected the rights of holders of any class of claims; and

(6) include any other appropriate provision not inconsistent with the applicable provisions of this title.

(c) In a case concerning an individual, a plan proposed by an entity other than the debtor may not provide for the use, sale, or lease of property exempted under section 522 of this title, unless the debtor consents to such use, sale, or lease.

(d) Notwithstanding subsection (a) of this section and sections 506(b), 1129(a)(7), and 1129(b) of this title, if it is proposed in a plan to cure a default the amount necessary to cure the default shall be determined in accordance with the underlying agreement and applicable nonbankruptcy law.

UNOFFICIAL COMMENTS

Section 1123(a) is mandatory; it establishes what a chapter 11 plan must contain. Section 1123(b) is permissive; it provides what a chapter 11 plan may contain.

In a very real sense, section 1126 on acceptance and section 1129 on confirmation also affect the contents of the plan. Since a plan will only become effective with the requisite creditor acceptance and court confirmation, the contents of a plan are very much affected by what creditors will accept and what the court will confirm.

Chapter 11 cases in which the debtor is an individual are comparatively uncommon. Exam coverage of the differences between a chapter 11 case in which the debtor is an individual is more common (because it is so easy to write an exam question exploiting those differences.)

The two most important assets of most individuals are her (1) house and (2) car. With respect to "the debtor's principal residence," section 1123(b)(5) is similar to section 1322(b)(2). There is no chapter 11 counterpart to section 1325(a) provision regarding motor vehicles.

There is no chapter 13 counterpart to section 1126.

OTHER SECTIONS

Section 1123 repeatedly uses the term "class." Classification of claims is governed by section 1122.

Section 1123 repeatedly uses the term "impair." That term is explained in section 1124.

Think about a sale pursuant to section 363(b) as an alternative to a chapter 11 plan that provides for the "sale of all or substantially all" pursuant to section 1123(b)(4).

And, think about how the time deadlines in section 365(d) limit the practical significance of section 1123(b)(2).

§ 1124. Impairment of claims or interests

Except as provided in section 1123(a)(4) of this title, a class of claims or interests is impaired under a plan unless, with respect to each claim or interest of such class, the plan—

   (1) leaves unaltered the legal, equitable, and contractual rights to which such claim or interest entitles the holder of such claim or interest; or

   (2) notwithstanding any contractual provision or applicable law that entitles the holder of such claim or interest to demand or receive accelerated payment of such claim or interest after the occurrence of a default—

      (A) cures any such default that occurred before or after the commencement of the case under this title, other than a default of a kind specified in section 365(b)(2) of this title or of a kind that section 365(b)(2) expressly does not require to be cured;

      (B) reinstates the maturity of such claim or interest as such maturity existed before such default;

      (C) compensates the holder of such claim or interest for any damages incurred as a result of any reasonable reliance by such holder on such contractual provision or such applicable law;

      (D) if such claim or such interest arises from any failure to perform a nonmonetary obligation, other than a default arising from failure to operate a nonresidential real property lease subject to section 365(b)(1)(A), compensates the holder of such claim or such interest (other than the debtor or an insider) for any actual pecuniary loss incurred by such holder as a result of such failure; and

      (E) does not otherwise alter the legal, equitable, or contractual rights to which such claim or interest entitles the holder of such claim or interest.

UNOFFICIAL COMMENTS

Notice the focus in section 1124 is on whether a "class of claims" is impaired, not whether a claim is impaired.

The key to understanding "impaired" is understanding the word "unaltered"—a term not defined in the Bankruptcy Code but regularly used by the cases applying section 1124. And, understanding "impaired" is one of the keys to understanding the chapter 11 plan process.

OTHER SECTIONS

Look to section 1122 for information on classification of claims.

Reading section 1126(f) together with section 1123(a)(3), we see that a chapter 11 plan is not required to impair all classes of claims but that the plan must "specify the treatment" of impaired classes.

Impairment is relevant in determining which classes of claims have to accept a plan under sections 1126 and 1129.

§ 1125. Postpetition disclosure and solicitation

(a) In this section—

(1) "adequate information" means information of a kind, and in sufficient detail, as far as is reasonably practicable in light of the nature and history of the debtor and the condition of the debtor's books and records, including a discussion of the potential material Federal tax consequences of the plan to the debtor, any successor to the debtor, and a hypothetical investor typical of the holders of claims or interests in the case, that would enable such a hypothetical investor of the relevant class to make an informed judgment about the plan, but adequate information need not include such information about any other possible or proposed plan and in determining whether a disclosure statement provides adequate information, the court shall consider the complexity of the case, the benefit of additional information to creditors and other parties in interest, and the cost of providing additional information; and

(2) "investor typical of holders of claims or interests of the relevant class" means investor having—

(A) a claim or interest of the relevant class;

(B) such a relationship with the debtor as the holders of other claims or interests of such class generally have; and

(C) such ability to obtain such information from sources other than the disclosure required by this section as holders of claims or interests in such class generally have.

(b) An acceptance or rejection of a plan may not be solicited after the commencement of the case under this title from a holder of a claim or interest with respect to such claim or interest, unless, at the time of or before such solicitation, there is transmitted to such holder the plan or a summary of the plan, and a written disclosure statement approved, after notice and a hearing, by the court as containing adequate information. The court may approve a disclosure statement without a valuation of the debtor or an appraisal of the debtor's assets.

(c) The same disclosure statement shall be transmitted to each holder of a claim or interest of a particular class, but there may be transmitted different disclosure statements, differing in amount, detail, or kind of information, as between classes.

(d) Whether a disclosure statement required under subsection (b) of this section contains adequate information is not governed by any otherwise applicable nonbankruptcy law, rule, or regulation, but an agency or official whose duty is to administer or enforce such a law, rule, or regulation may be heard on the issue of whether a disclosure statement contains adequate information. Such an agency or official may not appeal from, or otherwise seek review of, an order approving a disclosure statement.

(e) A person that solicits acceptance or rejection of a plan, in good faith and in compliance with the applicable provisions of this title, or that participates, in good faith and in compliance with the applicable provisions of this title, in the offer, issuance, sale, or purchase of a security, offered or sold under the plan, of the debtor, of an affiliate participating in a joint plan with the debtor, or of a newly organized successor to the debtor under the plan, is not liable, on account of such solicitation or participation, for violation of any applicable law, rule, or regulation governing solicitation of acceptance or rejection of a plan or the offer, issuance, sale, or purchase of securities.

(f) Notwithstanding subsection (b), in a small business case—

    (1) the court may determine that the plan itself provides adequate information and that a separate disclosure statement is not necessary;

    (2) the court may approve a disclosure statement submitted on standard forms approved by the court or adopted under section 2075 of title 28; and

    (3)(A) the court may conditionally approve a disclosure statement subject to final approval after notice and a hearing;

        (B) acceptances and rejections of a plan may be solicited based on a conditionally approved disclosure statement if the debtor provides adequate information to each holder of a claim or interest that is solicited, but a conditionally approved disclosure statement shall be mailed not later than 25 days before the date of the hearing on confirmation of the plan; and

        (C) the hearing on the disclosure statement may be combined with the hearing on confirmation of a plan.

(g) Notwithstanding subsection (b), an acceptance or rejection of the plan may be solicited from a holder of a claim or interest if such solicitation complies with applicable nonbankruptcy law and if such holder was solicited before the commencement of the case in a manner complying with applicable nonbankruptcy law.

UNOFFICIAL COMMENT

Creditors vote on a chapter 11 plan and so should have some idea about what is in the plan and why the plan proponent thinks that the plan will work. Accordingly, section 1125 requires (i) preparation of a disclosure statement with "adequate information, (ii) court approval of that disclosure statement and (iii) distribution of that disclosure statement to creditors before they vote."

If you are concerned with a "pre-pack", then you are concerned about section 1125(g) which, in essence, reverses the order of (ii) and (iii) above. If you are looking at a pre-pack problem, then you also need to look at section 1126(b).

§ 1126. Acceptance of plan

    (a) The holder of a claim or interest allowed under section 502 of this title may accept or reject a plan. * * *

    (b) For the purposes of subsections (c) and (d) of this section, a holder of a claim or interest that has accepted or rejected the plan before the commencement of the case under this title is deemed to have accepted or rejected such plan, as the case may be, if—

    (1) the solicitation of such acceptance or rejection was in compliance with any applicable nonbankruptcy law, rule, or regulation governing the adequacy of disclosure in connection with such solicitation; or

    (2) if there is not any such law, rule, or regulation, such acceptance or rejection was solicited after disclosure to such holder of adequate information, as defined in section 1125(a) of this title.

    (c) A class of claims has accepted a plan if such plan has been accepted by creditors, other than any entity designated under subsection (e) of this section, that hold at least two-thirds in amount and more than one-half in number of the allowed claims of such class held by creditors, other than any entity designated under subsection (e) of this section, that have accepted or rejected such plan.

(d) A class of interests has accepted a plan if such plan has been accepted by holders of such interests, other than any entity designated under subsection (e) of this section, that hold at least two-thirds in amount of the allowed interests of such class held by holders of such interests, other than any entity designated under subsection (e) of this section, that have accepted or rejected such plan.

(e) On request of a party in interest, and after notice and a hearing, the court may designate any entity whose acceptance or rejection of such plan was not in good faith, or was not solicited or procured in good faith or in accordance with the provisions of this title.

(f) Notwithstanding any other provision of this section, a class that is not impaired under a plan, and each holder of a claim or interest of such class, are conclusively presumed to have accepted the plan, and solicitation of acceptances with respect to such class from the holders of claims or interests of such class is not required.

(g) Notwithstanding any other provision of this section, a class is deemed not to have accepted a plan if such plan provides that the claims or interests of such class do not entitle the holders of such claims or interests to receive or retain any property under the plan on account of such claims or interests.

UNOFFICIAL COMMENT

In applying the numerical requirements of section 1126(c), please pay special attention to the final phrase "that have accepted or rejected such plan." If there are 23 claims in a class but only 11 vote on the plan, then the requirement of "more than one-half in number" means 6 or more.

When you see the verb "designate" in section 1126(c) and (e). think "disregard" or "throw out."

OTHER SECTIONS

Classification of claims is explained in section 1122. Impairment is explained in section 1124.

Creditor acceptance of a plan is an important part of court approval of a plan under section 1129(a)(8), 1129(a)(10) and 1129(b).

Look to Form 14 on page 283 infra to see how creditors vote on a plan.

§ 1127. Modification of plan

(a) The proponent of a plan may modify such plan at any time before confirmation, but may not modify such plan so that such plan as modified fails to meet the requirements of sections 1122 and 1123 of this title. After the proponent of a plan files a modification of such plan with the court, the plan as modified becomes the plan.

(b) The proponent of a plan or the reorganized debtor may modify such plan at any time after confirmation of such plan and before substantial consummation of such plan, but may not modify such plan so that such plan as modified fails to meet the requirements of sections 1122 and 1123 of this title. Such plan as modified under this subsection becomes the plan only if circumstances warrant such modification and the court, after notice and a hearing, confirms such plan as modified, under section 1129 of this title.

(c) The proponent of a modification shall comply with section 1125 of this title with respect to the plan as modified.

(d) Any holder of a claim or interest that has accepted or rejected a plan is deemed to have accepted or rejected, as the case may be, such plan as modified, unless, within the time fixed by the court, such holder changes such holder's previous acceptance or rejection.

(e) If the debtor is an individual, the plan may be modified at any time after confirmation of the plan but before the completion of payments under the plan, whether or not the plan has been substantially consummated, upon request of the debtor, the trustee, the United States trustee, or the holder of an allowed unsecured claim, to—

> **(1)** increase or reduce the amount of payments on claims of a particular class provided for by the plan;

> **(2)** extend or reduce the time period for such payments; or

> **(3)** alter the amount of the distribution to a creditor whose claim is provided for by the plan to the extent necessary to take account of any payment of such claim made other than under the plan.

(f)(1) Sections 1121 through 1128 and the requirements of section 1129 apply to any modification under subsection (e).

> **(2)** The plan, as modified, shall become the plan only after there has been disclosure under section 1125 as the court may direct, notice and a hearing, and such modification is approved.

§ 1128. Confirmation hearing

(a) After notice, the court shall hold a hearing on confirmation of a plan.

(b) A party in interest may object to confirmation of a plan.

§ 1129. Confirmation of plan

(a) The court shall confirm a plan only if all of the following requirements are met:

> **(1)** The plan complies with the applicable provisions of this title.

> **(2)** The proponent of the plan complies with the applicable provisions of this title.

> **(3)** The plan has been proposed in good faith and not by any means forbidden by law.

> **(4)** Any payment made or to be made by the proponent, by the debtor, or by a person issuing securities or acquiring property under the plan, for services or for costs and expenses in or in connection with the case, or in connection with the plan and incident to the case, has been approved by, or is subject to the approval of, the court as reasonable.

> **(5)(A)(i)** The proponent of the plan has disclosed the identity and affiliations of any individual proposed to serve, after confirmation of the plan, as a director, officer, or voting trustee of the debtor, an affiliate of the debtor participating in a joint plan with the debtor, or a successor to the debtor under the plan; and

>> **(ii)** the appointment to, or continuance in, such office of such individual, is consistent with the interests of creditors and equity security holders and with public policy; and

> **(B)** the proponent of the plan has disclosed the identity of any insider that will be employed or retained by the reorganized debtor, and the nature of any compensation for such insider.

(6) Any governmental regulatory commission with jurisdiction, after confirmation of the plan, over the rates of the debtor has approved any rate change provided for in the plan, or such rate change is expressly conditioned on such approval.

(7) With respect to each impaired class of claims or interests—

    (A) each holder of a claim or interest of such class—

        (i) has accepted the plan; or

        (ii) will receive or retain under the plan on account of such claim or interest property of a value, as of the effective date of the plan, that is not less than the amount that such holder would so receive or retain if the debtor were liquidated under chapter 7 of this title on such date; or

    (B) if section 1111(b)(2) of this title applies to the claims of such class, each holder of a claim of such class will receive or retain under the plan on account of such claim property of a value, as of the effective date of the plan, that is not less than the value of such holder's interest in the estate's interest in the property that secures such claims.

(8) With respect to each class of claims or interests—

    (A) such class has accepted the plan; or

    (B) such class is not impaired under the plan.

(9) Except to the extent that the holder of a particular claim has agreed to a different treatment of such claim, the plan provides that—

    (A) with respect to a claim of a kind specified in section 507(a)(2) or 507(a)(3) of this title, on the effective date of the plan, the holder of such claim will receive on account of such claim cash equal to the allowed amount of such claim;

    (B) with respect to a class of claims of a kind specified in section 507(a)(1), 507(a)(4), 507(a)(5), 507(a)(6), or 507(a)(7) of this title, each holder of a claim of such class will receive—

        (i) if such class has accepted the plan, deferred cash payments of a value, as of the effective date of the plan, equal to the allowed amount of such claim; or

        (ii) if such class has not accepted the plan, cash on the effective date of the plan equal to the allowed amount of such claim;

    (C) with respect to a claim of a kind specified in section 507(a)(8) of this title, the holder of such claim will receive on account of such claim regular installment payments in cash—

        (i) of a total value, as of the effective date of the plan, equal to the allowed amount of such claim;

        (ii) over a period ending not later than 5 years after the date of the order for relief under section 301, 302, or 303; and

        (iii) in a manner not less favorable than the most favored nonpriority unsecured claim provided for by the plan (other than cash payments made to a class of creditors under section 1122(b)); and

(D) with respect to a secured claim which would otherwise meet the description of an unsecured claim of a governmental unit under section 507(a)(8), but for the secured status of that claim, the holder of that claim will receive on account of that claim, cash payments, in the same manner and over the same period, as prescribed in subparagraph (C).

(10) If a class of claims is impaired under the plan, at least one class of claims that is impaired under the plan has accepted the plan, determined without including any acceptance of the plan by any insider.

(11) Confirmation of the plan is not likely to be followed by the liquidation, or the need for further financial reorganization, of the debtor or any successor to the debtor under the plan, unless such liquidation or reorganization is proposed in the plan.

(12) All fees payable under section 1930 of title 28, as determined by the court at the hearing on confirmation of the plan, have been paid or the plan provides for the payment of all such fees on the effective date of the plan.

(13) The plan provides for the continuation after its effective date of payment of all retiree benefits, as that term is defined in section 1114 of this title, at the level established pursuant to subsection (e)(1)(B) or (g) of section 1114 of this title, at any time prior to confirmation of the plan, for the duration of the period the debtor has obligated itself to provide such benefits.

(14) If the debtor is required by a judicial or administrative order, or by statute, to pay a domestic support obligation, the debtor has paid all amounts payable under such order or such statute for such obligation that first become payable after the date of the filing of the petition.

(15) In a case in which the debtor is an individual and in which the holder of an allowed unsecured claim objects to the confirmation of the plan—

(A) the value, as of the effective date of the plan, of the property to be distributed under the plan on account of such claim is not less than the amount of such claim; or

(B) the value of the property to be distributed under the plan is not less than the projected disposable income of the debtor (as defined in section 1325(b)(2)) to be received during the 5-year period beginning on the date that the first payment is due under the plan, or during the period for which the plan provides payments, whichever is longer.

(16) All transfers of property under the plan shall be made in accordance with any applicable provisions of nonbankruptcy law that govern the transfer of property by a corporation or trust that is not a moneyed, business, or commercial corporation or trust.

(b)(1) Notwithstanding section 510(a) of this title, if all of the applicable requirements of subsection (a) of this section other than paragraph (8) are met with respect to a plan, the court, on request of the proponent of the plan, shall confirm the plan notwithstanding the requirements of such paragraph if the plan does not discriminate unfairly, and is fair and equitable, with respect to each class of claims or interests that is impaired under, and has not accepted, the plan.

(2) For the purpose of this subsection, the condition that a plan be fair and equitable with respect to a class includes the following requirements:

(A) With respect to a class of secured claims, the plan provides—

(i)(I) that the holders of such claims retain the liens securing such claims, whether the property subject to such liens is retained by the debtor or transferred to another entity, to the extent of the allowed amount of such claims; and

(II) that each holder of a claim of such class receive on account of such claim deferred cash payments totaling at least the allowed amount of such claim, of a value, as of the effective date of the plan, of at least the value of such holder's interest in the estate's interest in such property;

(ii) for the sale, subject to section 363(k) of this title, of any property that is subject to the liens securing such claims, free and clear of such liens, with such liens to attach to the proceeds of such sale, and the treatment of such liens on proceeds under clause (i) or (iii) of this subparagraph; or

(iii) for the realization by such holders of the indubitable equivalent of such claims.

(B) With respect to a class of unsecured claims—

(i) the plan provides that each holder of a claim of such class receive or retain on account of such claim property of a value, as of the effective date of the plan, equal to the allowed amount of such claim; or

(ii) the holder of any claim or interest that is junior to the claims of such class will not receive or retain under the plan on account of such junior claim or interest any property, except that in a case in which the debtor is an individual, the debtor may retain property included in the estate under section 1115, subject to the requirements of subsection (a)(14) of this section.

(C) With respect to a class of interests—

(i) the plan provides that each holder of an interest of such class receive or retain on account of such interest property of a value, as of the effective date of the plan, equal to the greatest of the allowed amount of any fixed liquidation preference to which such holder is entitled, any fixed redemption price to which such holder is entitled, or the value of such interest; or

(ii) the holder of any interest that is junior to the interests of such class will not receive or retain under the plan on account of such junior interest any property.

(c) Notwithstanding subsections (a) and (b) of this section and except as provided in section 1127(b) of this title, the court may confirm only one plan, unless the order of confirmation in the case has been revoked under section 1144 of this title. If the requirements of subsections (a) and (b) of this section are met with respect to more than one plan, the court shall consider the preferences of creditors and equity security holders in determining which plan to confirm.

(d) Notwithstanding any other provision of this section, on request of a party in interest that is a governmental unit, the court may not confirm a plan if the principal purpose of the plan is the avoidance of taxes or the avoidance of the application of section

5 of the Securities Act of 1933. In any hearing under this subsection, the governmental unit has the burden of proof on the issue of avoidance.

(e) In a small business case, the court shall confirm a plan that complies with the applicable provisions of this title and that is filed in accordance with section 1121(e) not later than 45 days after the plan is filed unless the time for confirmation is extended in accordance with section 1121(e)(3).

UNOFFICIAL COMMENTS

"Confirmation" is another way of saying "court approval of a plan." And, court approval of a plan is required even if the creditor approval is unanimous.

Subsection (a) of section 1129 has 16 numbered requirements. Law school classes that cover section 1129(a) typically cover 4 of the 16: (7) which is often referred to as the "best interests" requirement, (11) which is often referred as to the "feasibility" requirement and (8) and (10).

If you read 1129(a)(8) and (10) together, then section 1129(a)(10) does not seem to add anything to section 1129(a)(8). You need to read both (a)(8) and (a)(10) together with the prefatory language in section 1129(b).

In essence, section 1129(a)(10) which requires acceptance by the requisite majorities of at least one of the impaired classes of claim is the minimum that must always be met. While, in the real world, section 1129(a)(8) which requires acceptance by the requisite majorities of all impaired classes is usually met, a plan can be confirmed under section 1129(b) if all the requirements of section 1129(a) other than 1129(a)(8) are met and the additional requirements of section 1129(b) are also met.

Confirmation under section 1129(b) is generally referred to as "cram down." The term "cram down" does not appear in the Bankruptcy Code. It describes court-imposed changes on a class of claims that were not approved by the requisite majorities of the class.

Again, you can do section 1129(b) only if all of the requirements of section 1129(a) other than section 1129(a)(8) have been satisfied. And, in doing section 1129(b), you have to do two additional requirements with respect to each class that has not accepted the plan.

First, "not discriminate unfairly." A plan may discriminate among classes. E.g., class 3 gets cash, class 4 gets notes. No express statutory ban on treating the various classes differently. If, however, a class does not accept the plan, it will be necessary under section 1129(b) to show that the plan does not discriminate "unfairly" against that class. No statutory definition of "unfairly."

Second, "fair and equitable" (also known as the "absolute priority rule"). That gets you into section 1129(b)(2). In doing section 1129(b)(2), notice separate requirements apply depending on whether the non-assenting class is (A) secured claims or (B) unsecured claims or (C) "interests." Also, note that the prefatory language uses the verb "includes," not "is" or "means" so that merely satisfying (A) or (B) or (C) might not satisfy the requirement of "fair and equitable."

To the extent that law school bankruptcy classes cover section 1129(b)(2), the coverage is generally limited to section 1129(b)(2)(A). In applying section 1129(b)(2)(A) to a non-assenting class of secured claims, it is important to know (1) the value of the collateral and (2) the appropriate cram down interest rate ("value as of the effective date of the plan"). It is also necessary to know (1) whether there been a section 1111(b) election and (2) what a section 1111(b) election means and (3) what "totaling at least the allowed amount of such claim" and "value, as of the effective date of the plan, of at least the value of such holder's interest" mean when there has been a section 1111(b) election.

Chapter 11 cases in which the debtor is an individual are comparatively uncommon. Coverage of the differences between a chapter 11 case in which the debtor is an individual is more common (because it is so easy to write an exam question exploiting those differences.) The two most important assets of most individuals are her (1) car and (2) house. There is no section 1129 counterpart to section 1325(a) provision regarding motor vehicles With respect to "the debtor's principal residence," section 1123(b)(5) is similar to section 1322(b)(2).

SUBCHAPTER III—POSTCONFIRMATION MATTERS

§ 1141. Effect of confirmation

(a) Except as provided in subsections (d)(2) and (d)(3) of this section, the provisions of a confirmed plan bind the debtor, any entity issuing securities under the plan, any entity acquiring property under the plan, and any creditor, equity security holder, or general partner in the debtor, whether or not the claim or interest of such creditor, equity security holder, or general partner is impaired under the plan and whether or not such creditor, equity security holder, or general partner has accepted the plan.

(b) Except as otherwise provided in the plan or the order confirming the plan, the confirmation of a plan vests all of the property of the estate in the debtor.

(c) Except as provided in subsections (d)(2) and (d)(3) of this section and except as otherwise provided in the plan or in the order confirming the plan, after confirmation of a plan, the property dealt with by the plan is free and clear of all claims and interests of creditors, equity security holders, and of general partners in the debtor.

(d)(1) Except as otherwise provided in this subsection, in the plan, or in the order confirming the plan, the confirmation of a plan—

    (A) discharges the debtor from any debt that arose before the date of such confirmation, and any debt of a kind specified in section 502(g), 502(h), or 502(i) of this title, whether or not—

        (i) a proof of the claim based on such debt is filed or deemed filed under section 501 of this title;

        (ii) such claim is allowed under section 502 of this title; or

        (iii) the holder of such claim has accepted the plan; and

    (B) terminates all rights and interests of equity security holders and general partners provided for by the plan.

(2) A discharge under this chapter does not discharge a debtor who is an individual from any debt excepted from discharge under section 523 of this title.

(3) The confirmation of a plan does not discharge a debtor if—

    (A) the plan provides for the liquidation of all or substantially all of the property of the estate;

    (B) the debtor does not engage in business after consummation of the plan; and

    (C) the debtor would be denied a discharge under section 727(a) of this title if the case were a case under chapter 7 of this title.

166

(4) The court may approve a written waiver of discharge executed by the debtor after the order for relief under this chapter.

(5) In a case in which the debtor is an individual—

    (A) unless after notice and a hearing the court orders otherwise for cause, confirmation of the plan does not discharge any debt provided for in the plan until the court grants a discharge on completion of all payments under the plan;

    (B) at any time after the confirmation of the plan, and after notice and a hearing, the court may grant a discharge to the debtor who has not completed payments under the plan if—

        (i) the value, as of the effective date of the plan, of property actually distributed under the plan on account of each allowed unsecured claim is not less than the amount that would have been paid on such claim if the estate of the debtor had been liquidated under chapter 7 on such date; and

        (ii) modification of the plan under section 1127 is not practicable; and

* * *

UNOFFICIAL COMMENTS

Look to section 1141(a) to see who is affected by plan confirmation—"notice the phrases whether or not such creditor * * * has accepted the plan."

Look to section 1141(d) to see the primary effect of confirmation—a discharge. One more time. In chapter 11, unlike chapter 13, the debtor receives a discharge when the court confirms the plan, not when the debtor completes its plan payment obligations. The payment obligations of a chapter 11 debtor are replaced by its plan obligations. Compare the general discharge of section 1141(d)(1)(A) with the more limited discharge for individual debtors in section 1141(d)(2).

In determining whether the discharge should be denied because of section 1141(d)(3) notice the conjunction "and" which connects (A) with (B) with (C) and in applying (C) pay special attention to 727(a)(1).

OTHER SECTIONS

Section 524(a) deals with the effect of a discharge generally.

Section 1141(d)(5) was adapted from section 1328.

§ 1142. Implementation of plan

(a) Notwithstanding any otherwise applicable nonbankruptcy law, rule, or regulation relating to financial condition, the debtor and any entity organized or to be organized for the purpose of carrying out the plan shall carry out the plan and shall comply with any orders of the court.

(b) The court may direct the debtor and any other necessary party to execute or deliver or to join in the execution or delivery of any instrument required to effect a transfer of property dealt with by a confirmed plan, and to perform any other act, including the satisfaction of any lien, that is necessary for the consummation of the plan.

§ 1143. Distribution

If a plan requires presentment or surrender of a security or the performance of any other act as a condition to participation in distribution under the plan, such action shall be taken not later than five years after the date of the entry of the order of confirmation. Any entity that has not within such time presented or surrendered such entity's security or taken any such other action that the plan requires may not participate in distribution under the plan.

§ 1144. Revocation of an order of confirmation

On request of a party in interest at any time before 180 days after the date of the entry of the order of confirmation, and after notice and a hearing, the court may revoke such order if and only if such order was procured by fraud. An order under this section revoking an order of confirmation shall—

(1) contain such provisions as are necessary to protect any entity acquiring rights in good faith reliance on the order of confirmation; and

(2) revoke the discharge of the debtor.

§ 1145. Exemption from securities laws

(a) Except with respect to an entity that is an underwriter as defined in subsection (b) of this section, section 5 of the Securities Act of 1933 and any State or local law requiring registration for offer or sale of a security or registration or licensing of an issuer of, underwriter of, or broker or dealer in, a security do not apply to—

(1) the offer or sale under a plan of a security of the debtor, of an affiliate participating in a joint plan with the debtor, or of a successor to the debtor under the plan—

(A) in exchange for a claim against, an interest in, or a claim for an administrative expense in the case concerning, the debtor or such affiliate; or

(B) principally in such exchange and partly for cash or property;

(2) the offer of a security through any warrant, option, right to subscribe, or conversion privilege that was sold in the manner specified in paragraph (1) of this subsection, or the sale of a security upon the exercise of such a warrant, option, right, or privilege;

(3) the offer or sale, other than under a plan, of a security of an issuer other than the debtor or an affiliate, if—

(A) such security was owned by the debtor on the date of the filing of the petition;

(B) the issuer of such security is—

(i) required to file reports under section 13 or 15(d) of the Securities Exchange Act of 1934; and

(ii) in compliance with the disclosure and reporting provision of such applicable section; and

(C) such offer or sale is of securities that do not exceed—

(i) during the two-year period immediately following the date of the filing of the petition, four percent of the securities of such class outstanding on such date; and

      (ii) during any 180-day period following such two-year period, one percent of the securities outstanding at the beginning of such 180-day period; or

* * *

§1146. Special tax provisions

    (a) The issuance, transfer, or exchange of a security, or the making or delivery of an instrument of transfer under a plan confirmed under section 1129 of this title, may not be taxed under any law imposing a stamp tax or similar tax.

    (b) The court may authorize the proponent of a plan to request a determination, limited to questions of law, by a State or local governmental unit charged with responsibility for collection or determination of a tax on or measured by income, of the tax effects, under section 346 of this title and under the law imposing such tax, of the plan. In the event of an actual controversy, the court may declare such effects after the earlier of—

      (1) the date on which such governmental unit responds to the request under this subsection; or

      (2) 270 days after such request.

* * *

CHAPTER 12—ADJUSTMENT OF DEBTS OF A FAMILY FARMER OR FISHERMAN WITH REGULAR ANNUAL INCOME

SUBCHAPTER I—OFFICERS, ADMINISTRATION, AND THE ESTATE

SUBCHAPTER II—THE PLAN

§ 1201. Stay of action against codebtor

(a) Except as provided in subsections (b) and (c) of this section, after the order for relief under this chapter, a creditor may not act, or commence or continue any civil action, to collect all or any part of a consumer debt of the debtor from any individual that is liable on such debt with the debtor, or that secured such debt, unless—

    (1) such individual became liable on or secured such debt in the ordinary course of such individual's business; or

    (2) the case is closed, dismissed, or converted to a case under chapter 7 of this title.

(b) A creditor may present a negotiable instrument, and may give notice of dishonor of such an instrument.

(c) On request of a party in interest and after notice and a hearing, the court shall grant relief from the stay provided by subsection (a) of this section with respect to a creditor, to the extent that—

    (1) as between the debtor and the individual protected under subsection (a) of this section, such individual received the consideration for the claim held by such creditor;

    (2) the plan filed by the debtor proposes not to pay such claim; or

    (3) such creditor's interest would be irreparably harmed by continuation of such stay.

(d) Twenty days after the filing of a request under subsection (c)(2) of this section for relief from the stay provided by subsection (a) of this section, such stay is terminated with respect to the party in interest making such request, unless the debtor or any individual that is liable on such debt with the debtor files and serves upon such party in interest a written objection to the taking of the proposed action.

* * *

§ 1207. Property of the estate

(a) Property of the estate includes, in addition to the property specified in *section 541* of this title—

    (1) all property of the kind specified in such section that the debtor acquires after the commencement of the case but before the case is closed, dismissed, or converted to a case under chapter 7 of this title, whichever occurs first; and

    (2) earnings from services performed by the debtor after the commencement of the case but before the case is closed, dismissed, or converted to a case under chapter 7 of this title, whichever occurs first.

(b) Except as provided in *section 1204*, a confirmed plan, or an order confirming a plan, the debtor shall remain in possession of all property of the estate

* * *

§ 1221. Filing of plan

The debtor shall file a plan not later than 90 days after the order for relief under this chapter, except that the court may extend such period if the need for an extension is attributable to circumstances for which the debtor should not justly be held accountable.

§ 1222. Contents of plan

(a) The plan shall—

(1) provide for the submission of all or such portion of future earnings or other future income of the debtor to the supervision and control of the trustee as is necessary for the execution of the plan;

(2) provide for the full payment, in deferred cash payments, of all claims entitled to priority under *section 507*, unless—

    (A) the claim is a claim owed to a governmental unit that arises as a result of the sale, transfer, exchange, or other disposition of any farm asset used in the debtor's farming operation, in which case the claim shall be treated as an unsecured claim that is not entitled to priority under *section 507*, but the debt shall be treated in such manner only if the debtor receives a discharge; or

    (B) the holder of a particular claim agrees to a different treatment of that claim;

(3) if the plan classifies claims and interests, provide the same treatment for each claim or interest within a particular class unless the holder of a particular claim or interest agrees to less favorable treatment; and

(4) notwithstanding any other provision of this section, a plan may provide for less than full payment of all amounts owed for a claim entitled to priority under *section 507(a)(1)(B)* only if the plan provides that all of the debtor's projected disposable income for a 5-year period beginning on the date that the first payment is due under the plan will be applied to make payments under the plan.

(b) Subject to subsections (a) and (c) of this section, the plan may—

(1) designate a class or classes of unsecured claims, as provided in *section 1122* of this title, but may not discriminate unfairly against any class so designated; however, such plan may treat claims for a consumer debt of the debtor if an individual is liable on such consumer debt with the debtor differently than other unsecured claims;

(2) modify the rights of holders of secured claims, or of holders of unsecured claims, or leave unaffected the rights of holders of any class of claims;

(3) provide for the curing or waiving of any default;

(4) provide for payments on any unsecured claim to be made concurrently with payments on any secured claim or any other unsecured claim;

(5) provide for the curing of any default within a reasonable time and maintenance of payments while the case is pending on any unsecured claim or secured claim on which the last payment is due after the date on which the final payment under the plan is due;

(6) subject to *section 365* of this title, provide for the assumption, rejection, or assignment of any executory contract or unexpired lease of the debtor not previously rejected under such section;

(7) provide for the payment of all or part of a claim against the debtor from property of the estate or property of the debtor;

(8) provide for the sale of all or any part of the property of the estate or the distribution of all or any part of the property of the estate among those having an interest in such property;

(9) provide for payment of allowed secured claims consistent with *section 1225(a)(5)* of this title, over a period exceeding the period permitted under section 1222(c);

(10) provide for the vesting of property of the estate, on confirmation of the plan or at a later time, in the debtor or in any other entity;

(11) provide for the payment of interest accruing after the date of the filing of the petition on unsecured claims that are nondischargeable under *section 1228(a)*, except that such interest may be paid only to the extent that the debtor has disposable income available to pay such interest after making provision for full payment of all allowed claims; and

(12) include any other appropriate provision not inconsistent with this title.

(c) Except as provided in subsections (b)(5) and (b)(9), the plan may not provide for payments over a period that is longer than three years unless the court for cause approves a longer period, but the court may not approve a period that is longer than five years.

(d) Notwithstanding subsection (b)(2) of this section and *sections 506(b)* and *1225(a)(5)* of this title, if it is proposed in a plan to cure a default, the amount necessary to cure the default, shall be determined in accordance with the underlying agreement and applicable nonbankruptcy law.

* * *

§ 1225. Confirmation of plan

(a) Except as provided in subsection (b), the court shall confirm a plan if—

(1) the plan complies with the provisions of this chapter and with the other applicable provisions of this title;

(2) any fee, charge, or amount required under chapter 123 of title 28, or by the plan, to be paid before confirmation, has been paid;

(3) the plan has been proposed in good faith and not by any means forbidden by law;

(4) the value, as of the effective date of the plan, of property to be distributed under the plan on account of each allowed unsecured claim is not less than the amount that would be paid on such claim if the estate of the debtor were liquidated under chapter 7 of this title on such date;

(5) with respect to each allowed secured claim provided for by the plan—

(A) the holder of such claim has accepted the plan;

(B)(i) the plan provides that the holder of such claim retain the lien securing such claim; and

(ii) the value, as of the effective date of the plan, of property to be distributed by the trustee or the debtor under the plan on account of such claim is not less than the allowed amount of such claim; or

(C) the debtor surrenders the property securing such claim to such holder;

(6) the debtor will be able to make all payments under the plan and to comply with the plan; and

(7) the debtor has paid all amounts that are required to be paid under a domestic support obligation and that first become payable after the date of the filing of the petition if the debtor is required by a judicial or administrative order, or by statute, to pay such domestic support obligation.

(b)(1) If the trustee or the holder of an allowed unsecured claim objects to the confirmation of the plan, then the court may not approve the plan unless, as of the effective date of the plan—

(A) the value of the property to be distributed under the plan on account of such claim is not less than the amount of such claim;

(B) the plan provides that all of the debtor's projected disposable income to be received in the three-year period, or such longer period as the court may approve under *section 1222(c)*, beginning on the date that the first payment is due under the plan will be applied to make payments under the plan; or

(C) the value of the property to be distributed under the plan in the 3-year period, or such longer period as the court may approve under *section 1222(c)*, beginning on the date that the first distribution is due under the plan is not less than the debtor's projected disposable income for such period.

(2) For purposes of this subsection, "disposable income" means income which is received by the debtor and which is not reasonably necessary to be expended—

(A) for the maintenance or support of the debtor or a dependent of the debtor or for a domestic support obligation that first becomes payable after the date of the filing of the petition; or

(B) for the payment of expenditures necessary for the continuation, preservation, and operation of the debtor's business.

(c) After confirmation of a plan, the court may order any entity from whom the debtor receives income to pay all or any part of such income to the trustee.

* * *

§ 1228. Discharge

(a) Subject to subsection (d), as soon as practicable after completion by the debtor of all payments under the plan, and in the case of a debtor who is required by a judicial or administrative order, or by statute, to pay a domestic support obligation, after such debtor certifies that all amounts payable under such order or such statute that are due on or before the date of the certification (including amounts due before the petition was filed, but only to the extent provided for by the plan) have been paid, other than payments to holders of allowed claims provided for under *section 1222(b)(5)* or *1222(b)(9)* of this

173

title, unless the court approves a written waiver of discharge executed by the debtor after the order for relief under this chapter, the court shall grant the debtor a discharge of all debts provided for by the plan allowed under *section 503* of this title or disallowed under *section 502* of this title, except any debt—

> **(1)** provided for under *section 1222(b)(5)* or *1222(b)(9)* of this title; or

> **(2)** of the kind specified in *section 523(a)* of this title.

(b) Subject to subsection (d), at any time after the confirmation of the plan and after notice and a hearing, the court may grant a discharge to a debtor that has not completed payments under the plan only if—

> **(1)** the debtor's failure to complete such payments is due to circumstances for which the debtor should not justly be held accountable;

> **(2)** the value, as of the effective date of the plan, of property actually distributed under the plan on account of each allowed unsecured claim is not less than the amount that would have been paid on such claim if the estate of the debtor had been liquidated under chapter 7 of this title on such date; and

> **(3)** modification of the plan under *section 1229* of this title is not practicable.

(c) A discharge granted under subsection (b) of this section discharges the debtor from all unsecured debts provided for by the plan or disallowed under *section 502* of this title, except any debt—

> **(1)** provided for under *section 1222(b)(5)* or *1222(b)(9)* of this title; or

> **(2)** of a kind specified in *section 523(a)* of this title.

(d) On request of a party in interest before one year after a discharge under this section is granted, and after notice and a hearing, the court may revoke such discharge only if—

> **(1)** such discharge was obtained by the debtor through fraud; and

> **(2)** the requesting party did not know of such fraud until after such discharge was granted.

(e) After the debtor is granted a discharge, the court shall terminate the services of any trustee serving in the case.

(f) The court may not grant a discharge under this chapter unless the court after notice and a hearing held not more than 10 days before the date of the entry of the order granting the discharge finds that there is no reasonable cause to believe that—

> **(1)** *section 522(q)(1)* may be applicable to the debtor; and

> **(2)** there is pending any proceeding in which the debtor may be found guilty of a felony of the kind described in *section 522(q)(1)(A)* or liable for a debt of the kind described in *section 522(q)(1)(B)*. Title 11

CHAPTER 13—ADJUSTMENT OF DEBTS OF AN INDIVIDUAL WITH REGULAR INCOME

SUBCHAPTER I—OFFICERS, ADMINISTRATION, AND THE ESTATE

SUBCHAPTER I—OFFICERS, ADMINISTRATION, AND THE ESTATE

§ 1301. Stay of action against codebtor

(a) Except as provided in subsections (b) and (c) of this section, after the order for relief under this chapter, a creditor may not act, or commence or continue any civil action, to collect all or any part of a consumer debt of the debtor from any individual that is liable on such debt with the debtor, or that secured such debt, unless—

　　(1) such individual became liable on or secured such debt in the ordinary course of such individual's business; or

　　(2) the case is closed, dismissed, or converted to a case under chapter 7 or 11 of this title. * * *

(c) On request of a party in interest and after notice and a hearing, the court shall grant relief from the stay provided by subsection (a) of this section with respect to a creditor, to the extent that—

　　(1) as between the debtor and the individual protected under subsection (a) of this section, such individual received the consideration for the claim held by such creditor;

　　(2) the plan filed by the debtor proposes not to pay such claim; or

　　(3) such creditor's interest would be irreparably harmed by continuation of such stay.

(d) Twenty days after the filing of a request under subsection (c)(2) of this section for relief from the stay provided by subsection (a) of this section, such stay is terminated with respect to the party in interest making such request, unless the debtor or any individual that is liable on such debt with the debtor files and serves upon such party in interest a written objection to the taking of the proposed action.

OTHER SECTIONS

Always important to look at section 101 for definitions: consumer debt, debtor, individual with regular income. Section 101 does not tell us what "request" means. Rule 4001 infra at page 226, tells us that "request" means "motion."

Section 109(e) governs eligibility to be a chapter 13 debtor. Who files for chapter 13 will also be affected by section 707, which limits access to chapter 7.

Section 362 imposes the automatic stay.

§ 1302. Trustee

(a) If the United States trustee appoints an individual under section 586(b) of title 28 to serve as standing trustee in cases under this chapter and if such individual qualifies under section 322 of this title, then such individual shall serve as trustee in the case. Otherwise, the United States trustee shall appoint one disinterested person to serve as trustee in the case or the United States trustee may serve as a trustee in the case.

(b) The trustee shall—

    (1) perform the duties specified in sections 704(2), 704(3), 704(4), 704(5), 704(6), 704(7), and 704(9) of this title;

    (2) appear and be heard at any hearing that concerns—

        (A) the value of property subject to a lien;

        (B) confirmation of a plan; or

        (C) modification of the plan after confirmation;

* * *

    (4) advise, other than on legal matters, and assist the debtor in performance under the plan;

    (5) ensure that the debtor commences making timely payments under section 1326 of this title; and

* * *

(c) If the debtor is engaged in business, then in addition to the duties specified in subsection (b) of this section, the trustee shall perform the duties specified in sections 1106(a)(3) and 1106(a)(4) of this title.

* * *

UNOFFICIAL COMMENTS

In chapter 7 or chapter 11, a person is appointed to serve as a trustee in a specific case. In chapter 13, a person is appointed to serve as "standing trustee in [all] cases."

Note that the chapter 13 trustee is required to appear at "any" hearing on court confirmation of the chapter 13 plan. In most districts, in most chapter 13 cases, there is no actual confirmation hearing. Cf. section 102. And if the bankruptcy judge actually holds a hearing and hears from anyone at the "hearing" it will usually be the chapter 13 trustee.

The chapter 13 trustee is also charged with monitoring a chapter 13 debtor's plan payments. She is usually the most important professional in a chapter 13 case.

§ 1303. Rights and powers of debtor

Subject to any limitations on a trustee under this chapter, the debtor shall have, exclusive of the trustee, the rights and powers of a trustee under sections 363(b), 363(d), 363(e), 363(f), and 363(/), of this title.

OTHER SECTIONS

Compare with sections 1107 and 1108.

§ 1304. Debtor engaged in business

(a) A debtor that is self-employed and incurs trade credit in the production of income from such employment is engaged in business.

(b) Unless the court orders otherwise, a debtor engaged in business may operate the business of the debtor and, subject to any limitations on a trustee under sections 363(c) and 364 of this title and to such limitations or conditions as the court prescribes, shall have, exclusive of the trustee, the rights and powers of the trustee under such sections.

(c) A debtor engaged in business shall perform the duties of the trustee specified in section 704(a)(8) of this title.

§ 1305. Filing and allowance of postpetition claims

(a) A proof of claim may be filed by any entity that holds a claim against the debtor—

(1) for taxes that become payable to a governmental unit while the case is pending; or

(2) that is a consumer debt, that arises after the date of the order for relief under this chapter, and that is for property or services necessary for the debtor's performance under the plan.

(b) Except as provided in subsection (c) of this section, a claim filed under subsection (a) of this section shall be allowed or disallowed under section 502 of this title, but shall be determined as of the date such claim arises, and shall be allowed under section 502(a), 502(b), or 502(c) of this title, or disallowed under section 502(d) or 502(e) of this title, the same as if such claim had arisen before the date of the filing of the petition.

(c) A claim filed under subsection (a)(2) of this section shall be disallowed if the holder of such claim knew or should have known that prior approval by the trustee of the debtor's incurring the obligation was practicable and was not obtained.

UNOFFICIAL COMMENT

The key word to notice is the word "may." Generally, a holder of a claim does not have a choice of waiting to recover after the bankruptcy case is over instead of participating in the bankruptcy distribution. Section 1305 gives that choice to holders of certain kinds of postpetition claims.

OTHER SECTIONS

Section 101 defines terms such as "consumer debt."

Section 1328(d)(2) provides an exception from discharge for certain section 1305 claims.

§ 1306. Property of the estate

(a) Property of the estate includes, in addition to the property specified in section 541 of this title—

    (1) all property of the kind specified in such section that the debtor acquires after the commencement of the case but before the case is closed, dismissed, or converted to a case under chapter 7, 11, or 12 of this title, whichever occurs first; and

    (2) earnings from services performed by the debtor after the commencement of the case but before the case is closed, dismissed, or converted to a case under chapter 7, 11, or 12 of this title, whichever occurs first.

(b) Except as provided in a confirmed plan or order confirming a plan, the debtor shall remain in possession of all property of the estate.

OTHER SECTIONS

Read section 1306 together with section 541—especially 541(a)(6).

Section 1115 is adapted from section 1306.

Property of the estate in chapters 13 and 11 is different from property of the estate in a chapter 7 bankruptcy case. If a chapter 13 case is converted to chapter 7, look to section 348(f) in determining what is property of the estate in a chapter 7 case.

§ 1307. Conversion or dismissal

(a) The debtor may convert a case under this chapter to a case under chapter 7 of this title at any time. Any waiver of the right to convert under this subsection is unenforceable.

(b) On request of the debtor at any time, if the case has not been converted under section 706, 1112, or 1208 of this title, the court shall dismiss a case under this chapter. Any waiver of the right to dismiss under this subsection is unenforceable.

(c) Except as provided in subsection (f) of this section, on request of a party in interest or the United States trustee and after notice and a hearing, the court may convert a case under this chapter to a case under chapter 7 of this title, or may dismiss a case under this chapter, whichever is in the best interests of creditors and the estate, for cause, including—

    (1) unreasonable delay by the debtor that is prejudicial to creditors;

    (2) nonpayment of any fees and charges required under chapter 123 of title 28;

    (3) failure to file a plan timely under section 1321 of this title;

    (4) failure to commence making timely payments under section 1326 of this title;

    (5) denial of confirmation of a plan under section 1325 of this title and denial of a request made for additional time for filing another plan or a modification of a plan;

    (6) material default by the debtor with respect to a term of a confirmed plan;

    (7) revocation of the order of confirmation under section 1330 of this title, and denial of confirmation of a modified plan under section 1329 of this title;

    (8) termination of a confirmed plan by reason of the occurrence of a condition specified in the plan other than completion of payments under the plan;

(9) only on request of the United States trustee, failure of the debtor to file, within fifteen days, or such additional time as the court may allow, after the filing of the petition commencing such case, the information required by paragraph (1) of section 521(a);

(10) only on request of the United States trustee, failure to timely file the information required by paragraph (2) of section 521(a); or

(11) failure of the debtor to pay any domestic support obligation that first becomes payable after the date of the filing of the petition.

(d) Except as provided in subsection (f) of this section, at any time before the confirmation of a plan under section 1325 of this title, on request of a party in interest or the United States trustee and after notice and a hearing, the court may convert a case under this chapter to a case under chapter 11 or 12 of this title.

(e) Upon the failure of the debtor to file a tax return under section 1308, on request of a party in interest or the United States trustee and after notice and a hearing, the court shall dismiss a case or convert a case under this chapter to a case under chapter 7 of this title, whichever is in the best interest of the creditors and the estate.

(f) The court may not convert a case under this chapter to a case under chapter 7, 11, or 12 of this title if the debtor is a farmer, unless the debtor requests such conversion.

(g) Notwithstanding any other provision of this section, a case may not be converted to a case under another chapter of this title unless the debtor may be a debtor under such chapter.

OTHER SECTIONS

Look to section 109(g) for the effect of section 1307(b) dismissal on eligibility for later bankruptcy relief. Section 348 governs the legal effects of conversion of a case from one chapter to another. Look to section 349 for legal effects of dismissal.

* * *

§ 1308. Filing of prepetition of tax returns

(a) Not later than the day before the date on which the meeting of the creditors is first scheduled to be held under *section 341(a)*, if the debtor was required to file a tax return under applicable nonbankruptcy law, the debtor shall file with appropriate tax authorities all tax returns for all taxable periods ending during the 4-year period ending on the date of the filing of the petition.

(b)(1) Subject to paragraph (2), if the tax returns required by subsection (a) have not been filed by the date on which the meeting of creditors is first scheduled to be held under *section 341(a)*, the trustee may hold open that meeting for a reasonable period of time to allow the debtor an additional period of time to file any unfiled returns, but such additional period of time shall not extend beyond—

(A) for any return that is past due as of the date of the filing of the petition, the date that is 120 days after the date of that meeting; or

(B) for any return that is not past due as of the date of the filing of the petition, the later of—

(i) the date that is 120 days after the date of that meeting; or

(ii) the date on which the return is due under the last automatic extension of time for filing that return to which the debtor is entitled, and for which request is timely made, in accordance with applicable nonbankruptcy law.

(2) After notice and a hearing, and order entered before the tolling of any applicable filing period determined under paragraph (1), if the debtor demonstrates by a preponderance of the evidence that the failure to file a return as required under paragraph (1) is attributable to circumstances beyond the control of the debtor, the court may extend the filing period established by the trustee under this subsection for—

(A) a period of not more than 30 days for returns described in paragraph (1)(A); and

(B) a period not to extend after the applicable extended due date for a return described in paragraph (1)(B) * * *

* * *

SUBCHAPTER II—THE PLAN

§ 1321. Filing of plan

The debtor shall file a plan.

UNOFFICIAL COMMENTS

In chapter 11 cases, there are circumstances in which creditors can file plans. In chapter 13 cases, only the debtor can file the plan.

The time constraints of chapter 13 are very different from chapter 11. Under Rule 3015, a chapter 13 plan must be filed within 15 days after the commencement of the case, unless the court extends the time for cause.

OTHER SECTIONS

Section 1322 deals with the contents of a plan. For an example of a chapter 13 plan, see page 363 et seq.

§ 1322. Contents of plan

(a) The plan

(1) shall provide for the submission of all or such portion of future earnings or other future income of the debtor to the supervision and control of the trustee as is necessary for the execution of the plan;

(2) shall provide for the full payment, in deferred cash payments, of all claims entitled to priority under section 507 of this title, unless the holder of a particular claim agrees to a different treatment of such claim;

(3) if the plan classifies claims, shall provide the same treatment for each claim within a particular class; and.

(4) notwithstanding any other provision of this section, may provide for less than full payment of all amounts owed for a claim entitled to priority under section 507(a)(1)(B) only if the plan provides that all of the debtor's projected disposable income for a 5-year period beginning on the date that the first payment is due under the plan will be applied to make payments under the plan.

(b) Subject to subsections (a) and (c) of this section, the plan may—

(1) designate a class or classes of unsecured claims, as provided in section 1122 of this title, but may not discriminate unfairly against any class so designated; however, such plan may treat claims for a consumer debt of the debtor if an individual is liable on such consumer debt with the debtor differently than other unsecured claims;

(2) modify the rights of holders of secured claims, other than a claim secured only by a security interest in real property that is the debtor's principal residence, or of holders of unsecured claims, or leave unaffected the rights of holders of any class of claims; *not home mortgage*

(3) provide for the curing or waiving of any default;

(4) provide for payments on any unsecured claim to be made concurrently with payments on any secured claim or any other unsecured claim;

(5) notwithstanding paragraph (2) of this subsection, provide for the curing of any default within a reasonable time and maintenance of payments while the case is pending on any unsecured claim or secured claim on which the last payment is due after the date on which the final payment under the plan is due;

(6) provide for the payment of all or any part of any claim allowed under section 1305 of this title;

(7) subject to section 365 of this title, provide for the assumption, rejection, or assignment of any executory contract or unexpired lease of the debtor not previously rejected under such section;

(8) provide for the payment of all or part of a claim against the debtor from property of the estate or property of the debtor;

(9) provide for the vesting of property of the estate, on confirmation of the plan or at a later time, in the debtor or in any other entity;

(10) provide for the payment of interest accruing after the date of the filing of the petition on unsecured claims that are nondischargeable under section 1328(a), except that such interest may be paid only to the extent that the debtor has disposable income available to pay such interest after making provision for full payment of all allowed claims; and

(11) include any other appropriate provision not inconsistent with this title.

(c) Notwithstanding subsection (b)(2) and applicable nonbankruptcy law—

(1) a default with respect to, or that gave rise to, a lien on the debtor's principal residence may be cured under paragraph (3) or (5) of subsection (b) until such residence is sold at a foreclosure sale that is conducted in accordance with applicable nonbankruptcy law; and

(2) in a case in which the last payment on the original payment schedule for a claim secured only by a security interest in real property that is the debtor's principal residence is due before the date on which the final payment under the plan is due, the plan may provide for the payment of the claim as modified pursuant to section 1325(a)(5) of this title.

Can de-accaerate by statute at any time pnwr to freclosure sale.

(d)(1) If the current monthly income of the debtor and the debtor's spouse combined, when multiplied by 12, is not less than—

    (A) in the case of a debtor in a household of 1 person, the median family income of the applicable State for 1 earner;

    (B) in the case of a debtor in a household of 2, 3, or 4 individuals, the highest median family income of the applicable State for a family of the same number or fewer individuals; or

    (C) in the case of a debtor in a household exceeding 4 individuals, the highest median family income of the applicable State for a family of 4 or fewer individuals, plus $675 per month for each individual in excess of 4, the plan may not provide for payments over a period that is longer than 5 years.

    (2) If the current monthly income of the debtor and the debtor's spouse combined, when multiplied by 12, is less than—

    (A) in the case of a debtor in a household of 1 person, the median family income of the applicable State for 1 earner;

    (B) in the case of a debtor in a household of 2, 3, or 4 individuals, the highest median family income of the applicable State for a family of the same number or fewer individuals; or

    (C) in the case of a debtor in a household exceeding 4 individuals, the highest median family income of the applicable State for a family of 4 or fewer individuals, plus $625 per month for each individual in excess of 4,

the plan may not provide for payments over a period that is longer than 3 years, unless the court, for cause, approves a longer period, but the court may not approve a period that is longer than 5 years.

    (e) Notwithstanding subsection (b)(2) of this section and sections 506(b) and 1325(a)(5) of this title, if it is proposed in a plan to cure a default, the amount necessary to cure the default, shall be determined in accordance with the underlying agreement and applicable nonbankruptcy law.

* * *

UNOFFICIAL COMMENTS

    Notice that this section contemplates that a chapter 13 plan will treat secured claims differently from unsecured claims, priority claims different from other unsecured claims, claims secured only by the debtor's principal residence different from other secured claims.

OTHER SECTIONS

    Section 1322, like every section, needs to be read together with the definitions of section 101: "consumer debt", "current monthly income", "median family income." And the explanation of "secured claim" in section 506(a).

    A plan has no legal effect unless and until it is confirmed by the court. Accordingly, section 1322 needs to be read together with the section 1325 requirements for court approval. Note that section 1325 not only deals separately with claims secured only by the debtor's principal residence but also deals separately with most claims secured by motor vehicles.

    Section 1325(b)(2) defines "disposable income" but limits the definition to "for purposes of this subsection."

    The phrase "not discriminate unfairly" in section 1322(b)(1) also appears in section 1129(b).

And, much of section 1322(d) also appears in section 707(b).

Looking at Form 22C on page 297 et seq. infra will help you understand what section 1322(d) is about. More specifically, Census Bureau Median Family Income By Family Size give you the specifics of "median family income."

§ 1323. Modification of plan before confirmation

(a) The debtor may modify the plan at any time before confirmation, but may not modify the plan so that the plan as modified fails to meet the requirements of section 1322 of this title.

(b) After the debtor files a modification under this section, the plan as modified becomes the plan.

(c) Any holder of a secured claim that has accepted or rejected the plan is deemed to have accepted or rejected, as the case may be, the plan as modified, unless the modification provides for a change in the rights of such holder from what such rights were under the plan before modification, and such holder changes such holder's previous acceptance or rejection.

§ 1324. Confirmation hearing

(a) Except as provided in subsection (b) and after notice, the court shall hold a hearing on confirmation of the plan. A party in interest may object to confirmation of the plan.

(b) The hearing on confirmation of the plan may be held not earlier than 20 days and not later than 45 days after the date of the meeting of creditors under section 341(a), unless the court determines that it would be in the best interests of the creditors and the estate to hold such hearing at an earlier date and there is no objection to such earlier date.

§ 1325. Confirmation of plan ~Disposible income –~

(a) Except as provided in subsection (b), the court shall confirm a plan if—

(1) the plan complies with the provisions of this chapter and with the other applicable provisions of this title;

(2) any fee, charge, or amount required under chapter 123 of title 28, or by the plan, to be paid before confirmation, has been paid;

(3) the plan has been proposed in good faith and not by any means forbidden by law;

(4) the value, as of the effective date of the plan, of property to be distributed under the plan on account of each allowed unsecured claim is not less than the amount that would be paid on such claim if the estate of the debtor were liquidated under chapter 7 of this title on such date; ~best interest pln~

(5) with respect to each allowed secured claim provided for by the plan—

(A) the holder of such claim has accepted the plan;

(B)(i) the plan provides that—

(I) the holder of such claim retain the lien securing such claim until the earlier of—

~If above median income we define reasonable expenses according to the means test.~

     (aa) the payment of the underlying debt determined under nonbankruptcy law; or

     (bb) discharge under section 1328; and

    (II) if the case under this chapter is dismissed or converted without completion of the plan, such lien shall also be retained by such holder to the extent recognized by applicable nonbankruptcy law;

   (ii) the value, as of the effective date of the plan, of property to be distributed under the plan on account of such claim is not less than the allowed amount of such claim; and

   (iii) if—

    (I) property to be distributed pursuant to this subsection is in the form of periodic payments, such payments shall be in equal monthly amounts; and

    (II) the holder of the claim is secured by personal property, the amount of such payments shall not be less than an amount sufficient to provide to the holder of such claim adequate protection during the period of the plan; or

  (C) the debtor surrenders the property securing such claim to such holder;

 (6) the debtor will be able to make all payments under the plan and to comply with the plan;

 (7) the action of the debtor in filing the petition was in good faith;

 (8) the debtor has paid all amounts that are required to be paid under a domestic support obligation and that first become payable after the date of the filing of the petition if the debtor is required by a judicial or administrative order, or by statute, to pay such domestic support obligation; and

 (9) the debtor has filed all applicable Federal, State, and local tax returns as required by section 1308.

For purposes of paragraph (5), section 506 shall not apply to a claim described in that paragraph if the creditor has a purchase money security interest securing the debt that is the subject of the claim, the debt was incurred within the 910-day period preceding the date of the filing of the petition, and the collateral for that debt consists of a motor vehicle (as defined in section 30102 of title 49) acquired for the personal use of the debtor, or if collateral for that debt consists of any other thing of value, if the debt was incurred during the 1-year period preceding that filing;

 (b)(1) If the trustee or the holder of an allowed unsecured claim objects to the confirmation of the plan, then the court may not approve the plan unless, as of the effective date of the plan—

  (A) the value of the property to be distributed under the plan on account of such claim is not less than the amount of such claim; or

  (B) the plan provides that all of the debtor's projected disposable income to be received in the applicable commitment period beginning on the date that the first payment is due under the plan will be applied to make payments to unsecured creditors under the plan.

(2) For purposes of this subsection, the term "disposable income" means current monthly income received by the debtor (other than child support payments, foster care payments, or disability payments for a dependent child made in accordance with applicable nonbankruptcy law to the extent reasonably necessary to be expended for such child) less amounts reasonably necessary to be expended—

(A)(i) for the maintenance or support of the debtor or a dependent of the debtor, or for a domestic support obligation, that first becomes payable after the date the petition is filed; and

(ii) for charitable contributions (that meet the definition of "charitable contribution" under section 548(d)(3) to a qualified religious or charitable entity or organization (as defined in section 548(d)(4)) in an amount not to exceed 15 percent of gross income of the debtor for the year in which the contributions are made); and

(B) if the debtor is engaged in business, for the payment of expenditures necessary for the continuation, preservation, and operation of such business.

(3) Amounts reasonably necessary to be expended under paragraph (2), other than subparagraph (A)(ii) of paragraph (2), shall be determined in accordance with subparagraphs (A) and (B) of section 707(b)(2), if the debtor has current monthly income, when multiplied by 12, greater than—

(A) in the case of a debtor in a household of 1 person, the median family income of the applicable State for 1 earner;

(B) in the case of a debtor in a household of 2, 3, or 4 individuals, the highest median family income of the applicable State for a family of the same number or fewer individuals; or

(C) in the case of a debtor in a household exceeding 4 individuals, the highest median family income of the applicable State for a family of 4 or fewer individuals, plus $675 per month for each individual in excess of 4.

(4) For purposes of this subsection, the "applicable commitment period"—

(A) subject to subparagraph (B), shall be—

(i) 3 years; or

(ii) not less than 5 years, if the current monthly income of the debtor and the debtor's spouse combined, when multiplied by 12, is not less than—

(I) in the case of a debtor in a household of 1 person, the median family income of the applicable State for 1 earner;

(II) in the case of a debtor in a household of 2, 3, or 4 individuals, the highest median family income of the applicable State for a family of the same number or fewer individuals; or

(III) in the case of a debtor in a household exceeding 4 individuals, the highest median family income of the applicable State for a family of 4 or fewer individuals, plus $675 per month for each individual in excess of 4; and

(B) may be less than 3 or 5 years, whichever is applicable under subparagraph (A), but only if the plan provides for payment in full of all allowed unsecured claims over a shorter period.

(c) After confirmation of a plan, the court may order any entity from whom the debtor receives income to pay all or any part of such income to the trustee.

UNOFFICIAL COMMENTS

Remember section 102's definition of "hearing." In most chapter 13 cases, there is no actual confirmation hearing.

Remember also that in chapter 13, unlike chapter 11, the only opportunity creditors have to participate in the plan process is to object to confirmation of the plan pursuant to section 1324. Generally, objections to a chapter 13 plan come from the standing chapter 13 trustee and come to the debtor's attorney by informal communications, rather than filed pleadings.

Regardless of whether the chapter 13 trustee or any creditor objects to the plan, the court must apply the nine numbered requirements in section 1325(a). Section 1325(a)(4) is generally referred to as a "best interest of creditors" test; similar language appears in section 1129(a). Similarly, the language for plan treatment of secured claims in section 1325(a)(5)(B)(ii) is similar to language in section 1129(b).

The unnumbered paragraph at the end of section 1325(a)(9), the "hanging paragraph", is not similar to any other statutory language anywhere. It is hard to understand and apply and likely to be on your exam.

OTHER SECTIONS

Section 1325, like every section, needs to be read together with the definitions of section 101: "consumer debt," "current monthly income," "median family income." And read together with the explanation of "secured claim" in section 506(a). And read together with the explanation of the "means test" in section 707(b)(2)(A) and (B) which is to be used in calculating "disposable income" under section 1325(b)(3) and "applicable commitment period" in section 1325(b)(4).

Also, it might be helpful to look at Form 22C on page 297 infra. All chapter 13 debtors must complete this form.

You can get a better sense of what "means testing" means by also looking at Form 22A on page 287 infra. Individual debtors filing for chapter 7 relief will complete this form for "means testing" purposes.

Some of the information needed to complete this form, such as the debtor's current monthly income, will come from the debtor's own personal records. Other information comes from data collected by the Census Bureau and Internal Revenue Service. The U.S. Trustee website, www.usdoj.gov/ust/eo/bapcpa/meanstesting.htm reproduces this data, such as Census Bureau Median Income By Family Size.

§ 1326. Payments

(a)(1) Unless the court orders otherwise, the debtor shall commence making payments not later than 30 days after the date of the filing of the plan or the order for relief, whichever is earlier, in the amount—

> **(A)** proposed by the plan to the trustee; * * *

> **(C)** that provides adequate protection directly to a creditor holding an allowed claim secured by personal property to the extent the claim is attributable to the purchase of such property by the debtor for that portion of the obligation that becomes due after the order for relief, reducing the payments under subparagraph (A) by the amount so paid and providing the trustee with evidence of such payment, including the amount and date of payment.

> **(2)** A payment made under paragraph (1)(A) shall be retained by the trustee until confirmation or denial of confirmation. If a plan is confirmed, the trustee shall distribute any such payment in accordance with the plan as soon as is practicable. If a

plan is not confirmed, the trustee shall return any such payments not previously paid and not yet due and owing to creditors pursuant to paragraph (3) to the debtor, after deducting any unpaid claim allowed under section 503(b).

* * *

§ 1327. Effect of confirmation

(a) The provisions of a confirmed plan bind the debtor and each creditor, whether or not the claim of such creditor is provided for by the plan, and whether or not such creditor has objected to, has accepted, or has rejected the plan.

(b) Except as otherwise provided in the plan or the order confirming the plan, the confirmation of a plan vests all of the property of the estate in the debtor.

(c) Except as otherwise provided in the plan or in the order confirming the plan, the property vesting in the debtor under subsection (b) of this section is free and clear of any claim or interest of any creditor provided for by the plan.

UNOFFICIAL COMMENT

In chapter 13 cases, like chapter 11 cases involving individuals, confirmation of the plan alone does not result in a discharge. Instead, discharge is keyed to plan payments.

§ 1328. Discharge

(a) Subject to subsection (d), as soon as practicable after completion by the debtor of all payments under the plan, and in the case of a debtor who is required by a judicial or administrative order, or by statute, to pay a domestic support obligation, after such debtor certifies that all amounts payable under such order or such statute that are due on or before the date of the certification (including amounts due before the petition was filed, but only to the extent provided for by the plan) have been paid, unless the court approves a written waiver of discharge executed by the debtor after the order for relief under this chapter, the court shall grant the debtor a discharge of all debts provided for by the plan or disallowed under section 502 of this title, except any debt—

(1) provided for under section 1322(b)(5);

(2) of the kind specified in section 507(a)(8)(C) or in paragraph (1)(B), (1)(C), (2), (3), (4), (5), (8), or (9) of section 523(a);

(3) for restitution, or a criminal fine, included in a sentence on the debtor's conviction of a crime; or

(4) for restitution, or damages, awarded in a civil action against the debtor as a result of willful or malicious injury by the debtor that caused personal injury to an individual or the death of an individual.

(b) Subject to subsection (d), at any time after the confirmation of the plan and after notice and a hearing, the court may grant a discharge to a debtor that has not completed payments under the plan only if— *exemptions*

(1) the debtor's failure to complete such payments is due to circumstances for which the debtor should not justly be held accountable;

(2) the value, as of the effective date of the plan, of property actually distributed under the plan on account of each allowed unsecured claim is not less than the

187

amount that would have been paid on such claim if the estate of the debtor had been liquidated under chapter 7 of this title on such date; and

    (3) modification of the plan under section 1329 of this title is not practicable.

    (c) A discharge granted under subsection (b) of this section discharges the debtor from all unsecured debts provided for by the plan or disallowed under section 502 of this title, except any debt—

    (1) provided for under section 1322(b)(5) of this title; or

    (2) of a kind specified in section 523(a) of this title.

    (d) Notwithstanding any other provision of this section, a discharge granted under this section does not discharge the debtor from any debt based on an allowed claim filed under section 1305(a)(2) of this title if prior approval by the trustee of the debtor's incurring such debt was practicable and was not obtained.

    (e) On request of a party in interest before one year after a discharge under this section is granted, and after notice and a hearing, the court may revoke such discharge only if—

    (1) such discharge was obtained by the debtor through fraud; and

    (2) the requesting party did not know of such fraud until after such discharge was granted.

    (f) Notwithstanding subsections (a) and (b), the court shall not grant a discharge of all debts provided for in the plan or disallowed under section 502, if the debtor has received a discharge—

    (1) in a case filed under chapter 7, 11, or 12 of this title during the 4-year period preceding the date of the order for relief under this chapter, or

    (2) in a case filed under chapter 13 of this title during the 2-year period preceding the date of such order.

    (g)(1) The court shall not grant a discharge under this section to a debtor unless after filing a petition the debtor has completed an instructional course concerning personal financial management described in section 111.

* * *

    (3) The United States trustee (or the bankruptcy administrator, if any) who makes a determination described in paragraph (2) shall review such determination not later than 1 year after the date of such determination, and not less frequently than annually thereafter.

    (h) The court may not grant a discharge under this chapter unless the court after notice and a hearing held not more than 10 days before the date of the entry of the order granting the discharge finds that there is no reasonable cause to believe that—

    (1) section 522(q)(1) may be applicable to the debtor; and

    (2) there is pending any proceeding in which the debtor may be found guilty of a felony of the kind described in section 522(q)(1)(A) or liable for a debt of the kind described in section 522(q)(1)(B).

* * *

UNOFFICIAL COMMENTS

This section provides for two different kinds of discharge. A debtor who meets all of her plan payment obligations gets a discharge under section 1328(a). A debtor who because of a court-recognized hardship is not able to complete plan payments gets a section 1328(b) discharge; a section 1328(b) discharge is, cleverly enough, generally referred to as a "hardship discharge."

A section 1328(a) discharge is more favorable to debtors than a section 1328(b) hardship discharge. As a careful reading of section 1328(a)(2) and section 1328(c)(2) reveal, all section 523 exceptions to discharge apply to a debtor who receives a section 1328(b) discharge but not all apply to a debtor who receives a section 1328(a) discharge.

OTHER SECTIONS

Section 524(a) sets out the effect of a discharge. Under section 727(a)(9), a chapter 13 discharge may affect the debtor's ability to obtain a discharge in a subsequent chapter 7 case.

Before using section 1328(b) for a debtor who is not able to meet her plan payment obligations, think about using section 1329 to modify the plan provisions regarding payment obligations.

§ 1329. Modification of plan after confirmation

(a) At any time after confirmation of the plan but before the completion of payments under such plan, the plan may be modified, upon request of the debtor, the trustee, or the holder of an allowed unsecured claim, to—

(1) increase or reduce the amount of payments on claims of a particular class provided for by the plan;

(2) extend or reduce the time for such payments;

(3) alter the amount of the distribution to a creditor whose claim is provided for by the plan to the extent necessary to take account of any payment of such claim other than under the plan; or

(4) reduce amounts to be paid under the plan by the actual amount expended by the debtor to purchase health insurance for the debtor (and for any dependent of the debtor if such dependent does not otherwise have health insurance coverage) if the debtor documents the cost of such insurance and demonstrates that—

(A) such expenses are reasonable and necessary;

(B)(i) if the debtor previously paid for health insurance, the amount is not materially larger than the cost the debtor previously paid or the cost necessary to maintain the lapsed policy; or

(ii) if the debtor did not have health insurance, the amount is not materially larger than the reasonable cost that would be incurred by a debtor who purchases health insurance, who has similar income, expenses, age, and health status, and who lives in the same geographical location with the same number of dependents who do not otherwise have health insurance coverage; and

(C) the amount is not otherwise allowed for purposes of determining disposable income under section 1325(b) of this title;

and upon request of any party in interest, files proof that a health insurance policy was purchased.

(b)(1) Sections 1322(a), 1322(b), and 1323(c) of this title and the requirements of section 1325(a) of this title apply to any modification under subsection (a) of this section.

(2) The plan as modified becomes the plan unless, after notice and a hearing, such modification is disapproved.

(c) A plan modified under this section may not provide for payments over a period that expires after the applicable commitment period under section 1325(b)(1)(B) after the time that the first payment under the original confirmed plan was due, unless the court, for cause, approves a longer period, but the court may not approve a period that expires after five years after such time.

§ 1330. Revocation of an order of confirmation

(a) On request of a party in interest at any time within 180 days after the date of the entry of an order of confirmation under section 1325 of this title, and after notice and a hearing, the court may revoke such order if such order was procured by fraud.

(b) If the court revokes an order of confirmation under subsection (a) of this section, the court shall dispose of the case under section 1307 of this title, unless, within the time fixed by the court, the debtor proposes and the court confirms a modification of the plan under section 1329 of this title.

CHAPTER 15—
ANCILLARY AND OTHER CROSS-BORDER CASES

SUBCHAPTER I—GENERAL PROVISIONS

§ 1501. Purpose and scope of application

(a) The purpose of this chapter is to incorporate the Model Law on Cross-Border Insolvency so as to provide effective mechanisms for dealing with cases of cross-border insolvency with the objectives of—

(1) cooperation between—

(A) courts of the United States, United States trustees, trustees, examiners, debtors, and debtors in possession; and

(B) the courts and other competent authorities of foreign countries involved in cross-border insolvency cases;

(2) greater legal certainty for trade and investment;

(3) fair and efficient administration of cross-border insolvencies that protects the interests of all creditors, and other interested entities, including the debtor;

(4) protection and maximization of the value of the debtor's assets; and

(5) facilitation of the rescue of financially troubled businesses, thereby protecting investment and preserving employment.

(b) This chapter applies where—

(1) assistance is sought in the United States by a foreign court or a foreign representative in connection with a foreign proceeding;

(2) assistance is sought in a foreign country in connection with a case under this title;

(3) a foreign proceeding and a case under this title with respect to the same debtor are pending concurrently; or

191

(4) creditors or other interested persons in a foreign country have an interest in requesting the commencement of, or participating in, a case or proceeding under this title.

(c) This chapter does not apply to—

(1) a proceeding concerning an entity, other than a foreign insurance company, identified by exclusion in section 109(b);

(2) an individual, or to an individual and such individual's spouse, who have debts within the limits specified in section 109(e) and who are citizens of the United States or aliens lawfully admitted for permanent residence in the United States; or

(3) an entity subject to a proceeding under the Securities Investor Protection Act of 1970, a stockbroker subject to subchapter III of chapter 7 of this title, or a commodity broker subject to subchapter IV of chapter 7 of this title.

* * *

§ 1502. Definitions

For the purposes of this chapter, the term—

(1) "debtor" means an entity that is the subject of a foreign proceeding;

(2) "establishment" means any place of operations where the debtor carries out a nontransitory economic activity;

(3) "foreign court" means a judicial or other authority competent to control or supervise a foreign proceeding;

(4) "foreign main proceeding" means a foreign proceeding pending in the country where the debtor has the center of its main interests;

(5) "foreign nonmain proceeding" means a foreign proceeding, other than a foreign main proceeding, pending in a country where the debtor has an establishment;

(6) "trustee" includes a trustee, a debtor in possession in a case under any chapter of this title, or a debtor under chapter 9 of this title;

(7) "recognition" means the entry of an order granting recognition of a foreign main proceeding or foreign nonmain proceeding under this chapter; and

(8) "within the territorial jurisdiction of the United States", when used with reference to property of a debtor, refers to tangible property located within the territory of the United States and intangible property deemed under applicable nonbankruptcy law to be located within that territory, including any property subject to attachment or garnishment that may properly be seized or garnished by an action in a Federal or State court in the United States.

§ 1503. International obligations of the United States

To the extent that this chapter conflicts with an obligation of the United States arising out of any treaty or other form of agreement to which it is a party with one or more other countries, the requirements of the treaty or agreement prevail.

§ 1504. Commencement of ancillary case

A case under this chapter is commenced by the filing of a petition for recognition of a foreign proceeding under section 1515.

§ 1505. Authorization to act in a foreign country

A trustee or another entity (including an examiner) may be authorized by the court to act in a foreign country on behalf of an estate created under section 541. An entity authorized to act under this section may act in any way permitted by the applicable foreign law.

§ 1506. Public policy exception

Nothing in this chapter prevents the court from refusing to take an action governed by this chapter if the action would be manifestly contrary to the public policy of the United States.

§ 1507. Additional assistance

(a) Subject to the specific limitations stated elsewhere in this chapter the court, if recognition is granted, may provide additional assistance to a foreign representative under this title or under other laws of the United States.

(b) In determining whether to provide additional assistance under this title or under other laws of the United States, the court shall consider whether such additional assistance, consistent with the principles of comity, will reasonably assure—

(1) just treatment of all holders of claims against or interests in the debtor's property;

(2) protection of claim holders in the United States against prejudice and inconvenience in the processing of claims in such foreign proceeding;

(3) prevention of preferential or fraudulent dispositions of property of the debtor;

(4) distribution of proceeds of the debtor's property substantially in accordance with the order prescribed by this title; and

(5) if appropriate, the provision of an opportunity for a fresh start for the individual that such foreign proceeding concerns.

§ 1508. Interpretation

In interpreting this chapter, the court shall consider its international origin, and the need to promote an application of this chapter that is consistent with the application of similar statutes adopted by foreign jurisdictions.

SUBCHAPTER II—ACCESS OF FOREIGN REPRESENTATIVES AND CREDITORS TO THE COURT

§ 1509. Right of direct access

(a) A foreign representative may commence a case under section 1504 by filing directly with the court a petition for recognition of a foreign proceeding under section 1515.

(b) If the court grants recognition under section 1517, and subject to any limitations that the court may impose consistent with the policy of this chapter—

　(1) the foreign representative has the capacity to sue and be sued in a court in the United States;

　(2) the foreign representative may apply directly to a court in the United States for appropriate relief in that court; and

　(3) a court in the United States shall grant comity or cooperation to the foreign representative.

(c) A request for comity or cooperation by a foreign representative in a court in the United States other than the court which granted recognition shall be accompanied by a certified copy of an order granting recognition under section 1517.

(d) If the court denies recognition under this chapter, the court may issue any appropriate order necessary to prevent the foreign representative from obtaining comity or cooperation from courts in the United States.

(e) Whether or not the court grants recognition, and subject to sections 306 and 1510, a foreign representative is subject to applicable nonbankruptcy law.

(f) Notwithstanding any other provision of this section, the failure of a foreign representative to commence a case or to obtain recognition under this chapter does not affect any right the foreign representative may have to sue in a court in the United States to collect or recover a claim which is the property of the debtor.

§ 1510. Limited jurisdiction

The sole fact that a foreign representative files a petition under section 1515 does not subject the foreign representative to the jurisdiction of any court in the United States for any other purpose.

§ 1511. Commencement of case under section 301, 302 or 303

(a) Upon recognition, a foreign representative may commence—

　(1) an involuntary case under section 303; or

　(2) a voluntary case under section 301 or 302, if the foreign proceeding is a foreign main proceeding.

(b) The petition commencing a case under subsection (a) must be accompanied by a certified copy of an order granting recognition. The court where the petition for recognition has been filed must be advised of the foreign representative's intent to commence a case under subsection (a) prior to such commencement.

§ 1512. Participation of a foreign representative in a case under this title

Upon recognition of a foreign proceeding, the foreign representative in the recognized proceeding is entitled to participate as a party in interest in a case regarding the debtor under this title.

§ 1513. Access of foreign creditors to a case under this title

(a) Foreign creditors have the same rights regarding the commencement of, and participation in, a case under this title as domestic creditors.

(b)(1) Subsection (a) does not change or codify present law as to the priority of claims under section 507 or 726, except that the claim of a foreign creditor under those sections shall not be given a lower priority than that of general unsecured claims without priority solely because the holder of such claim is a foreign creditor.

(2)(A) Subsection (a) and paragraph (1) do not change or codify present law as to the allowability of foreign revenue claims or other foreign public law claims in a proceeding under this title.

(B) Allowance and priority as to a foreign tax claim or other foreign public law claim shall be governed by any applicable tax treaty of the United States, under the conditions and circumstances specified therein.

§ 1514. Notification to foreign creditors concerning a case under this title

(a) Whenever in a case under this title notice is to be given to creditors generally or to any class or category of creditors, such notice shall also be given to the known creditors generally, or to creditors in the notified class or category, that do not have addresses in the United States. The court may order that appropriate steps be taken with a view to notifying any creditor whose address is not yet known.

(b) Such notification to creditors with foreign addresses described in subsection (a) shall be given individually, unless the court considers that, under the circumstances, some other form of notification would be more appropriate. No letter or other formality is required.

(c) When a notification of commencement of a case is to be given to foreign creditors, such notification shall—

(1) indicate the time period for filing proofs of claim and specify the place for filing such proofs of claim;

(2) indicate whether secured creditors need to file proofs of claim; and

(3) contain any other information required to be included in such notification to creditors under this title and the orders of the court.

(d) Any rule of procedure or order of the court as to notice or the filing of a proof of claim shall provide such additional time to creditors with foreign addresses as is reasonable under the circumstances.

SUBCHAPTER III—RECOGNITION OF A FOREIGN PROCEEDING AND RELIEF

§ 1515. Application for recognition

(a) A foreign representative applies to the court for recognition of a foreign proceeding in which the foreign representative has been appointed by filing a petition for recognition.

(b) A petition for recognition shall be accompanied by—

(1) a certified copy of the decision commencing such foreign proceeding and appointing the foreign representative;

(2) a certificate from the foreign court affirming the existence of such foreign proceeding and of the appointment of the foreign representative; or

(3) in the absence of evidence referred to in paragraphs (1) and (2), any other evidence acceptable to the court of the existence of such foreign proceeding and of the appointment of the foreign representative.

(c) A petition for recognition shall also be accompanied by a statement identifying all foreign proceedings with respect to the debtor that are known to the foreign representative.

(d) The documents referred to in paragraphs (1) and (2) of subsection (b) shall be translated into English. The court may require a translation into English of additional documents.

§ 1516. Presumptions concerning recognition

(a) If the decision or certificate referred to in section 1515(b) indicates that the foreign proceeding is a foreign proceeding and that the person or body is a foreign representative, the court is entitled to so presume.

(b) The court is entitled to presume that documents submitted in support of the petition for recognition are authentic, whether or not they have been legalized.

(c) In the absence of evidence to the contrary, the debtor's registered office, or habitual residence in the case of an individual, is presumed to be the center of the debtor's main interests.

§ 1517. Order granting recognition

(a) Subject to section 1506, after notice and a hearing, an order recognizing a foreign proceeding shall be entered if—

(1) such foreign proceeding for which recognition is sought is a foreign main proceeding or foreign nonmain proceeding within the meaning of section 1502;

(2) the foreign representative applying for recognition is a person or body; and

(3) the petition meets the requirements of section 1515.

(b) Such foreign proceeding shall be recognized—

(1) as a foreign main proceeding if it is pending in the country where the debtor has the center of its main interests; or

(2) as a foreign nonmain proceeding if the debtor has an establishment within the meaning of section 1502 in the foreign country where the proceeding is pending.

(c) A petition for recognition of a foreign proceeding shall be decided upon at the earliest possible time. Entry of an order recognizing a foreign proceeding constitutes recognition under this chapter.

(d) The provisions of this subchapter do not prevent modification or termination of recognition if it is shown that the grounds for granting it were fully or partially lacking or have ceased to exist, but in considering such action the court shall give due weight to possible prejudice to parties that have relied upon the order granting recognition. A case under this chapter may be closed in the manner prescribed under section 350.

§ 1518. Subsequent information

From the time of filing the petition for recognition of a foreign proceeding, the foreign representative shall file with the court promptly a notice of change of status concerning—

(1) any substantial change in the status of such foreign proceeding or the status of the foreign representative's appointment; and

(2) any other foreign proceeding regarding the debtor that becomes known to the foreign representative.

§ 1519. Relief that may be granted upon filing petition for recognition

(a) From the time of filing a petition for recognition until the court rules on the petition, the court may, at the request of the foreign representative, where relief is urgently needed to protect the assets of the debtor or the interests of the creditors, grant relief of a provisional nature, including—

(1) staying execution against the debtor's assets;

(2) entrusting the administration or realization of all or part of the debtor's assets located in the United States to the foreign representative or another person authorized by the court, including an examiner, in order to protect and preserve the value of assets that, by their nature or because of other circumstances, are perishable, susceptible to devaluation or otherwise in jeopardy; and

(3) any relief referred to in paragraph (3), (4), or (7) of section 1521(a).

(b) Unless extended under section 1521(a)(6), the relief granted under this section terminates when the petition for recognition is granted.

(c) It is a ground for denial of relief under this section that such relief would interfere with the administration of a foreign main proceeding.

(d) The court may not enjoin a police or regulatory act of a governmental unit, including a criminal action or proceeding, under this section.

(e) The standards, procedures, and limitations applicable to an injunction shall apply to relief under this section.

(f) The exercise of rights not subject to the stay arising under section 362(a) pursuant to paragraph (6), (7), (17), or (27) of section 362(b) or pursuant to section 362(o) shall not be stayed by any order of a court or administrative agency in any proceeding under this chapter.

§ 1520. Effects of recognition of a foreign main proceeding

(a) Upon recognition of a foreign proceeding that is a foreign main proceeding—

(1) sections 361 and 362 apply with respect to the debtor and the property of the debtor that is within the territorial jurisdiction of the United States;

(2) sections 363, 549, and 552 apply to a transfer of an interest of the debtor in property that is within the territorial jurisdiction of the United States to the same extent that the sections would apply to property of an estate;

(3) unless the court orders otherwise, the foreign representative may operate the debtor's business and may exercise the rights and powers of a trustee under and to the extent provided by sections 363 and 552; and

(4) section 552 applies to property of the debtor that is within the territorial jurisdiction of the United States.

(b) Subsection (a) does not affect the right to commence an individual action or proceeding in a foreign country to the extent necessary to preserve a claim against the debtor.

(c) Subsection (a) does not affect the right of a foreign representative or an entity to file a petition commencing a case under this title or the right of any party to file claims or take other proper actions in such a case.

§ 1521. Relief that may be granted upon recognition

(a) Upon recognition of a foreign proceeding, whether main or nonmain, where necessary to effectuate the purpose of this chapter and to protect the assets of the debtor or the interests of the creditors, the court may, at the request of the foreign representative, grant any appropriate relief, including—

(1) staying the commencement or continuation of an individual action or proceeding concerning the debtor's assets, rights, obligations or liabilities to the extent they have not been stayed under section 1520(a);

(2) staying execution against the debtor's assets to the extent it has not been stayed under section 1520(a);

(3) suspending the right to transfer, encumber or otherwise dispose of any assets of the debtor to the extent this right has not been suspended under section 1520(a);

(4) providing for the examination of witnesses, the taking of evidence or the delivery of information concerning the debtor's assets, affairs, rights, obligations or liabilities;

(5) entrusting the administration or realization of all or part of the debtor's assets within the territorial jurisdiction of the United States to the foreign representative or another person, including an examiner, authorized by the court;

(6) extending relief granted under section 1519(a); and

(7) granting any additional relief that may be available to a trustee, except for relief available under sections 522, 544, 545, 547, 548, 550, and 724(a).

(b) Upon recognition of a foreign proceeding, whether main or nonmain, the court may, at the request of the foreign representative, entrust the distribution of all or part of the debtor's assets located in the United States to the foreign representative or another person, including an examiner, authorized by the court, provided that the court is satisfied that the interests of creditors in the United States are sufficiently protected.

(c) In granting relief under this section to a representative of a foreign nonmain proceeding, the court must be satisfied that the relief relates to assets that, under the law of the United States, should be administered in the foreign nonmain proceeding or concerns information required in that proceeding.

(d) The court may not enjoin a police or regulatory act of a governmental unit, including a criminal action or proceeding, under this section.

(e) The standards, procedures, and limitations applicable to an injunction shall apply to relief under paragraphs (1), (2), (3), and (6) of subsection (a).

(f) The exercise of rights not subject to the stay arising under section 362(a) pursuant to paragraph (6), (7), (17), or (27) of section 362(b) or pursuant to section 362(o) shall not be stayed by any order of a court or administrative agency in any proceeding under this chapter.

§ 1522. Protection of creditors and other interested persons

(a) The court may grant relief under section 1519 or 1521, or may modify or terminate relief under subsection (c), only if the interests of the creditors and other interested entities, including the debtor, are sufficiently protected.

(b) The court may subject relief granted under section 1519 or 1521, or the operation of the debtor's business under section 1520(a)(3), to conditions it considers appropriate, including the giving of security or the filing of a bond.

(c) The court may, at the request of the foreign representative or an entity affected by relief granted under section 1519 or 1521, or at its own motion, modify or terminate such relief.

(d) Section 1104(d) shall apply to the appointment of an examiner under this chapter. Any examiner shall comply with the qualification requirements imposed on a trustee by section 322.

§ 1523. Actions to avoid acts detrimental to creditors

(a) Upon recognition of a foreign proceeding, the foreign representative has standing in a case concerning the debtor pending under another chapter of this title to initiate actions under sections 522, 544, 545, 547, 548, 550, 553, and 724(a).

(b) When a foreign proceeding is a foreign nonmain proceeding, the court must be satisfied that an action under subsection (a) relates to assets that, under United States law, should be administered in the foreign nonmain proceeding.

§ 1524. Intervention by a foreign representative

Upon recognition of a foreign proceeding, the foreign representative may intervene in any proceedings in a State or Federal court in the United States in which the debtor is a party.

SUBCHAPTER IV—COOPERATION WITH FOREIGN COURTS AND FOREIGN REPRESENTATIVES

§ 1525. Cooperation and direct communication between the court and foreign courts or foreign representatives

(a) Consistent with section 1501, the court shall cooperate to the maximum extent possible with a foreign court or a foreign representative, either directly or through the trustee.

(b) The court is entitled to communicate directly with, or to request information or assistance directly from, a foreign court or a foreign representative, subject to the rights of a party in interest to notice and participation.

§ 1526. Cooperation and direct communication between the trustee and foreign courts or foreign representatives

(a) Consistent with section 1501, the trustee or other person, including an examiner, authorized by the court, shall, subject to the supervision of the court, cooperate to the maximum extent possible with a foreign court or a foreign representative.

(b) The trustee or other person, including an examiner, authorized by the court is entitled, subject to the supervision of the court, to communicate directly with a foreign court or a foreign representative.

§ 1527. Forms of cooperation

Cooperation referred to in sections 1525 and 1526 may be implemented by any appropriate means, including—

(1) appointment of a person or body, including an examiner, to act at the direction of the court;

(2) communication of information by any means considered appropriate by the court;

(3) coordination of the administration and supervision of the debtor's assets and affairs;

(4) approval or implementation of agreements concerning the coordination of proceedings; and

(5) coordination of concurrent proceedings regarding the same debtor.

SUBCHAPTER V—CONCURRENT PROCEEDINGS

§ 1528. Commencement of a case under this title after recognition of a foreign main proceeding

After recognition of a foreign main proceeding, a case under another chapter of this title may be commenced only if the debtor has assets in the United States. The effects of such case shall be restricted to the assets of the debtor that are within the territorial jurisdiction of the United States and, to the extent necessary to implement cooperation and coordination under sections 1525, 1526, and 1527, to other assets of the debtor that are within the jurisdiction of the court under sections 541(a) of this title, and 1334(e) of title 28, to the extent that such other assets are not subject to the jurisdiction and control of a foreign proceeding that has been recognized under this chapter.

§ 1529. Coordination of a case under this title and a foreign proceeding

If a foreign proceeding and a case under another chapter of this title are pending concurrently regarding the same debtor, the court shall seek cooperation and coordination under sections 1525, 1526, and 1527, and the following shall apply:

(1) If the case in the United States pending at the time the petition for recognition of such foreign proceeding is filed—

(A) any relief granted under section 1519 or 1521 must be consistent with the relief granted in the case in the United States; and

(B) section 1520 does not apply even if such foreign proceeding is recognized as a foreign main proceeding.

(2) If a case in the United States under this title commences after recognition, or after the date of the filing of the petition for recognition, of such foreign proceeding—

(A) any relief in effect under section 1519 or 1521 shall be reviewed by the court and shall be modified or terminated if inconsistent with the case in the United States; and

(B) if such foreign proceeding is a foreign main proceeding, the stay and suspension referred to in section 1520(a) shall be modified or terminated if inconsistent with the relief granted in the case in the United States.

(3) In granting, extending, or modifying relief granted to a representative of a foreign nonmain proceeding, the court must be satisfied that the relief relates to assets that, under the laws of the United States, should be administered in the foreign nonmain proceeding or concerns information required in that proceeding.

(4) In achieving cooperation and coordination under sections 1528 and 1529, the court may grant any of the relief authorized under section 305.

§ 1530. Coordination of more than 1 foreign proceeding

In matters referred to in section 1501, with respect to more than 1 foreign proceeding regarding the debtor, the court shall seek cooperation and coordination under sections 1525, 1526, and 1527, and the following shall apply:

(1) Any relief granted under section 1519 or 1521 to a representative of a foreign nonmain proceeding after recognition of a foreign main proceeding must be consistent with the foreign main proceeding.

(2) If a foreign main proceeding is recognized after recognition, or after the filing of a petition for recognition, of a foreign nonmain proceeding, any relief in effect under section 1519 or 1521 shall be reviewed by the court and shall be modified or terminated if inconsistent with the foreign main proceeding.

(3) If, after recognition of a foreign nonmain proceeding, another foreign nonmain proceeding is recognized, the court shall grant, modify, or terminate relief for the purpose of facilitating coordination of the proceedings.

§ 1531. Presumption of insolvency based on recognition of a foreign main proceeding

In the absence of evidence to the contrary, recognition of a foreign main proceeding is, for the purpose of commencing a proceeding under section 303, proof that the debtor is generally not paying its debts as such debts become due.

§ 1532. Rule of payment in concurrent proceedings

Without prejudice to secured claims or rights in rem, a creditor who has received payment with respect to its claim in a foreign proceeding pursuant to a law relating to insolvency may not receive a payment for the same claim in a case under any other chapter of this title regarding the debtor, so long as the payment to other creditors of the same class is proportionately less than the payment the creditor has already received.

PART 2

BANKRUPTCY CRIMES
(TITLE 18 OF THE UNITED
STATES CODE)

PART 3

SELECTED RELATED PROVISIONS OF U.S. CODE TITLES 18 AND 28 TITLE 18 CRIMES AND CRIMINAL PROCEDURE

CHAPTER 9—BANKRUPTCY

CHAPTER 9—BANKRUPTCY

§ 151. Definition

As used in this chapter, the term "debtor" means a debtor concerning whom a petition has been filed under Title 11.

§ 152. Concealment of assets; false oaths and claims; bribery

A person who—

(1) knowingly and fraudulently conceals from a custodian, trustee, marshal, or other officer of the court charged with the control or custody of property, or, in connection with a case under title 11, from creditors or the United States Trustee, any property belonging to the estate of a debtor;

(2) knowingly and fraudulently makes a false oath or account in or in relation to any case under title 11;

(3) knowingly and fraudulently makes a false declaration, certificate, verification, or statement under penalty of perjury as permitted under section 1746 of title 28, in or in relation to any case under title 11;

(4) knowingly and fraudulently presents any false claim for proof against the estate of a debtor, or uses any such claim in any case under title 11, in a personal capacity or as or through an agent, proxy, or attorney;

(5) knowingly and fraudulently receives any material amount of property from a debtor after the filing of a case under title 11, with intent to defeat the provisions of title 11;

(6) knowingly and fraudulently gives, offers, receives, or attempts to obtain any money or property, remuneration, compensation, reward, advantage, or promise thereof for acting or forbearing to act in any case under title 11;

(7) in a personal capacity or as an agent or officer of any person or corporation, in contemplation of a case under title 11 by or against the person or any other person or corporation, or with intent to defeat the provisions of title 11, knowingly and

205

fraudulently transfers or conceals any of his property or the property of such other person or corporation;

    (8) after the filing of a case under title 11 or in contemplation thereof, knowingly and fraudulently conceals, destroys, mutilates, falsifies, or makes a false entry in any recorded information (including books, documents, records, and papers) relating to the property or financial affairs of a debtor; or

    (9) after the filing of a case under title 11, knowingly and fraudulently withholds from a custodian, trustee, marshal, or other officer of the court or a United States Trustee entitled to its possession, any recorded information (including books, documents, records, and papers) relating to the property or financial affairs of a debtor,

shall be fined under this title, imprisoned not more than 5 years, or both.

* * *

§ 156.   Knowing disregard of bankruptcy law or rule

    (a) Definitions.—In this section—

    (1) the term "bankruptcy petition preparer" means a person, other than the debtor's attorney or an employee of such an attorney, who prepares for compensation a document for filing; and

    (2) the term "document for filing" means a petition or any other document prepared for filing by a debtor in a United States bankruptcy court or a United States district court in connection with a case under title 11.

    (b) Offense.—If a bankruptcy case or related proceeding is dismissed because of a knowing attempt by a bankruptcy petition preparer in any manner to disregard the requirements of title 11, United States Code, or the Federal Rules of Bankruptcy Procedure, the bankruptcy petition preparer shall be fined under this title, imprisoned not more than 1 year, or both.

§ 157.   Bankruptcy fraud

    A person who, having devised or intending to devise a scheme or artifice to defraud and for the purpose of executing or concealing such a scheme or artifice or attempting to do so—

    (1) files a petition under title 11, including a fraudulent involuntary bankruptcy petition under section 303 of such title;

    (2) files a document in a proceeding under title 11; or

    (3) makes a false or fraudulent representation, claim, or promise concerning or in relation to a proceeding under title 11, at any time before or after the filing of the petition, or in relation to a proceeding falsely asserted to be pending under such title,

shall be fined under this title, imprisoned not more than 5 years, or both.

PART 3

BANKRUPTCY JURISDICTION, VENUE AND APPEALS
(TITLE 28)

TITLE 28
JUDICIARY AND JUDICIAL PROCEDURE

PART I—ORGANIZATION OF COURTS

CHAPTER 6—BANKRUPTCY JUDGES

PART II—DEPARTMENT OF JUSTICE

CHAPTER 39—UNITED STATES TRUSTEES

PART III—COURT OFFICERS AND EMPLOYEES

CHAPTER 57—GENERAL PROVISIONS APPLICABLE TO COURT OFFICERS AND EMPLOYEES

PART IV—JURISDICTION AND VENUE

CHAPTER 85—DISTRICT COURTS; JURISDICTION

CHAPTER 87—DISTRICT COURTS; VENUE

CHAPTER 89—DISTRICT COURTS; REMOVAL OF CASES FROM STATE COURTS

PART V—PROCEDURE

CHAPTER 123—FEES AND COSTS

CHAPTER 131—RULES OF COURTS

PART I—ORGANIZATION OF COURTS

CHAPTER 6—BANKRUPTCY JUDGES

§ 151. Designation of bankruptcy courts

In each judicial district, the bankruptcy judges in regular active service shall constitute a unit of the district court to be known as the bankruptcy court for that district. Each bankruptcy judge, as a judicial officer of the district court, may exercise the authority conferred under this chapter with respect to any action, suit, or proceeding and may preside alone and hold a regular or special session of the court, except as otherwise provided by law or by rule or order of the district court.

UNOFFICIAL COMMENTS

Sections 1334, 151 and 157 have to be read together. Preferably in that order. In section 1334, there is a Congressional grant of jurisdiction to district courts. In section 151, bankruptcy judges are made part of the district court. And, section 157 establishes the procedures for determining what a bankruptcy judge does and what a district judge does.

§ 152. Appointment of bankruptcy judges

(a)(1) Each bankruptcy judge to be appointed for a judicial district, as provided in paragraph (2), shall be appointed by the court of appeals of the United States for the circuit in which such district is located. Such appointments shall be made after considering the recommendations of the Judicial Conference submitted pursuant to subsection (b). Each bankruptcy judge shall be appointed for a term of fourteen years, subject to the provisions of subsection (e). However, upon the expiration of the term, a bankruptcy judge may, with the approval of the judicial council of the circuit, continue to perform the duties of the office until the earlier of the date which is 180 days after the expiration of the term or the date of the appointment of a successor. Bankruptcy judges shall serve as judicial officers of the United States district court established under Article III of the Constitution.

(2) The bankruptcy judges appointed pursuant to this section shall be appointed for the several judicial districts as follows:

Districts	Judges
Alabama:	
Northern	5
Middle	2
Southern	2
Alaska	2
Arizona	7
Arkansas:	
Eastern and Western	3
California:	
Northern	9
Eastern	6

* * *

§ 157. Procedures

(a) Each district court may provide that any or all cases under title 11 and any or all proceedings arising under title 11 or arising in or related to a case under title 11 shall be referred to the bankruptcy judges for the district.

(b)(1) Bankruptcy judges may hear and determine all cases under title 11 and all core proceedings arising under title 11, or arising in a case under title 11, referred under subsection (a) of this section, and may enter appropriate orders and judgments, subject to review under section 158 of this title.

(2) Core proceedings include, but are not limited to—

(A) matters concerning the administration of the estate;

(B) allowance or disallowance of claims against the estate or exemptions from property of the estate, and estimation of claims or interests for the purposes of confirming a plan under chapter 11, 12, or 13 of title 11 but not the liquidation or estimation of contingent or unliquidated personal injury tort or wrongful death claims against the estate for purposes of distribution in a case under title 11;

(C) counterclaims by the estate against persons filing claims against the estate;

(D) orders in respect to obtaining credit;

(E) orders to turn over property of the estate;

(F) proceedings to determine, avoid, or recover preferences;

(G) motions to terminate, annul, or modify the automatic stay;

(H) proceedings to determine, avoid, or recover fraudulent conveyances;

(I) determinations as to the dischargeability of particular debts;

(J) objections to discharges;

(K) determinations of the validity, extent, or priority of liens;

(L) confirmations of plans;

(M) orders approving the use or lease of property, including the use of cash collateral;

(N) orders approving the sale of property other than property resulting from claims brought by the estate against persons who have not filed claims against the estate;

(O) other proceedings affecting the liquidation of the assets of the estate or the adjustment of the debtor-creditor or the equity security holder relationship, except personal injury tort or wrongful death claims; and

(P) recognition of foreign proceedings and other matters under chapter 15 of title 11.

(3) The bankruptcy judge shall determine, on the judge's own motion or on timely motion of a party, whether a proceeding is a core proceeding under this subsection or is a proceeding that is otherwise related to a case under title 11. A determination that a proceeding is not a core proceeding shall not be made solely on the basis that its resolution may be affected by State law.

(4) Non-core proceedings under section 157(b)(2)(B) of title 28, United States Code, shall not be subject to the mandatory abstention provisions of section 1334(c)(2).

(5) The district court shall order that personal injury tort and wrongful death claims shall be tried in the district court in which the bankruptcy case is pending, or in the district court in the district in which the claim arose, as determined by the district court in which the bankruptcy case is pending.

(c)(1) A bankruptcy judge may hear a proceeding that is not a core proceeding but that is otherwise related to a case under title 11. In such proceeding, the bankruptcy judge shall submit proposed findings of fact and conclusions of law to the district court, and any final order or judgment shall be entered by the district judge after considering the bankruptcy judge's proposed findings and conclusions and after reviewing de novo those matters to which any party has timely and specifically objected.

(2) Notwithstanding the provisions of paragraph (1) of this subsection, the district court, with the consent of all the parties to the proceeding, may refer a proceeding related to a case under title 11 to a bankruptcy judge to hear and determine and to enter appropriate orders and judgments, subject to review under section 158 of this title.

(d) The district court may withdraw, in whole or in part, any case or proceeding referred under this section, on its own motion or on timely motion of any party, for cause shown. The district court shall, on timely motion of a party, so withdraw a proceeding if the court determines that resolution of the proceeding requires consideration of both title 11 and other laws of the United States regulating organizations or activities affecting interstate commerce.

(e) If the right to a jury trial applies in a proceeding that may be heard under this section by a bankruptcy judge, the bankruptcy judge may conduct the jury trial if specially designated to exercise such jurisdiction by the district court and with the express consent of all the parties.

UNOFFICIAL COMMENTS

Sections 1334, 151 and 157 have to be read together. In section 1334, there is a Congressional grant of jurisdiction to district courts. In section 151, bankruptcy judges are made part of the district court. And, section 157 establishes the procedures for determining what a bankruptcy judge does and what a district judge does.

Local rules set out the steps required for withdrawal of reference.

In each judicial district, there is a general order, generally referring bankruptcy matters to bankruptcy judges. In light of these general reference orders and sections 151 and 1334, every time you see the phrase "district court" in the title 28 provisions allocating judicial power over bankruptcy matters, think "bankruptcy judge."

Matters that do not come within the term "core proceedings" as explained in section 157(b)(2) are generally called "non-core proceedings."

The Supreme Court in *Stein v. Marshall*, held that section 157(b)(2)(C) as applied to state-law based counterclaims was unconstitutional.

§ 158. Appeals

(a) The district courts of the United States shall have jurisdiction to hear appeals[1]

(1) from final judgments, orders, and decrees;

(2) from interlocutory orders and decrees issued under section 1121(d) of title 11 increasing or reducing the time periods referred to in section 1121 of such title; and

(3) with leave of the court, from other interlocutory orders and decrees;

and, with leave of the court, from interlocutory orders and decrees, of bankruptcy judges entered in cases and proceedings referred to the bankruptcy judges under section 157 of this title. An appeal under this subsection shall be taken only to the district court for the judicial district in which the bankruptcy judge is serving.

(b)(1) The judicial council of a circuit shall establish a bankruptcy appellate panel service composed of bankruptcy judges of the districts in the circuit who are appointed by the judicial council in accordance with paragraph (3), to hear and determine, with the consent of all the parties, appeals under subsection (a) unless the judicial council finds that—

(A) there are insufficient judicial resources available in the circuit; or

(B) establishment of such service would result in undue delay or increased cost to parties in cases under title 11.

* * *

(d)(1) The courts of appeals shall have jurisdiction of appeals from all final decisions, judgments, orders, and decrees entered under subsections (a) and (b) of this section.

* * *

(D) An appeal under this paragraph does not stay any proceeding of the bankruptcy court, the district court, or the bankruptcy appellate panel from which the appeal is taken, unless the respective bankruptcy court, district court, or bankruptcy appellate panel, or the court of appeals in which the appeal in pending, issues a stay of such proceeding pending the appeal.

* * *

PART II—DEPARTMENT OF JUSTICE

CHAPTER 39—UNITED STATES TRUSTEES

Sec.

§ 581. United States trustees

(a) The Attorney General shall appoint one United States trustee for each of the following regions composed of Federal judicial districts * * *

---

[1] So in original.

(b) Each United States trustee shall be appointed for a term of five years. On the expiration of his term, a United States trustee shall continue to perform the duties of his office until his successor is appointed and qualifies.

(c) Each United States trustee is subject to removal by the Attorney General.

PART III—COURT OFFICERS AND EMPLOYEES

CHAPTER 57—GENERAL PROVISIONS APPLICABLE TO COURT OFFICERS AND EMPLOYEES

§ 959. Trustees and receivers suable; management; State laws

(a) Trustees, receivers or managers of any property, including debtors in possession, may be sued, without leave of the court appointing them, with respect to any of their acts or transactions in carrying on business connected with such property. Such actions shall be subject to the general equity power of such court so far as the same may be necessary to the ends of justice, but this shall not deprive a litigant of his right to trial by jury.

(b) Except as provided in section 1166 of title 11, a trustee, receiver or manager appointed in any cause pending in any court of the United States, including a debtor in possession, shall manage and operate the property in his possession as such trustee, receiver or manager according to the requirements of the valid laws of the State in which such property is situated, in the same manner that the owner or possessor thereof would be bound to do if in possession thereof.

PART IV—JURISDICTION AND VENUE

CHAPTER 85—DISTRICT COURTS; JURISDICTION

§ 1334. Bankruptcy cases and proceedings

(a) Except as provided in subsection (b) of this section, the district courts shall have original and exclusive jurisdiction of all cases under title 11.

(b) Except as provided in subsection (e)(2), and notwithstanding any Act of Congress that confers exclusive jurisdiction on a court or courts other than the district courts, the district courts shall have original but not exclusive jurisdiction of all civil proceedings arising under title 11, or arising in or related to cases under title 11.

(c)(1) Except with respect to a case under chapter 15 of title 11, nothing in this section prevents a district court in the interest of justice, or in the interest of comity with State courts or respect for State law, from abstaining from hearing a particular proceeding arising under title 11 or arising in or related to a case under title 11.

(2) Upon timely motion of a party in a proceeding based upon a State law claim or State law cause of action, related to a case under title 11 but not arising under title 11 or arising in a case under title 11, with respect to which an action could not have been commenced in a court of the United States absent jurisdiction under this section, the district court shall abstain from hearing such proceeding if an action is commenced, and can be timely adjudicated, in a State forum of appropriate jurisdiction.

(d) Any decision to abstain or not to abstain made under subsection (c) (other than a decision not to abstain in a proceeding described in subsection (c)(2)) is not reviewable by appeal or otherwise by the court of appeals under section 158(d), 1291, or 1292 of this title or by the Supreme Court of the United States under section 1254 of this title. Subsection (c) and this subsection shall not be construed to limit the applicability of the stay provided for by section 362 of title 11, United States Code, as such section applies to an action affecting the property of the estate in bankruptcy.

(e) The district court in which a case under title 11 is commenced or is pending shall have exclusive jurisdiction—

    (1) of all the property, wherever located, of the debtor as of the commencement of such case, and of property of the estate; and

    (2) over all claims or causes of action that involve construction of section 327 of title 11, United States Code, or rules relating to disclosure requirements under section 327.

UNOFFICIAL COMMENT

Sections 1334, 151 and 157 have to be read together. In section 1334, there is a Congressional grant of jurisdiction to district courts. In section 151, bankruptcy judges are made part of the district court. And, section 157 establishes the procedures for determining what a bankruptcy judge does and what a district judge does.

In each judicial district, there is a general order, generally referring bankruptcy matters to bankruptcy judges. In light of these general reference orders and section 151, every time you see the phrase "district court" in the title 28 provisions allocating judicial power over bankruptcy matters, think "bankruptcy judge."

CHAPTER 87—DISTRICT COURTS; VENUE

Sec.

§ 1408. Venue of Cases under Title 11

Except as provided in section 1410 of this title, a case under title 11 may be commenced in the district court for the district—

    (1) in which the domicile, residence, principal place of business in the United States, or principal assets in the United States, of the person or entity that is the subject of such case have been located for the one hundred and eighty days immediately preceding such commencement, or for a longer portion of such one-hundred-and-eighty-day period than the domicile, residence, or principal place of business, in the United States, or principal assets in the United States, of such person were located in any other district; or

(2) in which there is pending a case under title 11 concerning such person's affiliate, general partner, or partnership.

UNOFFICIAL COMMENT

If you professor has written law review articles about big case bankruptcy filings in Delaware, then it is important to read this section and those articles.

§ 1409. Venue of proceedings arising under title 11 or arising in or related to cases under title 11

(a) Except as otherwise provided in subsections (b) and (d), a proceeding arising under title 11 or arising in or related to a case under title 11 may be commenced in the district court in which such case is pending.

(b) Except as provided in subsection (d) of this section, a trustee in a case under title 11 may commence a proceeding arising in or related to such case to recover a money judgment of or property worth less than $1,100 or a consumer debt of less than $16,425, or a debt (excluding a consumer debt) against a noninsider of less than $10,950, only in the district court for the district in which the defendant resides.

* * *

(d) A trustee may commence a proceeding arising under title 11 or arising in or related to a case under title 11 based on a claim arising after the commencement of such case from the operation of the business of the debtor only in the district court for the district where a State or Federal court sits in which, under applicable nonbankruptcy venue provisions, an action on such claim may have been brought.

(e) A proceeding arising under title 11 or arising in or related to a case under title 11, based on a claim arising after the commencement of such case from the operation of the business of the debtor, may be commenced against the representative of the estate in such case in the district court for the district where the State or Federal court sits in which the party commencing such proceeding may, under applicable nonbankruptcy venue provisions, have brought an action on such claim, or in the district court in which such case is pending.

* * *

§ 1411. Jury trials

(a) Except as provided in subsection (b) of this section, this chapter and title 11 do not affect any right to trial by jury that an individual has under applicable nonbankruptcy law with regard to a personal injury or wrongful death tort claim.

(b) The district court may order the issues arising under section 303 of title 11 to be tried without a jury.

§ 1412. Change of venue

A district court may transfer a case or proceeding under title 11 to a district court for another district, in the interest of justice or for the convenience of the parties.

CHAPTER 89—DISTRICT COURTS; REMOVAL OF CASES FROM STATE COURTS

Sec.
1452.   Removal of Claims Related to Bankruptcy Cases

§ 1452. Removal of claims related to bankruptcy cases

(a) A party may remove any claim or cause of action in a civil action other than a proceeding before the United States Tax Court or a civil action by a governmental unit to enforce such governmental unit's police or regulatory power, to the district court for the district where such civil action is pending, if such district court has jurisdiction of such claim or cause of action under section 1334 of this title.

(b) The court to which such claim or cause of action is removed may remand such claim or cause of action on any equitable ground. An order entered under this subsection remanding a claim or cause of action, or a decision to not remand, is not reviewable by appeal or otherwise by the court of appeals under section 158(d), 1291, or 1292 of this title or by the Supreme Court of the United States under section 1254 of this title.

PART V—PROCEDURE

CHAPTER 123—FEES AND COSTS

Sec.
1930.   Bankruptcy Fees

§ 1930. Bankruptcy fees

(a) The parties commencing a case under title 11 shall pay to the clerk of the district court or the clerk of the bankruptcy court, if one has been certified pursuant to section 156(b) of this title, the following filing fees:

(1) For a case commenced under—

(A) chapter 7 of title 11, $245, and

(B) chapter 13 of title 11, $235.

* * *

(3) For a case commenced under chapter 11 of title 11 that does not concern a railroad, as defined in section 101 of title 11, $1,000.

* * *

(5) For a case commenced under chapter 12 of title 11, $200.

(6) In addition to the filing fee paid to the clerk, a quarterly fee shall be paid to the United States trustee, for deposit in the Treasury, in each case under chapter 11 of title 11 for each quarter (including any fraction thereof) until the case is converted or dismissed, whichever occurs first. The fee shall be $ 30,000 for each quarter in which disbursements total $30,000,000 or more. The fee shall be payable on the last day of the calendar month following the calendar quarter for which the fee is owed.

* * *

(f)(1) Under the procedures prescribed by the Judicial Conference of the United States, the district court or the bankruptcy court may waive the filing fee in a case under chapter 7 of title 11 for an individual if the court determines that such individual has income less than 150 percent of the income official poverty line (as defined by the Office of Management and Budget, and revised annually in accordance with section 673(2) of the Omnibus Budget Reconciliation Act of 1981) applicable to a family of the size involved and is unable to pay that fee in installments. . . .

CHAPTER 131—RULES OF COURTS

Sec.
2075.   Bankruptcy Rules

§ 2075. Bankruptcy rules

The Supreme Court shall have the power to prescribe by general rules, the forms of process, writs, pleadings, and motions, and the practice and procedure in cases under title 11.

Such rules shall not abridge, enlarge, or modify any substantive right.

The Supreme Court shall transmit to Congress not later than May 1 of the year in which a rule prescribed under this section is to become effective a copy of the proposed rule. The rule shall take effect no earlier than December 1 of the year in which it is transmitted to Congress unless otherwise provided by law.

The bankruptcy rules promulgated under this section shall prescribe a form for the statement required under section 707(b)(2)(C) of title 11 and may provide general rules on the content of such statement.

PART 4

FEDERAL RULES OF BANKRUPTCY PROCEDURE

FEDERAL RULES OF BANKRUPTCY PROCEDURE[1]

PART I—COMMENCEMENT OF CASE: PROCEEDINGS RELATING TO PETITION AND ORDER FOR RELIEF

Rule

Rule 1015. Consolidation or Joint Administration of Cases Pending in Same Court

* * *

(b) Cases involving two or more related debtors

If a joint petition or two or more petitions are pending in the same court by or against (1) a husband and wife, or (2) a partnership and one or more of its general partners, or (3) two or more general partners, or (4) a debtor and an affiliate, the court may order a joint administration of the estates. Prior to entering an order the court shall give consideration to protecting creditors of different estates against potential conflicts of interest. An order directing joint administration of individual cases of a husband and wife shall, if one spouse has elected the exemptions under § 522(b)(2) of the Code and the other has elected the exemptions under § 522(b)(3), fix a reasonable time within which either may amend the election so that both shall have elected the same exemptions. The order shall notify the debtors that unless they elect the same exemptions within the time fixed by the court, they will be deemed to have elected the exemptions provided by § 522(b)(2).

---

[1]   Most of the provisions of the Bankruptcy Abuse Prevention and Consumer Protection Act ("BAPCPA") became effective in October of 2005.

Promulgation of Bankruptcy Rules is normally a three-year process. As a result, the Advisory Committee on Bankruptcy Rules has prepared Interim Rules designed to implement the changes mandated by BAPCA. These Interim Rules have legal effect because local courts have adopted the Interim Rules.

In this book, we use italics to indicate language added by the Interim Rules.

* * *

PART II—OFFICERS AND ADMINISTRATION; NOTICES; MEETINGS; EXAMINATIONS; ELECTIONS; ATTORNEYS AND ACCOUNTANTS

Rule 2002. Notices to Creditors, Equity Security Holders, Administrators in Foreign Proceedings, Persons Against Whom Provisional Relief is Sought in Ancillary and Other Cross-Border Cases, United States, and United States Trustee

(a) Twenty-one-day notices to parties in interest

Except as provided in subdivisions (h), (i), (/), (p), and (q) of this rule, the clerk, or some other person as the court may direct, shall give the debtor, the trustee, all creditors and indenture trustees at least 21 days' notice by mail of:

(1) the meeting of creditors under § 341 or § 1104(b) of the Code, which notice, unless the court orders otherwise, shall include the debtor's employer identification number, social security number, and any other federal taxpayer identification number;

(2) a proposed use, sale, or lease of property of the estate other than in the ordinary course of business, unless the court for cause shown shortens the time or directs another method of giving notice;

(3) the hearing on approval of a compromise or settlement of a controversy other than approval of an agreement pursuant to *Rule 4001(d)*, unless the court for cause shown directs that notice not be sent;

(4) in a chapter 7 liquidation, a chapter 11 reorganization case, or a chapter 12 family farmer debt adjustment case, the hearing on the dismissal of the case or the conversion of the case to another chapter, unless the hearing is under § 707(a)(3) or § 707(b) or is on dismissal of the case for failure to pay the filing fee;

(5) the time fixed to accept or reject a proposed modification of a plan;

(6) a hearing on any entity's request for compensation or reimbursement of expenses if the request exceeds $1,000;

(7) the time fixed for filing proofs of claims pursuant to *Rule 3003(c)*; and

(8) the time fixed for filing objections and the hearing to consider confirmation of a chapter 12 plan.

* * *

Rule 2004. Examination

(a) Examination on motion

On motion of any party in interest, the court may order the examination of any entity.

(b) Scope of examination

The examination of an entity under this rule or of the debtor under § 343 of the Code may relate only to the acts, conduct, or property or to the liabilities and financial condition of the debtor, or to any matter which may affect the administration of the debtor's estate, or to the debtor's right to a discharge. In a family farmer's debt adjustment case under chapter 12, an individual's debt adjustment case under chapter 13, or a reorganization case under chapter 11 of the Code, other than for the reorganization of a railroad, the examination may also relate to the operation of any business and the desirability of its continuance, the source of any money or property acquired or to be acquired by the debtor for purposes of consummating a plan and the consideration given or offered therefor, and any other matter relevant to the case or to the formulation of a plan.

* * *

(d) Time and place of examination of debtor

The court may for cause shown and on terms as it may impose order the debtor to be examined under this rule at any time or place it designates, whether within or without the district wherein the case is pending.

* * *

PART III—CLAIMS AND DISTRIBUTION TO CREDITORS AND EQUITY INTEREST HOLDERS; PLANS

Rule 3012. Valuation of Security

The court may determine the value of a claim secured by a lien on property in which the estate has an interest on motion of any party in interest and after a hearing on notice to the holder of the secured claim and any other entity as the court may direct.

Rule 3014. Election Under § 1111(b) by Secured Creditor in Chapter 9 Municipality or Chapter 11 Reorganization Case

An election of application of § 1111(b)(2) of the Code by a class of secured creditors in a chapter 9 or 11 case may be made at any time prior to the conclusion of the hearing on the disclosure statement or within such later time as the court may fix. If the disclosure statement is conditionally approved pursuant to Rule 3017.1, and a final hearing on the disclosure statement is not held, the election of application of § 1111(b)(2) may be made not later than the date fixed pursuant to Rule 3017.1(a)(2) or another date the court may fix. The election shall be in writing and signed unless made at the hearing on the disclosure statement. The election, if made by the majorities required by § 1111(b)(1)(A)(i), shall be binding on all members of the class with respect to the plan.

* * *

PART IV—THE DEBTOR: DUTIES AND BENEFITS

Rule 4001. Relief from Automatic Stay; Prohibiting or Conditioning the Use, Sale, or Lease of Property; Use of Cash Collateral; Obtaining Credit; Agreements

(a) Relief from stay; prohibiting or conditioning the use, sale, or lease of property

(1) Motion

A motion for relief from an automatic stay provided by the Code or a motion to prohibit or condition the use, sale, or lease of property pursuant to § 363(e) shall be made in accordance with Rule 9014 and shall be served on any committee elected pursuant to § 705 or appointed pursuant to § 1102 of the Code or its authorized agent, or, if the case is a chapter 9 municipality case or a chapter 11 reorganization case and no committee of unsecured creditors has been appointed pursuant to § 1102, on the creditors included on the list filed pursuant to Rule 1007(d), and on such other entities as the court may direct.

(2) Ex parte relief

Relief from a stay under § 362(a) or a request to prohibit or condition the use, sale, or lease of property pursuant to § 363(e) may be granted without prior notice only if (A) it clearly appears from specific facts shown by affidavit or by a verified motion that immediate and irreparable injury, loss, or damage will result to the movant before the adverse party or the attorney for the adverse party can be heard in opposition, and (B) the movant's attorney certifies to the court in writing the efforts, if any, which have been made to give notice and the reasons why notice should not be required. The party obtaining relief under this subdivision and § 362(f) or § 363(e) shall immediately give oral notice thereof to the trustee or debtor in possession and to the debtor and forthwith mail or otherwise transmit to such adverse party or parties a copy of the order granting relief. On two days notice to the party who obtained relief from the stay without notice or on shorter notice to that party as the court may prescribe, the adverse party may appear and move reinstatement of the stay or reconsideration of the order prohibiting or conditioning the use, sale, or lease of property. In that event, the court shall proceed expeditiously to hear and determine the motion.

(3) Stay of order

An order granting a motion for relief from an automatic stay made in accordance with Rule 4001(a)(1) is stayed until the expiration of 14 days after the entry of the order, unless the court orders otherwise.

(b) Use of cash collateral

(1) Motion; Service.

(A) Motion. A motion for authority to use cash collateral shall be made in accordance with Rule 9014 and shall be accompanied by a proposed form of order.

(B) Contents. The motion shall consist of or (if the motion is more than five pages in length) begin with a concise statement of the relief requested, not to exceed five pages, that lists or summarizes, and sets out the location within the relevant documents of, all material provisions, including:

> **(i)** the name of each entity with an interest in the cash collateral;

> **(ii)** the purposes for the use of the cash collateral;

> **(iii)** the material terms, including duration, of the use of the cash collateral; and

> **(iv)** any liens, cash payments, or other adequate protection that will be provided to each entity with an interest in the cash collateral or, if no additional adequate protection is proposed, an explanation of why each entity's interest is adequately protected.

(C) Service. The motion shall be served on: (1) any entity with an interest in the cash collateral; (2) any committee elected under § 705 or appointed under § 1102 of the Code, or its authorized agent, or, if the case is a chapter 9 municipality case or a chapter 11 reorganization case and no committee of unsecured creditors has been appointed under § 1102, the creditors included on the list filed under Rule 1007(d); and (3) any other entity that the court directs.

* * *

(c) Obtaining credit

(A) Motion. A motion for authority to obtain credit shall be made in accordance with Rule 9014 and shall be accompanied by a copy of the credit agreement and a proposed form of order.

(B) Contents. The motion shall consist of or (if the motion is more than five pages in length) begin with a concise statement of the relief requested, not to exceed five pages, that lists or summarizes, and sets out the location within the relevant documents of, all material provisions of the proposed credit agreement and form of order, including interest rate, maturity, events of default, liens, borrowing limits, and borrowing conditions. If the proposed credit agreement or form of order includes any of the provisions listed below, the concise statement shall also: briefly list or summarize each one; identify its specific location in the proposed agreement and form of order; and identify any such provision that is proposed to remain in effect if interim approval is granted, but final relief is denied, as provided under Rule 4001(c)(2). In addition, the motion shall describe the nature and extent of each provision listed below:

(i) a grant of priority or a lien on property of the estate under § 364(c) or (d);

(ii) the providing of adequate protection or priority for a claim that arose before the commencement of the case, including the granting of a lien on property of the estate to secure the claim, or the use of property of the estate or credit obtained under § 364 to make cash payments on account of the claim;

(iii) a determination of the validity, enforceability, priority, or amount of a claim that arose before the commencement of the case, or of any lien securing the claim;

(iv) a waiver or modification of Code provisions or applicable rules relating to the automatic stay;

(v) a waiver or modification of any entity's authority or right to file a plan, seek an extension of time in which the debtor has the exclusive right to file a plan, request the use of cash collateral under § 363(c), or request authority to obtain credit under § 364;

(vi) the establishment of deadlines for filing a plan of reorganization, for approval of a disclosure statement, for a hearing on confirmation, or for entry of a confirmation order;

(vii) a waiver or modification of the applicability of nonbankruptcy law relating to the perfection of a lien on property of the estate, or on the foreclosure or other enforcement of the lien;

(viii) a release, waiver, or limitation on any claim or other cause of action belonging to the estate or the trustee, including any modification of the statute of limitations or other deadline to commence an action;

(ix) the indemnification of any entity;

(x) a release, waiver, or limitation of any right under § 506(c); or

(xi) the granting of a lien on any claim or cause of action arising under §§ 544, 545, 547, 548, 549, 553(b), 723(a), or 724(a).

* * *

Rule 4002. Duties of Debtor

(a) In general

In addition to performing other duties prescribed by the Code and rules, the debtor shall:

(1) attend and submit to an examination at the times ordered by the court;

(2) attend the hearing on a complaint objecting to discharge and testify, if called as a witness;

(3) inform the trustee immediately in writing as to the location of real property in which the debtor has an interest and the name and address of every person holding money or property subject to the debtor's withdrawal or order if a schedule of property has not yet been filed pursuant to Rule 1007;

(4) cooperate with the trustee in the preparation of an inventory, the examination of proofs of claim, and the administration of the estate; and

(5) file a statement of any change of the debtor's address.

(b) Individual debtor's duty to provide documentation

(1) Personal Identification. Every individual debtor shall bring to the meeting of creditors under § 341:

(A) a picture identification issued by a government unit, or other personal identifying information that establishes the debtor's identity; and

(B) evidence of social security number(s), or a written statement that such documentation does not exist.

(2) Financial Information. Every individual debtor shall bring to the meeting of creditors under 341 and make available to the trustee the following documents or copies of them, or provide a written statement that the documentation does not exist or is not in the debtor's possession:

(A) evidence of current income such as the most recent payment advice;

(B) unless the trustee or the United States trustee instructs otherwise, statements for each of the debtor's depository and investment accounts, including checking, savings, and money market accounts, mutual funds and brokerage accounts for the time period that includes the date of the filing of the petition; and

(C) documentation of monthly expenses claimed by the debtor when required by § 707(b)(2)(A) or (B).

(3) Tax Return. At least 7 days before the first date set for the meeting of creditors under § 341, the debtor shall provide to the trustee a copy of the debtor's Federal income tax return for the most recent tax year ending immediately before the commencement of the case and for which a return was filed, including any attachments, or a transcript of the tax return, or provide a written statement that the documentation does not exist.

(4) Tax Returns Provided to Creditors. If a creditor, at least 14 days before the first date set for the meeting of creditors under § 341, requests a copy of the debtor's tax return that is to be provided to the trustee under subdivision (b)(3), the debtor shall provide to the requesting creditor a copy of the return, including any attachments, or a transcript of the tax return, or provide a written statement that the documentation does not exist at least 7 days before the first date set for the meeting of creditors under § 341.

(5) The debtor's obligation to provide tax returns under Rule 4002(b)(3) and (b)(4) is subject to procedures for safeguarding the confidentiality of tax information established by the Director of the Administrative Office of the United States Courts.

Rule 4003. Exemptions

(a) Claim of exemptions

A debtor shall list the property claimed as exempt under § 522 of the Code on the schedule of assets required to be filed by *Rule 1007*. If the debtor fails to claim exemptions or file the schedule within the time specified in *Rule 1007*, a dependent of the debtor may file the list within 30 days thereafter.

(b) Objecting to a claim of exemptions

(1) Except as provided in paragraphs (2) and (3), a party in interest may file an objection to the list of property claimed as exempt within 30 days after the meeting of creditors held under § 341(a) is concluded or within 30 days after any amendment to the list or supplemental schedules is filed, whichever is later. The court may, for cause, extend the time for filing objections if, before the time to object expires, a party in interest files a request for an extension.

(2) The trustee may file an objection to a claim of exemption at any time prior to one year after the closing of the case if the debtor fraudulently asserted the claim of exemption. The trustee shall deliver or mail the objection to the debtor and the debtor's attorney, and to any person filing the list of exempt property and that person's attorney.

(3) An objection to a claim of exemption based on § 522(q) shall be filed before the closing of the case. If an exemption is first claimed after a case is reopened, an objection shall be filed before the reopened case is closed.

(4) A copy of any objection shall be delivered or mailed to the trustee, the debtor and the debtor's attorney, and the person filing the list and that person's attorney.

(c) Burden of proof

In any hearing under this rule, the objecting party has the burden of proving that the exemptions are not properly claimed. After hearing on notice, the court shall determine the issues presented by the objections.

* * *

Rule 4007. Determination of Dischargeability of a Debt

(a) Persons entitled to file complaint

A debtor or any creditor may file a complaint to obtain a determination of the dischargeability of any debt.

(b) Time for commencing proceeding other than under § 523(c) of the Code

A complaint other than under § 523(c) may be filed at any time. A case may be reopened without payment of an additional filing fee for the purpose of filing a complaint to obtain a determination under this rule.

(c) Time for filing complaint under § 523(c) in a chapter 7 liquidation, chapter 11 reorganization, chapter 12 family farmer's debt adjustment case, or chapter 13 individual's debt adjustment case; notice of time fixed

Except as provided in subdivision (d), a complaint to determine the dischargeability of a debt under § 523(c) shall be filed no later than 60 days after the first date set for the meeting of creditors under § 341(a). The court shall give all creditors no less than 30 days' notice of the time so fixed in the manner provided in Rule 2002. On motion of a party in interest, after hearing on notice, the court may for cause extend the time fixed under this subdivision. The motion shall be filed before the time has expired.

(d) Time for filing complaint under § 523(a)(6) in chapter 13 individual's debt adjustment case; notice of time fixed

On motion by a debtor for a discharge under § 1328(b), the court shall enter an order fixing the time to file a complaint to determine the dischargeability of any debt under § 523(a)(6) and shall give no less than 30 days' notice of the time fixed to all creditors in the manner provided in Rule 2002. On motion of any party in interest after hearing on notice the court may for cause extend the time fixed under this subdivision. The motion shall be filed before the time has expired.

* * *

Rule 4008. Filing of Reaffirmation Agreement; Statement in Support of Reaffirmation Agreement

(a) Filing of reaffirmation agreement

A reaffirmation agreement shall be filed no later than 60 days after the first date set for the meeting of creditors under § 341(a) of the Code. . . . The court may, at any time and in its discretion, enlarge the time to file reaffirmation agreement.

(b) Statement in support of reaffirmation agreement

The debtor's statement required under § 524(k)(6)(A) of the Code shall be accompanied by a statement of the total income and expenses stated on schedules I and J. If there is a difference between the total income and expenses stated on those schedules and the statement required under § 524(k)(6)(A), the statement required by this subdivision shall include an explanation of the difference.

* * *

PART VII—ADVERSARY PROCEEDINGS

Rule 7001. Scope of Rules of Part VII

An adversary proceeding is governed by the rules of this Part VII. The following are adversary proceedings:

(1) a proceeding to recover money or property, other than a proceeding to compel the debtor to deliver property to the trustee, or a proceeding under § 554(b) or § 725 of the Code, Rule 2017, or Rule 6002;

(2) a proceeding to determine the validity, priority, or extent of a lien or other interest in property, other than a proceeding under Rule 4003(d);

(3) a proceeding to obtain approval under § 363(h) for the sale of both the interest of the estate and of a co-owner in property;

(4) a proceeding to object to or revoke a discharge;

(5) a proceeding to revoke an order of confirmation of a chapter 11, chapter 12, or chapter 13 plan;

(6) a proceeding to determine the dischargeability of a debt;

(7) a proceeding to obtain an injunction or other equitable relief, except when a chapter 9, chapter 11, chapter 12, or chapter 13 plan provides for the relief;

(8) a proceeding to subordinate any allowed claim or interest, except when a chapter 9, chapter 11, chapter 12, or chapter 13 plan provides for subordination;

(9) a proceeding to obtain a declaratory judgment relating to any of the foregoing; or

(10) a proceeding to determine a claim or cause of action removed under 28 U.S.C. § 1452.

* * *

PART IX—GENERAL PROVISIONS

Rule 9014. Contested Matters

(a) Motion. In a contested matter not otherwise governed by these rules, relief shall be requested by motion, and reasonable notice and opportunity for hearing shall be afforded the party against whom relief is sought. No response is required under this rule unless the court directs otherwise. * * *

(d) Testimony of witnesses. Testimony of witnesses with respect to disputed material factual issues shall be taken in the same manner as testimony in an adversary proceeding.

PART 5

OFFICIAL BANKRUPTCY FORMS

OFFICIAL BANKRUPTCY FORMS

Form Number 1

B1 (Official Form 1) (12/07)

United States Bankruptcy Court _____ DISTRICT OF _____		Voluntary Petition
Name of Debtor (if individual, enter Last, First, Middle):		Name of Joint Debtor (Spouse) (Last, First, Middle):
All Other Names used by the Debtor in the last 8 years (include married, maiden, and trade names):		All Other Names used by the Joint Debtor in the last 8 years (include married, maiden, and trade names):
Last four digits of Social-Security/Complete EIN or other Tax-I.D. No. (if more than one, state all):		Last four digits of Social-Security/Complete EIN or other Tax-I.D. No. (if more than one, state all):
Street Address of Debtor (No. and Street, City, and State): ZIP CODE		Street Address of Joint Debtor (No. and Street, City, and State): ZIP CODE
County of Residence or of the Principal Place of Business:		County of Residence or of the Principal Place of Business:
Mailing Address of Debtor (if different from street address): ZIP CODE		Mailing Address of Joint Debtor (if different from street address): ZIP CODE
Location of Principal Assets of Business Debtor (if different from street address above): ZIP CODE		

Type of Debtor
(Form of Organization)
(Check **one** box.)

☐ Individual (includes Joint Debtors)
 See Exhibit D on page 2 of this form.
☐ Corporation (includes LLC and LLP)
☐ Partnership
☐ Other (If debtor is not one of the above entities, check this box and state type of entity below.)

_____

Nature of Business
(Check **one** box.)

☐ Health Care Business
☐ Single Asset Real Estate as defined in 11 U.S.C. § 101(51B)
☐ Railroad
☐ Stockbroker
☐ Commodity Broker
☐ Clearing Bank
☐ Other

Tax-Exempt Entity
(Check box, if applicable.)

☐ Debtor is a tax-exempt organization under Title 26 of the United States Code (the Internal Revenue Code).

Chapter of Bankruptcy Code Under Which the Petition is Filed (Check **one** box.)

☐ Chapter 7
☐ Chapter 9
☐ Chapter 11
☐ Chapter 12
☐ Chapter 13

☐ Chapter 15 Petition for Recognition of a Foreign Main Proceeding
☐ Chapter 15 Petition for Recognition of a Foreign Nonmain Proceeding

Nature of Debts
(Check one box.)

☐ Debts are primarily consumer debts, defined in 11 U.S.C. § 101(8) as "incurred by an individual primarily for a personal, family, or house-hold purpose."
☐ Debts are primarily business debts.

Filing Fee (Check one box.)

☐ Full Filing Fee attached.

☐ Filing Fee to be paid in installments (applicable to individuals only). Must attach signed application for the court's consideration certifying that the debtor is unable to pay fee except in installments. Rule 1006(b). See Official Form 3A.

☐ Filing Fee waiver requested (applicable to chapter 7 individuals only). Must attach signed application for the court's consideration. See Official Form 3B.

Chapter 11 Debtors

Check one box:
☐ Debtor is a small business debtor as defined in 11 U.S.C. § 101(51D).
☐ Debtor is not a small business debtor as defined in 11 U.S.C. § 101(51D).

Check if:
☐ Debtor's aggregate noncontingent liquidated debts (excluding debts owed to insiders or affiliates) are less than $2,190,000.
- -
Check all applicable boxes:
☐ A plan is being filed with this petition.
☐ Acceptances of the plan were solicited prepetition from one or more classes of creditors, in accordance with 11 U.S.C. § 1126(b).

Statistical/Administrative Information

☐ Debtor estimates that funds will be available for distribution to unsecured creditors.
☐ Debtor estimates that, after any exempt property is excluded and administrative expenses paid, there will be no funds available for distribution to unsecured creditors.

THIS SPACE IS FOR COURT USE ONLY

Estimated Number of Creditors

☐ 1-49	☐ 50-99	☐ 100-199	☐ 200-999	☐ 1,000-5,000	☐ 5,001-10,000	☐ 10,001-25,000	☐ 25,001-50,000	☐ 50,001-100,000	☐ Over 100,000

Estimated Assets

☐ $0 to $50,000	☐ $50,001 to $100,000	☐ $100,001 to $500,000	☐ $500,001 to $1 million	☐ $1,000,001 to $10 million	☐ $10,000,001 to $50 million	☐ $50,000,001 to $100 million	☐ $100,000,001 to $500 million	☐ $500,000,001 to $1 billion	☐ More than $1 billion

Estimated Liabilities

☐ $0 to $50,000	☐ $50,001 to $100,000	☐ $100,001 to $500,000	☐ $500,001 to $1 million	☐ $1,000,001 to $10 million	☐ $10,000,001 to $50 million	☐ $50,000,001 to $100 million	☐ $100,000,001 to $500 million	☐ $500,000,001 to $1 billion	☐ More than $1 billion

B1 (Official Form 1) (12/07)   Page 2

Voluntary Petition *(This page must be completed and filed in every case.)*	Name of Debtor(s):	

All Prior Bankruptcy Cases Filed Within Last 8 Years (If more than two, attach additional sheet.)

Location Where Filed:	Case Number:	Date Filed:
Location Where Filed:	Case Number:	Date Filed:

Pending Bankruptcy Case Filed by any Spouse, Partner, or Affiliate of this Debtor (If more than one, attach additional sheet.)

Name of Debtor:	Case Number:	Date Filed:
District:	Relationship:	Judge:

Exhibit A	Exhibit B
(To be completed if debtor is required to file periodic reports (e.g., forms 10K and 10Q) with the Securities and Exchange Commission pursuant to Section 13 or 15(d) of the Securities Exchange Act of 1934 and is requesting relief under chapter 11.)	(To be completed if debtor is an individual whose debts are primarily consumer debts.) I, the attorney for the petitioner named in the foregoing petition, declare that I have informed the petitioner that [he or she] may proceed under chapter 7, 11, 12, or 13 of title 11, United States Code, and have explained the relief available under each such chapter. I further certify that I have delivered to the debtor the notice required by 11 U.S.C. § 342(b).
☐ Exhibit A is attached and made a part of this petition.	X _____ Signature of Attorney for Debtor(s) (Date)

Exhibit C

Does the debtor own or have possession of any property that poses or is alleged to pose a threat of imminent and identifiable harm to public health or safety?

☐   Yes, and Exhibit C is attached and made a part of this petition.

☐   No.

Exhibit D

(To be completed by every individual debtor. If a joint petition is filed, each spouse must complete and attach a separate Exhibit D.)

☐   Exhibit D completed and signed by the debtor is attached and made a part of this petition.

If this is a joint petition:

☐   Exhibit D also completed and signed by the joint debtor is attached and made a part of this petition.

Information Regarding the Debtor - Venue
(Check any applicable box.)

☐   Debtor has been domiciled or has had a residence, principal place of business, or principal assets in this District for 180 days immediately preceding the date of this petition or for a longer part of such 180 days than in any other District.

☐   There is a bankruptcy case concerning debtor's affiliate, general partner, or partnership pending in this District.

☐   Debtor is a debtor in a foreign proceeding and has its principal place of business or principal assets in the United States in this District, or has no principal place of business or assets in the United States but is a defendant in an action or proceeding [in a federal or state court] in this District, or the interests of the parties will be served in regard to the relief sought in this District.

Certification by a Debtor Who Resides as a Tenant of Residential Property
(Check all applicable boxes.)

☐   Landlord has a judgment against the debtor for possession of debtor's residence. (If box checked, complete the following.)

_____
(Name of landlord that obtained judgment)

_____
(Address of landlord)

☐   Debtor claims that under applicable nonbankruptcy law, there are circumstances under which the debtor would be permitted to cure the entire monetary default that gave rise to the judgment for possession, after the judgment for possession was entered, and

☐   Debtor has included with this petition the deposit with the court of any rent that would become due during the 30-day period after the filing of the petition.

☐   Debtor certifies that he/she has served the Landlord with this certification. (11 U.S.C. § 362(l)).

B1 (Official Form) 1 (12/07)	Page 3
Voluntary Petition *(This page must be completed and filed in every case.)*	Name of Debtor(s):

Signatures

Signature(s) of Debtor(s) (Individual/Joint)	Signature of a Foreign Representative
I declare under penalty of perjury that the information provided in this petition is true and correct. [If petitioner is an individual whose debts are primarily consumer debts and has chosen to file under chapter 7] I am aware that I may proceed under chapter 7, 11, 12 or 13 of title 11, United States Code, understand the relief available under each such chapter, and choose to proceed under chapter 7. [If no attorney represents me and no bankruptcy petition preparer signs the petition] I have obtained and read the notice required by 11 U.S.C. § 342(b). I request relief in accordance with the chapter of title 11, United States Code, specified in this petition. X _____ Signature of Debtor X _____ Signature of Joint Debtor _____ Telephone Number (if not represented by attorney) _____ Date	I declare under penalty of perjury that the information provided in this petition is true and correct, that I am the foreign representative of a debtor in a foreign proceeding, and that I am authorized to file this petition. (Check only one box.) ☐ I request relief in accordance with chapter 15 of title 11, United States Code. Certified copies of the documents required by 11 U.S.C. § 1515 are attached. ☐ Pursuant to 11 U.S.C. § 1511, I request relief in accordance with the chapter of title 11 specified in this petition. A certified copy of the order granting recognition of the foreign main proceeding is attached. X _____ (Signature of Foreign Representative) _____ (Printed Name of Foreign Representative) _____ Date
Signature of Attorney*	**Signature of Non-Attorney Bankruptcy Petition Preparer**
X _____ Signature of Attorney for Debtor(s) _____ Printed Name of Attorney for Debtor(s) _____ Firm Name _____ Address _____ _____ _____ Telephone Number _____ Date *In a case in which § 707(b)(4)(D) applies, this signature also constitutes a certification that the attorney has no knowledge after an inquiry that the information in the schedules is incorrect.	I declare under penalty of perjury that: (1) I am a bankruptcy petition preparer as defined in 11 U.S.C. § 110; (2) I prepared this document for compensation and have provided the debtor with a copy of this document and the notices and information required under 11 U.S.C. §§ 110(b), 110(h), and 342(b); and, (3) if rules or guidelines have been promulgated pursuant to 11 U.S.C. § 110(h) setting a maximum fee for services chargeable by bankruptcy petition preparers, I have given the debtor notice of the maximum amount before preparing any document for filing for a debtor or accepting any fee from the debtor, as required in that section. Official Form 19 is attached. _____ Printed Name and title, if any, of Bankruptcy Petition Preparer _____ Social-Security number (If the bankruptcy petition preparer is not an individual, state the Social-Security number of the officer, principal, responsible person or partner of the bankruptcy petition preparer.) (Required by 11 U.S.C. § 110.) _____ Address X _____ _____ Date Signature of bankruptcy petition preparer or officer, principal, responsible person, or partner whose Social-Security number is provided above. Names and Social-Security numbers of all other individuals who prepared or assisted in preparing this document unless the bankruptcy petition preparer is not an individual. If more than one person prepared this document, attach additional sheets conforming to the appropriate official form for each person. *A bankruptcy petition preparer's failure to comply with the provisions of title 11 and the Federal Rules of Bankruptcy Procedure may result in fines or imprisonment or both. 11 U.S.C. § 110; 18 U.S.C. § 156.*
Signature of Debtor (Corporation/Partnership)	
I declare under penalty of perjury that the information provided in this petition is true and correct, and that I have been authorized to file this petition on behalf of the debtor. The debtor requests the relief in accordance with the chapter of title 11, United States Code, specified in this petition. X _____ Signature of Authorized Individual _____ Printed Name of Authorized Individual _____ Title of Authorized Individual _____ Date	

Form Number 6

Form 6. Schedules

B6 Cover (Form 6 Cover) (12/07)

Summary of Schedules

Statistical Summary of Certain Liabilities and Related Data (28 U.S.C. § 159)

B6 Summary (Official Form 6—Summary) (12/07)

United States Bankruptcy Court
_____ District Of _____

In re _____   Case No. _____
　　　　　　　Debtor

　　　　　　　　　　　　　　　　　　　Chapter _____

SUMMARY OF SCHEDULES

Indicate as to each schedule whether that schedule is attached and state the number of pages in each. Report the totals from Schedules A, B, D, E, F, I, and J in the boxes provided. Add the amounts from Schedules A and B to determine the total amount of the debtor's assets. Add the amounts of all claims from Schedules D, E, and F to determine the total amount of the debtor's liabilities. Individual debtors also must complete the "Statistical Summary of Certain Liabilities and Related Data" if they file a case under chapter 7, 11, or 13.

NAME OF SCHEDULE	ATTACHED (YES/NO)	NO. OF SHEETS	ASSETS	LIABILITIES	OTHER
A—Real Property			$		
B—Personal Property	.		$		
C—Property Claimed As Exempt					
D—Creditors Holding Secured Claims				$	
E—Creditors Holding Unsecured Priority Claims (Total of Claims on Schedule E)				$	
F—Creditors Holding Unsecured Nonpriority Claims				$	
G—Executory Contracts and Unexpired Leases					
H—Codebtors					
I—Current Income of Individual Debtor(s)					$
J—Current Expenditures of Individual Debtor(s)					$
TOTAL			$	$	

B6 Summary (Official Form 6—Summary) (12/07)

United States Bankruptcy Court

_____ District Of _____

In re _____   Case No. _____
                      Debtor

                                             Chapter _____

STATISTICAL SUMMARY OF CERTAIN LIABILITIES
AND RELATED DATA (28 U.S.C. § 159)

If you are an individual debtor whose debts are primarily consumer debts, as defined in § 101(8) of the Bankruptcy Code (11 U.S.C. § 101(8)), filing a case under chapter 7, 11 or 13, you must report all information requested below.

☐ Check this box if you are an individual debtor whose debts are NOT primarily consumer debts. You are not required to report any information here.

This information is for statistical purposes only under 28 U.S.C. § 159.

Summarize the following types of liabilities, as reported in the Schedules, and total them.

Type of Liability	Amount	
Domestic Support Obligations (from Schedule E)	$	
Taxes and Certain Other Debts Owed to Governmental Units (from Schedule E)	$	
Claims for Death or Personal Injury While Debtor Was Intoxicated (from Schedule E) (whether disputed or undisputed)	$	
Student Loan Obligations (from Schedule F)	$	
Domestic Support, Separation Agreement, and Divorce Decree Obligations Not Reported on Schedule E	$	
Obligations to Pension or Profit–Sharing, and Other Similar Obligations (from Schedule F)	$	
TOTAL	$	
State the following:		
Average Income (from Schedule I, Line 16)	$	
Average Expenses (from Schedule J, Line 18)	$	
Current Monthly Income (from Form 22A Line 12; **OR**, Form 22B Line 11; **OR**, Form 22C Line 20)	$	
State the following:		
1. Total from Schedule D, "UNSECURED PORTION, IF ANY" column		$
2. Total from Schedule E, "AMOUNT ENTITLED TO PRIORITY" column.	$	
3. Total from Schedule E, "AMOUNT NOT ENTITLED TO PRIORITY, IF ANY" column		$
4. Total from Schedule F		$
5. Total of non-priority unsecured debt (sum of 1, 3, and 4)		$

B6A (Official Form 6A) (12/07)

In re _____, Case No. _____
　　　　　　Debtor　　　　　　　　　　　　　(If known)

SCHEDULE A—REAL PROPERTY

Except as directed below, list all real property in which the debtor has any legal, equitable, or future interest, including all property owned as a cotenant, community property, or in which the debtor has a life estate. Include any property in which the debtor holds rights and powers exercisable for the debtor's own benefit. If the debtor is married, state whether the husband, wife, both, or the marital community own the property by placing an "H," "W," "J," or "C" in the column labeled "Husband, Wife, Joint, or Community." If the debtor holds no interest in real property, write "None" under "Description and Location of Property."

Do not include interests in executory contracts and unexpired leases on this schedule. List them in Schedule G—Executory Contracts and Unexpired Leases.

If an entity claims to have a lien or hold a secured interest in any property, state the amount of the secured claim. See Schedule D. If no entity claims to hold a secured interest in the property, write "None" in the column labeled "Amount of Secured Claim."

If the debtor is an individual or if a joint petition is filed, state the amount of any exemption claimed in the property only in Schedule C—Property Claimed as Exempt.

DESCRIPTION AND LOCATION OF PROPERTY	NATURE OF DEBTOR'S INTEREST IN PROPERTY	HUSBAND, WIFE, JOINT, OR COMMUNITY	CURRENT VALUE OF DEBTOR'S INTEREST IN PROPERTY, WITHOUT DEDUCTING ANY SECURED CLAIM OR EXEMPTION	AMOUNT OF SECURED CLAIM

Total ▶ $

(Report also on Summary of Schedules.)

240

B6B (Official Form 6B) (12/07)

In re _____, Case No. _____
            Debtor   (If known)

SCHEDULE B—PERSONAL PROPERTY

Except as directed below, list all personal property of the debtor of whatever kind. If the debtor has no property in one or more of the categories, place an "x" in the appropriate position in the column labeled "None." If additional space is needed in any category, attach a separate sheet properly identified with the case name, case number, and the number of the category. If the debtor is married, state whether the husband, wife, both, or the marital community own the property by placing an "H," "W," "J," or "C" in the column labeled "Husband, Wife, Joint, or Community." If the debtor is an individual or a joint petition is filed, state the amount of any exemptions claimed only in Schedule C—Property Claimed as Exempt.

Do not list interests in executory contracts and unexpired leases on this schedule. List them in Schedule G—Executory Contracts and Unexpired Leases.

If the property is being held for the debtor by someone else, state that person's name and address under "Description and Location of Property."

If the property is being held for a minor child, simply state the child's initials and the name and address of the child's parent or guardian, such as "A.B., a minor child, by John Doe, guardian." Do not disclose the child's name. See, 11 U.S.C. § 112 and Fed. R. Bankr. P. 1007(m).

B6B (Official Form 6B) (12/07)—Cont.

TYPE OF PROPERTY	N O N E	DESCRIPTION AND LOCATION OF PROPERTY	HUSBAND—WIFE	JOINT	COMMUNITY	CURRENT VALUE OF DEBTOR'S INTEREST IN PROPERTY, WITHOUT DEDUCTING ANY SECURED CLAIM OR EXEMPTION
1. Cash on hand.						
2. Checking, savings or other financial accounts, certificates of deposit, or shares in banks, savings and loan, thrift, building and loan, and homestead associations, or credit unions, brokerage houses, or cooperatives.						
3. Security deposits with public utilities, telephone companies, landlords, and others.						
4. Household goods and furnishings, including audio, video, and computer equipment.						
5. Books; pictures and other art objects; antiques; stamp, coin, record, tape, compact disc, and other collections or collectibles.						
6. Wearing apparel.						
7. Furs and jewelry.						
8. Firearms and sports, photographic, and other hobby equipment.						
9. Interests in insurance policies. Name insurance company of each policy and itemize surrender or refund value of each.						
10. Annuities. Itemize and name each issuer.						
11. Interests in an education IRA as defined in 26 U.S.C. § 530(b)(1) or under a qualified State tuition plan as defined in 26 U.S.C. § 529(b)(1). Give particulars. (File separately the record(s) of any such interest(s). 11 U.S.C. § 521(c)).						

B6B (Official Form 6B) (12/07) - Cont.

In re _____ ,   Case No. _____ ,
            Debtor   (If known)

SCHEDULE B-PERSONAL PROPERTY
(Continuation Sheet)

TYPE OF PROPERTY	N O N E	DESCRIPTION AND LOCATION OF PROPERTY	HUSBAND, WIFE, JOINT, OR COMMUNITY	CURRENT VALUE OF DEBTOR'S INTEREST IN PROPERTY, WITHOUT DEDUCTING ANY SECURED CLAIM OR EXEMPTION
12. Interests In IRA, ERISA, Keogh, or other pension or profit sharing plans. Give particulars.				
13. Stock and interests in incorporated and unincorporated businesses. Itemize.				
14. Interests in partnerships or joint ventures. Itemize.				
15. Government and corporate bonds and other negotiable and nonnegotiable instruments.				
16. Accounts receivable.				
17. Alimony, maintenance, support, and property settlements to which the debtor is or may be entitled. Give particulars.				
18. Other liquidated debts owed to debtor including tax refunds. Give particulars.				
19. Equitable or future interests, life estates, and rights or powers exercisable for the benefit of the debtor other than those listed In Schedule A— Real Property.				
20. Contingent and noncontingent interests in estate of a decedent, death benefit plan, life insurance policy, or trust.				
21. Other contingent and unliquidated claims of every nature, including tax refunds, counterclaims of the debtor, and rights to setoff claims. Give estimated value of each.				
22. Patents, copyrights, and other intellectual property. Give particulars.				
23. Licenses, franchises, and other general Intangibles. Give particulars.				

243

B6B (Official Form 6B) (12/07)—Cont.

In re _____   Case No. _____,
          Debtor   (If known)

SCHEDULE B-PERSONAL PROPERTY
(Continuation Sheet)

TYPE OF PROPERTY	NONE	DESCRIPTION AND LOCATION OF PROPERTY	HUSBAND, WIFE, JOINT, OR COMMUNITY	CURRENT VALUE OF DEBTOR'S INTEREST IN PROPERTY, WITHOUT DEDUCTING ANY SECURED CLAIM OR EXEMPTION
24. Customer lists or other compilations containing personally identifiable information (as defined in 11 U.S.C. § 101(41A)) provided to the debtor by individuals in connection with obtaining a product or service from the debtor primarily for personal, family, or household purposes.				
25. Automobiles, trucks, trailers, and other vehicles and accessories.				
26. Boats, motors, and accessories.				
27. Aircraft and accessories.				
28. Office equipment, furnishings, and supplies.				
29. Machinery, fixtures, equipment, and supplies used in business.				
30. Inventory.				
31. Animals.				
32. Crops—growing or harvested. Give particulars.				
33. Farming equipment and implements.				
34. Farm supplies, chemicals, and feed.				
35. Other personal property of any kind not already listed. Itemize.				

_____ continuation sheets attached   Total ▶ | $

(Include amounts from any continuation sheets attached. Report total also on Summary of Schedules.)

B6C (Official Form 6C) (12/12)   (08/11 publication draft)

In re _____ ,   Case No. _____
              Debtor   **(If known)**

SCHEDULE C - PROPERTY CLAIMED AS EXEMPT

Debtor claims the exemptions to which debtor is entitled under: □   Check if debtor claims a homestead exemption that exceeds
(Check one box) $146,450.*
□   11 U.S.C. § 522(b)(2)
□   11 U.S.C. § 522(b)(3)

DESCRIPTION OF PROPERTY	CURRENT MARKET VALUE OF PROPERTY WITHOUT DEDUCTING EXEMPTIONS	SPECIFY LAW PROVIDING EACH EXEMPTION	VALUE OF CLAIMED EXEMPTION (Check only one box for each exemption.)
			□ Exemption limited to $_____ □ Full fair market value of the exempted property
			□ Exemption limited to $_____ □ Full fair market value of the exempted property
			□ Exemption limited to $_____ □ Full fair market value of the exempted property
			□ Exemption limited to $_____ □ Full fair market value of the exempted property
			□ Exemption limited to $_____ □ Full fair market value of the exempted property
			□ Exemption limited to $_____ □ Full fair market value of the exempted property
			□ Exemption limited to $_____ □ Full fair market value of the exempted property
			□ Exemption limited to $_____ □ Full fair market value of the exempted property

* Amount subject to adjustment on 4/1/13, and every three years thereafter with respect to cases commenced on or after the date of adjustment.

B6D (Official Form 6D) (12/07)

In re _____,   Case No. _____,
              Debtor   (If known)

SCHEDULE D—CREDITORS HOLDING SECURED CLAIMS

State the name, mailing address, including zip code, and last four digits of any account number of all entities holding claims secured by property of the debtor as of the date of filing of the petition. The complete account number of any account the debtor has with the creditor is useful to the trustee and the creditor and may be provided if the debtor chooses to do so. List creditors holding all types of secured interests such as judgment liens, garnishments, statutory liens, mortgages, deeds of trust, and other security interests.

List creditors in alphabetical order to the extent practicable. If a minor child is the creditor, state the child's initials and the name and address of the child's parent or guardian, such as "A.B., a minor child, by John Doe, guardian." Do not disclose the child's name. See, 11 U.S.C. § 112 and Fed. R. Bankr. P. 1007(m). If all secured creditors will not fit on this page, use the continuation sheet provided.

If any entity other than a spouse in a joint case may be jointly liable on a claim, place an "X" in the column labeled "Codebtor," include the entity on the appropriate schedule of creditors, and complete Schedule H—Codebtors. If a joint petition is filed, state whether the husband, wife, both of them, or the marital community may be liable on each claim by placing an "H," "W," "J," or "C" in the column labeled "Husband, Wife, Joint, or Community."

If the claim is contingent, place an "X" in the column labeled "Contingent." If the claim is unliquidated, place an "X" in the column labeled "Unliquidated." If the claim is disputed, place an "X" in the column labeled "Disputed." (You may need to place an "X" in more than one of these three columns.)

Total the columns labeled "Amount of Claim Without Deducting Value of Collateral" and "Unsecured Portion, if Any" in the boxes labeled "Total(s)" on the last sheet of the completed schedule. Report the total from the column labeled "Amount of Claim Without Deducting Value of Collateral" also on the Summary of Schedules and, if the debtor is an individual with primarily consumer debts, report the total from the column labeled "Unsecured Portion, if Any" on the Statistical Summary of Certain Liabilities and Related Data.

☐ Check this box if debtor has no creditors holding secured claims to report on this Schedule D.

B6D (Official Form 6D) (12/07)—Cont.

CREDITOR'S NAME AND MAILING ADDRESS INCLUDING ZIP CODE AND AN ACCOUNT NUMBER (See Instructions Above.)	CODEBTOR	HUSBAND, WIFE, JOINT, OR COMMUNITY	DATE CLAIM WAS INCURRED, NATURE OF LIEN, AND DESCRIPTION AND VALUE OF PROPERTY SUBJECT TO LIEN	CONTINGENT	UNLIQUIDATED	DISPUTED	AMOUNT OF CLAIM WITHOUT DEDUCTING VALUE OF COLLATERAL	UNSECURED PORTION, IF ANY
ACCOUNT NO.								
			VALUE $					
ACCOUNT NO.								
			VALUE $					
ACCOUNT NO.								
			VALUE $					
ACCOUNT NO.								
			VALUE $					
___continuation sheets attached			Subtotal ▶ (Total of this page)				$	$
			Total ▶ (Use only on last page)				$	$
							(Report also on Summary of Schedules.)	(If applicable, report also on Statistical Summary of Certain Liabilities and Related Data.)

B6D (Official Form 6D) (12/07)- Cont.

In re _____　　Case No. _____
　　　　　　　Debtor　　　　　　　　　　　　　　　　　　　　　　(If known)

SCHEDULE D—CREDITORS HOLDING SECURED CLAIMS
(Continuation Sheet)

CREDITOR'S NAME AND MAILING ADDRESS INCLUDING ZIP CODE AND AN ACCOUNT NUMBER (See Instructions Above)	CODEBTOR	HUSBAND, WIFE, JOINT, OR COMMUNITY		DATE CLAIM WAS INCURRED, NATURE OF LIEN, AND DESCRIPTION AND VALUE OF PROPERTY SUBJECT TO LIEN	CONTINGENT	UNLIQUIDATED	DISPUTED	AMOUNT OF CLAIM WITHOUT DEDUCTING VALUE OF COLLATERAL	UNSECURED PORTION, IF ANY
ACCOUNT NO.									
				VALUE $					
ACCOUNT NO.									
				VALUE $					
ACCOUNT NO.									
				VALUE $					
ACCOUNT NO.									
				VALUE $					
ACCOUNT NO.									
				VALUE $					

Sheet no. ___ of ___ continuation sheets attached to Schedule of Creditors Holding Secured Claims

Subtotal(s) ▶ (Total(s) of this page(s))　$　　$

Total(s) ▶ (Use only on last page)　$　　$

(Report also on Summary of Schedules.)　(If applicable, report also on Statistical Summary of Certain Liabilities and Related Data.)

B6E (Official Form 6E) (12/07)

In re _____,   Case No. _____,
           Debtor   (If known)

SCHEDULE E—CREDITORS HOLDING
UNSECURED PRIORITY CLAIMS

A complete list of claims entitled to priority, listed separately by type of priority, is to be set forth on the sheets provided. Only holders of unsecured claims entitled to priority should be listed in this schedule. In the boxes provided on the attached sheets, state the name, mailing address, including zip code, and last four digits of the account number, if any, of all entities holding priority claims against the debtor or the property of the debtor, as of the date of the filing of the petition. Use a separate continuation sheet for each type of priority and label each with the type of priority.

The complete account number of any account the debtor has with the creditor is useful to the trustee and the creditor and may be provided if the debtor chooses to do so. If a minor child is a creditor, state the child's initials and the name and address of the child's parent or guardian, such as "A.B., a minor child, by John Doe, guardian." Do not disclose the child's name. See, 11 U.S.C. § 112 and Fed.R.Bankr.P. 1007(m).

If any entity other than a spouse in a joint case may be jointly liable on a claim, place an "X" in the column labeled "Codebtor," include the entity on the appropriate schedule of creditors, and complete Schedule H-Codebtors. If a joint petition is filed, state whether the husband, wife, both of them, or the marital community may be liable on each claim by placing an "H,""W,""J," or "C" in the column labeled "Husband, Wife, Joint, or Community." If the claim is contingent, place an "X" in the column labeled "Contingent." If the claim is unliquidated, place an "X" in the column labeled "Unliquidated." If the claim is disputed, place an "X" in the column labeled "Disputed." (You may need to place an "X" in more than one of these three columns.)

Report the total of claims listed on each sheet in the box labeled "Subtotals" on each sheet. Report the total of all claims listed on this Schedule E in the box labeled "Total" on the last sheet of the completed schedule. Report this total also on the Summary of Schedules.

Report the total of amounts entitled to priority listed on each sheet in the box labeled "Subtotals" on each sheet. Report the total of all amounts entitled to priority listed on this Schedule E in the box labeled "Totals" on the last sheet of the completed schedule. Individual debtors with primarily consumer debts report this total also on the Statistical Summary of Certain Liabilities and Related Data.

Report the total of amounts not entitled to priority listed on each sheet in the box labeled "Subtotals" on each sheet. Report the total of all amounts not entitled to priority listed on this Schedule E in the box labeled "Totals" on the last sheet of the completed schedule. Individual debtors with primarily consumer debts report this total also on the Statistical Summary of Certain Liabilities and Related Data.

☐ Check this box if debtor has no creditors holding unsecured priority claims to report on this Schedule E.

TYPES OF PRIORITY CLAIMS (Check the appropriate box(es) below if claims in that category are listed on the attached sheets.)

☐ **Domestic Support Obligations**

Claims for domestic support that are owed to or recoverable by a spouse, former spouse, or child of the debtor, or the parent, legal guardian, or responsible relative of such a child, or a governmental unit to whom such a domestic support claim has been assigned to the extent provided in 11 U.S.C. § 507(a)(1).

☐ **Extensions of credit in an involuntary case**

Claims arising in the ordinary course of the debtor's business or financial affairs after the commencement of the case but before the earlier of the appointment of a trustee or the order for relief. 11 U.S.C. § 507(a)(3).

☐ **Wages, salaries, and commissions**

Wages, salaries, and commissions, including vacation, severance, and sick leave pay owing to employees and commissions owing to qualifying independent sales representatives up to $10,950* per person earned within 180 days immediately preceding the filing of the original petition, or the cessation of business, whichever occurred first, to the extent provided in 11 U.S.C. § 507(a)(4).

☐ **Contributions to employee benefit plans**

Money owed to employee benefit plans for services rendered within 180 days immediately preceding the filing of the original petition, or the cessation of business, whichever occurred first, to the extent provided in 11 U.S.C. § 507(a)(5).

☐ **Certain farmers and fishermen**

Claims of certain farmers and fishermen, up to $5,400* per farmer or fisherman, against the debtor, as provided in 11 U.S.C. § 507(a)(6).

☐ **Deposits by individuals**

Claims of individuals up to $2,425* for deposits for the purchase, lease, or rental of property or services for personal, family, or household use, that were not delivered or provided. 11 U.S.C. § 507(a)(7).

☐ **Taxes and Certain Other Debts Owed to Governmental Units**

Taxes, customs duties, and penalties owing to federal, state, and local governmental units as set forth in 11 U.S.C. § 507(a)(8).

☐ **Commitments to Maintain the Capital of an Insured Depository Institution**

Claims based on commitments to the FDIC, RTC, Director of the Office of Thrift Supervision, Comptroller of the Currency, or Board of Governors of the Federal Reserve System, or their predecessors or successors, to maintain the capital of an insured depository institution. 11 U.S.C. § 507(a)(9).

☐ **Claims for Death or Personal Injury While Debtor Was Intoxicated**

Claims for death or personal injury resulting from the operation of a motor vehicle or vessel while the debtor was intoxicated from using alcohol, a drug, or another substance. 11 U.S.C. § 507(a)(10).

* Amounts are subject to adjustment on April 1, 2010, and every three years thereafter with respect to cases commenced on or after the date of adjustment.

_____ continuation sheets attached

B6E (Official Form 6E) (12/07) - Cont.

In re _____   Case No. _____
         Debtor   (If known)

SCHEDULE E—CREDITORS HOLDING UNSECURED PRIORITY CLAIMS
(Continuation Sheet)

Type of Priority for Claims Listed on This Sheet

CREDITOR'S NAME, MAILING ADDRESS INCLUDING ZIP CODE, AND ACCOUNT NUMBER (See instructions above.)	CODEBTOR	HUSBAND, WIFE, JOINT, OR COMMUNITY	DATE CLAIM WAS INCURRED AND CONSIDERATION FOR CLAIM	CONTINGENT	UNLIQUIDATED	DISPUTED	AMOUNT OF CLAIM	AMOUNT ENTITLED TO PRIORITY	AMOUNT NOT ENTITLED TO PRIORITY, IF ANY
Account No.									
Account No.									
Account No.									
Account No.									
Account No.									
Sheet no. ___ of ___ continuation sheets attached to Schedule of Creditors Holding Priority Claims			Subtotals ▶ (Totals of this page)				$	$	
			Total ▶ (Use only on last page of the completed Schedule E. Report also on the Summary of Schedules.)				$		
			Totals ▶ (Use only on last page of the completed Schedule E. If applicable, report also on the Statistical Summary of Certain Liabilities and Related Data.)					$	$

B6F (Official Form 6F) (12/07)

In re _____,   Case No. _____
                Debtor   (if known)

SCHEDULE F—CREDITORS HOLDING UNSECURED
NONPRIORITY CLAIMS

State the name, mailing address, including zip code, and last four digits of any account number, of all entities holding unsecured claims without priority against the debtor or the property of the debtor, as of the date of filing of the petition. The complete account number of any account the debtor has with the creditor is useful to the trustee and the creditor and may be provided if the debtor chooses to do so. If a minor child is a creditor, state the child's initials and the name and address of the child's parent or guardian, such as "A.B., a minor child, by John Doe, guardian." Do not disclose the child's name. See, 11 U.S.C. § 112 and Fed.R.Bankr.P. 1007(m). Do not include claims listed in Schedules D and E. If all creditors will not fit on this page, use the continuation sheet provided.

If any entity other than a spouse in a joint case may be jointly liable on a claim, place an "X" in the column labeled "Codebtor," include the entity on the appropriate schedule of creditors, and complete Schedule H—Codebtors. If a joint petition is filed, state whether the husband, wife, both of them, or the marital community may be liable on each claim by placing an "H," "W," "J," or "C" in the column labeled "Husband, Wife, Joint, or Community."

If the claim is contingent, place an "X" in the column labeled "Contingent." If the claim is unliquidated, place an "X" in the column labeled "Unliquidated." If the claim is disputed, place an "X" in the column labeled "Disputed." (You may need to place an "X" in more than one of these three columns.)

Report the total of all claims listed on this schedule in the box labeled "Total" on the last sheet of the completed schedule. Report this total also on the Summary of Schedules and, if the debtor is an individual with primarily consumer debts, report this total also on the Statistical Summary of Certain Liabilities and Related Data.

☐ Check this box if debtor has no creditors holding unsecured claims to report on this Schedule F.

CREDITOR'S NAME, MAILING ADDRESS INCLUDING ZIP CODE, AND ACCOUNT NUMBER (See instructions above.)	CODEBTOR	HUSBAND WIFE	JOINT	COMMUNITY	CONTINGENT	UNLIQUIDATED	DISPUTED	AMOUNT OF CLAIM
ACCOUNT NO.								
ACCOUNT NO.								
ACCOUNT NO.								
ACCOUNT NO.								
Subtotal ▶								$
Total ▶								$

_____ continuation sheets attached

(Use only on last page of the completed Schedule F.)
(Report also on Summary of Schedule and, if applicable, on the Statistical Summary of Certain Liabilities and Related Data.)

B6F (Official Form 6F) (12/07) — Cont.

In re _____,   Case No. _____,
               Debtor   (If known)

SCHEDULE F—CREDITORS HOLDING UNSECURED NONPRIORITY CLAIMS
(Continuation Sheet)

CREDITOR'S NAME, MAILING ADDRESS INCLUDING ZIP CODE, AND ACCOUNT NUMBER (See instructions above.)	CODEBTOR	HUSBAND, WIFE, JOINT, OR COMMUNITY	DATE CLAIM WAS INCURRED AND CONSIDERATION FOR CLAIM. IF CLAIM IS SUBJECT TO SETOFF, SO STATE.	CONTINGENT	UNLIQUIDATED	DISPUTED	AMOUNT OF CLAIM
ACCOUNT NO.							
ACCOUNT NO.							
ACCOUNT NO.							
ACCOUNT NO.							
ACCOUNT NO.							

Sheet no. ___ of ___ continuation sheets attached to Schedule of Creditors Holding Unsecured Nonpriority Claims

                                     Subtotal ▶ $

                                     Total ▶ $
(Use only on last page of the completed Schedule F.)
(Report also on Summary of Schedules and, if applicable on the Statistical Summary of Certain Liabilities and Related Data.)

B6G (Official Form 6G) (12/07)

In re _____,   Case No. _____
　　　　　Debtor　　　　　　　　　　　　　　　(If known)

SCHEDULE G—EXECUTORY CONTRACTS
AND UNEXPIRED LEASES

Describe all executory contracts of any nature and all unexpired leases of real or personal property. Include any timeshare interests. State nature of debtor's interest in contract, i.e., "Purchaser," "Agent," etc. State whether debtor is the lessor or lessee of a lease. Provide the names and complete mailing addresses of all other parties to each lease or contract described. If a minor child is a party to one of the leases or contracts, state the child's initials and the name and address of the child's parent or guardian, such as "A.B., a minor child, by John Doe, guardian." Do not disclose the child's name. See, 11 U.S.C. § 112 and Fed. R. Bankr. P. 1007(m).

☐ Check this box if debtor has no executory contracts or unexpired leases.

NAME AND MAILING ADDRESS, INCLUDING ZIP CODE, OF OTHER PARTIES TO LEASE OR CONTRACT.	DESCRIPTION OF CONTRACT OR LEASE AND NATURE OF DEBTOR'S INTEREST, STATE WHETHER LEASE IS FOR NONRESIDENTIAL REAL PROPERTY, STATE CONTRACT NUMBER OF ANY GOVERNMENT CONTRACT.

B6H (Official Form B6H) (12/07)

In re _____,　　Case No. _____
　　　　　　　Debtor　　　　　　　　　　　　　　　　　　　　(if known)

SCHEDULE H—CODEBTORS

Provide the information requested concerning any person or entity, other than a spouse in a joint case, that is also liable on any debts listed by the debtor in the schedules of creditors. Include all guarantors and co-signers. If the debtor resides or resided in a community property state, commonwealth, or territory (including Alaska, Arizona, California, Idaho, Louisiana, Nevada, New Mexico, Puerto Rico, Texas, Washington, or Wisconsin) within the eight-year period immediately preceding the commencement of the case, identify the name of the debtor's spouse and of any former spouse who resides or resided with the debtor in the community property state, commonwealth, or territory. Include all names used by the nondebtor spouse during the eight years immediately preceding the commencement of this case. If a minor child is a codebtor or a creditor, state the child's initials and the name and address of the child's parent or guardian, such as "A.B., a minor child, by John Doe, guardian." Do not disclose the child's name. See, 11 U.S.C. § 112 and Fed. R. Bankr. P. 1007(m).

☐ Check this box if debtor has no codebtors.

NAME AND ADDRESS OF CODEBTOR	NAME AND ADDRESS OF CREDITOR

B6I (Official Form 6I (12/07))

In re _____,   Case No. _____
                          Debtor   (If known)

SCHEDULE I—CURRENT INCOME OF INDIVIDUAL DEBTOR(S)

The column labeled "Spouse" must be completed in all cases filed by joint debtors and by every married debtor, whether or not a joint petition is filed, unless the spouses are separated and a joint petition is not filed. Do not state the name of any minor child. The average monthly income calculated on this form may differ from the current monthly income calculated on Form 22A, 22B, or 22C.

Debtor's Marital Status:	DEPENDENTS OF DEBTOR AND SPOUSE	
	RELATIONSHIP(S):	AGE(S):
Employment:	DEBTOR	SPOUSE
Occupation		
Name of Employer		
How long employed		
Address of Employer		

INCOME: (Estimate of average or projected monthly income at time case filed)   DEBTOR   SPOUSE

1. Monthly gross wages, salary, and commissions
       (Prorate if not paid monthly) $_____ $_____
2. Estimate monthly overtime $_____ $_____

3. SUBTOTAL $_____ $_____
4. LESS PAYROLL DEDUCTIONS
       a. Payroll taxes and social security $_____ $_____
       b. Insurance $_____ $_____
       c. Union dues $_____ $_____
       d. Other (Specify): _____ $_____ $_____

5. SUBTOTAL OF PAYROLL DEDUCTIONS $_____ $_____
6. TOTAL NET MONTHLY TAKE HOME PAY $_____ $_____
7. Regular income from operation of business or profession
       or farm. (Attach detailed statement)
8. Income from real property $_____ $_____
9. Interest and dividends $_____ $_____
10. Alimony, maintenance or support payments payable to the
       debtor for the debtor's use or that of dependents listed
       above. $_____ $_____
11. Social security or government assistance
       (Specify): _____ $_____ $_____
12. Pension or retirement income $_____ $_____
13. Other monthly income
       (Specify): _____ $_____ $_____

14. SUBTOTAL OF LINES 7 THROUGH 13 $_____ $_____
15. AVERAGE MONTHLY INCOME (Add amounts on lines 6 and 14) $_____ $_____
16. COMBINED AVERAGE MONTHLY INCOME: (Combine col-
       umn totals from line 15) $_____ $_____

(Report also on Summary of Schedules and, if applicable, on Statistical Summary of Certain Liabilities and Related Data)

17. Describe any increase or decrease in income reasonably anticipated to occur within the year following the filing of this document:
_____
_____

B6J (Official Form 6J) (12/07)

In re _____,   Case No. _____
                Debtor   (If known)

SCHEDULE J—CURRENT EXPENDITURES
OF INDIVIDUAL DEBTOR(S)

Complete this schedule by estimating the average or projected monthly expenses of the debtor and the debtor's family at time case filed. Prorate any payments made bi-weekly, quarterly, semi-annually, or annually to show monthly rate. The average monthly expenses calculated on this form may differ from the deductions from income allowed on Form 22A or 22C.

☐ Check this box if a joint petition is filed and debtor's spouse maintains a separate household. Complete a separate schedule of expenditures labeled "Spouse."

1. Rent or home mortgage payment (include lot rented for mobile home) $_____
    a.   Are real estate taxes included?   Yes _____ No _____
    b.   Is property insurance included?   Yes _____ No _____
2. Utilities: a.   Electricity and heating fuel $_____
           b.   Water and sewer $_____
           c.   Telephone $_____
           d.   Other _____ $_____
3. Home maintenance (repairs and upkeep) $_____
4. Food $_____
5. Clothing $_____
6. Laundry and dry cleaning $_____
7. Medical and dental expenses $_____
8. Transportation (not including car payments) $_____
9. Recreation, clubs and entertainment, newspapers, magazines, etc. $_____
10. Charitable contributions $_____
11. Insurance (not deducted from wages or included in home mortgage payments)
    a.   Homeowner's or renter's $_____
    b.   Life $_____
    c.   Health $_____
    d.   Auto $_____
    e.   Other _____ $_____
12. Taxes (not deducted from wages or included in home mortgage payments) (Specify) _____ $_____
13. Installment payments: (In chapter 11, 12, and 13 cases, do not list payments to be included in the plan)
    a.   Auto $_____
    b.   Other _____ $_____
    c.   Other _____ $_____
14. Alimony, maintenance, and support paid to others $_____
15. Payments for support of additional dependents not living at your home $_____
16. Regular expenses from operation of business, profession, or farm (attach detailed statement) $_____
17. Other _____ $_____
18. AVERAGE MONTHLY EXPENSES (Total lines 1-17. Report also on Summary of Schedules and, if applicable, on the Statistical Summary of Certain Liabilities and Related Data.) $_____
19. Describe any increase or decrease in expenditures reasonably anticipated to occur within the year following the filing of this document:

_____

20. STATEMENT OF MONTHLY NET INCOME
    a.   Average monthly income from Line 15 of Schedule I $_____
    b.   Average monthly expenses from Line 18 above $_____
    c.   Monthly net income (a. minus b.) $_____

B6 Declaration (Official Form 6—Declaration) (12/07)

In re _____, Case No. _____
                  Debtor   (if known)

DECLARATION CONCERNING DEBTOR'S SCHEDULES
DECLARATION UNDER PENALTY OF PERJURY
BY INDIVIDUAL DEBTOR

I declare under penalty of perjury that I have read the foregoing summary and schedules, consisting of _____ sheets, and that they are true and correct to the best of my knowledge, information, and belief.

Date: _____   Signature: _____
                                                              Debtor

Date: _____   Signature: _____
                                                        (Joint Debtor, if any)

[If joint case, both spouses must sign.]

··

DECLARATION AND SIGNATURE OF NON-ATTORNEY BANKRUPTCY PETITION PREPARER (See 11 U.S.C. § 110)

I declare under penalty of perjury that: (1) I am a bankruptcy petition preparer as defined in 11 U.S.C. § 110; (2) I prepared this document for compensation and have provided the debtor with a copy of this document and the notices and information required under 11 U.S.C. §§ 110(b), 110(h) and 342(b); and, (3) if rules or guidelines have been promulgated pursuant to 11 U.S.C. § 110(h) setting a maximum fee for services chargeable by bankruptcy petition preparers, I have given the debtor notice of the maximum amount before preparing any document for filing for a debtor or accepting any fee from the debtor, as required by that section.

_____   _____
Printed or Typed Name and Title, if any,   Social Security No.
of Bankruptcy Petition Preparer   *(Required by 11 U.S.C. § 110.)*

If the bankruptcy petition preparer is not an individual, state the name, title (if any), address, and social security number of the officer, principal, responsible person, or partner who signs this document.

_____

_____

Address

X_____   _____
Signature of Bankruptcy Petition Preparer   Date

Names and Social Security numbers of all other individuals who prepared or assisted in preparing this document, unless the bankruptcy petition preparer is not an individual:

If more than one person prepared this document, attach additional signed sheets conforming to the appropriate Official Form for each person.

A bankruptcy petition preparer's failure to comply with the provisions of title 11 and the Federal Rules of Bankruptcy Procedure may result in fines or imprisonment or both. 11 U.S.C. § 110; 18 U.S.C. § 156.

··

OFFICIAL BANKRUPTCY FORMS

Form Number 7

B 7 (Official Form 7) (12/12)   (08/11 publication draft)

UNITED STATES BANKRUPTCY COURT

_____ **DISTRICT OF** _____

In re: _____,   Case No. _____
                    Debtor   (if known)

STATEMENT OF FINANCIAL AFFAIRS

This statement is to be completed by every debtor. Spouses filing a joint petition may file a single statement on which the information for both spouses is combined. If the case is filed under chapter 12 or chapter 13, a married debtor must furnish information for both spouses whether or not a joint petition is filed, unless the spouses are separated and a joint petition is not filed. An individual debtor engaged in business as a sole proprietor, partner, family farmer, or self-employed professional, should provide the information requested on this statement concerning all such activities as well as the individual's personal affairs. To indicate payments, transfers and the like to minor children, state the child's initials and the name and address of the child's parent or guardian, such as "A.B., a minor child, by John Doe, guardian." Do not disclose the child's name. See, 11 U.S.C. §112 and Fed. R. Bankr. P. 1007(m).

Questions 1 - 18 are to be completed by all debtors. Debtors that are or have been in business, as defined below, also must complete Questions 19 - 25. **If the answer to an applicable question is "None," mark the box labeled "None."** If additional space is needed for the answer to any question, use and attach a separate sheet properly identified with the case name, case number (if known), and the number of the question.

DEFINITIONS

"In business." A debtor is "in business" for the purpose of this form if the debtor is a corporation or partnership. An individual debtor is "in business" for the purpose of this form if the debtor is or has been, within six years immediately preceding the filing of this bankruptcy case, any of the following: an officer, director, managing executive, or owner of 5 percent or more of the voting or equity securities of a corporation; a partner, other than a limited partner, of a partnership; a sole proprietor or self-employed full-time or part-time. An individual debtor also may be "in business" for the purpose of this form if the debtor engages in a trade, business, or other activity, other than as an employee, to supplement income from the debtor's primary employment.

"Insider." The term "insider" includes but is not limited to: relatives of the debtor; general partners of the debtor and their relatives; corporations of which the debtor is an officer, director, or person in control; officers, directors, and any persons in control of a corporate debtor and their relatives; affiliates of the debtor and insiders of such affiliates; and any managing agent of the debtor. 11 U.S.C. § 101(2), (31).

---

1. **Income from employment or operation of business**

None
☐

State the gross amount of income the debtor has received from employment, trade, or profession, or from operation of the debtor's business, including part-time activities either as an employee or in independent trade or business, from the beginning of this calendar year to the date this case was commenced. State also the gross amounts received during the **two years** immediately preceding this calendar year. (A debtor that maintains, or has maintained, financial records on the basis of a fiscal rather than a calendar year may report fiscal year income. Identify the beginning and ending dates of the debtor's fiscal year.) If a joint petition is filed, state income for each spouse separately. (Married debtors filing under chapter 12 or chapter 13 must state income of both spouses whether or not a joint petition is filed, unless the spouses are separated and a joint petition is not filed.)

AMOUNT   SOURCE

B 7 (12/12)   (08/11 publication draft)

2. Income other than from employment or operation of business

State the amount of income received by the debtor other than from employment, trade, profession, operation of the debtor's business during the **two years** immediately preceding the commencement of this case. Give particulars. If a joint petition is filed, state income for each spouse separately. (Married debtors filing under chapter 12 or chapter 13 must state income for each spouse whether or not a joint petition is filed, unless the spouses are separated and a joint petition is not filed.)

AMOUNT   SOURCE

---

3. Payments to creditors

Complete a. or b., as appropriate, and c.

a. *Individual or joint debtor(s) with primarily consumer debts:* List all payments on loans, installment purchases of goods or services, and other debts to any creditor made within **90 days** immediately preceding the commencement of this case unless the aggregate value of all property that constitutes or is affected by such transfer is less than $600. Indicate with an asterisk (*) any payments that were made to a creditor on account of a domestic support obligation or as part of an alternative repayment schedule under a plan by an approved nonprofit budgeting and credit counseling agency. (Married debtors filing under chapter 12 or chapter 13 must include payments by either or both spouses whether or not a joint petition is filed, unless the spouses are separated and a joint petition is not filed.)

NAME AND ADDRESS OF CREDITOR	DATES OF PAYMENTS	AMOUNT PAID	AMOUNT STILL OWING

b. *Debtor whose debts are not primarily consumer debts: List each payment or other transfer to any creditor made* within **90 days** immediately preceding the commencement of the case unless the aggregate value of all property that constitutes or is affected by such transfer is less than $5,850*. If the debtor is an individual, indicate with an asterisk (*) any payments that were made to a creditor on account of a domestic support obligation or as part of an alternative repayment schedule under a plan by an approved nonprofit budgeting and credit counseling agency. (Married debtors filing under chapter 12 or chapter 13 must include payments and other transfers by either or both spouses whether or not a joint petition is filed, unless the spouses are separated and a joint petition is not filed.)

NAME AND ADDRESS OF CREDITOR	DATES OF PAYMENTS/ TRANSFERS	AMOUNT PAID OR VALUE OF TRANSFERS	AMOUNT STILL OWING

---

*Amount subject to adjustment on 4/01/13, and every three years thereafter with respect to cases commenced on or after the date of adjustment.

B 7 (12/12)   (08/11 publication draft)

None

☐   c. *All debtors:* List all payments made within **one year** immediately preceding the commencement of this case to or for the benefit of creditors who are or were insiders. (Married debtors filing under chapter 12 or chapter 13 must include payments by either or both spouses whether or not a joint petition is filed, unless the spouses are separated and a joint petition is not filed.)

NAME AND ADDRESS OF CREDITOR AND RELATIONSHIP TO DEBTOR	DATE OF PAYMENT	AMOUNT PAID	AMOUNT STILL OWING

---

4. Suits and administrative proceedings, executions, garnishments and attachments

None

☐   a. List all suits and administrative proceedings to which the debtor is or was a party within **one year** immediately preceding the filing of this bankruptcy case. (Married debtors filing under chapter 12 or chapter 13 must include information concerning either or both spouses whether or not a joint petition is filed, unless the spouses are separated and a joint petition is not filed.)

CAPTION OF SUIT AND CASE NUMBER	NATURE OF PROCEEDING	COURT OR AGENCY AND LOCATION	STATUS OR DISPOSITION

None

☐   b. Describe all property that has been attached, garnished or seized under any legal or equitable process within **one year** immediately preceding the commencement of this case. (Married debtors filing under chapter 12 or chapter 13 must include information concerning property of either or both spouses whether or not a joint petition is filed, unless the spouses are separated and a joint petition is not filed.)

NAME AND ADDRESS OF PERSON FOR WHOSE BENEFIT PROPERTY WAS SEIZED	DATE OF SEIZURE	DESCRIPTION AND VALUE OF PROPERTY

---

5. Repossessions, foreclosures and returns

None

☐   List all property that has been repossessed by a creditor, sold at a foreclosure sale, transferred through a deed in lieu of foreclosure or returned to the seller, within **one year** immediately preceding the commencement of this case. (Married debtors filing under chapter 12 or chapter 13 must include information concerning property of either or both spouses whether or not a joint petition is filed, unless the spouses are separated and a joint petition is not filed.)

NAME AND ADDRESS OF CREDITOR OR SELLER	DATE OF REPOSSESSION, FORECLOSURE SALE, TRANSFER OR RETURN	DESCRIPTION AND VALUE OF PROPERTY

B 7 (12/12)   (08/11 publication draft)

6. Assignments and receiverships

None ☐ a. Describe any assignment of property for the benefit of creditors made within **120 days** immediately preceding the commencement of this case. (Married debtors filing under chapter 12 or chapter 13 must include any assignment by either or both spouses whether or not a joint petition is filed, unless the spouses are separated and a joint petition is not filed.)

NAME AND ADDRESS OF ASSIGNEE	DATE OF ASSIGNMENT	TERMS OF ASSIGNMENT OR SETTLEMENT

None ☐ b. List all property which has been in the hands of a custodian, receiver, or court-appointed official within **one year** immediately preceding the commencement of this case. (Married debtors filing under chapter 12 or chapter 13 must include information concerning property of either or both spouses whether or not a joint petition is filed, unless the spouses are separated and a joint petition is not filed.)

NAME AND ADDRESS OF CUSTODIAN	NAME AND LOCATION OF COURT CASE TITLE & NUMBER	DATE OF ORDER	DESCRIPTION AND VALUE OF PROPERTY

---

7. Gifts

None ☐ List all gifts or charitable contributions made within **one year** immediately preceding the commencement of this case except ordinary and usual gifts to family members aggregating less than $200 in value per individual family member and charitable contributions aggregating less than $100 per recipient. (Married debtors filing under chapter 12 or chapter 13 must include gifts or contributions by either or both spouses whether or not a joint petition is filed, unless the spouses are separated and a joint petition is not filed.)

NAME AND ADDRESS OF PERSON OR ORGANIZATION	RELATIONSHIP TO DEBTOR, IF ANY	DATE OF GIFT	DESCRIPTION AND VALUE OF GIFT

---

8. Losses

None ☐ List all losses from fire, theft, other casualty or gambling within **one year** immediately preceding the commencement of this case **or since the commencement of this case**. (Married debtors filing under chapter 12 or chapter 13 must include losses by either or both spouses whether or not a joint petition is filed, unless the spouses are separated and a joint petition is not filed.)

DESCRIPTION AND VALUE OF PROPERTY	DESCRIPTION OF CIRCUMSTANCES AND, IF LOSS WAS COVERED IN WHOLE OR IN PART BY INSURANCE, GIVE PARTICULARS	DATE OF LOSS

B 7 (12/12)   (08/11 publication draft)

9. Payments related to debt counseling or bankruptcy

None
☐

List all payments made or property transferred by or on behalf of the debtor to any persons, including attorneys, for consultation concerning debt consolidation, relief under the bankruptcy law or preparation of a petition in bankruptcy within **one year** immediately preceding the commencement of this case.

NAME AND ADDRESS OF PAYEE	DATE OF PAYMENT, NAME OF PAYER IF OTHER THAN DEBTOR	AMOUNT OF MONEY OR DESCRIPTION AND VALUE OF PROPERTY

10. Other transfers

None
☐

a. List all other property, other than property transferred in the ordinary course of the business or financial affairs of the debtor, transferred either absolutely or as security within **two years** immediately preceding the commencement of this case. (Married debtors filing under chapter 12 or chapter 13 must include transfers by either or both spouses whether or not a joint petition is filed, unless the spouses are separated and a joint petition is not filed.)

NAME AND ADDRESS OF TRANSFEREE, RELATIONSHIP TO DEBTOR	DATE	DESCRIBE PROPERTY TRANSFERRED AND VALUE RECEIVED

None
☐

b. List all property transferred by the debtor within **ten years** immediately preceding the commencement of this case to a self-settled trust or similar device of which the debtor is a beneficiary.

NAME OF TRUST OR OTHER DEVICE	DATE(S) OF TRANSFER(S)	AMOUNT OF MONEY OR DESCRIPTION AND VALUE OF PROPERTY OR DEBTOR'S INTEREST IN PROPERTY

11. Closed financial accounts

None
☐

List all financial accounts and instruments held in the name of the debtor or for the benefit of the debtor which were closed, sold, or otherwise transferred within **one year** immediately preceding the commencement of this case. Include checking, savings, or other financial accounts, certificates of deposit, or other instruments; shares and share accounts held in banks, credit unions, pension funds, cooperatives, associations, brokerage houses and other financial institutions. (Married debtors filing under chapter 12 or chapter 13 must include information concerning accounts or instruments held by or for either or both spouses whether or not a joint petition is filed, unless the spouses are separated and a joint petition is not filed.)

NAME AND ADDRESS OF INSTITUTION	TYPE OF ACCOUNT, LAST FOUR DIGITS OF ACCOUNT NUMBER, AND AMOUNT OF FINAL BALANCE	AMOUNT AND DATE OF SALE OR CLOSING

B 7 (12/12)   (08/11 publication draft)

12. Safe deposit boxes

None ☐

List each safe deposit or other box or depository in which the debtor has or had securities, cash, or other valuables within **one year** immediately preceding the commencement of this case. (Married debtors filing under chapter 12 or chapter 13 must include boxes or depositories of either or both spouses whether or not a joint petition is filed, unless the spouses are separated and a joint petition is not filed.)

NAME AND ADDRESS OF BANK OR OTHER DEPOSITORY	NAMES AND ADDRESSES OF THOSE WITH ACCESS TO BOX OR DEPOSITORY	DESCRIPTION OF CONTENTS	DATE OF TRANSFER OR SURRENDER, IF ANY

13. Setoffs

None ☐

List all setoffs made by any creditor, including a bank, against a debt or deposit of the debtor within **90 days** preceding the commencement of this case. (Married debtors filing under chapter 12 or chapter 13 must include information concerning either or both spouses whether or not a joint petition is filed, unless the spouses are separated and a joint petition is not filed.)

NAME AND ADDRESS OF CREDITOR	DATE OF SETOFF	AMOUNT OF SETOFF

14. Property held for another person

None ☐

List all property owned by another person that the debtor holds or controls.

NAME AND ADDRESS OF OWNER	DESCRIPTION AND VALUE OF PROPERTY	LOCATION OF PROPERTY

15. Prior address of debtor

None ☐

If debtor has moved within **three years** immediately preceding the commencement of this case, list all premises which the debtor occupied during that period and vacated prior to the commencement of this case. If a joint petition is filed, report also any separate address of either spouse.

ADDRESS	NAME USED	DATES OF OCCUPANCY

OFFICIAL BANKRUPTCY FORMS

B 7 (12/12)   (08/11 publication draft)

16. Spouses and Former Spouses

None ☐   If the debtor resides or resided in a community property state, commonwealth, or territory (including Alaska, Arizona, California, Idaho, Louisiana, Nevada, New Mexico, Puerto Rico, Texas, Washington, or Wisconsin) within **eight years** immediately preceding the commencement of the case, identify the name of the debtor's spouse and of any former spouse who resides or resided with the debtor in the community property state.

NAME

---

17. Environmental Information.

For the purpose of this question, the following definitions apply:

"Environmental Law" means any federal, state, or local statute or regulation regulating pollution, contamination, releases of hazardous or toxic substances, wastes or material into the air, land, soil, surface water, groundwater, or other medium, including, but not limited to, statutes or regulations regulating the cleanup of these substances, wastes, or material.

"Site" means any location, facility, or property as defined under any Environmental Law, whether or not presently or formerly owned or operated by the debtor, including, but not limited to, disposal sites.

"Hazardous Material" means anything defined as a hazardous waste, hazardous substance, toxic substance, hazardous material, pollutant, or contaminant or similar term under an Environmental Law.

None ☐   a. List the name and address of every site for which the debtor has received notice in writing by a governmental unit that it may be liable or potentially liable under or in violation of an Environmental Law. Indicate the governmental unit, the date of the notice, and, if known, the Environmental Law:

SITE NAME AND ADDRESS	NAME AND ADDRESS OF GOVERNMENTAL UNIT	DATE OF NOTICE	ENVIRONMENTAL LAW

None ☐   b. List the name and address of every site for which the debtor provided notice to a governmental unit of a release of Hazardous Material. Indicate the governmental unit to which the notice was sent and the date of the notice.

SITE NAME AND ADDRESS	NAME AND ADDRESS OF GOVERNMENTAL UNIT	DATE OF NOTICE	ENVIRONMENTAL LAW

None ☐   c. List all judicial or administrative proceedings, including settlements or orders, under any Environmental Law with respect to which the debtor is or was a party. Indicate the name and address of the governmental unit that is or was a party to the proceeding, and the docket number.

NAME AND ADDRESS OF GOVERNMENTAL UNIT	DOCKET NUMBER	STATUS OR DISPOSITION

---

18 . Nature, location and name of business

None ☐   a. *If the debtor is an individual,* list the names, addresses, taxpayer-identification numbers, nature of the businesses, and beginning and ending dates of all businesses in which the debtor was an officer, director, partner, or managing executive of a corporation, partner in a partnership, sole proprietor, or was self-employed in a trade, profession, or

B 7 (12/12)   (08/11 publication draft)

other activity either full- or part-time within **six years** immediately preceding the commencement of this case, or in which the debtor owned 5 percent or more of the voting or equity securities within **six years** immediately preceding the commencement of this case.

If the debtor is a partnership, list the names, addresses, taxpayer-identification numbers, nature of the businesses, and beginning and ending dates of all businesses in which the debtor was a partner or owned 5 percent or more of the voting or equity securities, within **six years** immediately preceding the commencement of this case.

If the debtor is a corporation, list the names, addresses, taxpayer-identification numbers, nature of the businesses, and beginning and ending dates of all businesses in which the debtor was a partner or owned 5 percent or more of the voting or equity securities within **six years** immediately preceding the commencement of this case.

NAME	LAST FOUR DIGITS OF SOCIAL-SECURITY OR OTHER INDIVIDUAL TAXPAYER-I.D. NO. (ITIN)/ COMPLETE EIN	ADDRESS	NATURE OF BUSINESS	BEGINNING AND ENDING DATES

None
☐

b. Identify any business listed in response to subdivision a., above, that is "single asset real estate" as defined in 11 U.S.C. § 101.

NAME	ADDRESS

The following questions are to be completed by every debtor that is a corporation or partnership and by any individual debtor who is or has been, within **six years** immediately preceding the commencement of this case, any of the following: an officer, director, managing executive, or owner of more than 5 percent of the voting or equity securities of a corporation; a partner, other than a limited partner, of a partnership, a sole proprietor, or self-employed in a trade, profession, or other activity, either full- or part-time.

*(An individual or joint debtor should complete this portion of the statement **only** if the debtor is or has been in business, as defined above, within six years immediately preceding the commencement of this case. A debtor who has not been in business within those six years should go directly to the signature page.)*

---

19. Books, records and financial statements

None
☐

a. List all bookkeepers and accountants who within **two years** immediately preceding the filing of this bankruptcy case kept or supervised the keeping of books of account and records of the debtor.

NAME AND ADDRESS	DATES SERVICES RENDERED

None
☐

b. List all firms or individuals who within **two years** immediately preceding the filing of this bankruptcy case have audited the books of account and records, or prepared a financial statement of the debtor.

NAME	ADDRESS	DATES SERVICES RENDERED

B 7 (12/12)   (08/11 publication draft)

None
☐ c. List all firms or individuals who at the time of the commencement of this case were in possession of the
books of account and records of the debtor. If any of the books of account and records are not available, explain.

NAME   ADDRESS

None
☐ d. List all financial institutions, creditors and other parties, including mercantile and trade agencies, to whom a
financial statement was issued by the debtor within **two years** immediately preceding the commencement of this case.

NAME AND ADDRESS   DATE ISSUED

---

20. Inventories

None
☐ a. List the dates of the last two inventories taken of your property, the name of the person who supervised the
taking of each inventory, and the dollar amount and basis of each inventory.

DATE OF INVENTORY   INVENTORY SUPERVISOR   DOLLAR AMOUNT
OF INVENTORY
(Specify cost, market or other basis)

None
☐ b. List the name and address of the person having possession of the records of each of the inventories reported
in a., above.

DATE OF INVENTORY   NAME AND ADDRESSES
OF CUSTODIAN
OF INVENTORY RECORDS

---

21. Current Partners, Officers, Directors and Shareholders

None
☐ a. If the debtor is a partnership, list the nature and percentage of partnership interest of each member of the
partnership.

NAME AND ADDRESS   NATURE OF INTEREST   PERCENTAGE OF INTEREST

None
☐ b.   If the debtor is a corporation, list all officers and directors of the corporation, and each stockholder who
directly or indirectly owns, controls, or holds 5 percent or more of the voting or equity securities of the
corporation.

                                                  NATURE AND PERCENTAGE
NAME AND ADDRESS   TITLE   OF STOCK OWNERSHIP

B 7 (12/12)   (08/11 publication draft)

22 . Former partners, officers, directors and shareholders

None
☐

a.   If the debtor is a partnership, list each member who withdrew from the partnership within **one year** immediately preceding the commencement of this case.

NAME   ADDRESS   DATE OF WITHDRAWAL

None
☐

b.   If the debtor is a corporation, list all officers or directors whose relationship with the corporation terminated within **one year** immediately preceding the commencement of this case.

NAME AND ADDRESS   TITLE   DATE OF TERMINATION

23 . Withdrawals from a partnership or distributions by a corporation

None
☐

If the debtor is a partnership or corporation, list all withdrawals or distributions credited or given to an insider, including compensation in any form, bonuses, loans, stock redemptions, options exercised and any other perquisite during **one year** immediately preceding the commencement of this case.

NAME & ADDRESS   DATE AND PURPOSE   AMOUNT OF MONEY
OF RECIPIENT,   OF WITHDRAWAL.   OR DESCRIPTION
RELATIONSHIP TO DEBTOR   AND VALUE OF PROPERTY

24. Tax Consolidation Group.

None
☐

If the debtor is a corporation, list the name and federal taxpayer-identification number of the parent corporation of any consolidated group for tax purposes of which the debtor has been a member at any time within **six years** immediately preceding the commencement of the case.

NAME OF PARENT CORPORATION   TAXPAYER-IDENTIFICATION NUMBER (EIN)

25. Pension Funds.

None
☐

If the debtor is not an individual, list the name and federal taxpayer-identification number of any pension fund to which the debtor, as an employer, has been responsible for contributing at any time within **six years** immediately preceding the commencement of the case.

NAME OF PENSION FUND   TAXPAYER-IDENTIFICATION NUMBER (EIN)

* * * * * *

269

B 7 (12/12)   (08/11 publication draft)

[If completed by an individual or individual and spouse]

I declare under penalty of perjury that I have read the answers contained in the foregoing statement of financial affairs and any attachments thereto and that they are true and correct.

Date _____   Signature of Debtor _____

Date _____   Signature of Joint Debtor (if any) _____

[If completed on behalf of a partnership or corporation]

I declare under penalty of perjury that I have read the answers contained in the foregoing statement of financial affairs and any attachments thereto and that they are true and correct to the best of my knowledge, information and belief.

Date _____   Signature _____

                    Print Name and Title _____

[An individual signing on behalf of a partnership or corporation must indicate position or relationship to debtor.]

____ continuation sheets attached

Penalty for making a false statement: Fine of up to $500,000 or imprisonment for up to 5 years, or both. 18 U.S.C. §§ 152 and 3571

DECLARATION AND SIGNATURE OF NON-ATTORNEY BANKRUPTCY PETITION PREPARER (See 11 U.S.C. § 110)

I declare under penalty of perjury that: (1) I am a bankruptcy petition preparer as defined in 11 U.S.C. § 110; (2) I prepared this document for compensation and have provided the debtor with a copy of this document and the notices and information required under 11 U.S.C. §§ 110(b), 110(h), and 342(b); and, (3) if rules or guidelines have been promulgated pursuant to 11 U.S.C. § 110(h) setting a maximum fee for services chargeable by bankruptcy petition preparers, I have given the debtor notice of the maximum amount before preparing any document for filing for a debtor or accepting any fee from the debtor, as required by that section.

_____   _____
Printed or Typed Name and Title, if any, of Bankruptcy Petition Preparer   Social-Security No. (Required by 11 U.S.C. § 110.)

If the bankruptcy petition preparer is not an individual, state the name, title (if any), address, and social-security number of the officer, principal, responsible person, or partner who signs this document.

_____
Address

_____   _____
Signature of Bankruptcy Petition Preparer   Date

Names and Social-Security numbers of all other individuals who prepared or assisted in preparing this document unless the bankruptcy petition preparer is not an individual:

If more than one person prepared this document, attach additional signed sheets conforming to the appropriate Official Form for each person.

A bankruptcy petition preparer's failure to comply with the provisions of title 11 and the Federal Rules of Bankruptcy Procedure may result in fines or imprisonment or both. 18 U.S.C. § 156.

Form Number 8

Form 8. Individual Debtor's Statement of Intention

B8 (Official Form 8) (12/08)

UNITED STATES BANKRUPTCY COURT

In re _____, Case No. _____
                Debtor   Chapter 7

CHAPTER 7 INDIVIDUAL DEBTOR'S STATEMENT OF INTENTION

PART A—Debts secured by property of the estate. *(Part A must be fully completed for EACH debt which is secured by property of the estate. Attach additional pages if necessary.)*

Property No. 1	
Creditor's Name:	**Describe Property Securing Debt:**

Property will be *(check one)*:
☐ Surrendered   ☐ Retained

If retaining the property, I intend to *(check at least one)*:
☐ Redeem the property
☐ Reaffirm the debt
☐ Other. Explain _____ (for example, avoid lien using 11 U.S.C. § 522(f)).

Property is *(check one)*:
☐ Claimed as exempt   ☐ Not claimed as exempt

Property No. 2 *(if necessary)*	
Creditor's Name:	**Describe Property Securing Debt:**

Property will be *(check one)*:
☐ Surrendered   ☐ Retained

If retaining the property, I intend to *(check at least one)*:
☐ Redeem the property
☐ Reaffirm the debt
☐ Other. Explain _____ (for example, avoid lien using 11 U.S.C. § 522(f)).

Property is *(check one)*:
☐ Claimed as exempt   ☐ Not claimed as exempt

B8 (Official Form 8) (12/08)

PART B—Personal property subject to unexpired leases. *(All three columns of Part B must be completed for each unexpired lease. Attach additional pages if necessary.)*

Property No. 1		
Lessor's Name:	**Describe Leased Property:**	Lease will be Assumed pursuant to 11 U.S.C. § 365(p)(2): ☐ YES ☐ NO

Property No. 2 *(if necessary)*		
Lessor's Name:	**Describe Leased Property:**	Lease will be Assumed pursuant to 11 U.S.C. § 365(p)(2): ☐ YES ☐ NO

Property No. 3 *(if necessary)*		
Lessor's Name:	**Describe Leased Property:**	Lease will be Assumed pursuant to 11 U.S.C. § 365(p)(2): ☐ YES ☐ NO

___ continuation sheets attached *(if any)*

I declare under penalty of perjury that the above indicates my intention as to any property of my estate securing a debt and/or personal property subject to an unexpired lease.

Date: _____

_____
Signature of Debtor

_____
Signature of Joint Debtor

B8 (Official Form 8) (12/08)

CHAPTER 7 INDIVIDUAL DEBTOR'S STATEMENT OF INTENTION
(Continuation Sheet)

PART A—Continuation

Property No.	
Creditor's Name:	**Describe Property Securing Debt:**

Property will be *(check one)*:
☐ Surrendered   ☐ Retained

If retaining the property, I intend to *(check at least one)*:
☐ Redeem the property
☐ Reaffirm the debt
☐ Other. Explain _____ (for example, avoid lien using 11 U.S.C. § 522(f)).

Property is *(check one)*:
☐ Claimed as exempt   ☐ Not claimed as exempt

PART B—Continuation

Property No.		
Lessor's Name:	**Describe Leased Property:**	Lease will be Assumed pursuant to 11 U.S.C. § 365(p)(2): ☐ YES ☐ NO

Property No.		
Lessor's Name:	**Describe Leased Property:**	Lease will be Assumed pursuant to 11 U.S.C. § 365(p)(2): ☐ YES ☐ NO

(Added Aug. 1, 1991; and amended Mar. 1995; Oct. 1, 1997; Dec. 1, 2003; Aug. 11, 2005, eff. Oct. 17, 2005; Dec. 1, 2008.)

OFFICIAL BANKRUPTCY FORMS

Form Number 9F

B9F (Official Form 9F) (Chapter 11 Corporation/Partnership Case) (12/08)

UNITED STATES BANKRUPTCY COURT _____ District of _____

Notice of
Chapter 11 Bankruptcy Case, Meeting of Creditors, & Deadlines

or

[A chapter 11 bankruptcy case concerning the debtor(s) listed below was filed on _____ (date).]

[A bankruptcy case concerning the debtor(s) listed below was originally filed under chapter _____ on _____ (date) and was converted to a case under chapter 11 on _____ (date).]

You may be a creditor of the debtor. This notice lists important deadlines. You may want to consult an attorney to protect your rights. All documents filed in the case may be inspected at the bankruptcy clerk's office at the address listed below.

NOTE: The staff of the bankruptcy clerk's office cannot give legal advice.

See Reverse Side For Important Explanations

Debtor(s) (name(s) and address):	Case Number:
	Last four digits of Social-Security or Individual Taxpayer-ID (ITIN) No(s)./Complete EIN:
All other names used by the Debtor(s) in the last 8 years (include trade names):	Attorney for Debtor(s) (name and address):
	Telephone number:

Meeting of Creditors

Date: / / Time: ( ) A.M. ( ) P.M. Location:

Deadline to File a Proof of Claim

Proof of Claim must be *received* by the bankruptcy clerk's office by the following deadline:

Notice of deadline will be sent at a later time.

Creditor with a Foreign Address:

A creditor to whom this notice is sent at a foreign address should read the information under "Claims" on the reverse side.

Deadline to File a Complaint to Determine Dischargeability of Certain Debts:

Creditors May Not Take Certain Actions:

In most instances, the filing of the bankruptcy case automatically stays certain collection and other actions against the debtor and the debtor's property. Under certain circumstances, the stay may be limited to 30 days or not exist at all, although the debtor can request the court to extend or impose a stay. If you attempt to collect a debt or take other action in violation of the Bankruptcy Code, you may be penalized. Consult a lawyer to determine your rights in this case.

Address of the Bankruptcy Clerk's Office:	For the Court:
	Clerk of the Bankruptcy Court:
Telephone number:	
Hours Open:	Date:

EXPLANATIONS

B9F (Official Form
9F) (12/08)

Filing of Chapter 11 Bankruptcy Case	A bankruptcy case under Chapter 11 of the Bankruptcy Code (title 11, United States Code) has been filed in this court by or against the debtor(s) listed on the front side, and an order for relief has been entered. Chapter 11 allows a debtor to reorganize or liquidate pursuant to a plan. A plan is not effective unless confirmed by the court. You may be sent a copy of the plan and a disclosure statement telling you about the plan, and you might have the opportunity to vote on the plan. You will be sent notice of the date of the confirmation hearing, and you may object to confirmation of the plan and attend the confirmation hearing. Unless a trustee is serving, the debtor will remain in possession of the debtor's property and may continue to operate any business.
Legal Advice	The staff of the bankruptcy clerk's office cannot give legal advice. Consult a lawyer to determine your rights in this case.
Creditors Generally May Not Take Certain Actions	Prohibited collection actions are listed in Bankruptcy Code § 362. Common examples of prohibited actions include contacting the debtor by telephone, mail, or otherwise to demand repayment; taking actions to collect money or obtain property from the debtor; repossessing the debtor's property; and starting or continuing lawsuits or foreclosures. Under certain circumstances, the stay may be limited to 30 days or not exist at all, although the debtor can request the court to extend or impose a stay.
Meeting of Creditors	A meeting of creditors is scheduled for the date, time, and location listed on the front side. *The debtor's representative must be present at the meeting to be questioned under oath by the trustee and by creditors.* Creditors are welcome to attend, but are not required to do so. The meeting may be continued and concluded at a later date without further notice. The court, after notice and a hearing, may order that the United States trustee not convene the meeting if the debtor has filed a plan for which the debtor solicited acceptances before filing the case.
Claims	A Proof of Claim is a signed statement describing a creditor's claim. If a Proof of Claim form is not included with this notice, you can obtain one at any bankruptcy clerk's office. You may look at the schedules that have been or will be filed at the bankruptcy clerk's office. If your claim is scheduled and is *not* listed as disputed, contingent, or unliquidated, it will be allowed in the amount scheduled unless you filed a Proof of Claim or you are sent further notice about the claim. Whether or not your claim is scheduled, you are permitted to file a Proof of Claim. If your claim is not listed at all *or* if your claim is listed as disputed, contingent, or unliquidated, then you must file a Proof of Claim or you might not be paid any money on your claim and may be unable to vote on a plan. The court has not yet set a deadline to file a Proof of Claim. If a deadline is set, you *will* be sent another notice. A secured creditor retains rights in its collateral regardless of whether that creditor files a Proof of Claim. Filing a Proof of Claim submits the creditor to the jurisdiction of the bankruptcy court, with consequences a lawyer can explain. For example, a secured creditor who files a Proof of Claim may surrender important nonmonetary rights, including the right to a jury trial. **Filing Deadline for a Creditor with a Foreign Address:** The deadline for filing claims will be set in a later court order and will apply to all creditors unless the order provides otherwise. If notice of the order setting the deadline is sent to a creditor at a foreign address, the creditor may file a motion requesting the court to extend the deadline.
Discharge of Debts	Confirmation of a chapter 11 plan may result in a discharge of debts, which may include all or part of your debt. *See* Bankruptcy Code § 1141(d). A discharge means that you may never try to collect the debt from the debtor, except as provided in the plan. If you believe that a debt owed to you is not dischargeable under Bankruptcy Code § 1141(d)(6)(A), you must start a lawsuit by filing a complaint in the bankruptcy clerk's office by the "Deadline to File a Complaint to Determine Dischargeability of Certain Debts" listed on the front side. The bankruptcy clerk's office must receive the complaint and any required filing fee by that deadline.
Bankruptcy Clerk's Office	Any paper that you file in this bankruptcy case should be filed at the bankruptcy clerk's office at the address listed on the front side. You may inspect all papers filed, including the list of the debtor's property and debts and the list of the property claimed as exempt, at the bankruptcy clerk's office.
Creditor with a Foreign Address	Consult a lawyer familiar with United States bankruptcy law if you have any questions regarding your rights in this case.

Proof of Claim
Form Number 10

B 10 (Official Form 10) (12/11)   (08/10 publication draft)

UNITED STATES BANKRUPTCY COURT _____ DISTRICT OF _____	PROOF OF CLAIM

Name of Debtor:

Case Number:

NOTE: *Do not use this form to make a claim for an administrative expense that arises after the bankruptcy filing. You may file a request for payment of an administrative expense according to 11 U.S.C. § 503.*

Name of Creditor (the person or other entity to whom the debtor owes money or property):

Name and address where notices should be sent:

Telephone number: email:

COURT USE ONLY

☐ Check this box if this claim amends a previously filed claim.

Court Claim Number:_____
(*If known*)

Filed on:_____

Name and address where payment should be sent (if different from above):

Telephone number: email:

☐ Check this box if you are aware that anyone else has filed a proof of claim relating to this claim. Attach copy of statement giving particulars.

☐ Check this box if you are the debtor or trustee in this case.

1. Amount of Claim as of Date Case Filed: $_____

If all or part of the claim is secured, complete item 4.

If all or part of the claim is entitled to priority, complete item 5.

☐ Check this box if the claim includes interest or other charges in addition to the principal amount of the claim. Attach a statement that itemizes interest or charges.

2. Basis for Claim: _____
(See instruction #2)

3. Last four digits of any number by which creditor identifies debtor: _____

3a. Debtor may have scheduled account as: _____
(See instruction #3a)

3b. Uniform Claim Identifier (optional): _____
(See instruction #3b)

4. Secured Claim (See instruction #4)
Check the appropriate box if the claim is secured by a lien on property or a right of setoff, attach required redacted documents, and provide the requested information.

Nature of property or right of setoff: ☐ Real Estate ☐ Motor Vehicle ☐ Other
Describe:

Value of Property: $_____

Annual Interest Rate ____% ☐ Fixed or ☐ Variable
(when case was filed)

Amount of arrearage and other charges, as of the time case was filed, included in secured claim, if any:
$_____

Basis for perfection: _____

Amount of Secured Claim: $_____

Amount Unsecured: $_____

5. Amount of Claim Entitled to Priority under 11 U.S.C. §507(a). If any part of the claim falls into one of the following categories, check the box specifying the priority and state the amount.

☐ Domestic support obligations under 11 U.S.C. §507(a)(1)(A) or (a)(1)(B).

☐ Wages, salaries, or commissions (up to $11,725*) earned within 180 days before the case was filed or the debtor's business ceased, whichever is earlier – 11 U.S.C. §507 (a)(4).

☐ Contributions to an employee benefit plan – 11 U.S.C. §507 (a)(5).

☐ Up to $2,600* of deposits toward purchase, lease, or rental of property or services for personal, family, or household use – 11 U.S.C. §507(a)(7).

☐ Taxes or penalties owed to governmental units – 11 U.S.C. §507 (a)(8).

☐ Other – Specify applicable paragraph of 11 U.S.C. §507 (a)(__).

Amount entitled to priority:
$_____

Amounts are subject to adjustment on 4/1/13 and every 3 years thereafter with respect to cases commenced on or after the date of adjustment.

6. Credits. The amount of all payments on this claim has been credited for the purpose of making this proof of claim. (See instruction #6)

B 10 (Official Form 10) (12/11)   (08/10 publication draft)

7. Documents: Attached are redacted copies of any documents that support the claim, such as promissory notes, purchase orders, invoices, itemized statements of running accounts, contracts, judgments, mortgages, and security agreements. If the claim is secured, box 4 has been completed, and redacted copies of documents providing evidence of perfection of a security interest are attached. *(See instruction #7, and the definition of "redacted.")*

DO NOT SEND ORIGINAL DOCUMENTS. ATTACHED DOCUMENTS MAY BE DESTROYED AFTER SCANNING.

If the documents are not available, please explain:

8. Signature: (See instruction #8)

Check the appropriate box.

☐ I am the creditor.   ☐ I am the creditor's authorized agent.   ☐ I am the trustee, or the debtor,   ☐ I am a guarantor, surety, indorser, or other codebtor.
(Attach copy of power of attorney, if any.)   (See Bankruptcy Rule 3004.)   (See Bankruptcy Rule 3005.)

I declare under penalty of perjury that the information provided in this claim is true and correct to the best of my knowledge, information, and reasonable belief.

Print Name: _____
Title: _____
Company: _____
Address and telephone number (if different from notice address above): _____   (Signature)   (Date)

Telephone number: _____ email: _____
Penalty for presenting fraudulent claim: Fine of up to $500,000 or imprisonment for up to 5 years, or both. 18 U.S.C. §§ 152 and 3571.

INSTRUCTIONS FOR PROOF OF CLAIM FORM

The instructions and definitions below are general explanations of the law. In certain circumstances, such as bankruptcy cases not filed voluntarily by the debtor, exceptions to these general rules may apply.

Items to be completed in Proof of Claim form

Court, Name of Debtor, and Case Number:
Fill in the federal judicial district in which the bankruptcy case was filed (for example, Central District of California), the debtor's full name, and the case number. If the creditor received a notice of the case from the bankruptcy court, all of this information is at the top of the notice.

Creditor's Name and Address:
Fill in the name of the person or entity asserting a claim and the name and address of the person who should receive notices issued during the bankruptcy case. A separate space is provided for the payment address if it differs from the notice address. The creditor has a continuing obligation to keep the court informed of its current address. See Federal Rule of Bankruptcy Procedure (FRBP) 2002(g).

1. Amount of Claim as of Date Case Filed:
State the total amount owed to the creditor on the date of the bankruptcy filing. Follow the instructions concerning whether to complete items 4 and 5. Check the box if interest or other charges are included in the claim.

2. Basis for Claim:
State the type of debt or how it was incurred. Examples include goods sold, money loaned, services performed, personal injury/wrongful death, car loan, mortgage note, and credit card. If the claim is based on delivering health care goods or services, limit the disclosure of the goods or services so as to avoid embarrassment or the disclosure of confidential health care information. You may be required to provide additional disclosure if an interested party objects to the claim.

3. Last Four Digits of Any Number by Which Creditor Identifies Debtor:
State only the last four digits of the debtor's account or other number used by the creditor to identify the debtor.

3a. Debtor May Have Scheduled Account As:
Report a change in the creditor's name, a transferred claim, or any other information that clarifies a difference between this proof of claim and the claim as scheduled by the debtor.

3b. Uniform Claim Identifier:
If you use a uniform claim identifier, you may report it here. A uniform claim identifier is an optional 24-character identifier that certain large creditors use to facilitate electronic payment in chapter 13 cases.

4. Secured Claim:
Check whether the claim is fully or partially secured. Skip this section if the claim is entirely unsecured. (See Definitions.) If the claim is secured, check the box for the nature and value of property that secures the claim, attach copies of lien documentation, and state, as of the date of the bankruptcy filing, the annual interest rate (and whether it is fixed or variable), and the amount past due on the claim.

5. Amount of Claim Entitled to Priority Under 11 U.S.C. §507(a).
If any portion of the claim falls into any category shown, check the appropriate box(es) and state the amount entitled to priority. (See Definitions.) A claim may be partly priority and partly non-priority. For example, in some of the categories, the law limits the amount entitled to priority.

6. Credits:
An authorized signature on this proof of claim serves as an acknowledgment that when calculating the amount of the claim, the creditor gave the debtor credit for any payments received toward the debt.

7. Documents:
Attach redacted copies of any documents that show the debt exists and a lien secures the debt. You must also attach copies of documents that evidence perfection of any security interest. FRBP 3001(c) and (d). If the claim is based on delivering health care goods or services, limit disclosing confidential health care information. Do not send original documents, as attachments may be destroyed after scanning.

8. Date and Signature:
The individual completing this proof of claim must sign and date it. FRBP 9011. If the claim is filed electronically, FRBP 5005(a)(2) authorizes courts to establish local rules specifying what constitutes a signature. If you sign this form, you declare under penalty of perjury that the information provided is true and correct to the best of your knowledge, information, and reasonable belief. Your signature is also a certification that the claim meets the requirements of FRBP 9011(b). Whether the claim is filed electronically or in person, if your name is on the signature line, you are responsible for the declaration. Print the name and title, if any, of the creditor or other person authorized to file this claim. State the filer's address and telephone number if it differs from the address given on the top of the form for purposes of receiving notices. If the claim is filed by an authorized agent, attach a complete copy of any power of attorney, and provide both the name of the individual filing the claim and the name of the agent. If the authorized agent is a servicer, identify the corporate servicer as the company. Criminal penalties apply for making a false statement on a proof of claim.

B 10 (Official Form 10) (12/11)   (08/10 publication draft)

DEFINITIONS

INFORMATION

Debtor
A debtor is the person, corporation, or other entity that has filed a bankruptcy case.

Creditor
A creditor is a person, corporation, or other entity to whom the debtor owes a debt that was incurred before the date of the bankruptcy filing. See 11 U.S.C. §101 (10).

Claim
A claim is the creditor's right to receive payment for a debt owed by the debtor on the date of the bankruptcy filing. See 11 U.S.C. §101 (5). A claim may be secured or unsecured.

Proof of Claim
A proof of claim is a form used by the creditor to indicate the amount of the debt owed by the debtor on the date of the bankruptcy filing. The creditor must file the form with the clerk of the same bankruptcy court in which the bankruptcy case was filed.

Secured Claim Under 11 U.S.C. §506(a)
A secured claim is one backed by a lien on property of the debtor. The claim is secured so long as the creditor has the right to be paid from the property prior to other creditors. The amount of the secured claim cannot exceed the value of the property. Any amount owed to the creditor in excess of the value of the property is an unsecured claim. Examples of liens on property include a mortgage on real estate or a security interest in a car. A lien may be voluntarily granted by a debtor or may be obtained through a court proceeding. In some states, a court judgment is a lien.

A claim also may be secured if the creditor owes the debtor money (has a right to setoff).

Unsecured Claim
An unsecured claim is one that does not meet the requirements of a secured claim. A claim may be partly unsecured if the amount of the claim exceeds the value of the property on which the creditor has a lien.

Claim Entitled to Priority Under 11 U.S.C. §507(a)
Priority claims are certain categories of unsecured claims that are paid from the available money or property in a bankruptcy case before other unsecured claims.

Redacted
A document has been redacted when the person filing it has masked, edited out, or otherwise deleted, certain information. A creditor must show only the last four digits of any social-security, individual's tax-identification, or financial-account number, only the initials of a minor's name, and only the year of any person's date of birth. If the claim is based on the delivery of health care goods or services, limit the disclosure of the goods or services so as to avoid embarrassment or the disclosure of confidential health care information.

Evidence of Perfection
Evidence of perfection may include a mortgage, lien, certificate of title, financing statement, or other document showing that the lien has been filed or recorded.

Acknowledgment of Filing of Claim
To receive acknowledgment of your filing, you may either enclose a stamped self-addressed envelope and a copy of this proof of claim or you may access the court's PACER system (www.pacer.psc.uscourts.gov) for a small fee to view your filed proof of claim.

Offers to Purchase a Claim
Certain entities are in the business of purchasing claims for an amount less than the face value of the claims. One or more of these entities may contact the creditor and offer to purchase the claim. Some of the written communications from these entities may easily be confused with official court documentation or communications from the debtor. These entities do not represent the bankruptcy court or the debtor. The creditor has no obligation to sell its claim. However, if the creditor decides to sell its claim, any transfer of such claim is subject to FRBP 3001(e), any applicable provisions of the Bankruptcy Code (11 U.S.C. § 101 et seq.), and any applicable orders of the bankruptcy court.

B 10 (Attachment A) (12/11)   (08/10 publication draft)

Mortgage Proof of Claim Attachment

If you file a claim secured by a security interest in the debtor's principal residence, you must use this form as an attachment to your proof of claim. See Bankruptcy Rule 3001(c)(2).

Name of debtor: _____	Case number: _____
Name of creditor: _____	Last four digits of any number you use to identify the debtor's account: ___ ___ ___ ___

Part 1: Statement of Principal and Interest Due as of the Petition Date

Itemize the principal and interest due on the claim as of the petition date (included in the Amount of Claim listed in Item 1 on your Proof of Claim form).

1. Principal due $ _____

2. Interest due

Interest rate	From mm/dd/yyyy	To mm/dd/yyyy	Amount
_____ %	__/__/__	__/__/__	$ _____
_____ %	__/__/__	__/__/__	$ _____
_____ %	__/__/__	__/__/__	+ $ _____

Total interest due as of the petition date $ _____   Copy total here ▶   + $ _____

3. Total principal and interest due $ _____

Part 2: Statement of Prepetition Fees, Expenses, and Charges

Itemize the fees, expenses, and charges incurred in connection with the claim as of the petition date (included in the Amount of Claim listed in Item 1 on the Proof of Claim form).

Description	Dates Incurred	Amount
Late charges	_____	$ _____
Non-sufficient funds (NSF) fees	_____	$ _____
Attorney's fees	_____	$ _____
Filing fees and court costs	_____	$ _____
Advertisement costs	_____	$ _____
Sheriff/auctioneer fees	_____	$ _____
Title costs	_____	$ _____
Recording fees	_____	$ _____
Appraisal/broker's price opinion fees	_____	$ _____
Property inspection fees	_____	$ _____
Tax advances (non-escrow)	_____	$ _____
Insurance advances (non-escrow)	_____	$ _____
Escrow shortage or deficiency (not included in payments due)	_____	$ _____
Property preservation expenses. Specify: _____	_____	$ _____
Other. Specify: _____	_____	$ _____
Other. Specify: _____	_____	$ _____
Other. Specify: _____	_____	+ $ _____

Total prepetition fees, expenses, and charges. Add all of the amounts listed above. $ _____

B 10 (Attachment A) (12/11)   (08/10 publication draft)

Part 3. Statement of Amount Necessary to Cure Default as of the Petition Date

Does the installment payment amount include an escrow deposit?

❏ No

❏ Yes. Attach to the Proof of Claim form an escrow account statement prepared as of the petition date in a form consistent
with applicable nonbankruptcy law.

1. Installment payments due	Date last payment received by creditor	__/__/__	
	Number of installment payments due	_____	
2. Amount of installment payments due	____ installments @	$ _____	
	____ installments @	$ _____	
	____ installments @	+ $ _____	
	Total installment payments due as of the petition date	$ _____	Copy total here ▶ $ _____
	Add total prepetition fees, expenses, and charges		Copy total from Part 2 here ▶ + $ _____
	Subtract total of unapplied funds (funds received but not credited to account)		- $ _____
	Total amount necessary to cure default as of the petition date		$ _____
			Copy total onto Item 4 of Proof of Claim form

B 10 (Supplement 1) (12/11)   (08/10 publication draft)

United States Bankruptcy Court

_____ District of _____

In re _____ ,   Case No. _____
          Debtor
                                                        Chapter 13

Notice of Mortgage Payment Change

If you file a claim secured by a security interest in the debtor's principal residence provided for under the debtor's plan pursuant to
§ 1322(b)(5), you must use this form to give notice of any changes in the installment payment amount. File this form as a supplement
to your proof of claim at least 21 days before the new payment amount is due. See Bankruptcy Rule 3002.1.

Name of creditor: _____   Court claim no. (if known): _____

Last four digits of any number   Date of payment change:
you use to identify the debtor's   __ __ __ __   Must be at least 21 days after date   __/__/__
account: of this notice

                                                        New total payment: $ _____
                                                        Principal, interest, and escrow, if
                                                        any

Part 1: Escrow Account Payment Adjustment

Will there be a change in the debtor's escrow account payment?

❏ No
❏ Yes. Attach a copy of the escrow account statement, prepared according to applicable nonbankruptcy law. Describe the basis
for the change. If a statement is not attached, explain why: _____

        Current escrow payment: $ _____   New escrow payment: $ _____

Part 2: Mortgage Payment Adjustment

Will the debtor's principal and interest payment change based on an adjustment to the interest rate in the debtor's variable-rate
note?

❏ No
❏ Yes. Attach a copy of the rate change notice, prepared according to applicable nonbankruptcy law. Describe the basis for the
change. If a notice is not attached, explain why: _____

        Current interest rate: _____%   New interest rate: _____%

        Current principal and interest payment:$ _____   New principal and interest payment:$ _____

Part 3: Other Payment Change

Will there be a change in the debtor's mortgage payment for a reason not listed above?

❏ No
❏ Yes. Attach a copy of any documents describing the basis for the change, such as a repayment plan or loan modification
agreement. (Court approval may be required before the payment change can take effect.)

        Reason for change: _____

        Current mortgage payment: $ _____   New mortgage payment: $ _____

B 10 (Supplement 1) (12/11)   (08/10 publication draft)

Part 4: Sign Here

The person completing this Notice must sign it. Sign and print your name and your title, if any, and state your address and telephone number if different from the notice address listed on the proof of claim to which this Supplement applies.

Check the appropriate box.

☐ I am the creditor.   ☐ I am the creditor's authorized agent.
(Attach copy of power of attorney, if any.)

I declare under penalty of perjury that the information provided in this claim is true and correct to the best of my knowledge, information, and reasonable belief.

x _____   Date ___/___/_____
Signature

Print: _____   Title _____
First Name   Middle Name   Last Name

Company _____

Address _____
Number   Street

City   State   ZIP Code

Contact phone (_____) _____ - _____   Email _____

B 10 (Supplement 1) (Committee Note) (12/11)   (08/10 publication draft)

COMMITTEE NOTE

This form is new and applies in chapter 13 cases. It implements Rule 3002.1, which requires the holder of a claim secured by a security interest in the debtor's principal residence – or the holder's agent – to provide notice at least 21 days prior to a change in the amount of the ongoing mortgage installment payments. The form requires the holder of the claim to indicate the basis for the changed payment amount and when it will take effect. The notice must be filed as a supplement to the claim holder's proof of claim, and it must be served on the debtor, debtor's counsel, and the trustee.

The individual completing the form must sign and date it. By doing so, he or she declares under penalty of perjury that the information provided is true and correct to the best of that individual's knowledge, information, and reasonable belief. The signature is also a certification that the standards of FRBP 9011(b) are satisfied.

B 10 (Supplement 2) (12/11)   (08/10 publication draft)

UNITED STATES BANKRUPTCY COURT

_____ District of _____

In re _____,   Case No. _____
     Debtor

                                                 Chapter 13

Notice of Postpetition Mortgage Fees, Expenses, and Charges

If you hold a claim secured by a security interest in the debtor's principal residence, you must use this form to give notice of any postpetition fees, expenses, and charges that you assert are recoverable against the debtor or against the debtor's principal residence. File this form as a supplement to your proof of claim. See Bankruptcy Rule 3002.1.

Name of creditor: _____   Court claim no. (if known): _____

Last four digits of any number you use to
identify the debtor's account: __ __ __ __

Does this notice supplement a prior notice of postpetition fees,
expenses, and charges?

  ❑ No
  ❑ Yes. Date of the last notice: ____/____/____

Part 1: Itemize Postpetition Fees, Expenses, and Charges

Itemize the fees, expenses, and charges incurred on the debtor's mortgage account after the petition was filed. Do not include any escrow account disbursements or any amounts previously itemized in a notice filed in this case or ruled on by the bankruptcy court.

Description	Dates Incurred	Amount
Late charges	_____	$ _____
Non-sufficient funds (NSF) fees	_____	$ _____
Attorney fees	_____	$ _____
Filing fees and court costs	_____	$ _____
Bankruptcy/Proof of claim fees	_____	$ _____
Appraisal/Broker's price opinion fees	_____	$ _____
Property inspection fees	_____	$ _____
Tax advances (non-escrow)	_____	$ _____
Insurance advances (non-escrow)	_____	$ _____
Property preservation expenses. Specify:_____	_____	$ _____
Other. Specify:_____	_____	$ _____
Other. Specify:_____	_____	$ _____
Other. Specify:_____	_____	$ _____
Other. Specify:_____	_____	$ _____

The debtor or trustee may challenge whether the fees, expenses, and charges you listed are required to be paid. See 11 U.S.C. § 1322(b)(5) and Bankruptcy Rule 3002.1.

B 10 (Supplement 2) (12/11)   (08/10 publication draft)

Part 2: Sign Here

The person completing this Notice must sign it. Sign and print your name and your title, if any, and state your address and telephone number if different from the notice address listed on the proof of claim to which this Supplement applies.

Check the appropriate box.

❑ I am the creditor.   ❑ I am the creditor's authorized agent.
                   (Attach copy of power of attorney, if any.)

I declare under penalty of perjury that the information provided in this claim is true and correct to the best of my knowledge, information, and reasonable belief.

X _____   Date __/__/__
   Signature

Print: _____   Title _____
      First Name   Middle Name   Last Name

Company _____

Address _____
      Number   Street
     _____
      City   State ZIP Code

Contact phone (___) ___-____   Email _____

Form Number 14

Official Form 14
(12/03)

Form 14. CLASS [   ] BALLOT FOR ACCEPTING OR REJECTING PLAN OF REORGANIZATION

[Caption as in Form 16A]

CLASS [   ] BALLOT FOR ACCEPTING OR REJECTING PLAN OF REORGANIZATION

[Proponent] filed a plan of reorganization dated *[Date]* (the "Plan") for the Debtor in this case. The Court has *[conditionally]* approved a disclosure statement with respect to the Plan (the "Disclosure Statement"). The Disclosure Statement provides information to assist you in deciding how to vote your ballot. If you do not have a Disclosure Statement, you may obtain a copy from *[name, address, telephone number and telecopy number of proponent/proponent's attorney.]* Court approval of the disclosure statement does not indicate approval of the Plan by the Court.

You should review the Disclosure Statement and the Plan before you vote. You may wish to seek legal advice concerning the Plan and your classification and treatment under the Plan. Your *[claim] [equity interest]* has been placed in class [   ] under the Plan. If you hold claims or equity interests in more than one class, you will receive a ballot for each class in which you are entitled to vote.

If your ballot is not received by [*name and address of proponent's attorney or other appropriate address]* on or before *[date]*, and such deadline is not extended, your vote will not count as either an acceptance or rejection of the Plan.

If the Plan is confirmed by the Bankruptcy Court it will be binding on you whether or not you vote.

ACCEPTANCE OR REJECTION OF THE PLAN

[At this point the ballot should provide for voting by the particular class of creditors or equity holders receiving the ballot using one of the following alternatives;]

[If the voter is the holder of a secured, priority, or unsecured nonpriority claim:]

The undersigned, the holder of a Class [   ] claim against the Debtor in the unpaid amount of Dollars ($)

[or, if the voter is the holder of a bond, debenture, or other debt security:]

The undersigned, the holder of a Class [   ] claim against the Debtor, consisting of Dollars ($) principal amount of *[describe bond, debenture, or other debt security]* of the Debtor (For purposes of this Ballot, it is not necessary and you should not adjust the principal amount for any accrued or unmatured interest.)

[or, if the voter is the holder of an equity interest:]

The undersigned, the holder of Class [   ] equity interest in the Debtor, consisting of _____ shares or other interests of *[describe equity interest]* in the Debtor

Official Form 14 continued
(12/03)

[In each case, the following language should be included:]

    (Check one box only)

       [ ] ACCEPTS THE PLAN   [ ] REJECTS THE PLAN

Dated: _____

                Print or type name: _____

                Signature: _____

                Title (if corporation or partnership) _____

                Address: _____

                                  _____

RETURN THIS BALLOT TO:

[Name and address of proponent's attorney or other appropriate address]

Form Number 18

B18 (Official Form 18) (12/07)

United States Bankruptcy Court

_____ District Of _____

In re _____,
[Set forth here all names including married,
maiden, and trade names used by debtor within
last 8 years.]
                    Debtor

Address _____

_____

Last four digits of Social-Security or other Individual Taxpayer-
Identification No(s)(if any).: _____

Employer Tax-Identification No(s).(EIN) [if any]:_____

)
)
)
)
)   Case No. _____
)
)
)
)
)   Chapter 7
)
)
)
)
)
)

DISCHARGE OF DEBTOR

It appearing that the debtor is entitled to a discharge, **IT IS ORDERED:** The debtor is granted a discharge under section 727 of title 11, United States Code, (the Bankruptcy Code).

Dated: _____

BY THE COURT

_____
United States Bankruptcy Judge

SEE THE BACK OF THIS ORDER FOR IMPORTANT INFORMATION.

B18 (Official Form 18) (12/07) - Cont.

EXPLANATION OF BANKRUPTCY DISCHARGE
IN A CHAPTER 7 CASE

This court order grants a discharge to the person named as the debtor. It is not a dismissal of the case and it does not determine how much money, if any, the trustee will pay to creditors.

Collection of Discharged Debts Prohibited

The discharge prohibits any attempt to collect from the debtor a debt that has been discharged. For example, a creditor is not permitted to contact a debtor by mail, phone, or otherwise, to file or continue a lawsuit, to attach wages or other property, or to take any other action to collect a discharged debt from the debtor. *[In a case involving community property:* There are also special rules that protect certain community property owned by the debtor's spouse, even if that spouse did not file a bankruptcy case.] A creditor who violates this order can be required to pay damages and attorney's fees to the debtor.

However, a creditor may have the right to enforce a valid lien, such as a mortgage or security interest, against the debtor's property after the bankruptcy, if that lien was not avoided or eliminated in the bankruptcy case. Also, a debtor may voluntarily pay any debt that has been discharged.

Debts that are Discharged

The chapter 7 discharge order eliminates a debtor's legal obligation to pay a debt that is discharged. Most, but not all, types of debts are discharged if the debt existed on the date the bankruptcy case was filed. (If this case was begun under a different chapter of the Bankruptcy Code and converted to chapter 7, the discharge applies to debts owed when the bankruptcy case was converted.)

Debts that are Not Discharged.

Some of the common types of debts which are not discharged in a chapter 7 bankruptcy case are:

a. Debts for most taxes;

b. Debts incurred to pay nondischargeable taxes;

c. Debts that are domestic support obligations;

d. Debts for most student loans;

e. Debts for most fines, penalties, forfeitures, or criminal restitution obligations;

f. Debts for personal injuries or death caused by the debtor's operation of a motor vehicle, vessel, or aircraft while intoxicated;

g. Some debts which were not properly listed by the debtor;

h. Debts that the bankruptcy court specifically has decided or will decide in this bankruptcy case are not discharged;

i. Debts for which the debtor has given up the discharge protections by signing a reaffirmation agreement in compliance with the Bankruptcy Code requirements for reaffirmation of debts; and

j. Debts owed to certain pension, profit sharing, stock bonus, other retirement plans, or to the Thrift Savings Plan for federal employees for certain types of loans from these plans.

This information is only a general summary of the bankruptcy discharge. There are exceptions to these general rules. Because the law is complicated, you may want to consult an attorney to determine the exact effect of the discharge in this case.

Form Number 22A

B 22A (Official Form 22A) (Chapter 7) (12/12)   (08/11 publication draft)

In re _____
                 Debtor(s)

Case Number: _____
                 (If known)

According to the information required to be entered on this statement (check one box as directed in Part I, III, or VI of this statement):

☐ **The presumption arises.**
☐ **The presumption does not arise.**
☐ **The presumption is temporarily inapplicable.**

CHAPTER 7 STATEMENT OF CURRENT MONTHLY INCOME AND MEANS-TEST CALCULATION

In addition to Schedules I and J, this statement must be completed by every individual chapter 7 debtor. If none of the exclusions in Part I applies, joint debtors may complete one statement only. If any of the exclusions in Part I applies, joint debtors should complete separate statements if they believe this is required by § 707(b)(2)(C).

Part I. MILITARY AND NON-CONSUMER DEBTORS

1A	**Disabled Veterans.** If you are a disabled veteran described in the Declaration in this Part 1A, (1) check the box at the beginning of the Declaration, (2) check the box for "The presumption does not arise" at the top of this statement, and (3) complete the verification in Part VIII. Do not complete any of the remaining parts of this statement. ☐ **Declaration of Disabled Veteran.** By checking this box, I declare under penalty of perjury that I am a disabled veteran (as defined in 38 U.S.C. § 3741(1)) whose indebtedness occurred primarily during a period in which I was on active duty (as defined in 10 U.S.C. § 101(d)(1)) or while I was performing a homeland defense activity (as defined in 32 U.S.C. §901(1)).
1B	**Non-consumer Debtors.** If your debts are not primarily consumer debts, check the box below and complete the verification in Part VIII. Do not complete any of the remaining parts of this statement. ☐ **Declaration of non-consumer debts.** By checking this box, I declare that my debts are not primarily consumer debts.

1C	**Reservists and National Guard Members; active duty or homeland defense activity.** Members of a reserve component of the Armed Forces and members of the National Guard who were called to active duty (as defined in 10 U.S.C. § 101(d)(1)) after September 11, 2001, for a period of at least 90 days, or who have performed homeland defense activity (as defined in 32 U.S.C. § 901(1)) for a period of at least 90 days, are excluded from all forms of means testing during the time of active duty or homeland defense activity and for 540 days thereafter (the "exclusion period"). If you qualify for this temporary exclusion, (1) check the appropriate boxes and complete any required information in the Declaration of Reservists and National Guard Members below, (2) check the box for "The presumption is temporarily inapplicable" at the top of this statement, and (3) complete the verification in Part VIII. **During your exclusion period you are not required to complete the balance of this form, but you must complete the form no later than 14 days after the date on which your exclusion period ends, unless the time for filing a motion raising the means test presumption expires in your case before your exclusion period ends.**
	
	☐ **Declaration of Reservists and National Guard Members.** By checking this box and making the appropriate entries below, I declare that I am eligible for a temporary exclusion from means testing because, as a member of a reserve component of the Armed Forces or the National Guard
	
	    a. ☐ I was called to active duty after September 11, 2001, for a period of at least 90 days and
	        ☐ I remain on active duty /or/
	        ☐ I was released from active duty on _____, which is less than 540 days before this bankruptcy case was filed;
	
	        OR
	
	    b. ☐ I am performing homeland defense activity for a period of at least 90 days /or/
	        ☐ I performed homeland defense activity for a period of at least 90 days, terminating on _____, which is less than 540 days before this bankruptcy case was filed.

B 22A (Official Form 22A) (Chapter 7) (12/12)   (08/11 publication draft)

Part II. CALCULATION OF MONTHLY INCOME FOR § 707(b)(7) EXCLUSION

		Column A Debtor's Income	Column B Spouse's Income
2	**Marital/filing status.** Check the box that applies and complete the balance of this part of this statement as directed. a. ☐ Unmarried. **Complete only Column A ("Debtor's Income") for Lines 3-11.** b. ☐ Married, not filing jointly, with declaration of separate households. By checking this box, debtor declares under penalty of perjury: "My spouse and I are legally separated under applicable non-bankruptcy law or my spouse and I are living apart other than for the purpose of evading the requirements of § 707(b)(2)(A) of the Bankruptcy Code." **Complete only Column A ("Debtor's Income") for Lines 3-11.** c. ☐ Married, not filing jointly, without the declaration of separate households set out in Line 2.b above. **Complete both Column A ("Debtor's Income") and Column B ("Spouse's Income") for Lines 3-11.** d. ☐ Married, filing jointly. **Complete both Column A ("Debtor's Income") and Column B ("Spouse's Income") for Lines 3-11.**		
	All figures must reflect average monthly income received from all sources, derived during the six calendar months prior to filing the bankruptcy case, ending on the last day of the month before the filing. If the amount of monthly income varied during the six months, you must divide the six-month total by six, and enter the result on the appropriate line.		
3	**Gross wages, salary, tips, bonuses, overtime, commissions.**	$	$
4	**Income from the operation of a business, profession or farm.** Subtract Line b from Line a and enter the difference in the appropriate column(s) of Line 4. If you operate more than one business, profession or farm, enter aggregate numbers and provide details on an attachment. Do not enter a number less than zero. **Do not include any part of the business expenses entered on Line b as a deduction in Part V.** a. Gross receipts — $ b. Ordinary and necessary business expenses — $ c. Business income — Subtract Line b from Line a	$	$
5	**Rent and other real property income.** Subtract Line b from Line a and enter the difference in the appropriate column(s) of Line 5. Do not enter a number less than zero. **Do not include any part of the operating expenses entered on Line b as a deduction in Part V.** a. Gross receipts — $ b. Ordinary and necessary operating expenses — $ c. Rent and other real property income — Subtract Line b from Line a	$	$
6	**Interest, dividends and royalties.**	$	$
7	**Pension and retirement income.**	$	$
8	**Any amounts paid by another person or entity, on a regular basis, for the household expenses of the debtor or the debtor's dependents, including child support paid for that purpose.** Do not include alimony or separate maintenance payments or amounts paid by your spouse if Column B is completed. Each regular payment should be reported in only one column; if a payment is listed in Column A, do not report that payment in Column B.	$	$
9	**Unemployment compensation.** Enter the amount in the appropriate column(s) of Line 9. However, if you contend that unemployment compensation received by you or your spouse was a benefit under the Social Security Act, do not list the amount of such compensation in Column A or B, but instead state the amount in the space below: Unemployment compensation claimed to be a benefit under the Social Security Act Debtor $ _____ Spouse $ _____	$	$

B 22A (Official Form 22A) (Chapter 7) (12/12)   (08/11 publication draft)

10	**Income from all other sources.** Specify source and amount. If necessary, list additional sources on a separate page. **Do not include alimony or separate maintenance payments paid by your spouse if Column B is completed, but include all other payments of alimony or separate maintenance.** Do not include any benefits received under the Social Security Act or payments received as a victim of a war crime, crime against humanity, or as a victim of international or domestic terrorism.			
	a.		$	
	b.		$	
	Total and enter on Line 10		$	$
11	**Subtotal of Current Monthly Income for § 707(b)(7).** Add Lines 3 thru 10 in Column A, and, if Column B is completed, add Lines 3 through 10 in Column B. Enter the total(s).		$	$
12	**Total Current Monthly Income for § 707(b)(7).** If Column B has been completed, add Line 11, Column A to Line 11, Column B, and enter the total. If Column B has not been completed, enter the amount from Line 11, Column A.		$	

Part III. APPLICATION OF § 707(b)(7) EXCLUSION

13	**Annualized Current Monthly Income for § 707(b)(7).** Multiply the amount from Line 12 by the number 12 and enter the result.	$
14	**Applicable median family income.** Enter the median family income for the applicable state and household size. (This information is available by family size at www.usdoj.gov/ust/ or from the clerk of the bankruptcy court.) a. Enter debtor's state of residence: _____ b. Enter debtor's household size: _____	$
15	**Application of Section 707(b)(7).** Check the applicable box and proceed as directed. ☐ **The amount on Line 13 is less than or equal to the amount on Line 14.** Check the box for "The presumption does not arise" at the top of page 1 of this statement, and complete Part VIII; do not complete Parts IV, V, VI or VII. ☐ **The amount on Line 13 is more than the amount on Line 14.** Complete the remaining parts of this statement.	

Complete Parts IV, V, VI, and VII of this statement only if required. (See Line 15.)

Part IV. CALCULATION OF CURRENT MONTHLY INCOME FOR § 707(b)(2)

16	**Enter the amount from Line 12.**		$
17	**Marital adjustment.** If you checked the box at Line 2.c, enter on Line 17 the total of any income listed in Line 11, Column B that was NOT paid on a regular basis for the household expenses of the debtor or the debtor's dependents. Specify in the lines below the basis for excluding the Column B income (such as payment of the spouse's tax liability or the spouse's support of persons other than the debtor or the debtor's dependents) and the amount of income devoted to each purpose. If necessary, list additional adjustments on a separate page. If you did not check box at Line 2.c, enter zero.		
	a.	$	
	b.	$	
	c.	$	
	Total and enter on Line 17.		$
18	**Current monthly income for § 707(b)(2).** Subtract Line 17 from Line 16 and enter the result.		$

289

B 22A (Official Form 22A) (Chapter 7) (12/12)   (08/11 publication draft)

Part V. CALCULATION OF DEDUCTIONS FROM INCOME

Subpart A: Deductions under Standards of the Internal Revenue Service (IRS)

19A	**National Standards: food, clothing and other items.** Enter in Line 19A the "Total" amount from IRS National Standards for Food, Clothing and Other Items for the applicable number of persons. (This information is available at www.usdoj.gov/ust/ or from the clerk of the bankruptcy court.) The applicable number of persons is the number that would currently be allowed as exemptions on your federal income tax return, plus the number of any additional dependents whom you support.	$
19B	**National Standards: health care.** Enter in Line a1 below the amount from IRS National Standards for Out-of-Pocket Health Care for persons under 65 years of age, and in Line a2 the IRS National Standards for Out-of-Pocket Health Care for persons 65 years of age or older. (This information is available at www.usdoj.gov/ust/ or from the clerk of the bankruptcy court.) Enter in Line b1 the applicable number of persons who are under 65 years of age, and enter in Line b2 the applicable number of persons who are 65 years of age or older. (The applicable number of persons in each age category is the number in that category that would currently be allowed as exemptions on your federal income tax return, plus the number of any additional dependents whom you support.) Multiply Line a1 by Line b1 to obtain a total amount for persons under 65, and enter the result in Line c1. Multiply Line a2 by Line b2 to obtain a total amount for persons 65 and older, and enter the result in Line c2. Add Lines c1 and c2 to obtain a total health care amount, and enter the result in Line 19B.	

Persons under 65 years of age			Persons 65 years of age or older			
a1.	Allowance per person		a2.	Allowance per person		
b1.	Number of persons		b2.	Number of persons		
c1.	Subtotal		c2.	Subtotal		$

20A	**Local Standards: housing and utilities; non-mortgage expenses.** Enter the amount of the IRS Housing and Utilities Standards; non-mortgage expenses for the applicable county and family size. (This information is available at www.usdoj.gov/ust/ or from the clerk of the bankruptcy court). The applicable family size consists of the number that would currently be allowed as exemptions on your federal income tax return, plus the number of any additional dependents whom you support.	$
20B	**Local Standards: housing and utilities; mortgage/rent expense.** Enter, in Line a below, the amount of the IRS Housing and Utilities Standards; mortgage/rent expense for your county and family size (this information is available at www.usdoj.gov/ust/ or from the clerk of the bankruptcy court) (the applicable family size consists of the number that would currently be allowed as exemptions on your federal income tax return, plus the number of any additional dependents whom you support); enter on Line b the total of the Average Monthly Payments for any debts secured by your home, as stated in Line 42; subtract Line b from Line a and enter the result in Line 20B. **Do not enter an amount less than zero.**	

a.	IRS Housing and Utilities Standards; mortgage/rental expense	$	
b.	Average Monthly Payment for any debts secured by your home, if any, as stated in Line 42	$	
c.	Net mortgage/rental expense	Subtract Line b from Line a.	$

21	**Local Standards: housing and utilities; adjustment.** If you contend that the process set out in Lines 20A and 20B does not accurately compute the allowance to which you are entitled under the IRS Housing and Utilities Standards, enter any additional amount to which you contend you are entitled, and state the basis for your contention in the space below: _____ _____	$

B 22A (Official Form 22A) (Chapter 7) (12/12)   (08/11 publication draft)

22A	**Local Standards: transportation; vehicle operation/public transportation expense.** You are entitled to an expense allowance in this category regardless of whether you pay the expenses of operating a vehicle and regardless of whether you use public transportation. Check the number of vehicles for which you pay the operating expenses or for which the operating expenses are included as a contribution to your household expenses in Line 8. ☐ 0 ☐ 1 ☐ 2 or more. If you checked 0, enter on Line 22A the "Public Transportation" amount from IRS Local Standards: Transportation. If you checked 1 or 2 or more, enter on Line 22A the "Operating Costs" amount from IRS Local Standards: Transportation for the applicable number of vehicles in the applicable Metropolitan Statistical Area or Census Region. (These amounts are available at www.usdoj.gov/ust/ or from the clerk of the bankruptcy court.)	$
22B	**Local Standards: transportation; additional public transportation expense.** If you pay the operating expenses for a vehicle and also use public transportation, and you contend that you are entitled to an additional deduction for your public transportation expenses, enter on Line 22B the "Public Transportation" amount from IRS Local Standards: Transportation. (This amount is available at www.usdoj.gov/ust/ or from the clerk of the bankruptcy court.)	$
23	**Local Standards: transportation ownership/lease expense; Vehicle 1.** Check the number of vehicles for which you claim an ownership/lease expense. (You may not claim an ownership/lease expense for more than two vehicles.) ☐ 1 ☐ 2 or more. Enter, in Line a below, the "Ownership Costs" for "One Car" from the IRS Local Standards: Transportation (available at www.usdoj.gov/ust/ or from the clerk of the bankruptcy court); enter in Line b the total of the Average Monthly Payments for any debts secured by Vehicle 1, as stated in Line 42; subtract Line b from Line a and enter the result in Line 23. **Do not enter an amount less than zero.**	
	a.	IRS Transportation Standards, Ownership Costs	$	
	b.	Average Monthly Payment for any debts secured by Vehicle 1, as stated in Line 42	$	
	c.	Net ownership/lease expense for Vehicle 1	Subtract Line b from Line a.	$
24	**Local Standards: transportation ownership/lease expense; Vehicle 2.** Complete this Line only if you checked the "2 or more" Box in Line 23. Enter, in Line a below, the "Ownership Costs" for "One Car" from the IRS Local Standards: Transportation (available at www.usdoj.gov/ust/ or from the clerk of the bankruptcy court); enter in Line b the total of the Average Monthly Payments for any debts secured by Vehicle 2, as stated in Line 42; subtract Line b from Line a and enter the result in Line 24. **Do not enter an amount less than zero.**	
	a.	IRS Transportation Standards, Ownership Costs	$	
	b.	Average Monthly Payment for any debts secured by Vehicle 2, as stated in Line 42	$	
	c.	Net ownership/lease expense for Vehicle 2	Subtract Line b from Line a.	$
25	**Other Necessary Expenses: taxes.** Enter the total average monthly expense that you actually incur for all federal, state and local taxes, other than real estate and sales taxes, such as income taxes, self-employment taxes, social-security taxes, and Medicare taxes. **Do not include real estate or sales taxes.**	$
26	**Other Necessary Expenses: involuntary deductions for employment.** Enter the total average monthly payroll deductions that are required for your employment, such as retirement contributions, union dues, and uniform costs. **Do not include discretionary amounts, such as voluntary 401(k) contributions.**	$
27	**Other Necessary Expenses: life insurance.** Enter total average monthly premiums that you actually pay for term life insurance for yourself. **Do not include premiums for insurance on your dependents, for whole life or for any other form of insurance.**	$
28	**Other Necessary Expenses: court-ordered payments.** Enter the total monthly amount that you are required to pay pursuant to the order of a court or administrative agency, such as spousal or child support payments. **Do not include payments on past due obligations included in Line 44.**	$

B 22A (Official Form 22A) (Chapter 7) (12/12)   (08/11 publication draft)

29	**Other Necessary Expenses: education for employment or for a physically or mentally challenged child.** Enter the total average monthly amount that you actually expend for education that is a condition of employment and for education that is required for a physically or mentally challenged dependent child for whom no public education providing similar services is available.	$
30	**Other Necessary Expenses: childcare.** Enter the total average monthly amount that you actually expend on childcare—such as baby-sitting, day care, nursery and preschool. **Do not include other educational payments.**	$
31	**Other Necessary Expenses: health care.** Enter the total average monthly amount that you actually expend on health care that is required for the health and welfare of yourself or your dependents, that is not reimbursed by insurance or paid by a health savings account, and that is in excess of the amount entered in Line 19B. **Do not include payments for health insurance or health savings accounts listed in Line 34.**	$
32	**Other Necessary Expenses: telecommunication services.** Enter the total average monthly amount that you actually pay for telecommunication services other than your basic home telephone and cell phone service— such as pagers, call waiting, caller id, special long distance, internet service, or business cell phone service— to the extent necessary for your health and welfare or that of your dependents or for the production of income if not reimbursed by your employer. **Do not include any amount previously deducted.**	$
33	**Total Expenses Allowed under IRS Standards.** Enter the total of Lines 19 through 32.	$

Subpart B: Additional Living Expense Deductions
Note: Do not include any expenses that you have listed in Lines 19-32

34	**Health Insurance, Disability Insurance, and Health Savings Account Expenses.** List the monthly expenses in the categories set out in lines a-c below that are reasonably necessary for yourself, your spouse, or your dependents.		
	a. Health Insurance	$	
	b. Disability Insurance	$	
	c. Health Savings Account	$	
	Total and enter on Line 34 **If you do not actually expend this total amount**, state your actual total average monthly expenditures in the space below: $ _____		$
35	**Continued contributions to the care of household or family members.** Enter the total average actual monthly expenses that you will continue to pay for the reasonable and necessary care and support of an elderly, chronically ill, or disabled member of your household or member of your immediate family who is unable to pay for such expenses.		$
36	**Protection against family violence.** Enter the total average reasonably necessary monthly expenses that you actually incurred to maintain the safety of your family under the Family Violence Prevention and Services Act or other applicable federal law. The nature of these expenses is required to be kept confidential by the court.		$
37	**Home energy costs.** Enter the total average monthly amount, in excess of the allowance specified by IRS Local Standards for Housing and Utilities, that you actually expend for home energy costs. **You must provide your case trustee with documentation of your actual expenses, and you must demonstrate that the additional amount claimed is reasonable and necessary.**		$
38	**Education expenses for dependent children less than 18.** Enter the total average monthly expenses that you actually incur, not to exceed $147.92* per child, for attendance at a private or public elementary or secondary school by your dependent children less than 18 years of age. **You must provide your case trustee with documentation of your actual expenses, and you must explain why the amount claimed is reasonable and necessary and not already accounted for in the IRS Standards.**		$

*Amount subject to adjustment on 4/01/13, and every three years thereafter with respect to cases commenced on or after the date of adjustment.

292

39	**Additional food and clothing expense.** Enter the total average monthly amount by which your food and clothing expenses exceed the combined allowances for food and clothing (apparel and services) in the IRS National Standards, not to exceed 5% of those combined allowances. (This information is available at www.usdoj.gov/ust/ or from the clerk of the bankruptcy court.) **You must demonstrate that the additional amount claimed is reasonable and necessary.**	$
40	**Continued charitable contributions.** Enter the amount that you will continue to contribute in the form of cash or financial instruments to a charitable organization as defined in 26 U.S.C. § 170(c)(1)-(2).	$
41	**Total Additional Expense Deductions under § 707(b).** Enter the total of Lines 34 through 40	$

Subpart C: Deductions for Debt Payment

42	**Future payments on secured claims.** For each of your debts that is secured by an interest in property that you own, list the name of the creditor, identify the property securing the debt, state the Average Monthly Payment, and check whether the payment includes taxes or insurance. The Average Monthly Payment is the total of all amounts scheduled as contractually due to each Secured Creditor in the 60 months following the filing of the bankruptcy case, divided by 60. If necessary, list additional entries on a separate page. Enter the total of the Average Monthly Payments on Line 42.	

	Name of Creditor	Property Securing the Debt	Average Monthly Payment	Does payment include taxes or insurance?	
a.			$	☐ yes ☐ no	
b.			$	☐ yes ☐ no	
c.			$	☐ yes ☐ no	
			Total: Add Lines a, b and c.		$

43	**Other payments on secured claims.** If any of debts listed in Line 42 are secured by your primary residence, a motor vehicle, or other property necessary for your support or the support of your dependents, you may include in your deduction 1/60th of any amount (the "cure amount") that you must pay the creditor in addition to the payments listed in Line 42, in order to maintain possession of the property. The cure amount would include any sums in default that must be paid in order to avoid repossession or foreclosure. List and total any such amounts in the following chart. If necessary, list additional entries on a separate page.	

	Name of Creditor	Property Securing the Debt	1/60th of the Cure Amount	
a.			$	
b.			$	
c.			$	
			Total: Add Lines a, b and c	$

44	**Payments on prepetition priority claims.** Enter the total amount, divided by 60, of all priority claims, such as priority tax, child support and alimony claims, for which you were liable at the time of your bankruptcy filing. **Do not include current obligations, such as those set out in Line 28.**	$

B 22A (Official Form 22A) (Chapter 7) (12/12)   (08/11 publication draft)

45	**Chapter 13 administrative expenses.** If you are eligible to file a case under chapter 13, complete the following chart, multiply the amount in line a by the amount in line b, and enter the resulting administrative expense.	

45	a.	Projected average monthly chapter 13 plan payment.	$
	b.	Current multiplier for your district as determined under schedules issued by the Executive Office for United States Trustees. (This information is available at www.usdoj.gov/ust/ or from the clerk of the bankruptcy court.)	x
	c.	Average monthly administrative expense of chapter 13 case	Total: Multiply Lines a and b $

46	**Total Deductions for Debt Payment.** Enter the total of Lines 42 through 45.	$

Subpart D: Total Deductions from Income

47	**Total of all deductions allowed under § 707(b)(2).** Enter the total of Lines 33, 41, and 46.	$

Part VI. DETERMINATION OF § 707(b)(2) PRESUMPTION

48	**Enter the amount from Line 18** (Current monthly income for § 707(b)(2))	$
49	**Enter the amount from Line 47** (Total of all deductions allowed under § 707(b)(2))	$
50	**Monthly disposable income under § 707(b)(2).** Subtract Line 49 from Line 48 and enter the result	$
51	**60-month disposable income under § 707(b)(2).** Multiply the amount in Line 50 by the number 60 and enter the result.	$
52	**Initial presumption determination.** Check the applicable box and proceed as directed. ☐ **The amount on Line 51 is less than $7,025*.** Check the box for "The presumption does not arise" at the top of page 1 of this statement, and complete the verification in Part VIII. Do not complete the remainder of Part VI. ☐ **The amount set forth on Line 51 is more than $11,725*.** Check the box for "The presumption arises" at the top of page 1 of this statement, and complete the verification in Part VIII. You may also complete Part VII. Do not complete the remainder of Part VI. ☐ **The amount on Line 51 is at least $7,025*, but not more than $11,725*.** Complete the remainder of Part VI (Lines 53 through 55).	
53	**Enter the amount of your total non-priority unsecured debt**	$
54	**Threshold debt payment amount.** Multiply the amount in Line 53 by the number 0.25 and enter the result.	$
55	**Secondary presumption determination.** Check the applicable box and proceed as directed. ☐ **The amount on Line 51 is less than the amount on Line 54.** Check the box for "The presumption does not arise" at the top of page 1 of this statement, and complete the verification in Part VIII. ☐ **The amount on Line 51 is equal to or greater than the amount on Line 54.** Check the box for "The presumption arises" at the top of page 1 of this statement, and complete the verification in Part VIII. You may also complete Part VII.	

Part VII: ADDITIONAL EXPENSE CLAIMS

56	**Other Expenses.** List and describe any monthly expenses, not otherwise stated in this form, that are required for the health and welfare of you and your family and that you contend should be an additional deduction from your current monthly income under § 707(b)(2)(A)(ii)(I). If necessary, list additional sources on a separate page. All figures should reflect your average monthly expense for each item. Total the expenses.	

	Expense Description	Monthly Amount
a.		$
b.		$
c.		$
	Total: Add Lines a, b and c	$

*Amounts are subject to adjustment on 4/01/13, and every three years thereafter with respect to cases commenced on or after the date of adjustment.

B 22A (Official Form 22A) (Chapter 7) (12/12)   (08/11 publication draft)

	### Part VIII: VERIFICATION

57	I declare under penalty of perjury that the information provided in this statement is true and correct. *(If this is a joint case, both debtors must sign.)*
	
	Date: _____ Signature: _____
	                                (Debtor)
	
	Date: _____ Signature: _____
	                                (Joint Debtor, if any)

Form Number 22B

B 22B (Official Form 22B) (Chapter 11) (12/10)

In re _____
                      Debtor(s)

Case Number: _____
                      (If known)

CHAPTER 11 STATEMENT OF CURRENT MONTHLY INCOME

In addition to Schedules I and J, this statement must be completed by every individual chapter 11 debtor, whether or not filing jointly. Joint debtors may complete one statement only.

	Part I. CALCULATION OF CURRENT MONTHLY INCOME			
1	**Marital/filing status.** Check the box that applies and complete the balance of this part of this statement as directed. a. ☐ Unmarried. **Complete only Column A ("Debtor's Income") for Lines 2-10.** b. ☐ Married, not filing jointly. **Complete only Column A ("Debtor's Income") for Lines 2-10.** c. ☐ Married, filing jointly. **Complete both Column A ("Debtor's Income") and Column B ("Spouse's Income") for Lines 2-10.**			
	All figures must reflect average monthly income received from all sources, derived during the six calendar months prior to filing the bankruptcy case, ending on the last day of the month before the filing. If the amount of monthly income varied during the six months, you must divide the six-month total by six, and enter the result on the appropriate line.		**Column A** Debtor's Income	**Column B** Spouse's Income
2	**Gross wages, salary, tips, bonuses, overtime, commissions.**		$	$
3	**Net income from the operation of a business, profession, or farm.** Subtract Line b from Line a and enter the difference in the appropriate column(s) of Line 3. If more than one business, profession or farm, enter aggregate numbers and provide details on an attachment. Do not enter a number less than zero.			
	a.	Gross receipts	$	
	b.	Ordinary and necessary business expenses	$	
	c.	Business income	Subtract Line b from Line a.	$
4	**Net rental and other real property income.** Subtract Line b from Line a and enter the difference in the appropriate column(s) of Line 4. Do not enter a number less than zero.			
	a.	Gross receipts	$	
	b.	Ordinary and necessary operating expenses	$	
	c.	Rent and other real property income	Subtract Line b from Line a.	$
5	**Interest, dividends, and royalties.**		$	$
6	**Pension and retirement income.**		$	$
7	**Any amounts paid by another person or entity, on a regular basis, for the household expenses of the debtor or the debtor's dependents, including child support paid for that purpose.** Do not include alimony or separate maintenance payments or amounts paid by the debtor's spouse if Column B is completed. Each regular payment should be reported in only one column; if a payment is listed in Column A, do not report that payment in Column B.		$	$
8	**Unemployment compensation.** Enter the amount in the appropriate column(s) of Line 8. However, if you contend that unemployment compensation received by you or your spouse was a benefit under the Social Security Act, do not list the amount of such compensation in Column A or B, but instead state the amount in the space below:			
	Unemployment compensation claimed to be a benefit under the Social Security Act	Debtor $ _____ Spouse $ _____	$	$

B 22B (Official Form 22B) (Chapter 11) (12/10)   2

9	**Income from all other sources**. Specify source and amount. If necessary, list additional sources on a separate page. Total and enter on Line 9. **Do not include alimony or separate maintenance payments paid by your spouse if Column B is completed, but include all other payments of alimony or separate maintenance. Do not include** any benefits received under the Social Security Act or payments received as a victim of a war crime, crime against humanity, or as a victim of international or domestic terrorism.		
	a. $		
	b. $	$	$
10	**Subtotal of current monthly income.** Add Lines 2 thru 9 in Column A, and, if Column B is completed, add Lines 2 through 9 in Column B. Enter the total(s).	$	$
11	**Total current monthly income.** If Column B has been completed, add Line 10, Column A to Line 10, Column B, and enter the total. If Column B has not been completed, enter the amount from Line 10, Column A.	$	

Part II: VERIFICATION	

12	I declare under penalty of perjury that the information provided in this statement is true and correct. *(If this a joint case, both debtors must sign.)*
	
	 Date: _____ Signature: _____
	                                           (Debtor)
	
	 Date: _____ Signature: _____
	                                     (Joint Debtor, if any)

Form Number 22C

B 22C (Official Form 22C) (Chapter 13) (12/12)   (08/11 publication draft)

In re _____

       Debtor(s)

Case Number: _____

       (If known)

<table>
<tr><td colspan="2">According to the calculations required by this statement:
☐ The applicable commitment period is 3 years.
☐ The applicable commitment period is 5 years.
☐ Disposable income is determined under § 1325(b)(3).
☐ Disposable income is not determined under § 1325(b)(3).
(Check the boxes as directed in Lines 17 and 23 of this statement.)</td></tr>
</table>

CHAPTER 13 STATEMENT OF CURRENT MONTHLY INCOME
AND CALCULATION OF COMMITMENT PERIOD AND DISPOSABLE INCOME

In addition to Schedules I and J, this statement must be completed by every individual chapter 13 debtor, whether or not filing jointly. Joint debtors may complete one statement only.

	Part I. REPORT OF INCOME			Column A Debtor's Income	Column B Spouse's Income
1	**Marital/filing status.** Check the box that applies and complete the balance of this part of this statement as directed. a. ☐ Unmarried. **Complete only Column A ("Debtor's Income") for Lines 2-10.** b. ☐ Married. **Complete both Column A ("Debtor's Income") and Column B ("Spouse's Income") for Lines 2-10.**				
	All figures must reflect average monthly income received from all sources, derived during the six calendar months prior to filing the bankruptcy case, ending on the last day of the month before the filing. If the amount of monthly income varied during the six months, you must divide the six-month total by six, and enter the result on the appropriate line.			Column A Debtor's Income	Column B Spouse's Income
2	**Gross wages, salary, tips, bonuses, overtime, commissions.**			$	$
3	**Income from the operation of a business, profession, or farm.** Subtract Line b from Line a and enter the difference in the appropriate column(s) of Line 3. If you operate more than one business, profession or farm, enter aggregate numbers and provide details on an attachment. Do not enter a number less than zero. **Do not include any part of the business expenses entered on Line b as a deduction in Part IV.**				
	a.	Gross receipts	$		
	b.	Ordinary and necessary business expenses	$		
	c.	Business income	Subtract Line b from Line a	$	$
4	**Rent and other real property income.** Subtract Line b from Line a and enter the difference in the appropriate column(s) of Line 4. Do not enter a number less than zero. **Do not include any part of the operating expenses entered on Line b as a deduction in Part IV.**				
	a.	Gross receipts	$		
	b.	Ordinary and necessary operating expenses	$		
	c.	Rent and other real property income	Subtract Line b from Line a	$	$
5	**Interest, dividends, and royalties.**			$	$
6	**Pension and retirement income.**			$	$
7	**Any amounts paid by another person or entity, on a regular basis, for the household expenses of the debtor or the debtor's dependents, including child support paid for that purpose.** Do not include alimony or separate maintenance payments or amounts paid by the debtor's spouse. Each regular payment should be reported in only one column; if a payment is listed in Column A, do not report that payment in Column B.			$	$

B 22C (Official Form 22C) (Chapter 13) (12/12)   (08/11 publication draft

8	**Unemployment compensation.** Enter the amount in the appropriate column(s) of Line 8. However, if you contend that unemployment compensation received by you or your spouse was a benefit under the Social Security Act, do not list the amount of such compensation in Column A or B, but instead state the amount in the space below: Unemployment compensation claimed to be a benefit under the Social Security Act Debtor $ _____ Spouse $ _____	$	$
9	**Income from all other sources.** Specify source and amount. If necessary, list additional sources on a separate page. Total and enter on Line 9. **Do not include** alimony or separate maintenance payments paid by your spouse, but include all other payments of alimony or separate maintenance. **Do not include** any benefits received under the Social Security Act or payments received as a victim of a war crime, crime against humanity, or as a victim of international or domestic terrorism. a. _____ $ _____ b. _____ $ _____	$	$
10	**Subtotal.** Add Lines 2 thru 9 in Column A, and, if Column B is completed, add Lines 2 through 9 in Column B. Enter the total(s).	$	$
11	**Total.** If Column B has been completed, add Line 10, Column A to Line 10, Column B, and enter the total. If Column B has not been completed, enter the amount from Line 10, Column A. $		

Part II. CALCULATION OF § 1325(b)(4) COMMITMENT PERIOD

12	Enter the amount from Line 11.	$
13	**Marital adjustment.** If you are married, but are not filing jointly with your spouse, AND if you contend that calculation of the commitment period under § 1325(b)(4) does not require inclusion of the income of your spouse, enter on Line 13 the amount of the income listed in Line 10, Column B that was NOT paid on a regular basis for the household expenses of you or your dependents and specify, in the lines below, the basis for excluding this income (such as payment of the spouse's tax liability or the spouse's support of persons other than the debtor or the debtor's dependents) and the amount of income devoted to each purpose. If necessary, list additional adjustments on a separate page. If the conditions for entering this adjustment do not apply, enter zero. a. _____ $ _____ b. _____ $ _____ c. _____ $ _____ Total and enter on Line 13.	$
14	Subtract Line 13 from Line 12 and enter the result.	$
15	**Annualized current monthly income for § 1325(b)(4).** Multiply the amount from Line 14 by the number 12 and enter the result.	$
16	**Applicable median family income.** Enter the median family income for applicable state and household size. (This information is available by family size at www.usdoj.gov/ust/ or from the clerk of the bankruptcy court.) a. Enter debtor's state of residence: _____ b. Enter debtor's household size: _____	$
17	**Application of § 1325(b)(4).** Check the applicable box and proceed as directed. ☐ **The amount on Line 15 is less than the amount on Line 16.** Check the box for "The applicable commitment period is 3 years" at the top of page 1 of this statement and continue with this statement. ☐ **The amount on Line 15 is not less than the amount on Line 16.** Check the box for "The applicable commitment period is 5 years" at the top of page 1 of this statement and continue with this statement.	

Part III. APPLICATION OF § 1325(b)(3) FOR DETERMINING DISPOSABLE INCOME

18	Enter the amount from Line 11.	$

19	**Marital adjustment.** If you are married, but are not filing jointly with your spouse, enter on Line 19 the total of any income listed in Line 10, Column B that was NOT paid on a regular basis for the household expenses of the debtor or the debtor's dependents. Specify in the lines below the basis for excluding the Column B income (such as payment of the spouse's tax liability or the spouse's support of persons other than the debtor or the debtor's dependents) and the amount of income devoted to each purpose. If necessary, list additional adjustments on a separate page. If the conditions for entering this adjustment do not apply, enter zero.	
	a. $ b. $ c. $	
	Total and enter on Line 19.	$
20	**Current monthly income for § 1325(b)(3).** Subtract Line 19 from Line 18 and enter the result.	$
21	**Annualized current monthly income for § 1325(b)(3).** Multiply the amount from Line 20 by the number 12 and enter the result.	$
22	**Applicable median family income.** Enter the amount from Line 16.	$
23	**Application of § 1325(b)(3).** Check the applicable box and proceed as directed. ☐ **The amount on Line 21 is more than the amount on Line 22.** Check the box for "Disposable income is determined under § 1325(b)(3)" at the top of page 1 of this statement and complete the remaining parts of this statement. ☐ **The amount on Line 21 is not more than the amount on Line 22.** Check the box for "Disposable income is not determined under § 1325(b)(3)" at the top of page 1 of this statement and complete Part VII of this statement. **Do not complete Parts IV, V, or VI.**	

Part IV. CALCULATION OF DEDUCTIONS FROM INCOME

Subpart A: Deductions under Standards of the Internal Revenue Service (IRS)

24A	**National Standards: food, apparel and services, housekeeping supplies, personal care, and miscellaneous.** Enter in Line 24A the "Total" amount from IRS National Standards for Allowable Living Expenses for the applicable number of persons. (This information is available at www.usdoj.gov/ust/ or from the clerk of the bankruptcy court.) The applicable number of persons is the number that would currently be allowed as exemptions on your federal income tax return, plus the number of any additional dependents whom you support.	$
24B	**National Standards: health care.** Enter in Line a1 below the amount from IRS National Standards for Out-of-Pocket Health Care for persons under 65 years of age, and in Line a2 the IRS National Standards for Out-of-Pocket Health Care for persons 65 years of age or older. (This information is available at www.usdoj.gov/ust/ or from the clerk of the bankruptcy court.) Enter in Line b1 the applicable number of persons who are under 65 years of age, and enter in Line b2 the applicable number of persons who are 65 years of age or older. (The applicable number of persons in each age category is the number in that category that would currently be allowed as exemptions on your federal income tax return, plus the number of any additional dependents whom you support.) Multiply Line a1 by Line b1 to obtain a total amount for persons under 65, and enter the result in Line c1. Multiply Line a2 by Line b2 to obtain a total amount for persons 65 and older, and enter the result in Line c2. Add Lines c1 and c2 to obtain a total health care amount, and enter the result in Line 24B.	

Persons under 65 years of age			Persons 65 years of age or older			
a1.	Allowance per person		a2.	Allowance per person		
b1.	Number of persons		b2.	Number of persons		
c1.	Subtotal		c2.	Subtotal		$

25A	**Local Standards: housing and utilities; non-mortgage expenses.** Enter the amount of the IRS Housing and Utilities Standards; non-mortgage expenses for the applicable county and family size. (This information is available at www.usdoj.gov/ust/ or from the clerk of the bankruptcy court). The applicable family size consists of the number that would currently be allowed as exemptions on your federal income tax return, plus the number of any additional dependents whom you support.	$

B 22C (Official Form 22C) (Chapter 13) (12/12)   (08/11 publication draft)

25B	**Local Standards: housing and utilities; mortgage/rent expense.** Enter, in Line a below, the amount of the IRS Housing and Utilities Standards; mortgage/rent expense for your county and family size (this information is available at www.usdoj.gov/ust/ or from the clerk of the bankruptcy court) (the applicable family size consists of the number that would currently be allowed as exemptions on your federal income tax return, plus the number of any additional dependents whom you support); enter on Line b the total of the Average Monthly Payments for any debts secured by your home, as stated in Line 47; subtract Line b from Line a and enter the result in Line 25B. **Do not enter an amount less than zero.**	

	a.	IRS Housing and Utilities Standards; mortgage/rent expense	$	
	b.	Average Monthly Payment for any debts secured by your home, if any, as stated in Line 47	$	
	c.	Net mortgage/rental expense	Subtract Line b from Line a.	$

26	**Local Standards: housing and utilities; adjustment.** If you contend that the process set out in Lines 25A and 25B does not accurately compute the allowance to which you are entitled under the IRS Housing and Utilities Standards, enter any additional amount to which you contend you are entitled, and state the basis for your contention in the space below: _____ _____ _____	$

27A	**Local Standards: transportation; vehicle operation/public transportation expense.** You are entitled to an expense allowance in this category regardless of whether you pay the expenses of operating a vehicle and regardless of whether you use public transportation. Check the number of vehicles for which you pay the operating expenses or for which the operating expenses are included as a contribution to your household expenses in Line 7. ☐ 0 ☐ 1 ☐ 2 or more. If you checked 0, enter on Line 27A the "Public Transportation" amount from IRS Local Standards: Transportation. If you checked 1 or 2 or more, enter on Line 27A the "Operating Costs" amount from IRS Local Standards: Transportation for the applicable number of vehicles in the applicable Metropolitan Statistical Area or Census Region. (These amounts are available at www.usdoj.gov/ust/ or from the clerk of the bankruptcy court.)	$

27B	**Local Standards: transportation; additional public transportation expense.** If you pay the operating expenses for a vehicle and also use public transportation, and you contend that you are entitled to an additional deduction for your public transportation expenses, enter on Line 27B the "Public Transportation" amount from IRS Local Standards: Transportation. (This amount is available at www.usdoj.gov/ust/ or from the clerk of the bankruptcy court.)	$

28	**Local Standards: transportation ownership/lease expense; Vehicle 1.** Check the number of vehicles for which you claim an ownership/lease expense. (You may not claim an ownership/lease expense for more than two vehicles.) ☐ 1 ☐ 2 or more. Enter, in Line a below, the "Ownership Costs" for "One Car" from the IRS Local Standards: Transportation (available at www.usdoj.gov/ust/ or from the clerk of the bankruptcy court); enter in Line b the total of the Average Monthly Payments for any debts secured by Vehicle 1, as stated in Line 47; subtract Line b from Line a and enter the result in Line 28. **Do not enter an amount less than zero.**	

	a.	IRS Transportation Standards, Ownership Costs	$	
	b.	Average Monthly Payment for any debts secured by Vehicle 1, as stated in Line 47	$	
	c.	Net ownership/lease expense for Vehicle 1	Subtract Line b from Line a.	$

B 22C (Official Form 22C) (Chapter 13) (12/12)   (08/11 publication draft

29	**Local Standards: transportation ownership/lease expense; Vehicle 2.** Complete this Line only if you checked the "2 or more" Box in Line 28. Enter, in Line a below, the "Ownership Costs" for "One Car" from the IRS Local Standards: Transportation (available at www.usdoj.gov/ust/ or from the clerk of the bankruptcy court); enter in Line b the total of the Average Monthly Payments for any debts secured by Vehicle 2, as stated in Line 47; subtract Line b from Line a and enter the result in Line 29. **Do not enter an amount less than zero.**		
	a. IRS Transportation Standards, Ownership Costs	S .	
	b. Average Monthly Payment for any debts secured by Vehicle 2, as stated in Line 47	S	
	c. Net ownership/lease expense for Vehicle 2	Subtract Line b from Line a.	$
30	**Other Necessary Expenses: taxes.** Enter the total average monthly expense that you actually incur for all federal, state, and local taxes, other than real estate and sales taxes, such as income taxes, self-employment taxes, social-security taxes, and Medicare taxes. **Do not include real estate or sales taxes.**		$
31	**Other Necessary Expenses: involuntary deductions for employment.** Enter the total average monthly deductions that are required for your employment, such as mandatory retirement contributions, union dues, and uniform costs. **Do not include discretionary amounts, such as voluntary 401(k) contributions.**		$
32	**Other Necessary Expenses: life insurance.** Enter total average monthly premiums that you actually pay for term life insurance for yourself. **Do not include premiums for insurance on your dependents, for whole life or for any other form of insurance.**		$
33	**Other Necessary Expenses: court-ordered payments.** Enter the total monthly amount that you are required to pay pursuant to the order of a court or administrative agency, such as spousal or child support payments. **Do not include payments on past due obligations included in Line 49.**		$
34	**Other Necessary Expenses: education for employment or for a physically or mentally challenged child.** Enter the total average monthly amount that you actually expend for education that is a condition of employment and for education that is required for a physically or mentally challenged dependent child for whom no public education providing similar services is available.		$
35	**Other Necessary Expenses: childcare.** Enter the total average monthly amount that you actually expend on childcare—such as baby-sitting, day care, nursery and preschool. **Do not include other educational payments.**		$
36	**Other Necessary Expenses: health care.** Enter the total average monthly amount that you actually expend on health care that is required for the health and welfare of yourself or your dependents, that is not reimbursed by insurance or paid by a health savings account, and that is in excess of the amount entered in Line 24B. **Do not include payments for health insurance or health savings accounts listed in Line 39.**		$
37	**Other Necessary Expenses: telecommunication services.** Enter the total average monthly amount that you actually pay for telecommunication services other than your basic home telephone and cell phone service—such as pagers, call waiting, caller id, special long distance, internet service, or business cell phone service—to the extent necessary for your health and welfare or that of your dependents or for the production of income if not reimbursed by your employer. **Do not include any amount previously deducted.**		$
38	**Total Expenses Allowed under IRS Standards.** Enter the total of Lines 24 through 37.		$

Subpart B: Additional Living Expense Deductions
Note: Do not include any expenses that you have listed in Lines 24-37

B 22C (Official Form 22C) (Chapter 13) (12/12)   (08/11 publication draft)

39	**Health Insurance, Disability Insurance, and Health Savings Account Expenses.** List the monthly expenses in the categories set out in lines a-c below that are reasonably necessary for yourself, your spouse, or your dependents.	

	a.	Health Insurance	$
	b.	Disability Insurance	$
	c.	Health Savings Account	$

Total and enter on Line 39 $

If you do not actually expend this total amount, state your actual total average monthly expenditures in the space below:

$ _____

40	**Continued contributions to the care of household or family members.** Enter the total average actual monthly expenses that you will continue to pay for the reasonable and necessary care and support of an elderly, chronically ill, or disabled member of your household or member of your immediate family who is unable to pay for such expenses. **Do not include payments listed in Line 34.**	$
41	**Protection against family violence.** Enter the total average reasonably necessary monthly expenses that you actually incur to maintain the safety of your family under the Family Violence Prevention and Services Act or other applicable federal law. The nature of these expenses is required to be kept confidential by the court.	$
42	**Home energy costs.** Enter the total average monthly amount, in excess of the allowance specified by IRS Local Standards for Housing and Utilities that you actually expend for home energy costs. **You must provide your case trustee with documentation of your actual expenses, and you must demonstrate that the additional amount claimed is reasonable and necessary.**	$
43	**Education expenses for dependent children under 18.** Enter the total average monthly expenses that you actually incur, not to exceed $147.92 per child, for attendance at a private or public elementary or secondary school by your dependent children less than 18 years of age. **You must provide your case trustee with documentation of your actual expenses, and you must explain why the amount claimed is reasonable and necessary and not already accounted for in the IRS Standards.**	$
44	**Additional food and clothing expense.** Enter the total average monthly amount by which your food and clothing expenses exceed the combined allowances for food and clothing (apparel and services) in the IRS National Standards, not to exceed 5% of those combined allowances. (This information is available at www.usdoj.gov/ust/ or from the clerk of the bankruptcy court.) **You must demonstrate that the additional amount claimed is reasonable and necessary.**	$
45	**Charitable contributions.** Enter the amount reasonably necessary for you to expend each month on charitable contributions in the form of cash or financial instruments to a charitable organization as defined in 26 U.S.C. § 170(c)(1)-(2). **Do not include any amount in excess of 15% of your gross monthly income.**	$
46	**Total Additional Expense Deductions under § 707(b).** Enter the total of Lines 39 through 45.	$

Subpart C: Deductions for Debt Payment

47	**Future payments on secured claims.** For each of your debts that is secured by an interest in property that you own, list the name of the creditor, identify the property securing the debt, state the Average Monthly Payment, and check whether the payment includes taxes or insurance. The Average Monthly Payment is the total of all amounts scheduled as contractually due to each Secured Creditor in the 60 months following the filing of the bankruptcy case, divided by 60. If necessary, list additional entries on a separate page. Enter the total of the Average Monthly Payments on Line 47.	

		Name of Creditor	Property Securing the Debt	Average Monthly Payment	Does payment include taxes or insurance?	
	a.			$	☐ yes ☐ no	
	b.			$	☐ yes ☐ no	
	c.			$	☐ yes ☐ no	
				Total: Add Lines a, b, and c		$

B 22C (Official Form 22C) (Chapter 13) (12/12)   (08/11 publication draft)

| 48 | **Other payments on secured claims.** If any of debts listed in Line 47 are secured by your primary residence, a motor vehicle, or other property necessary for your support or the support of your dependents, you may include in your deduction 1/60th of any amount (the "cure amount") that you must pay the creditor in addition to the payments listed in Line 47, in order to maintain possession of the property. The cure amount would include any sums in default that must be paid in order to avoid repossession or foreclosure. List and total any such amounts in the following chart. If necessary, list additional entries on a separate page. | |

		Name of Creditor	Property Securing the Debt	1/60th of the Cure Amount	
	a.			$	
	b.			$	
	c.			$	
				Total: Add Lines a, b, and c	$

| 49 | **Payments on prepetition priority claims.** Enter the total amount, divided by 60, of all priority claims, such as priority tax, child support and alimony claims, for which you were liable at the time of your bankruptcy filing. **Do not include current obligations, such as those set out in Line 33.** | $ |

| 50 | **Chapter 13 administrative expenses.** Multiply the amount in Line a by the amount in Line b, and enter the resulting administrative expense. | |

	a.	Projected average monthly chapter 13 plan payment.	$	
	b.	Current multiplier for your district as determined under schedules issued by the Executive Office for United States Trustees. (This information is available at www.usdoj.gov/ust/ or from the clerk of the bankruptcy court.)	x	
	c.	Average monthly administrative expense of chapter 13 case	Total: Multiply Lines a and b	$

| 51 | **Total Deductions for Debt Payment.** Enter the total of Lines 47 through 50. | $ |

Subpart D: Total Deductions from Income

| 52 | **Total of all deductions from income.** Enter the total of Lines 38, 46, and 51. | $ |

Part V. DETERMINATION OF DISPOSABLE INCOME UNDER § 1325(b)(2)

53	**Total current monthly income.** Enter the amount from Line 20.	$
54	**Support income.** Enter the monthly average of any child support payments, foster care payments, or disability payments for a dependent child, reported in Part 1, that you received in accordance with applicable nonbankruptcy law, to the extent reasonably necessary to be expended for such child.	$
55	**Qualified retirement deductions.** Enter the monthly total of (a) all amounts withheld by your employer from wages as contributions for qualified retirement plans, as specified in § 541(b)(7) and (b) all required repayments of loans from retirement plans, as specified in § 362(b)(19).	$
56	**Total of all deductions allowed under § 707(b)(2).** Enter the amount from Line 52.	$

B 22C (Official Form 22C) (Chapter 13) (12/12)   (08/11 publication draft

57	**Deduction for special circumstances.** If there are special circumstances that justify additional expenses for which there is no reasonable alternative, describe the special circumstances and the resulting expenses in lines a-c below. If necessary, list additional entries on a separate page. Total the expenses and enter the total in Line 57. **You must provide your case trustee with documentation of these expenses and you must provide a detailed explanation of the special circumstances that make such expenses necessary and reasonable.**

	Nature of special circumstances	Amount of expense	
a.		$	
b.		$	
c.		$	
		Total: Add Lines a, b, and c	$

58	**Total adjustments to determine disposable income.** Add the amounts on Lines 54, 55, 56, and 57 and enter the result.	$
59	**Monthly Disposable Income Under § 1325(b)(2).** Subtract Line 58 from Line 53 and enter the result.	$

Part VI: ADDITIONAL INFORMATION

60	**Other Expenses.** List and describe any monthly expenses, not otherwise stated in this form, that are required for the health and welfare of you and your family and that you contend should be an additional deduction from your current monthly income under § 707(b)(2)(A)(ii)(I). If necessary, list additional sources on a separate page. All figures should reflect your average monthly expense for each item. Total the expenses.

	Expense Description	Monthly Amount
a.		$
b.		$
c.		$
	Total: Add Lines a, b, and c	$

61	**Change in income or expenses.** If any change from the income or expenses you reported in this form has occurred or is virtually certain to occur during the 12-month period following the date of the filing of your petition, state in the space below: each line affected, the reason for the change, the date of the change, and the amount by which the income or expense reported on the affected line would be increased or decreased. For example, if the wages reported in Line 2 have increased or decreased, or are definitely scheduled to increase or decrease in the future, you would make an entry listing Line 2, the reason for the increase or decrease, the date it has occurred or will occur, and the amount of the change. Make a similar entry for increases or decreases in expenses reported earlier in this form. Add a separate page with additional lines, if necessary.

Line to change	Reason for change	Date of change	Increase (+) or decrease (-)	Amount of change
				$
				$
				$

Part VII: VERIFICATION

62	I declare under penalty of perjury that the information provided in this statement is true and correct. *(If this is a joint case, both debtors must sign.)*

Date: _____   Signature: _____
                                                 (Debtor)

Date: _____   Signature: _____
                                                 (Joint Debtor, if any)

Form Number 23

B 23 (Official Form 23) (12/10)

UNITED STATES BANKRUPTCY COURT

_____ District Of _____

In re _____,   Case No. _____
                     Debtor

                                                   Chapter _____

DEBTOR'S CERTIFICATION OF COMPLETION OF POSTPETITION INSTRUCTIONAL
COURSE CONCERNING PERSONAL FINANCIAL MANAGEMENT

Every individual debtor in a chapter 7, chapter 11 in which § 1141(d)(3) applies, or chapter 13 case must file this certification. If a joint petition is filed, each spouse must complete and file a separate certification. Complete one of the following statements and file by the deadline stated below:

☐ I, _____, the debtor in the above-styled case, hereby
        (Printed Name of Debtor)
certify that on _____ (Date), I completed an instructional course in personal financial management
provided by _____, an approved personal financial
                            (Name of Provider)
management provider.

   Certificate No. (if any):_____.

☐ I, _____, the debtor in the above-styled case, hereby
        (Printed Name of Debtor)
certify that no personal financial management course is required because of *[Check the appropriate box.]:*
       ☐ Incapacity or disability, as defined in 11 U.S.C. § 109(h);
       ☐ Active military duty in a military combat zone; or
       ☐ Residence in a district in which the United States trustee (or bankruptcy administrator) has determined that
the approved instructional courses are not adequate at this time to serve the additional individuals who would otherwise
be required to complete such courses.

Signature of Debtor: _____

Date: _____

_____

Instructions: Use this form only to certify whether you completed a course in personal financial management. (Fed. R. Bankr. P. 1007(b)(7).) Do NOT use this form to file the certificate given to you by your prepetition credit counseling provider and do NOT include with the petition when filing your case.

Filing Deadlines: In a chapter 7 case, file within 60 days of the first date set for the meeting of creditors under § 341 of the Bankruptcy Code. In a chapter 11 or 13 case, file no later than the last payment made by the debtor as required by the plan or the filing of a motion for a discharge under § 1141(d)(5)(B) or § 1328(b) of the Code. (See Fed. R. Bankr. P. 1007(c).)

PART 6

UNIFORM FRAUDULENT TRANSFER ACT

UNIFORM FRAUDULENT TRANSFER ACT*

§ 1. Definitions

As used in this [Act]:

(1) "Affiliate" means:

(i) a person who directly or indirectly owns, controls, or holds with power to vote, 20 percent or more of the outstanding voting securities of the debtor, other than a person who holds the securities,

(A) as a fiduciary or agent without sole discretionary power to vote the securities; or

(B) solely to secure a debt, if the person has not exercised the power to vote;

(ii) a corporation 20 percent or more of whose outstanding voting securities are directly or indirectly owned, controlled, or held with power to vote, by the debtor or a person who directly or indirectly owns, controls, or holds, with power to vote, 20 percent or more of the outstanding voting securities of the debtor, other than a person who holds the securities,

(A) as a fiduciary or agent without sole power to vote the securities; or

(B) solely to secure a debt, if the person has not in fact exercised the power to vote;

(iii) a person whose business is operated by the debtor under a lease or other agreement, or a person substantially all of whose assets are controlled by the debtor; or

(iv) a person who operates the debtor's business under a lease or other agreement or controls substantially all of the debtor's assets.

---

* Reproduced by permission of the National Conference of Commissioners on Uniform State Laws.

(2) "Asset" means property of a debtor, but the term does not include:

(i) property to the extent it is encumbered by a valid lien;

(ii) property to the extent it is generally exempt under nonbankruptcy law; or

(iii) an interest in property held in tenancy by the entireties to the extent it is not subject to process by a creditor holding a claim against only one tenant.

(3) "Claim" means a right to payment, whether or not the right is reduced to judgment, liquidated, unliquidated, fixed, contingent, matured, unmatured, disputed, undisputed, legal, equitable, secured, or unsecured.

(4) "Creditor" means a person who has a claim.

(5) "Debt" means liability on a claim.

(6) "Debtor" means a person who is liable on a claim.

(7) "Insider" includes:

(i) if the debtor is an individual,

(A) a relative of the debtor or of a general partner of the debtor;

(B) a partnership in which the debtor is a general partner;

(C) a general partner in a partnership described in clause (B); or

(D) a corporation of which the debtor is a director, officer, or person in control;

(ii) if the debtor is a corporation,

(A) a director of the debtor;

(B) an officer of the debtor;

(C) a person in control of the debtor;

(D) a partnership in which the debtor is a general partner;

(E) a general partner in a partnership described in clause (D); or

(F) a relative of a general partner, director, officer, or person in control of the debtor;

(iii) if the debtor is a partnership,

(A) a general partner in the debtor;

(B) a relative of a general partner in, a general partner of, or a person in control of the debtor;

(C) another partnership in which the debtor is a general partner;

(D) a general partner in a partnership described in clause (C); or

(E) a person in control of the debtor;

(iv) an affiliate, or an insider of an affiliate as if the affiliate were the debtor; and

(v) a managing agent of the debtor.

(8) "Lien" means a charge against or an interest in property to secure payment of a debt or performance of an obligation, and includes a security interest created by agreement, a judicial lien obtained by legal or equitable process or proceedings, a common-law lien, or a statutory lien.

(9) "Person" means an individual, partnership, corporation, association, organization, government or governmental subdivision or agency, business trust, estate, trust, or any other legal or commercial entity.

(10) "Property" means anything that may be the subject of ownership.

(11) "Relative" means an individual related by consanguinity within the third degree as determined by the common law, a spouse, or an individual related to a spouse within the third degree as so determined, and includes an individual in an adoptive relationship within the third degree.

(12) "Transfer" means every mode, direct or indirect, absolute or conditional, voluntary or involuntary, of disposing of or parting with an asset or an interest in an asset, and includes payment of money, release, lease, and creation of a lien or other encumbrance.

(13) "Valid lien" means a lien that is effective against the holder of a judicial lien subsequently obtained by legal or equitable process or proceedings.

§ 2. Insolvency

(a) A debtor is insolvent if the sum of the debtor's debts is greater than all of the debtor's assets at a fair valuation.

(b) A debtor who is generally not paying his [or her] debts as they become due is presumed to be insolvent.

(c) A partnership is insolvent under subsection (a) if the sum of the partnership's debts is greater than the aggregate, at a fair valuation, of all of the partnership's assets and the sum of the excess of the value of each general partner's nonpartnership assets over the partner's nonpartnership debts.

(d) Assets under this section do not include property that has been transferred, concealed, or removed with intent to hinder, delay, or defraud creditors or that has been transferred in a manner making the transfer voidable under this [Act].

(e) Debts under this section do not include an obligation to the extent it is secured by a valid lien on property of the debtor not included as an asset.

§ 3. Value

(a) Value is given for a transfer or an obligation if, in exchange for the transfer or obligation, property is transferred or an antecedent debt is secured or satisfied, but value does not include an unperformed promise made otherwise than in the ordinary course of the promisor's business to furnish support to the debtor or another person.

(b) For the purposes of Sections 4(a)(2) and 5, a person gives a reasonably equivalent value if the person acquires an interest of the debtor in an asset pursuant to a regularly conducted, noncollusive foreclosure sale or execution of a power of sale for the acquisition or disposition of the interest of the debtor upon default under a mortgage, deed of trust, or security agreement.

(c) A transfer is made for present value if the exchange between the debtor and the transferee is intended by them to be contemporaneous and is in fact substantially contemporaneous.

§ 4. Transfers Fraudulent as to Present and Future Creditors

(a) A transfer made or obligation incurred by a debtor is fraudulent as to a creditor, whether the creditor's claim arose before or after the transfer was made or the obligation was incurred, if the debtor made the transfer or incurred the obligation:

(1) with actual intent to hinder, delay, or defraud any creditor of the debtor; or

(2) without receiving a reasonably equivalent value in exchange for the transfer or obligation, and the debtor:

(i) was engaged or was about to engage in a business or a transaction for which the remaining assets of the debtor were unreasonably small in relation to the business or transaction; or

(ii) intended to incur, or believed or reasonably should have believed that he [or she] would incur, debts beyond his [or her] ability to pay as they became due.

(b) In determining actual intent under subsection (a)(1), consideration may be given, among other factors, to whether:

(1) the transfer or obligation was to an insider;

(2) the debtor retained possession or control of the property transferred after the transfer;

(3) the transfer or obligation was disclosed or concealed;

(4) before the transfer was made or obligation was incurred, the debtor had been sued or threatened with suit;

(5) the transfer was of substantially all the debtor's assets;

(6) the debtor absconded;

(7) the debtor removed or concealed assets;

(8) the value of the consideration received by the debtor was reasonably equivalent to the value of the asset transferred or the amount of the obligation incurred;

(9) the debtor was insolvent or became insolvent shortly after the transfer was made or the obligation was incurred;

(10) the transfer occurred shortly before or shortly after a substantial debt was incurred; and

(11) the debtor transferred the essential assets of the business to a lienor who transferred the assets to an insider of the debtor.

§ 5. Transfers Fraudulent as to Present Creditors

(a) A transfer made or obligation incurred by a debtor is fraudulent as to a creditor whose claim arose before the transfer was made or the obligation was incurred if the debtor made the transfer or incurred the obligation without receiving a reasonably equivalent value in exchange for the transfer or obligation and the debtor was insolvent at that time or the debtor became insolvent as a result of the transfer or obligation.

(b) A transfer made by a debtor is fraudulent as to a creditor whose claim arose before the transfer was made if the transfer was made to an insider for an antecedent debt, the debtor was insolvent at that time, and the insider had reasonable cause to believe that the debtor was insolvent.

§ 6. When Transfer is Made or Obligation is Incurred

For the purposes of this [Act]:

(1) a transfer is made:

(i) with respect to an asset that is real property other than a fixture, but including the interest of a seller or purchaser under a contract for the sale of the asset, when the transfer is so far perfected that a good-faith purchaser of the asset from the debtor against whom applicable law permits the transfer to be perfected cannot acquire an interest in the asset that is superior to the interest of the transferee; and

(ii) with respect to an asset that is not real property or that is a fixture, when the transfer is so far perfected that a creditor on a simple contract cannot acquire a judicial lien otherwise than under this [Act] that is superior to the interest of the transferee;

(2) if applicable law permits the transfer to be perfected as provided in paragraph (1) and the transfer is not so perfected before the commencement of an action for relief under this [Act], the transfer is deemed made immediately before the commencement of the action;

(3) if applicable law does not permit the transfer to be perfected as provided in paragraph (1), the transfer is made when it becomes effective between the debtor and the transferee;

(4) a transfer is not made until the debtor has acquired rights in the asset transferred;

(5) an obligation is incurred:

(i) if oral, when it becomes effective between the parties; or

(ii) if evidenced by a writing, when the writing executed by the obligor is delivered to or for the benefit of the obligee.

§ 7. Remedies of Creditors

(a) In an action for relief against a transfer or obligation under this [Act], a creditor, subject to the limitations in Section 8, may obtain:

(1) avoidance of the transfer or obligation to the extent necessary to satisfy the creditor's claim;

[(2) an attachment or other provisional remedy against the asset transferred or other property of the transferee in accordance with the procedure prescribed by [ ];]

(3) subject to applicable principles of equity and in accordance with applicable rules of civil procedure,

(i) an injunction against further disposition by the debtor or a transferee, or both, of the asset transferred or of other property;

(ii) appointment of a receiver to take charge of the asset transferred or of other property of the transferee; or

(iii) any other relief the circumstances may require.

(b) If a creditor has obtained a judgment on a claim against the debtor, the creditor, if the court so orders, may levy execution on the asset transferred or its proceeds.

§ 8. Defenses, Liability, and Protection of Transferee

(a) A transfer or obligation is not voidable under Section 4(a)(1) against a person who took in good faith and for a reasonably equivalent value or against any subsequent transferee or obligee.

(b) Except as otherwise provided in this section, to the extent a transfer is voidable in an action by a creditor under Section 7(a)(1), the creditor may recover judgment for the value of the asset transferred, as adjusted under subsection (c), or the amount necessary to satisfy the creditor's claim, whichever is less. The judgment may be entered against:

(1) the first transferee of the asset or the person for whose benefit the transfer was made; or

(2) any subsequent transferee other than a good faith transferee who took for value or from any subsequent transferee.

(c) If the judgment under subsection (b) is based upon the value of the asset transferred, the judgment must be for an amount equal to the value of the asset at the time of the transfer, subject to adjustment as the equities may require.

(d) Notwithstanding voidability of a transfer or an obligation under this [Act], a good-faith transferee or obligee is entitled, to the extent of the value given the debtor for the transfer or obligation, to

(1) a lien on or a right to retain any interest in the asset transferred;

(2) enforcement of any obligation incurred; or

(3) a reduction in the amount of the liability on the judgment.

(e) A transfer is not voidable under Section 4(a)(2) or Section 5 if the transfer results from:

(1) termination of a lease upon default by the debtor when the termination is pursuant to the lease and applicable law; or

(2) enforcement of a security interest in compliance with Article 9 of the Uniform Commercial Code.

(f) A transfer is not voidable under Section 5(b):

(1) to the extent the insider gave new value to or for the benefit of the debtor after the transfer was made unless the new value was secured by a valid lien;

(2) if made in the ordinary course of business or financial affairs of the debtor and the insider; or

(3) if made pursuant to a good-faith effort to rehabilitate the debtor and the transfer secured present value given for that purpose as well as an antecedent debt of the debtor.

§ 9. Extinguishment of [Claim for Relief] [Cause of Action]

A [claim for relief] [cause of action] with respect to a fraudulent transfer or obligation under this [Act] is extinguished unless action is brought:

(a) under Section 4(a)(1), within 4 years after the transfer was made or the obligation was incurred or, if later, within one year after the transfer or obligation was or could reasonably have been discovered by the claimant;

(b) under Section 4(a)(2) or 5(a), within 4 years after the transfer was made or the obligation was incurred; or

(c) under Section 5(b), within one year after the transfer was made or the obligation was incurred.

OTHER SECTIONS

Compare the "4 years" in section 9 with the "2 years" of section 548. Remember that section 544(b) incorporates state law, including section 9.

§ 10.   Supplementary Provisions

Unless displaced by the provisions of this [Act], the principles of law and equity, including the law merchant and the law relating to principal and agent, estoppel, laches, fraud, misrepresentation, duress, coercion, mistake, insolvency, or other validating or invalidating cause, supplement its provisions.

§ 11.   Uniformity of Application and Construction

This [Act] shall be applied and construed to effectuate its general purpose to make uniform the law with respect to the subject of this [Act] among states enacting it.

PART 7

UNIFORM COMMERCIAL CODE
(SELECTED SECTIONS)

UNIFORM COMMERCIAL CODE

Article 1. General Provisions

Official Text (as amended in 2003)

The American Law Institute and National Conference of Commissioners on Uniform State Laws

Part 2. General Definitions And Principles Of Interpretation

§ 1–201. General Definitions

* * *

(b) Subject to definitions contained in other articles of [the Uniform Commercial Code] that apply to particular articles or parts thereof:

* * *

(13) "Creditor" includes a general creditor, a secure creditor, a lien creditor, and any representative of creditors, including an assignee for the benefit of creditors, a trustee in bankruptcy, a receiver in equity, and an executor or administrator of an insolvent debtor's or assignor's estate.

* * *

(35) "Security interest" means an interest in personal property or fixtures which secures payment or performance of an obligation. "Security interest" includes any interest of a consignor and a buyer of accounts, chattel paper, a payment intangible, or a promissory note in a transaction that is subject to Article 9. "Security interest" does not include the special property interest of a buyer of goods on identification of those goods to a contract for sale under Section 2–401, but a buyer may also acquire a "security interest" by complying with Article 9. Except as otherwise provided in Section 2–505, the right of a seller or lessor of goods under Article 2 or 2A to retain or acquire possession of the goods is not a "security interest", but a seller or lessor may also acquire a "security interest" by complying with Article 9. The retention or reservation of title by a seller of goods notwithstanding shipment or delivery to the buyer under Section 2–401 is limited in effect to a reservation of a "security interest." Whether a transaction in the form of a lease creates a "security interest" is determined pursuant to Section 1–203.

* * *

Uniform Commercial Code

Article 2. Sales

Official Text

The American Law Institute and National Conference of Commissioners on Uniform State Laws

Part 7. Remedies

§ 2–702.   Seller's Remedies On Discovery Of Buyer's Insolvency

(1) If the seller discovers that the buyer is insolvent, the seller may refuse delivery except for cash including payment for all goods theretofore delivered under the contract, and stop delivery under Section 2–705.

(2) If the seller discovers that the buyer has received goods on credit while insolvent, the seller may reclaim the goods upon demand made within a reasonable time after the buyer's receipt of the goods. Except as provided in this subsection, the seller may not base a right to reclaim goods on the buyer's fraudulent or innocent misrepresentation of solvency or of intent to pay.

(3) The seller's right to reclaim under subsection (2) is subject to the rights of a buyer in ordinary course of business or other good-faith purchaser for value under Section 2–403. Successful reclamation of goods excludes all other remedies with respect to them.

Uniform Commercial Code

Article 9. Secured Transactions

Official Text (2005 Version)

The American Law Institute and National Conference of Commissioners on Uniform State Laws

Part 1. General Provisions

[Subpart 1. Short Title, Definitions, And General Concepts]

§ 9–102.   Definitions And Index Of Definitions

(a) [Article 9 definitions.] In this article:

* * *

(9) "Cash proceeds" means proceeds that are money, checks, deposit accounts, or the like.

* * *

(12) "Collateral" means the property subject to a security interest or agricultural lien. The term includes:

(A) proceeds to which a security interest attaches;

(B) accounts, chattel paper, payment intangibles, and promissory notes that have been sold; and

(C) goods that are the subject of a consignment.

(13) "Commercial tort claim" means a claim arising in tort with respect to which:

    (A) the claimant is an organization; or

    (B) the claimant is an individual and the claim:

        (i) arose in the course of the claimant's business or profession; and

        (ii) does not include damages arising out of personal injury to or the death of an individual.

* * *

(23) "Consumer goods" means goods that are used or bought for use primarily for personal, family, or household purposes.

* * *

(28) "Debtor" means:

    (A) a person having an interest, other than a security interest or other lien, in the collateral, whether or not the person is an obligor;

    (B) a seller of accounts, chattel paper, payment intangibles, or promissory notes; or

    (C) a consignee.

* * *

(44) "Goods" means all things that are movable when a security interest attaches. The term includes (i) fixtures, (ii) standing timber that is to be cut and removed under a conveyance or contract for sale, (iii) the unborn young of animals, (iv) crops grown, growing, or to be grown, even if the crops are produced on trees, vines, or bushes, and (v) manufactured homes. The term also includes a computer program embedded in goods and any supporting information provided in connection with a transaction relating to the program if (i) the program is associated with the goods in such a manner that it customarily is considered part of the goods, or (ii) by becoming the owner of the goods, a person acquires a right to use the program in connection with the goods. The term does not include a computer program embedded in goods that consist solely of the medium in which the program is embedded. The term also does not include accounts, chattel paper, commercial tort claims, deposit accounts, documents, general intangibles, instruments, investment property, letter-of-credit rights, letters of credit, money, or oil, gas, or other minerals before extraction.

* * *

(52) "Lien creditor" means:

    (A) a creditor that has acquired a lien on the property involved by attachment, levy, or the like;

    (B) an assignee for benefit of creditors from the time of assignment;

    (C) a trustee in bankruptcy from the date of the filing of the petition; or

    (D) a receiver in equity from the time of appointment.

* * *

(64) "Proceeds", * * * means the following property:

(A) whatever is acquired upon the sale, lease, license, exchange, or other disposition of collateral;

(B) whatever is collected on, or distributed on account of, collateral;

(C) rights arising out of collateral;

(D) to the extent of the value of collateral, claims arising out of the loss, nonconformity, or interference with the use of, defects or infringement of rights in, or damage to, the collateral; or

(E) to the extent of the value of collateral and to the extent payable to the debtor or the secured party, insurance payable by reason of the loss or nonconformity of, defects or infringement of rights in, or damage to, the collateral.

* * *

(72) "Secured party" means:

(A) a person in whose favor a security interest is created or provided for under a security agreement, whether or not any obligation to be secured is outstanding;

(B) a person that holds an agricultural lien;

(C) a consignor;

(D) a person to which accounts, chattel paper, payment intangibles, or promissory notes have been sold;

(E) a trustee, indenture trustee, agent, collateral agent, or other representative in whose favor a security interest or agricultural lien is created or provided for; or

(F) a person that holds a security interest arising under Section 2–401, 2–505, 2–711(3), 2A–508(5), 4–210, or 5–118.

(73) "Security agreement" means an agreement that creates or provides for a security interest.

§ 9–103.   Purchase-Money Security Interest; Application of Payments; Burden of Establishing

(a) [Definitions.] In this section:

(1) "purchase-money collateral" means goods or software that secures a purchase-money obligation incurred with respect to that collateral; and

(2) "purchase-money obligation" means an obligation of an obligor incurred as all or part of the price of the collateral or for value given to enable the debtor to acquire rights in or the use of the collateral if the value is in fact so used.

(b) [Purchase-money security interest in goods.] A security interest in goods is a purchase-money security interest:

(1) to the extent that the goods are purchase-money collateral with respect to that security interest;

(2) if the security interest is in inventory that is or was purchase-money collateral, also to the extent that the security interest secures a purchase-money

obligation incurred with respect to other inventory in which the secured party holds or held a purchase-money security interest; and

(3) also to the extent that the security interest secures a purchase-money obligation incurred with respect to software in which the secured party holds or held a purchase-money security interest.

(c) **[Purchase-money security interest in software.]** A security interest in software is a purchase-money security interest to the extent that the security interest also secures a purchase-money obligation incurred with respect to goods in which the secured party holds or held a purchase-money security interest if:

(1) the debtor acquired its interest in the software in an integrated transaction in which it acquired an interest in the goods; and

(2) the debtor acquired its interest in the software for the principal purpose of using the software in the goods.

(d) **[Consignor's inventory purchase-money security interest.]** The security interest of a consignor in goods that are the subject of a consignment is a purchase-money security interest in inventory.

(e) **[Application of payment in non-consumer-goods transaction.]** In a transaction other than a consumer-goods transaction, if the extent to which a security interest is a purchase-money security interest depends on the application of a payment to a particular obligation, the payment must be applied:

(1) in accordance with any reasonable method of application to which the parties agree;

(2) in the absence of the parties' agreement to a reasonable method, in accordance with any intention of the obligor manifested at or before the time of payment; or

(3) in the absence of an agreement to a reasonable method and a timely manifestation of the obligor's intention, in the following order:

(A) to obligations that are not secured; and

(B) if more than one obligation is secured, to obligations secured by purchase-money security interests in the order in which those obligations were incurred.

(f) **[No loss of status of purchase-money security interest in non-consumer-goods transaction.]** In a transaction other than a consumer-goods transaction, a purchase-money security interest does not lose its status as such, even if:

(1) the purchase-money collateral also secures an obligation that is not a purchase-money obligation;

(2) collateral that is not purchase-money collateral also secures the purchase-money obligation; or

(3) the purchase-money obligation has been renewed, refinanced, consolidated, or restructured.

(g) **[Burden of proof in non-consumer-goods transaction.]** In a transaction other than a consumer-goods transaction, a secured party claiming a purchase-money security interest has the burden of establishing the extent to which the security interest is a purchase-money security interest.

(h) **[Non-consumer-goods transactions; no inference.]** The limitation of the rules in subsections (e), (f), and (g) to transactions other than consumer-goods transactions is intended to leave to the court the determination of the proper rules in consumer-goods transactions. The court may not infer from that limitation the nature of the proper rule in consumer-goods transactions and may continue to apply established approaches.

* * *

Part 1. General Provisions

[Subpart 2. Applicability Of Article]

§ 9–109. Scope

(a) [General scope of article.] Except as otherwise provided in subsections (c) and (d), this article applies to:

(1) a transaction, regardless of its form, that creates a security interest in personal property or fixtures by contract;

(2) an agricultural lien;

(3) a sale of accounts, chattel paper, payment intangibles, or promissory notes;

(4) a consignment;

(5) a security interest arising under Section 2–401, 2–505, 2–711(3), or 2A–508(5), as provided in Section 9–110; and

(6) a security interest arising under Section 4–210 or 5–118.

* * *

Part 2. Effectiveness Of Security Agreement; Attachment Of Security
Interest; Rights Of Parties To Security Agreement

§ 9–201. General Effectiveness Of Security Agreement

(a) [General effectiveness.] Except as otherwise provided in [the Uniform Commercial Code], a security agreement is effective according to its terms between the parties, against purchasers of the collateral, and against creditors.

* * *

§ 9–204. After-Acquired Property; Future Advances

(a) [After-acquired collateral.] Except as otherwise provided in subsection (b), a security agreement may create or provide for a security interest in after-acquired collateral.

(b) [When after-acquired property clause not effective.] A security interest does not attach under a term constituting an after-acquired property clause to:

(1) consumer goods, other than an accession when given as additional security, unless the debtor acquires rights in them within 10 days after the secured party gives value; or

(2) a commercial tort claim.

(c) [Future advances and other value.] A security agreement may provide that collateral secures, or that accounts, chattel paper, payment intangibles, or promissory notes are sold in connection with, future advances or other value, whether or not the advances or value are given pursuant to commitment.

* * *

§ 9–315. Secured Party's Rights On Disposition Of Collateral And In Proceeds

(a) [Disposition of collateral: continuation of security interest.] Except as otherwise provided in this article and in Section 2–403(2):

(1) a security interest continues in collateral notwithstanding sale, lease, license, exchange, or other disposition thereof unless the secured party authorized the disposition free of the security interest; and

(2) a security interest attaches to any identifiable proceeds of collateral.

* * *

(c) [Perfection of security interest in proceeds.] A security interest in proceeds is a perfected security interest if the security interest in the original collateral was perfected.

(d) [Continuation of perfection.] A perfected security interest in proceeds becomes unperfected on the 21st day after the security interest attaches to the proceeds unless:

(1) the following conditions are satisfied:

(A) a filed financing statement covers the original collateral;

(B) the proceeds are collateral in which a security interest may be perfected by filing in the office in which the financing statement has been filed; and

(C) the proceeds are not acquired with cash proceeds;

(2) the proceeds are identifiable cash proceeds; or

(3) the security interest in the proceeds is perfected other than under subsection (c) when the security interest attaches to the proceeds or within 20 days thereafter.

(e) [When perfected security interest in proceeds becomes unperfected.] If a filed financing statement covers the original collateral, a security interest in proceeds which remains perfected under subsection (d)(1) becomes unperfected at the later of:

(1) when the effectiveness of the filed financing statement lapses under Section 9–515 or is terminated under Section 9–513; or

(2) the 21st day after the security interest attaches to the proceeds.

[Subpart 3. Priority]

§ 9–317. Interests That Take Priority Over Or Take Free Of Security Interest

(a) [Conflicting security interests and rights of lien creditors.] A security interest is subordinate to the rights of:

(1) a person entitled to priority under Section 9–322; and

(2) except as otherwise provided in subsection (e), a person that becomes a lien creditor before the earlier of the time:

(A) the security interest is perfected; or

(B) one of the conditions specified in Section 9-203(b)(3) is met and a financing statement covering the collateral is filed.

(b) [Buyers that receive delivery.] Except as otherwise provided in subsection (e), a buyer, other than a secured party, of tangible chattel paper, tangible documents, goods, instruments, or a security certificate takes free of a security interest if the buyer gives value and receives delivery of the collateral without knowledge of the security interest and before it is perfected.

* * *

(e) [Purchase-money security interest.] Except as otherwise provided in Sections 9-320 and 9-321, if a person files a financing statement with respect to a purchase-money security interest before or within 20 days after the debtor receives delivery of the collateral, the security interest takes priority over the rights of a buyer, lessee, or lien creditor which arise between the time the security interest attaches and the time of filing.

* * *

§ 9-609.   Secured Party's Right To Take Possession After Default

(a) [Possession; rendering equipment unusable; disposition on debtor's premises.] After default, a secured party:

(1) may take possession of the collateral; and

(2) without removal, may render equipment unusable and dispose of collateral on a debtor's premises under Section 9-610.

(b) [Judicial and nonjudicial process.] A secured party may proceed under subsection (a):

(1) pursuant to judicial process; or

(2) without judicial process, if it proceeds without breach of the peace.

(c) [Assembly of collateral.] If so agreed, and in any event after default, a secured party may require the debtor to assemble the collateral and make it available to the secured party at a place to be designated by the secured party which is reasonably convenient to both parties.

§ 9-610.   Disposition Of Collateral After Default

(a) [Disposition after default.] After default, a secured party may sell, lease, license, or otherwise dispose of any or all of the collateral in its present condition or following any commercially reasonable preparation or processing.

(b) [Commercially reasonable disposition.] Every aspect of a disposition of collateral, including the method, manner, time, place, and other terms, must be commercially reasonable. If commercially reasonable, a secured party may dispose of collateral by public or private proceedings, by one or more contracts, as a unit or in parcels, and at any time and place and on any terms.

* * *

§ 9–623. Right To Redeem Collateral

(a) [Persons that may redeem.] A debtor, any secondary obligor, or any other secured party or lienholder may redeem collateral.

(b) [Requirements for redemption.] To redeem collateral, a person shall tender:

(1) fulfillment of all obligations secured by the collateral; and

(2) the reasonable expenses and attorney's fees described in Section 9–615(a)(1).

(c) [When redemption may occur.] A redemption may occur at any time before a secured party:

(1) has collected collateral under Section 9–607;

(2) has disposed of collateral or entered into a contract for its disposition under Section 9–610; or

(3) has accepted collateral in full or partial satisfaction of the obligation it secures under Section 9–622.

* * *

PART 8
FEDERAL TAX LIEN ACT (TITLE 28)

FEDERAL TAX LIEN STATUTES
REVENUE CODE

Selected Sections

Sec.
6321. Lien for Taxes
6322. Period of Lien
6323. Validity and Priority

§ 6321. Lien for taxes

If any person liable to pay any tax neglects or refuses to pay the same after demand, the amount (including any interest, additional amount, addition to tax, or assessable penalty, together with any costs that may accrue in addition thereto) shall be a lien in favor of the United States upon all property and rights to property, whether real or personal, belonging to such person.

§ 6322. Period of lien

Unless another date is specifically fixed by law, the lien imposed by section 6321 shall arise at the time the assessment is made and shall continue until the liability for the amount so assessed (or a judgment against the taxpayer arising out of such liability) is satisfied or becomes unenforceable by reason of lapse of time.

§ 6323. Validity and priority against certain persons

(a) Purchasers, holders of security interests, mechanic's lienors, and judgment lien creditors.—The lien imposed by section 6321 shall not be valid as against any purchaser, holder of a security interest, mechanic's lienor, or judgment lien creditor until notice thereof which meets the requirements of subsection (f) has been filed by the Secretary. * * *

(c) Protection for certain commercial transactions financing agreements, etc.—

(1) In general.—To the extent provided in this subsection, even though notice of a lien imposed by section 6321 has been filed, such lien shall not be valid with respect to a security interest which came into existence after tax lien filing but which—

(A) is in qualified property covered by the terms of a written agreement entered into before tax lien filing and constituting—

(i) a commercial transactions financing agreement,

(ii) a real property construction or improvement financing agreement, or

(iii) an obligatory disbursement agreement, and

(B) is protected under local law against a judgment lien arising, as of the time of tax lien filing, out of an unsecured obligation.

(2) Commercial transactions financing agreement.—For purposes of this subsection—

331

(A) Definition.—The term "commercial transactions financing agreement" means an agreement (entered into by a person in the course of his trade or business)—

(i) to make loans to the taxpayer to be secured by commercial financing security acquired by the taxpayer in the ordinary course of his trade or business, or

(ii) to purchase commercial financing security (other than inventory) acquired by the taxpayer in the ordinary course of his trade or business;

but such an agreement shall be treated as coming within the term only to the extent that such loan or purchase is made before the 46th day after the date of tax lien filing or (if earlier) before the lender or purchaser had actual notice or knowledge of such tax lien filing.

(B) Limitation on qualified property.—The term "qualified property", when used with respect to a commercial transactions financing agreement, includes only commercial financing security acquired by the taxpayer before the 46th day after the date of tax lien filing.

(C) Commercial financing security defined.—The term "commercial financing security" means (i) paper of a kind ordinarily arising in commercial transactions, (ii) accounts receivable, (iii) mortgages on real property, and (iv) inventory.

(D) Purchaser treated as acquiring security interest.—A person who satisfies subparagraph (A) by reason of clause (ii) thereof shall be treated as having acquired a security interest in commercial financing security.

(3) Real property construction or improvement financing agreement.—For purposes of this subsection—

(A) Definition.—The term "real property construction or improvement financing agreement" means an agreement to make cash disbursements to finance—

(i) the construction or improvement of real property,

(ii) a contract to construct or improve real property, or

(iii) the raising or harvesting of a farm crop or the raising of livestock or other animals.

For purposes of clause (iii), the furnishing of goods and services shall be treated as the disbursement of cash.

(B) Limitation on qualified property.—The term "qualified property", when used with respect to a real property construction or improvement financing agreement, includes only—

(i) in the case of subparagraph (A)(i), the real property with respect to which the construction or improvement has been or is to be made,

(ii) in the case of subparagraph (A)(ii), the proceeds of the contract described therein, and

(iii) in the case of subparagraph (A)(iii), property subject to the lien imposed by section 6321 at the time of tax lien filing and the crop or the livestock or other animals referred to in subparagraph (A)(iii).

(4) Obligatory disbursement agreement.—For purposes of this subsection—

(A) Definition.—The term "obligatory disbursement agreement" means an agreement (entered into by a person in the course of his trade or business) to make disbursements, but such an agreement shall be treated as coming within the term only to the extent of disbursements which are required to be made by reason of the intervention of the rights of a person other than the taxpayer.

(B) Limitation on qualified property.—The term "qualified property", when used with respect to an obligatory disbursement agreement, means property subject to the lien imposed by section 6321 at the time of tax lien filing and (to the extent that the acquisition is directly traceable to the disbursements referred to in subparagraph (A)) property acquired by the taxpayer after tax lien filing.

(C) Special rules for surety agreements.—Where the obligatory disbursement agreement is an agreement ensuring the performance of a contract between the taxpayer and another person—

(i) the term "qualified property" shall be treated as also including the proceeds of the contract the performance of which was ensured, and

(ii) if the contract the performance of which was ensured was a contract to construct or improve real property, to produce goods, or to furnish services, the term "qualified property" shall be treated as also including any tangible personal property used by the taxpayer in the performance of such ensured contract.

(d) 45-day period for making disbursements.—Even though notice of a lien imposed by section 6321 has been filed, such lien shall not be valid with respect to a security interest which came into existence after tax lien filing by reason of disbursements made before the 46th day after the date of tax lien filing, or (if earlier) before the person making such disbursements had actual notice or knowledge of tax lien filing, but only if such security interest—

(1) is in property (A) subject, at the time of tax lien filing, to the lien imposed by section 6321, and (B) covered by the terms of a written agreement entered into before tax lien filing, and

(2) is protected under local law against a judgment lien arising, as of the time of tax lien filing, out of an unsecured obligation.

* * *

(f) Place for filing notice; form.—

(1) Place for filing.—The notice referred to in subsection (a) shall be filed—

(A) Under State laws.—

(i) Real property.—In the case of real property, in one office within the State (or the county, or other governmental subdivision), as designated by the laws of such State, in which the property subject to the lien is situated; and

(ii) Personal property.—In the case of personal property, whether tangible or intangible, in one office within the State (or the county, or other governmental subdivision), as designated by the laws of such State, in which the property subject to the lien is situated, except that State law merely conforming to or reenacting Federal law establishing a national filing system does not constitute a second office for filing as designated by the laws of such State; or

(B) With clerk of district court.—In the office of the clerk of the United States district court for the judicial district in which the property subject to the lien is situated, whenever the State has not by law designated one office which meets the requirements of subparagraph (A); or

(C) With Recorder of Deeds of the District of Columbia.—In the office of the Recorder of Deeds of the District of Columbia, if the property subject to the lien is situated in the District of Columbia.

(2) Situs of property subject to lien.—For purposes of paragraphs (1) and (4), property shall be deemed to be situated—

(A) Real property.—In the case of real property, at its physical location; or

(B) Personal property.—In the case of personal property, whether tangible or intangible, at the residence of the taxpayer at the time the notice of lien is filed.

For purposes of paragraph (2)(B), the residence of a corporation or partnership shall be deemed to be the place at which the principal executive office of the business is located, and the residence of a taxpayer whose residence is without the United States shall be deemed to be in the District of Columbia.

(3) Form.—The form and content of the notice referred to in subsection (a) shall be prescribed by the Secretary. Such notice shall be valid notwithstanding any other provision of law regarding the form or content of a notice of lien.

(4) Indexing required with respect to certain real property.—In the case of real property, if—

(A) under the laws of the State in which the real property is located, a deed is not valid as against a purchaser of the property who (at the time of purchase) does not have actual notice or knowledge of the existence of such deed unless the fact of filing of such deed has been entered and recorded in a public index at the place of filing in such a manner that a reasonable inspection of the index will reveal the existence of the deed, and

(B) there is maintained (at the applicable office under paragraph (1)) an adequate system for the public indexing of Federal tax liens,

then the notice of lien referred to in subsection (a) shall not be treated as meeting the filing requirements under paragraph (1) unless the fact of filing is entered and recorded in the index referred to in subparagraph (B) in such a manner that a reasonable inspection of the index will reveal the existence of the lien.

(5) National filing systems.—The filing of a notice of lien shall be governed solely by this title and shall not be subject to any other Federal law establishing a place or places for the filing of liens or encumbrances under a national filing system.

* * *

(h) Definitions.—For purposes of this section and section 6324—

(1) Security interest.—The term "security interest" means any interest in property acquired by contract for the purpose of securing payment or performance of an obligation or indemnifying against loss or liability. A security interest exists at any time (A) if, at such time, the property is in existence and the interest has become protected under local law against a subsequent judgment lien arising out of an unsecured obligation, and (B) to the extent that, at such time, the holder has parted with money or money's worth.

(2) Mechanic's lienor.—The term "mechanic's lienor" means any person who under local law has a lien on real property (or on the proceeds of a contract relating to real property) for services, labor, or materials furnished in connection with the construction or improvement of such property. For purposes of the preceding sentence, a person has a lien on the earliest date such lien becomes valid under local law against subsequent purchasers without actual notice, but not before he begins to furnish the services, labor, or materials.

* * *

(5) Tax lien filing.—The term "tax lien filing" means the filing of notice (referred to in subsection (a)) of the lien imposed by section 6321.

(6) Purchaser.—The term "purchaser" means a person who, for adequate and full consideration in money or money's worth, acquires an interest (other than a lien or security interest) in property which is valid under local law against subsequent purchasers without actual notice. In applying the preceding sentence for purposes of subsection (a) of this section, and for purposes of section 6324—

(A) a lease of property,

(B) a written executory contract to purchase or lease property,

(C) an option to purchase or lease property or any interest therein, or

(D) an option to renew or extend a lease of property,

which is not a lien or security interest shall be treated as an interest in property.

* * *

PART 9

OTHER MATERIALS: LOCAL BANKRUPTCY RULES, LOCAL BANKRUPTCY FORMS, BANKRUPTCY COURT ORDERS, AND PLEADINGS

UNITED STATES BANKRUPTCY COURT
CENTRAL DISTRICT OF CALIFORNIA

In re)

AUTOMATIC DISMISSAL OF CASES)   GENERAL ORDER 93-01
FOR FAILURE OF DEBTOR(S) TO)
APPEAR AT SCHEDULED SECTION)
341(a) MEETINGS OF CREDITORS)

To assist in the orderly conduct of the business of this Court, the Judges of the United States Bankruptcy Court for the Central District of California hereby enter General Order 93-01, dated June 1, 1993, which orders the automatic dismissal of Chapter 7 cases for failure of the debtor(s) to appear at scheduled Section 341(a) Meetings of Creditors.

IT IS ORDERED that pursuant to General Order 93-01, Chapter 7 cases that are filed or converted on or after April 5, 1993 shall be monitored for debtor's appearance at the Section 341(a) Meeting of Creditors. Upon notification from the assigned panel trustee that said debtor(s) failed to appear at the initial Section 341(a) Meeting of Creditors and any continuance thereof, the Clerk of Court is hereby ORDERED to enter an Order of Dismissal of the case with a 180-day prohibition of filing another case, unless leave of the Court is first obtained. The assigned panel trustee must file with the Court a Proof of Service of notification of any continued/rescheduled Section 341(a) Meeting of Creditors.

AO 72
(Rev. 8/82)

IT IS FURTHER ORDERED that General Order 93-01 vacates any requirement that the panel trustee file a Motion to Dismiss the Chapter 7 case for failure of the debtor(s) to appear at the Section 341(a) Meeting of Creditors.

DATED: _____MAY 26, 1993_____

CALVIN K. ASHLAND
Chief Judge, United States
Bankruptcy Court

AO 72
(Rev. 8/82)

<table>
<tr><td>Attorney or Party Name, Address, Telephone & FAX Numbers, and California State Bar Number</td><td>FOR COURT USE ONLY</td></tr>
<tr><td>☐ Individual appearing without counsel
☐ Attorney for Movant</td><td></td></tr>
</table>

UNITED STATES BANKRUPTCY COURT
CENTRAL DISTRICT OF CALIFORNIA

In re:	CHAPTER:
	CASE NO.:
Debtor(s).	DATE: TIME: CTRM: FLOOR:
Trustee.	

ORDER DENYING MOTION FOR RELIEF FROM THE AUTOMATIC STAY
UNDER 11 U.S.C. § 362
(MOVANT: _____)

1. The Motion was: ☐ Contested   ☐ Uncontested   ☐ Not Prosecuted

2. The description of the property (the "Property") to which this Order applies is as follows *(specify common description or street address)*:

3. The Motion is denied: ☐ without prejudice   ☐ with prejudice   on the following grounds:
   - ☐ Based upon the findings and conclusions made on the record at the hearing
   - ☐ Unexcused non-appearance by Movant
   - ☐ Lack of proper service
   - ☐ Lack of good cause shown for relief from stay
   - ☐ The automatic stay is no longer in effect under: ☐ 11 U.S.C. § 362(c)(2)(A)   ☐ 11 U.S.C. § 362(c)(2)(B)
     ☐ 11 U.S.C. § 362(c)(3)(A)   ☐ 11 U.S.C. § 362(c)(4)(A)
   - ☐ Other (specify):

4. ☐ Movant may not file another motion for relief from the stay in this case absent a court order authorizing re-filing.

Dated:

_____
UNITED STATES BANKRUPTCY JUDGE

This form is mandatory by Order of the United States Bankruptcy Court for the Central District of California.
Revised October 2005

F 4001-10.DENY

340

OTHER MATERIALS

In re	(SHORT TITLE)		CHAPTER:
		Debtor(s).	CASE NO.:

NOTICE OF ENTRY OF JUDGMENT OR ORDER
AND CERTIFICATE OF MAILING

TO ALL PARTIES IN INTEREST ON THE ATTACHED SERVICE LIST:

1. You are hereby notified, pursuant to Local Bankruptcy Rule 9021-1, that an ORDER DENYING MOTION FOR RELIEF FROM THE AUTOMATIC STAY UNDER 11 U.S.C. § 362 was entered on *(specify date)*:

2. I hereby certify that I mailed a copy of this notice and a true copy of the order or judgment to the persons and entities on the attached service list on *(specify date)*:

Dated:

JON D. CERETTO
Clerk of the Bankruptcy Court

By: _____
   Deputy Clerk

This form is mandatory by Order of the United States Bankruptcy Court for the Central District of California.
Revised October 2005   F 4001-10.DENY

341

Rule 6004-1   <u>**Sale and Sale Procedures Motions**</u>.

(a) <u>Applicability of Rule</u>. Except as otherwise provided in these Local Rules, this rule applies to motions to sell property of the estate under Bankruptcy Code section 363(b) ("Sale Motions") and motions seeking approval of sale, bid or auction procedures in anticipation of or in conjunction with a Sale Motion ("Sale Procedures Motions").

(b) <u>Sale Motions</u>. Except as otherwise provided in these Local Rules, the Code, the Bankruptcy Rules or an Order of the Court, all Sale Motions shall attach or include the following:

   (i)   A copy of the proposed purchase agreement, or a form of such agreement substantially similar to the one the debtor reasonably believes it will execute in connection with the proposed sale;

   (ii)   A copy of a proposed form of sale order;

   (iii) A request, if necessary, for the appointment of a consumer privacy ombudsman under Bankruptcy Code section 332; and

   (iv)   <u>Provisions to be Highlighted</u>. The Sale Motion must highlight material terms, including but not limited to (a) whether the proposed form of sale order and/or the underlying purchase agreement constitutes a sale or contains any provision of the type set forth below, (b) the location of any such provision in the proposed form of order or purchase agreement, and (c) the justification for the inclusion of such provision:

66

OTHER MATERIALS

(A) Sale to Insider. If the proposed sale is to an insider, as defined in Bankruptcy Code section 101(31), the Sale Motion must (a) identify the insider, (b) describe the insider's relationship to the debtor, and (c) set forth any measures taken to ensure the fairness of the sale process and the proposed transaction.

(B) Agreements with Management. If a proposed buyer has discussed or entered into any agreements with management or key employees regarding compensation or future employment, the Sale Motion must disclose (a) the material terms of any such agreements, and (b) what measures have been taken to ensure the fairness of the sale and the proposed transaction in the light of any such agreements.

(C) Releases. The Sale Motion must highlight any provisions pursuant to which an entity is being released or claims against any entity are being waived or otherwise satisfied.

(D) Private Sale/No Competitive Bidding. The Sale Motion must disclose whether an auction is contemplated, and highlight any provision in which the debtor has agreed not to solicit competing offers for the property subject to the Sale Motion or to otherwise limit shopping of the property.

(E) Closing and Other Deadlines. The Sale Motion must highlight any deadlines for the closing of the proposed sale or deadlines that are conditions to closing the proposed transaction.

(F) Good Faith Deposit. The Sale Motion must highlight whether the proposed purchaser has submitted or will be required to submit a good

67

faith deposit and, if so, the conditions under which such deposit may be forfeited.

(G) Interim Arrangements with Proposed Buyer. The Sale Motion must highlight any provision pursuant to which a debtor is entering into any interim agreements or arrangements with the proposed purchaser, such as interim management arrangements (which, if out of the ordinary course, also must be subject to notice and a hearing under section 363(b) of the Bankruptcy Code) and the terms of such agreements.

(H) Use of Proceeds. The Sale Motion must highlight any provision pursuant to which a debtor proposes to release sale proceeds on or after the closing without further Court order, or to provide for a definitive allocation of sale proceeds between or among various sellers or collateral.

(I) Tax Exemption. The Sale Motion must highlight any provision seeking to have the sale declared exempt from taxes under section 1146(a) of the Bankruptcy Code, the type of tax (e.g., recording tax, stamp tax, use tax, capital gains tax) for which the exemption is sought. It is not sufficient to refer simply to "transfer" taxes and the state or states in which the affected property is located.

(J) Record Retention. If the debtor proposes to sell substantially all of its assets, the Sale Motion must highlight whether the debtor will retain, or have reasonable access to, its books and records to enable it to administer its bankruptcy case.

(K) Sale of Avoidance Actions. The Sale Motion must highlight any provision pursuant to which

68

the debtor seeks to sell or otherwise limit its
rights to pursue avoidance claims under chapter
5 of the Bankruptcy Code.

(L) Requested Findings as to Successor Liability.
The Sale Motion should highlight any provision
limiting the proposed purchaser's successor
liability.

(M) Sale Free and Clear of Unexpired Leases. The
Sale Motion must highlight any provision by
which the debtor seeks to sell property free
and clear of a possessory leasehold interest,
license or other right.

(N) Credit Bid. The Sale Motion must highlight any
provision by which the debtor seeks to allow
credit bidding pursuant to Bankruptcy Code
section 363(k).

(O) Relief from Bankruptcy Rule 6004(h). The Sale
Motion must highlight any provision whereby the
debtor seeks relief from the ten-day stay
imposed by Bankruptcy Rule 6004(h).

(c) Sale Procedures Motions. A debtor may file a Sale
Procedures Motion seeking approval of an order (a "Sale
Procedures Order") approving bidding and auction procedures
either as part of the Sale Motion or by a separate motion
filed in anticipation of an auction and a proposed sale.

(i) Provisions to Highlight. The Sale Procedures Motion
should highlight the following provisions in any
Sale Procedures Order:

(A) Provisions Governing Qualification of Bidders.
Any provision governing an entity becoming a

69

qualified bidder, including but not limited to, an entity's obligation to:

(1) Deliver financial information by a stated deadline to the debtor and other key parties (ordinarily excluding other bidders).

(2) Demonstrate its financial wherewithal to consummate a sale.

(3) Maintain the confidentiality of information obtained from the debtor or other parties or execute a non-disclosure agreement.

(4) Make a non-binding expression of interest or execute a binding agreement.

(B) Provisions Governing Qualified Bids. Any provision governing a bid being a qualified bid, including, but not limited to:

(1) Any deadlines for submitting a bid and the ability of a bidder to modify a bid not deemed a qualified bid.

(2) Any requirements regarding the form of a bid, including whether a qualified bid must be (a) marked against the form of a stalking horse agreement or a template of the debtor's preferred sale terms, showing amendments and other modifications (including price and other terms), (b) for all of the same assets or may be for less than all of the assets proposed to be acquired by an initial, or stalking horse,

70

bidder or (c) remain open for a specified
period of time.

(3)   Any requirement that a bid include a good
      faith deposit, the amount of that deposit
      and under what conditions the good faith
      deposit is not refundable.

(4)   Any other conditions a debtor requires for
      a bid to be considered a qualified bid or
      to permit a qualified bidder to bid at an
      auction.

71

(C) <u>Provisions Providing Bid Protections to "Stalking Horse" or Initial Bidder.</u> Any provisions providing an initial or "stalking horse" bidder a form of bid protection, including, but not limited to the following:

    (1) <u>No-Shop or No-Solicitation Provisions.</u> Any limitations on a debtor's ability or right to solicit higher or otherwise better bids.

    (2) <u>Break-Up/Topping Fees and Expense Reimbursement.</u> Any agreement to provide or seek an order authorizing break-up or topping fees and/or expense reimbursement, and the terms and conditions under which any such fees or expense reimbursement would be paid.

    (3) <u>Bidding Increments.</u> Any requirement regarding the amount of the initial overbid and any successive bidding increments.

    (4) <u>Treatment of Break-Up and Topping Fees and Expense Reimbursement at Auction.</u> Any requirement that the stalking horse bidder receive a "credit" equal to the break-up or topping fee and or expense reimbursement when bidding at the auction and in such case whether the stalking horse is deemed to have waived any such fee and expense upon submitting a higher or otherwise better bid than its initial bid at the auction.

(D) <u>Modification of Bidding and Auction Procedures.</u> Any provision that would authorize a debtor, without further order of the Court, to modify

72

any procedures regarding bidding or conducting an auction.

    (E)   <u>Closing with Alternative Backup Bidders</u>. Any provision that would authorize the debtor to accept and close on alternative qualified bids received at an auction in the event that the bidder selected as the "successful bidder" at the conclusion of the auction fails to close the transaction within a specified period.

(ii)   <u>Provisions Governing the Auction</u>. Unless otherwise ordered by the Court, the Sale Procedures Order shall:

    (A)   Specify the date, time and place at which the auction will be conducted and the method for providing notice to parties of any changes thereto.

    (B)   Provide that each bidder participating at the auction will be required to confirm that it has not engaged in any collusion with respect to the bidding or the sale.

    (C)   State that the auction will be conducted openly and all creditors will be permitted to attend.

    (D)   Provide that bidding at the auction will be transcribed or videotaped.

73

OTHER MATERIALS

Delaware Local **Rule 4001-2** **Cash Collateral and Financing Orders**.

(a) <u>Motions</u>. Except as provided herein and elsewhere in these Local Rules, all cash collateral and financing requests under 11 U.S.C. §§ 363 and 364 shall be heard by motion filed under Fed. R. Bankr. P. 2002, 4001 and 9014 ("Financing Motions").

    (i) <u>Provisions to be Highlighted</u>. All Financing Motions must (a) recite whether the proposed form of order and/or underlying cash collateral stipulation or loan agreement contains any provision of the type indicated below, (b) identify the location of any such provision in the proposed form of order, cash collateral stipulation and/or loan agreement and (c) justify the inclusion of such provision:

        (A) Provisions that grant cross-collateralization protection (other than replacement liens or other adequate protection) to the prepetition secured creditors (<u>i.e.</u>, clauses that secure prepetition debt by postpetition assets in which the secured creditor would not otherwise have a security interest by virtue of its prepetition security agreement or applicable law);

        (B) Provisions or findings of fact that bind the estate or other parties in interest with respect to the validity, perfection or amount of the secured creditor's prepetition lien or the waiver of claims against the secured creditor without first giving parties in interest at least seventy-five (75) days from the entry of the order and the creditors' committee, if formed, at least sixty (60) days from the date of its formation to investigate such matters;

        (C) Provisions that seek to waive, without notice, whatever rights the estate may have under 11 U.S.C. § 506(c);

        (D) Provisions that immediately grant to the prepetition secured creditor liens on the debtor's claims and causes of action arising under 11 U.S.C. §§ 544, 545, 547, 548 and 549;

40

350

        (E)   Provisions that deem prepetition secured debt to be postpetition debt or that use postpetition loans from a prepetition secured creditor to pay part or all of that secured creditor's prepetition debt, other than as provided in 11 U.S.C. § 552(b);

        (F)   Provisions that provide disparate treatment for the professionals retained by a creditors' committee from those professionals retained by the debtor with respect to a professional fee carve-out; and

        (G)   Provisions that prime any secured lien without the consent of that lienor.

    (ii)   All Financing Motions shall also provide a summary of the essential terms of the proposed use of cash collateral and/or financing (e.g., the maximum borrowing available on a final basis, the interim borrowing limit, borrowing conditions, interest rate, maturity, events of default, use of funds limitations and protections afforded under 11 U.S.C. §§ 363 and 364).

(b)   <u>Interim Relief</u>. When Financing Motions are filed with the Court on or shortly after the petition date, the Court may grant interim relief pending review by interested parties of the proposed Debtor-in-Possession financing arrangements. Such interim relief shall be only what is necessary to avoid immediate and irreparable harm to the estate pending a final hearing. In the absence of extraordinary circumstances, the Court shall not approve interim financing orders that include any of the provisions previously identified in Local Rule 4001-2(a)(i)(A)-(F).

(c)   <u>Final Orders</u>. A final order shall be entered only after notice and a hearing under Fed. R. Bankr. P. 4001 and Local Rule 2002-1(b). Ordinarily, the final hearing shall be held at least seven (7) days following the organizational meeting of the creditors' committee contemplated by 11 U.S.C. § 1102.

41

OTHER MATERIALS

UNITED STATES BANKRUPTCY COURT
NORTHERN DISTRICT OF ILLINOIS
EASTERN DIVISION

In Re: Debtor(s))
)   Case No.
)

ORDER AND NOTICE SETTING TIME TO FILE CLAIMS

Debtor's counsel is directed, by _____, *to serve on all creditors a copy of this Order and to file proof of service with the Clerk.*

This bankruptcy case was filed on _____.

FOR CREDITORS WHO WISH TO FILE CLAIMS AGAINST THE BANKRUPTCY ESTATE

(a)   Claims of any governmental unit that arose prior to the case filing date are to be filed not later than 180 days after the order for relief, and

(b)   All other claims that arose prior to the case filing date are to be filed by _____.

All claims must be filed at the following address:

Clerk of the U.S. Bankruptcy Court
219 South Dearborn Street, Room 710
Chicago, IL 60604

If you fail to file a timely claim, your claim may not be allowed, and you may also be barred from voting on a proposed Plan of Reorganization and from receiving any distribution. However, under the law some parties need not file claims. See 11 U.S.C § 1111(a). Parties must rely on their own inspection of the schedules or advice of counsel to determine whether to file a claim.

FOR PARTIES WHO WISH TO OBJECT TO CLAIMS

All objections to claims must be filed and notice thereof served (a) on governmental creditors within 210 days after the date the petition was filed; and (b) on non-governmental claimants by _____. **If objections to claims are filed, claimants may appear for hearing on objections but are not required to do so unless the court so orders.**

ENTER:

_____
Judge

Dated:_____

Revised May 26, 2000   Form Order No. 16

OTHER MATERIALS

UNITED STATES BANKRUPTCY COURT
NORTHERN DISTRICT OF ILLINOIS
EASTERN DIVISION

In Re:)

)   Case No.

)

ORDER CONVERTING CASE UNDER CHAPTER 11
TO CASE UNDER CHAPTER 7

The Moving Party shall serve copies of this order on the Debtor, the Designated Person named in paragraph 3 below, and all professionals known to him who performed services in connection with the Chapter 11 case and shall file a proof of such service.

This case is before the court on a motion under 11 U.S.C. § 1112(b) to convert this Chapter 11 case to a case under Chapter 7 of the United States Bankruptcy Code, 11 U.S.C. §§ 101 *et seq.*, or, in the alternative, to dismiss the case. After notice and a hearing, the Court orders as follows:

1. This case is converted to a case under Chapter 7.

2. The Debtor and the Chapter 11 Trustee shall,
   a. On or before _____, account for and turn over to the Chapter 7 Trustee all records and property of the estate under their custody and control as required by Fed. R. Bankr. P. 1019(4);
   b. On or before _____, file a schedule of all unpaid debts incurred after the commencement of the Chapter 11 case (including the names and addresses of all creditors) as required by Fed. R. Bankr. P. 1019(5);
   c. On or before _____, file a final report and account as required by Fed. R. Bankr. P. 1019(5); and
   d. Within 15 days after the entry of this order, file the statements and schedules required by Fed. R. Bankr. P. 1019(1) and 1007(b), if such documents have not already been filed.

3. Pursuant to Fed. R. Bankr. P. 9001(5), the court designates _____ ("Designated Person") to perform the acts of the Debtor.

4. This matter is set for a status hearing on _____ at _____ in Courtroom No. _____ of the Everett McKinley Dirksen Federal Court House, 219 South Dearborn Street, Chicago, Illinois. At that hearing, the court will determine whether the Debtor /Designated Person/Chapter 11 Trustee have complied with this order and, if not, consider such requests for further relief as may be required to secure compliance with this order.

ENTER:

_____
                                 Judge

Dated: _____

                                  Form Order No. 20

convert11to7   ilnb: October 1,1999

OTHER MATERIALS

Trustee: ☐ Marshall ☐ Meyer
☐ Stearns ☐ Vaughn

UNITED STATES BANKRUPTCY COURT
NORTHERN DISTRICT OF ILLINOIS

In re:) Case No. _____ B _____
)
_____,   )
)
               Debtors.   ) Chapter 13 Plan, dated _____

☐ A check in this box indicates that the plan contains special provisions, set out in Section G. Otherwise, the plan includes no provisions deviating from the model plan adopted by the court at the time of the filing of this case.

Section A *Budget items*	1. As stated in the debtor's Schedule I and J, (a) the number of persons in the debtor's household is _____; (b) their ages are _____; (c) total household monthly income is $_____; and (d) total monthly household expenses are $_____, leaving $ 0.00 available monthly for plan payments. 2. The debtor's Schedule J includes $_____ for charitable contributions; the debtor represents that the debtor made substantially similar contributions for _____ months prior to filing this case.
Section B *General items*	1. The debtor assumes only the unexpired leases and executory contracts listed in Section G of this plan; all other unexpired leases and executory contracts are rejected. Both assumption and rejection are effective as of the date of plan confirmation. 2. Claims secured by a mortgage on real property of the debtor, set out in Section C or in Paragraph 2 of Section E of this plan, shall be treated as follows: (a) *Prepetition defaults.* If the debtor pays the cure amount specified in Paragraph 5 of Section E, while timely making all required postpetition payments, the mortgage will be reinstated according to its original terms, extinguishing any right of the mortgagee to recover any amount alleged to have arisen prior to the filing of the petition. (b) *Costs of collection.* Costs of collection, including attorneys' fees, incurred by the holder after the filing of this bankruptcy case and before the final payment of the cure amount specified in Paragraph 5 of Section E may be added to that cure amount pursuant to order of the court on motion of the holder. 3. The holder of any claim secured by a lien on property of the estate, other than a mortgage treated in Section C or in Paragraph 2 of Section E, shall retain the lien until the earlier of (a) payment of the underlying debt determined under nonbankruptcy law, or (b) discharge under 11 U.S.C. § 1328, at which time the lien shall terminate and be released by the creditor. 4. The debtor shall retain records, including all receipts, of all charitable donations listed in Schedule J.
Section C *Direct payment of claims by debtor*	☐ The debtor will make no direct payments to creditors holding prepetition claims. /or/ ☐ The debtor will make current monthly payments, as listed in the debtor's Schedule J-increased or decreased as necessary to reflect changes in variable interest rates, escrow requirements, collection costs, or similar matters-directly to the following creditors holding claims secured by a mortgage on the debtor's real property: Creditor: _____, monthly payment, $ _____; Creditor: _____, monthly payment, $ _____. *If this box is ☐ checked, additional direct mortgage payments are listed on the overflow page.*

354

OTHER MATERIALS

Section D *Payments by debtor to the trustee; plan term and comple-tion*	1. *Initial plan term.* The debtor will pay to the trustee $_____ monthly for _____ months [and $_____ monthly for an additional _____ months], for total payments, during the initial plan term, of $ 0.00 _____. [Enter this amount on Line 1 of Section H.] 2. *Adjustments to initial term.* If the amount paid by the debtor to the trustee during the initial plan term does not permit payment of general unsecured claims as specified in Paragraphs 8 and 9 of Section E, then the debtor shall make additional monthly payments, during the maximum plan term allowed by law, sufficient to permit the specified payments. 3. *Plan completion.* ☐ The plan will conclude before the end of the initial term, as adjusted by Paragraph 2, only at such time as all allowed claims are paid in full, with any interest required by the plan /or/ ☐ The plan will conclude before the end of the initial term at any time that the debtor pays to the trustee the full amounts specified in Paragraphs 1 and 2.
Section E *Disburse-ments by the trustee*	The trustee shall disburse payments received from the debtor under this plan as follows: 1. *Trustee's fees.* Payable monthly, as authorized; estimated at _____ % of plan payments; and during the initial plan term, totaling $ 0.00 _____. [Enter this amount on Line 2a of Section H.] 2. *Current mortgage payments.* Payable according to the terms of the mortgage, as set forth below, beginning with the first payment due after the filing of the case. Each of these payments shall be increased or de-creased by the trustee as necessary to reflect changes in variable interest rates, escrow requirements, or simi-lar matters; the trustee shall make the change in payments as soon as practicable after receipt of a notice of the change issued by the mortgage holder, but no later than 14 days after such receipt. The trustee shall no-tify the debtor of any such change at least 7 days before putting the change into effect. Any current mort-gage payment made by the debtor directly to the mortgagee shall be deducted from the amounts due to be paid by the trustee under this plan. (a) To creditor _____ , monthly payments of $_____ . These payments, over the term of the plan, are estimated to total $ 0.00 _____. (b) To creditor _____ , monthly payments of $_____ ; These payments, over the term of the plan, are estimated to total $ 0.00 _____. If this box ☐ is checked, additional current mortgage payments are listed on the overflow page. The total of all current mortgage payments to be made by the trustee under the plan is estimated to be $ 0.00 _____. [Enter this amount on Line 2b of Section H.] 3.1. *Other claims secured by value in collateral.* All secured claims, other than mortgage claims treated above and claims treated in Paragraph 3.2, are to be paid in full during the plan term, with interest at the annual percentage rates and in the fixed monthly amounts specified below regardless of contrary proofs of claim (subject to reduction with the consent of the creditor): (a) Creditor: _____ Collateral: _____ Amount of secured claim: $_____ APR _____ % Fixed monthly payment: $_____ ; Total estimated payments, including interest, on the claim: $ _____ ☐ Check if non-PMSI (b) Creditor: _____ Collateral: _____ Amount of secured claim:$_____ APR _____ % Fixed monthly payment: $_____ ; Total estimated payments, including interest, on the claim: $ _____ ☐ Check if non-PMSI

OTHER MATERIALS

Section E *Disburse-ments by the trustee*	If this box ☐ is checked, additional secured claims are listed on the overflow page. [All claims in the debtor's Schedule D, other than mortgages treated above and claims for which the collateral has no value, must be listed in this paragraph. The total of all payments on these secured claims, including interest, is estimated to be $ 0.00 _____. [Enter this amount on Line 2c of Section H.] 3.2. *Other secured claims treated as unsecured.* The following claims are secured by collateral that either has no value or that is fully encumbered by liens with higher priority. No payment will be made on these claims on account of their secured status, but to the extent that the claims are allowed, they will be paid as unsecured claims, pursuant to Paragraphs 6 and 8 of this section. (a) Creditor: _____ Collateral: _____ (b) Creditor: _____ Collateral: _____ If this box ☐ is checked, additional claims covered by this paragraph are listed on the overflow page. 4. *Priority claims of debtor's attorney.* Payable in amounts allowed by court order. The total claim of debtor's attorney is estimated to be $_____.[Enter this amount on Line 2d of Section H.] 5. *Mortgage arrears.* Payable as set forth below, regardless of contrary proofs of claim, except that the arrears payable may be reduced either with the consent of the mortgagee or by court order, entered on motion of the debtor with notice to the trustee and the mortgagee. Any such reduction shall be effective 14 days after either the trustee's receipt of a notice of reduction consented to by the mortgagee or the entry of a court order reducing the arrearage. (a) To creditor_____ , arrears of $ _____ payable monthly from available funds, pro rata with other mortgage arrears, ☐ without interest /or/ ☐ with interest at an annual percentage rate of _____%. These arrearage payments, over the term of the plan, are estimated to total $ _____. (b) To creditor_____ , arrears of $ _____ payable monthly from available funds, pro rata with other mortgage arrears, ☐ without interest /or/ ☐ with interest at an annual percentage rate of _____%. These arrearage payments, over the term of the plan, are estimated to total $ _____. If this box ☐ is checked, additional mortgage arrearage payments are listed on the overflow page. The total of all mortgage arrearage payments to be made by the trustee under the plan is estimated to be $ 0.00 _____. [Enter this amount on Line 2e of Section H.] 6. *Allowed priority claims other than those of the debtor's attorney.* Payable in full, without interest, on a pro rata basis. The total of all payments on non-attorney priority claims to be made by the trustee under the plan is estimated to be $ _____. [Enter this amount on Line 2f of Section H.] Any claim for which the proof of claim asserts both secured and priority status, but which is not identified as secured in Paragraphs 2, 3.1, or 3.2 of this section, will be treated under this paragraph to the extent that the claim is allowed as a priority claim. 7. *Specially classified unsecured claim.* A special class consisting of the following non-priority unsecured claim: shall be paid at _____% of the allowed amount. The total of all payments to this special class is estimated to be $_____. [Enter this amount on Line 2g of Section H.] Reason for the special class:_____ .

OTHER MATERIALS

	8. *General unsecured claims (GUCs)*. All allowed nonpriority unsecured claims, not specially classified, including unsecured deficiency claims under 11 U.S.C. § 506(a), shall be paid, pro rata, ☐ in full, /or / ☐ to the extent possible from the payments set out in Section D, but not less than _____ % of their allowed amount. [Enter minimum payment percentage on Line 4b of Section H.] Any claim for which the proof of claim asserts secured status, but which is not identified as secured in Paragraphs 2, 3.1, or 3.2 of this section, will be treated under this paragraph to the extent that the claim is allowed without priority. 9. *Interest*. ☐ Interest shall not be paid on unsecured claims /or ☐ interest shall be paid on unsecured claims, including priority and specially classified claims, at an annual percentage rate of _____ %. [Complete Line 4d of Section H to reflect interest payable.]
Section F *Priority*	The trustee shall pay the amounts specified in Section E of this Plan in the following order of priority, with claims in a given level of priority reduced proportionately in the event of insufficient plan payments: (1) trustee's fee; (2) current mortgage payments; (3) secured claims listed in Section E, Paragraph 3.1; (4) priority claims of the debtor's attorney; (5) mortgage arrears; (6) priority claims other than those of the debtor's attorney; (7) specially classified non-priority unsecured claims; and (8) general unsecured claims.
Section G *Special terms*	Notwithstanding anything to the contrary set forth above, this Plan shall include the provisions set forth in the box following the signatures. The provisions will not be effective unless there is a check in the notice box preceding Section A.
Section H *Summary of payments to and from the trustee*	(1) Total payments from the debtor to the Chapter 13 trustee (subject to Paragraph 2 of Section D) $ 0.00 (2) Estimated disbursements by the trustee for non-GUCs (general unsecured claims): (a) Trustee's Fees $ 0.00 (b) Current mortgage payments $ 0.00 (c) Payments of other allowed secured claims $ 0.00 (d) Priority payments to debtor's attorney $ 0.00 (e) Payments of mortgage arrears $ 0.00 (f) Payments of non-attorney priority claims $ 0.00 (g) Payments of specially classified unsecured claims $ 0.00 (h) Total [add Lines 2a through 2g] $ 0.00 (3) Estimated payments available for GUCs and interest during initial plan term [subtract Line 2h from Line 1] $ 0.00 (4) Estimated payments required after initial plan term: (a) Estimated total GUCs, including unsecured deficiency claims under § 506(a) $ _____ (b) Minimum GUC payment percentage 0 % (c) Estimated minimum GUC payment [multiply line 4a by line 4b] $ 0.00 (d) Estimated interest payments on unsecured claims $ _____ (e) Total of GUC and interest payments [add Lines 4c and 4d] $ 0.00 (f) Payments available during initial term [enter Line 3] $ 0.00 (g) Additional payments required [subtract Line 4f from line 4e] $ 0.00

	(5) Additional payments available:
	(a) Debtor's monthly payment less trustee's fees and current mortgage payments made by the trustee $ 0.00
	(b) Months in maximum plan term after initial term 60
	(c) Payments available *[multiply line 5a by line 5b]* $ 0.00
Section I *Payroll Control*	☐ A check in this box indicates that the debtor consents to immediate entry of an order directing the debtor's employer to deduct from the debtor's wages the amount specified in Paragraph 1 of Section D and to pay that amount to the trustee on the debtor's behalf. If this is a joint case, details of the deductions from each spouse's wages are set out in Section G.
Signatures	Debtor(s) [Sign only if not represented by an attorney] _____ _____ Date _____ Debtor's Attorney/s/ _____ Date _____
Attorney Information (name, address, telephone, etc.)	

Special Terms *[as provided in Section G]*

OTHER MATERIALS

Overflow Page *[Attach only if necessary]*

Section C **Direct payment of claims by debtor**	Creditor: _____, monthly payment, $ _____ ; Creditor: _____, monthly payment, $ _____ . Creditor: _____, monthly payment, $ _____ .

Section E
 	
Disburse-ments by the truste
	2. Current mortgage payments.
	(c) To creditor_____, monthly payments of $_____ .
	These payments, over the term of the plan, are estimated to total $ 0.00 .
	(d) To creditor_____, monthly payments of $_____ .
	These payments, over the term of the plan, are estimated to total $ 0.00 .
	(e) To creditor_____, monthly payments of $_____ .
	These payments, over the term of the plan, are estimated to total $ 0.00 .
	
	3.1 Other claims secured by value in collateral.
	(c) Creditor: _____ Collateral: _____
	    Amount of secured claim: $_____ APR ____ % ☐ Fixed monthly payment: $_____ ;
	    Total estimated payments, including interest, on the claim: $_____ . ☐ Check if non-PMSI
	(d) Creditor: _____ Collateral: _____
	    Amount of secured claim: $_____ APR ____ % ☐ Fixed monthly payment: $_____ ;
	    Total estimated payments, including interest, on the claim: $_____ . ☐ Check if non-PMSI
	(e) Creditor: _____ Collateral: _____
	    Amount of secured claim: $_____ APR ____ % ☐ Fixed monthly payment: $_____ ;
	    Total estimated payments, including interest, on the claim: $_____ . ☐ Check if non-PMSI
	(f) Creditor: _____ Collateral: _____
	    Amount of secured claim: $_____ APR ____ % ☐ Fixed monthly payment: $_____ ;
	    Total estimated payments, including interest, on the claim: $_____ . ☐ Check if non-PMSI
	
	3.2 Other secured claims treated as unsecured.
	(c) Creditor: _____ Collateral: _____
	(d) Creditor: _____ Collateral: _____
	(e) Creditor: _____ Collateral: _____
	(f) Creditor: _____ Collateral: _____
	
	5. Mortgage arrears.
	(c) To creditor_____ .
	arrears of $_____ , payable monthly from available funds, pro rata with other mortgage arrears,
	☐ without interest /or/ ☐ with interest at an annual percentage rate of _____%.
	These arrearage payments, over the term of the plan, are estimated to total $_____ .
	
	(d) To creditor_____ ,
	arrears of $_____ , payable monthly from available funds, pro rata with other mortgage arrears,
	☐ without interest /or/ ☐ with interest at an annual percentage rate of _____%.
	These arrearage payments, over the term of the plan, are estimated to total $_____ .
	
	(e) To creditor_____ ,
	arrears of $_____ , payable monthly from available funds, pro rata with other mortgage arrears,
	☐ without interest /or/ ☐ with interest at an annual percentage rate of _____%.
	These arrearage payments, over the term of the plan, are estimated to total $_____ .

OTHER MATERIALS

UNITED STATES BANKRUPTCY COURT
SOUTHERN DISTRICT OF FLORIDA
www.flsb.uscourts.gov

GUIDELINES FOR COMPENSATION FOR PROFESSIONAL SERVICES OR REIMBURSEMENT OF EXPENSES BY ATTORNEYS FOR CHAPTER 13 DEBTORS PURSUANT TO LOCAL RULE 2016-1(B)(2)(a)

The following Guidelines apply in all chapter 13 cases in the Southern District of Florida.

These Guidelines also apply to payments by other parties on behalf of debtors. Notwithstanding these Guidelines, any fees paid by debtors shall continue to be subject to the bankruptcy and local rules which govern payment of filing fees in installments.

(A) Compensation and Expenses Allowed Without Application to the Court. Limits on Compensation and Expenses Allowed. Without application to the court, attorneys for debtors in chapter 13 cases shall be permitted to charge an attorney's fee not to exceed, unless all payments have been vested to creditors by earlier order, a base fee of $3500.00 per case, whether individual or joint, and to receive expenses, including the filing fee and up to $150.00 in other estimated expenses.

The base fee shall be presumed to compensate debtor(s)' attorney for a level of service to debtors that at a minimum shall include the following services:

1. Verification of debtors' identity, social security number and eligibility for Chapter 13;
2. Timely preparation and filing of petition, schedules, statement of financial affairs, chapter 13 plan, all amendments and all required documents pursuant to the Bankruptcy Code, and Bankruptcy and Local Rules;
3. Service of copies of all filed plans to all creditors and interested parties;
4. Explanation to debtors regarding all debtors' responsibilities, including, but not limited to payments and attendance at the first meeting of creditors;
5. Preparation for and attendance at all first meetings of creditors;
6. Preparation of and attendance at all necessary pre-confirmation motions brought on behalf of debtors;
7. Timely review of all proofs of claim in accordance with Local Rule 2083-1(B);
8. Timely objection to all improper or invalid proofs of claim in accordance with Local Rule 2083-1(B);
9. Preparation for and attendance at all confirmation hearings;
10. Attendance at and defense of all motions against debtors until discharge, conversion or dismissal of the case;
11. Preparation, filing and service of notices of conversions or voluntary dismissals;
12. Preparation, filing and service of motions to deem mortgage current.

Without application to the court, upon filing and serving of an amended disclosure of compensation, pursuant to BR 2016(b), attorneys for debtors in chapter 13 cases may be

OTHER MATERIALS

permitted to charge an additional fee plus $25.00 in costs for the following services, if the retainer agreement authorizes these fees, not to exceed the following amounts:

1.	Post-confirmation modification of plan	$500
2.	Motion for hardship discharge	$500
3.	Motion to purchase, sell or refinance real property	$500
4.	Motion to rehear, vacate dismissal, shorten prejudice period or reinstate case	$500
5.	Motion to avoid lien	$500
6.	Motion to value a motor vehicle, a motor home, or a manufactured home	$500
7.	Motion to value real property	$750
8.	Home Mortgage Loan Modification	$500

The following conditions also apply:

(1) If the case is dismissed or converted prior to confirmation and if the retainer agreement so provides, the attorney for the debtor may request and receive fees from monies paid to the chapter 13 trustee without separate application to the court, but the total fee, including any fees previously paid, may not exceed $2,500.00, unless, pursuant to court order, plan payments were not returned to the debtor and were paid pursuant to the terms of the last filed plan.

(2) Reimbursement for general expenses, other than the filing fee, that exceed $150.00 shall require a separate application for reimbursement of expenses filed pursuant to paragraph (C) of these Guidelines. Reimbursement for expenses in excess of $150.00 shall be permitted only as allowed pursuant to section D, "Reimbursement of Expenses and Services", of the court's "Guidelines for Fee Applications for Professionals in the Southern District of Florida in Bankruptcy Cases".

Reimbursement for the following expenses shall also be permitted without a separate application for reimbursement:

1.	Court reporter expenses no greater than $125.00;	
2.	Interpreter fees no greater than $75.00;	
3.	Credit report retrieval fees no greater than $75.00.	

(B) Compensation and Expenses Requiring Application and Court Approval. Attorneys seeking compensation or expenses which exceed the limits set forth in paragraph (A) of these Guidelines shall submit the court's Local Form "Application for Compensation for Professional Services or Reimbursement of Expenses by Attorney for Chapter 13 Debtor" on or before the deadlines established by Local Rule 2016-1(C)(4). This requirement applies to initial fee applications as well as to additional or supplemental applications. The application shall:

(1) describe in detail the actual or estimated services or expenses for which compensation or reimbursement is sought; and

(2) include as an attachment a copy of the retainer agreement, if any.

CG-6 (rev. 02/24/12)

OTHER MATERIALS

(C) Requirement of Rights and Responsibilities Agreement Between Chapter 13 Debtor(s) and Chapter 13 Debtor(s)' Attorneys. As required by Local Rule 2016-1(B)(2), Chapter 13 debtors and their attorneys must execute the local form "Rights and Responsibilities Agreement Between Chapter 13 Debtor(s) and Chapter 13 Debtor(s)' Attorney for Cases Filed in the United States Bankruptcy Court, Southern District of Florida" prior to filing a chapter 13 case in this court. The form shall be retained by the parties and not filed with the court. A copy of the agreement must be made available to the chapter 13 trustee at the meeting of creditors.

CG-6 (rev. 02/24/12)

362

United States Bankruptcy Court
_____ District of _____

In re: Case No: _____

Debtor(s)

☐ Check if this is an
amended plan

Official Form XXXX Date: _____
Chapter 13 Plan

Check all that apply:

☐ **The plan seeks to limit the amount of a secured claim, which may result in a creditor's lien receiving a partial payment or no payment at all, as set out In Part 2, Section 7.**

☐ **The plan requests the avoidance of a judicial lien as set out in Part 2, Section 9.**

☐ **The plan requests the avoidance of a nonpossessory, nonpurchase-money security interest as set out in Part 2, Section 10.**

☐ **The plan sets out non-standard provisions in Part 10.**

Notice to Interested Parties: Your rights may be affected. Your claim may be reduced, modified, or eliminated.

You should read these papers carefully and discuss them with your attorney, if you have one in this bankruptcy case. If you do not have an attorney, you may wish to consult one.

If you oppose the Plan treatment of your claim or any provision of this Plan, you or your lawyer must file an objection to confirmation at least seven days before the hearing on confirmation, unless otherwise ordered by the Bankruptcy Court. The Bankruptcy Court may confirm this plan without further notice if no objection to confirmation is filed. See Bankruptcy Rule 3015.

Part 1: Plan Payments and Length of Plan

1. Debtor(s) will pay to the trustee $ _____ per month for _____ months, and

$ _____ per month for _____ months.

2. Payments to the trustee will be made from future earnings in the following manner:

☐ Debtor(s) will agree to entry of a payroll deduction order.

☐ Debtor(s) will make payments directly to the trustee.

3. Additional payments to the trustee will be made as follows (check all that apply):

❑ Debtor(s) will turn over to the trustee:

    ❑ any tax refunds received during the plan term

    ❑ any tax refunds in excess of $ _____ received during the plan term

❑ Other sources of funding, including the sale of property (describe source, amount and date when available):

_____

4. The estimated total amount of plan payments is $ _____.

5. The estimated term of the plan is _____ months.

Part 2: Treatment of Secured Claims

6. **Cure of Default and Maintenance of Payments.** The debtor(s) will cure the default and maintain the contractual installment payments on the secured claims listed below. The allowed claim for the arrearage amount, if any, will be paid under the plan, with interest if specified, at the rate stated.

Name of creditor	Collateral	Current Installment payment (including escrow payment)	Interest rate on arrearage (if applicable)	Amount of arrearage to be paid	Monthly plan payment on arrearage or other payment arrangement
		Payment: $_____ Disbursed by: ❑ Trustee ❑ Debtor(s)			
		Payment: $_____ Disbursed by: ❑ Trustee ❑ Debtor(s)			

7. **Determination of Allowed Secured Claims and Claim Modification.** The claims listed below are allowed secured claims only to the extent of the value of the creditor's interest in the collateral as provided under 11 U.S.C. § 506(a). Unless a creditor timely objects to confirmation, the value of the creditor's interest in the collateral shall be the amount of the allowed secured claim listed below, and it will be paid in full under the plan with interest at the rate stated below. The portion of any allowed claim that exceeds the amount of the allowed secured claim shall be treated as an unsecured claim under Part 4 of this plan. If the amount of a creditor's allowed secured claim is listed below as having no value, the creditor's allowed claim shall be treated in its entirety as an unsecured claim under Part 4 of this plan. The holder of any allowed secured claim, other than a mortgage treated in Part 2, Section 6, shall retain the lien until the earlier of (a) payment of the underlying debt determined under nonbankruptcy law, or (b) discharge under 11 U.S.C. § 1328(a), at which time the lien shall terminate and be released by the creditor. See Bankruptcy Rule 3015.

OTHER MATERIALS

Name of creditor	Amount of creditor's claim	Collateral	Value of collateral	Amount of claims senior to creditor's claim	Interest rate	Amount of creditor's secured claim to be paid	Monthly plan payment

8. **Secured Claims Not Subject to 11 U.S.C. § 506.** The claims listed below were either (1) incurred within 910 days before the petition date and secured by a purchase money security interest in a motor vehicle acquired for the personal use of the debtor or (2) incurred within one year of the petition date and secured by a purchase money security interest in any other thing of value. These claims will be paid in full under the plan with interest at the rate stated below.

Check if applicable:

❑ Other secured claims not subject to 11 U.S.C. § 506 that are not listed below are provided for in Part 10 below.

Name of creditor	Collateral	Interest rate	Amount of claim to be paid	Monthly plan payment

9. **Judicial Lien Avoidance.** The judicial liens securing the claims listed below impair exemptions to which the debtor(s) would have been entitled under 11 U. S. C. § 522(b). A judicial lien securing a claim listed below shall be avoided to the extent that the lien impairs such exemptions upon entry of the order confirming the plan. The amount of the lien that is avoided will be treated as an unsecured claim in Part 4. The amount of the lien that is not avoided will be paid in full as a secured claim under the plan. See 11 U. S. C. § 522(f) and Bankruptcy Rule 4003(d).

Name of creditor	Collateral	Judgment date and date of lien recording	Lien recording inform- ation	Amount of lien not avoided and paid as secured claim	Interest rate (If applicable)	Monthly plan payment (if applicable)
				a. Amount of judicial lien $ _____ b. Amount of all other liens $ _____ c. Value of claimed exemptions + $ _____ d. Total. Add a, b, and c $ _____ e. Value of debtor's interest in property $ _____ Extent of exemption impairment (check applicable box): ❑ **Line d is greater than Line e.** The entire lien is avoided. ❑ **Line d is less than Line e.** A portion of the lien is avoided. Amount of lien not avoided: $ _____		
				a. Amount of judicial lien $ _____ b. Amount of all other liens $ _____ c. Value of claimed exemptions + $ _____ d. Total. Add a, b, and c $ _____ e. Value of debtor's interest in property $ _____ Extent of exemption impairment (check applicable box): ❑ **Line d is greater than Line e.** The entire lien is avoided. ❑ **Line d is less than Line e.** A portion of the lien is avoided. Amount of lien not avoided: $ _____		

10. **Nonpossessory, Nonpurchase-money Security Interest Avoidance.** The nonpossessory, nonpurchase-money security interests securing the claims listed below impair exemptions to which the debtor(s) would have been entitled under 11 U. S. C. § 522(b). A security interest securing a claim listed below shall be avoided to the extent that the security interest impairs such exemptions upon entry of the order confirming the plan. The amount of the security interest that is avoided will be treated as an unsecured claim in Part 4. The amount of the security interest that is not avoided will be paid in full as a secured claim under the plan. See 11 U. S. C. § 522(f) and Bankruptcy Rule 4003(d).

Name of creditor	Collateral	Amount of security interest not avoided and paid as secured claim	Interest rate (If applicable)	Monthly plan payment (if applicable)
		a. Amount of security interest $ _____ b. Amount of all other liens $ _____ c. Value of claimed exemptions + $ _____ d. Total. Add a, b, and c $ _____ e. Value of debtor's interest in property $ _____ Extent of exemption impairment (check applicable box): ❑ **Line d is greater than Line e.** The entire security interest is avoided. ❑ **Line d is less than Line e.** A portion of the security interest is avoided. Amount of security interest not avoided: $ _____		

		a. Amount of security interest $ _____
		b. Amount of all other liens $ _____
		c. Value of claimed exemptions + $ _____
		d. Total. Add a, b, and c $ _____
		
		e. Value of debtor's interest in property $ _____
		
		Extent of exemption impairment (check applicable box):
		
		❏ **Line d is greater than Line e.** The entire
		   security interest is avoided.
		
		❏ **Line d is less than Line e.** A portion of the
		   security interest is avoided.
		
		Amount of security interest not avoided: $ _____		

11. **Surrender of Collateral.** The debtor(s) elect to surrender to the creditors listed below the personal or real property that is collateral for the claim. The debtor(s) consent to termination of the stay with respect to the collateral upon confirmation of the plan. Any allowed unsecured claim resulting from the disposition of the collateral will be treated in Part 4 below.

Name of creditor	Collateral

Part 3: Treatment of Administrative and Other Priority Claims

12. **Trustee's Fees.** Fees of the standing trustee will be paid in full, without interest. These fees are estimated to be _____% of plan payments; and during plan term, they are estimated to total $_____.

13. **Attorney's Fees.** Fees of the attorney, in the amount of $_____, will be paid in full, without interest.

14. **Other Priority Claims.** The allowed priority claims listed below will be paid in full.

Name of creditor	Basis for priority treatment	Amount to be paid

15. **Domestic Support Obligations Paid Less than Full Amount**. The allowed priority claims listed below based on a domestic support obligation will be paid less than the full amount of the claim in accordance with 11 U.S.C. § 1322(a)(4).

Name of creditor	Amount to be paid

16. **Interest.** Interest on allowed priority claims listed in line 15 will (check the applicable box):

   ☐ Not be paid

   ☐ Be paid at an annual percentage rate of _____ % in accordance with 11 U.S.C. § 1325(a)(4), and is estimated to total $ _____.

Part 4: Treatment of Nonpriority Unsecured Claims

17. **Cure of Default and Maintenance of Payments.** The debtor(s) will cure the default and maintain the contractual installment payments on the unsecured claims listed below on which the last payment is due after the final plan payment. The allowed claim for the arrearage amount will be paid under the plan.

Name of creditor	Current installment payment	Amount of arrearage to be paid
	Payment: $_____ Disbursed by: ☐ Trustee ☐ Debtor(s)	
	Payment: $_____ Disbursed by: ☐ Trustee ☐ Debtor(s)	

18. **Separately Classified Nonpriority Unsecured Claims.** The nonpriority unsecured allowed claims listed below are separately classified and will be treated as follows:

Name of creditor	Basis for separate classification	Treatment	Amount to be paid

368

19. **Nonpriority Unsecured Claims.** Nonpriority unsecured allowed claims that are not separately classified will be paid not less than (check the applicable box):

☐ The sum of $_____ to be distributed on a *pro rata* basis

☐ _____ percent of allowed claims

☐ The funds remaining after disbursements have been made to all other creditors provided for in this plan, to be distributed on a *pro rata* basis.

20. **Interest.** Interest on allowed unsecured claims, including separately classified claims, will (check the applicable box):

☐ Not be paid

☐ Be paid at an annual percentage rate of _____ % in accordance with 11 U.S.C. § 1325(a)(4), and is estimated to total $ _____.

Part 5: Executory Contracts and Unexpired Leases

21. All executory contracts and unexpired leases are rejected, except those listed below, which are assumed and will be treated as provided for below or under another specified provision of the plan.

Name of creditor	Property description	Treatment (refer to other plan section if applicable)	Current installment payment	Amount of arrearage to be paid
			Payment: $_____ Disbursed by: ☐ Trustee ☐ Debtor(s)	
			Payment: $_____ Disbursed by: ☐ Trustee ☐ Debtor(s)	

Part 6: Order of Distribution

22. The trustee will pay allowed claims in the following order:

1) _____

2) _____

3) _____

4) _____

5) _____

6) _____

7) _____

Part 7: Summary of Plan Disbursements

23. From the payments received from the debtor(s), the trustee will make the following estimated disbursements on allowed claims:

1) Current installment payments on secured claims (Part 2, Section 6 total): $ _____

2) Arrearage payments on secured claims (Part 2, Section 6 total): $ _____

3) Allowed secured claims (Part 2, Section 7 total): $ _____

4) Secured claims not subject to 11 U.S.C. § 506 (Part 2, Section 8 total): $ _____

5) Judicial liens not avoided (Part 2, Section 9 total): $ _____

6) Security interests not avoided (Part 2, Section 10 total): $ _____

7) Administrative and other priority claims (Part 3 total): $ _____

8) Current installment payments on unsecured debts (Part 4, Section 17 total): $ _____

9) Arrearage payments on unsecured debts (Part 4, Section 17 total): $ _____

10) Separately classified unsecured claims (Part 4, Section 18 total): $ _____

11) Nonpriority unsecured claims (Part 4, Section 19 total): $ _____

12) Interest on allowed unsecured claims (Part 4, Section 20 total): $ _____

13) Total of (1) through (12) above: $ _____

Part 8: Claims of Governmental Units

24. This plan is not binding with respect to any claim of a governmental unit that is (a) timely filed after confirmation of this plan, and (b) inconsistent with the treatment of such claim under this plan.

Part 9: Vesting of Property of the Estate

25. Property of the estate shall revest in the debtor(s) upon (check the applicable box):

□ Plan confirmation

□ Closing of case

□ Other: _____

Part 10: Non-standard Plan Provisions

In accordance with Bankruptcy Rule 3015(c), non-standard provisions are required to be set forth below.

Part 11: Signatures

Debtors (sign only if not represented by an attorney)

_____   Date _____

_____   Date _____

Debtors' Attorney

_____   Date _____